D1071574

FANTASIES OF IMPROVISATION

Fantasies of Improvisation

FREE PLAYING IN NINETEENTH-CENTURY MUSIC

Dana Gooley

OXFORD
UNIVERSITY PRESS

OXFORD
UNIVERSITY PRESS

Oxford University Press is a department of the University of Oxford. It furthers
the University's objective of excellence in research, scholarship, and education
by publishing worldwide. Oxford is a registered trade mark of Oxford University
Press in the UK and certain other countries.

Published in the United States of America by Oxford University Press
198 Madison Avenue, New York, NY 10016, United States of America.

Library of Congress Cataloging-in-Publication Data
Names: Gooley, Dana A. (Dana Andrew), 1969– author.
Title: Fantasies of improvisation : free playing in nineteenth-century music /
Dana Gooley.
Description: New York, NY : Oxford University Press, [2018] |
Includes bibliographical references and index.
Identifiers: LCCN 2017050199 (print) | LCCN 2017048569 (ebook) |
ISBN 9780190633585 (hardcover : alk. paper) | ISBN 9780190633592 (updf) |
ISBN 9780190633608 (epub)
Subjects: LCSH: Improvisation (Music)—History—19th century.
Classification: LCC ML430.7 .G67 2018 (ebook) | LCC ML430.7 (print) |
DDC 781.3/609034—dc23
LC record available at https://lccn.loc.gov/2017050199

This volume is published with the generous support of the Gustave Reese Endowment of the
American Musicological Society, funded in part by the National Endowment for the Humanities
and the Andrew W. Mellon Foundation.

9 8 7 6 5 4 3 2 1

Printed by Sheridan Books, Inc., United States of America

For Leah

Contents

List of Examples, Figures, and Tables ix
Acknowledgments xi
Abbreviations xv
A Note on Citations xvii

Prelude: *The Virtue of Improvisation* 1

1. *The School of Abbé Vogler: Weber and Meyerbeer* 25

2. *The Kapellmeister Network and the Performance of Community: Hummel, Moscheles, and Mendelssohn* 62

3. *Carl Loewe's Performative Romanticism* 116

4. *Schumann and the Economization of Musical Labor* 154

5. *Liszt and the Romantic Rhetoric of Improvisation* 198

6. *Improvisatoriness: The Regime of the Improvisation Imaginary* 243

Postlude: *Improvisation and Utopia* 277

INDEX 287

List of Examples, Figures, and Tables

Example 1.1 Opening section of "Finnish Melody" 32

Figure 1.1 Excerpt from Vogler's "Summa of Harmony" 35

Example 1.2 Haydn, "Betrachtung des Todes," opening 42

Example 1.3 Weber, *Variations sur un thème original*, op. 9 45

Example 1.4 Weber, *Variations sur "Vien' quà Dorina bella,"* op. 7, theme (excerpt) 47

Example 1.5 Weber, *Variations sur "Vien' quà Dorina bella"* 48

Example 2.1a "Escouto d'Jeannetto" from Dalayrac, *Les deux petits Savoyards* (1789) 83

Example 2.1b Beethoven, Symphony no. 7, theme of second movement 83

Table 3.1 Concert of Carl Loewe 124

Figure 3.1 First two strophes of Goethe's "Die Zauberlehrling" (The Sorcerer's Apprentice, 1797) 125

Example 3.1 First strophe of Loewe's setting of "Die Zauberlehrling" 126

Figure 3.2 First full strophe of Zelter's setting of "Die Zauberlehrling" 128

Example 3.2 Final measures of Loewe's setting of "Die Zauberlehrling" 129

Table 3.2 Table of known improvisations by Loewe 131

Figure 3.3 Cover page of Adolf Müller's song "Der Sänger" (1842) 143

Figure 3.4 Adolf Müller's working sheet for his dual poetry-song improvisation with Karoline Leonhardt-Lyser (1842) 144

Example 4.1 Schumann, *Variationen über den Namen "Abegg,"* op. 1 162

Example 4.2 Hummel, *Sonate* [in F♯ minor], op. 81, 1st mvmt 163

Example 4.3 Schumann, *Allegro*, op. 8 164

Example 4.4 From pedagogical "Preface" to *Studien für das Pianoforte, nach Capricen von Paganini bearbeitet*, op. 3 166

Example 4.5 Schumann, *Toccata*, op. 7, main figure 166

Example 4.6 Schumann, *Toccata*, chromatic figures 167

Example 4.7 Czerny, *Systematische Anleitung zum Fantasieren auf dem Pianoforte*, op. 200, ch. 1 167

Example 4.8 Schumann, *Toccata* 167

Example 4.9 Fréderic Kalkbrenner, *Traité d'harmonie du pianiste* (1849) 168

Example 4.10   Schumann, *Sonate* [in F♯ minor], op. 11, finale 168

Example 4.11   Schumann, *Variationen über den Namen "Abegg,"* finale 169

Example 4.12   Kalkbrenner, *Traité d'harmonie du pianiste* 171

Example 4.13   Himmel, melody of "An Alexis send'ich dich" 172

Example 5.1   Liszt, *Apparitions*, no. 3 217

Example 5.2   Liszt, *Harmonies poétiques et religieuses*, opening 217

Example 5.3   Liszt, *Apparitions*, no. 1 218

Acknowledgments

I WOULD LIKE to thank many friends, colleagues, and institutions for their contributions to the realization of this project. The book manuscript was completed with the generous support of a grant from the George A. and Eliza Gardner Howard Foundation, which enabled me to take an extra semester of leave. Suzanne Ryan at Oxford University Press has been an exceptionally supportive, wise, and alert editor. I thank her and her staff for their thoughtful and solicitous curatorial work. I wish there was a way to give anonymous readers more credit for the careful critical work they do with so little compensation. Anonymous readers, whoever you are: thank you for your suggestions, criticisms, and your selfless commitment to improving this work!

As the field of improvisation studies has grown over the past ten years I have enjoyed conferences and conversations with many brilliant and committed improvisologists. They include Bettina Brandl-Risi, Gabriela Brandstetter, Bruce Brubaker, Kai van Ekels, Melina Esse, Fabian Goppelsröder, George Lewis, Roger Moseley, Kevin Patton, Benjamin Piekut, Annette Richards, Clemens Risi, Alexander Stefaniak, and David Trippett. James Davies and Jim Samson have inspired me with brilliant and imaginative cultural archaeologies of keyboard practice in the early nineteenth century. I owe a very special thanks to Ken Hamilton, whose peerless knowledge of piano repertoire and romantic practice has been as valuable to me as his friendship and collegiality.

Some threads in this book originated in memorable exchanges with colleagues. Adeline Mueller alerted me to recent work on the history of childhood, which left a mark on the Liszt chapter. Jim Dennen strongly encouraged me to pursue the question of economy that is now a significant part of the Schumann chapter. Marc Perlman shared with me a paper he has written in the history of the term "improvisation," which helped shaped some of my larger lines of thought. Eric Schneeman tipped me off to the existence of the improvising poet Karoline Leonhardt-Lyser, who made an illuminating counter-case to Carl Loewe. I also received indispensable advice from Roe-Min Kok on the Schumann chapter, and from Nicolas Dufetel on the Liszt chapter. Shaena Weitz generously shared her original unpublished research into the journal *Le*

Pianiste and its advocacy of improvsation. Anston Bosman, in addition to being a great friend and interlocutor, helped workshop the book title.

I have had the opportunity to try out ideas and receive constructive feedback from engaging and challenging audiences at Cardiff University, Case Western Reserve University, Cornell University, Eastern Connecticut State University, Freie Universität Berlin, University of Chicago, University of Rochester, Universität Göttingen, University of California at Berkeley, and Washington University.

I began working on this book when I came to Brown University, and have benefited enormously from the supportive, stimulating environment there. The university provided me with valuable resources, including a Wendy J. Strothman Faculty Research Award that enabled me to research organ improvisers more deeply, and faculty fellowships from the Cogut Institute for the Humanities and the Pembroke Center for Teaching and Research on Women and Gender. I thank all my colleagues in the Music Department, the Orwig Music Library staff who kept sending new information my way, and the students in my courses Classical Improvisation and Critical Improvisation Studies, who constantly surprised me with their new inventions, digressions, and fantasies. For assistance with research, editing, and the preparation of music examples I was lucky to have the help of Brown students Nora Rothman, Maggie Qi, Mark Benis, and Devanney Haruta. Their diligence, intelligence, and sharp eyes for detail never ceased to impress me.

I am grateful to the hard-working staff members of the following institutions, who kindly helped me locate materials and arrange for reproductions: Archives nationales (Paris), Bibliothek im Rathaus (Vienna), Österreichische Nationalbibliothek (Vienna), Bibliothèque nationale de France (Paris), Bibliothek der Gesellschaft der Musikfreunde (Vienna), and Staatsbibliothek zu Berlin. Special thanks to Andrew Wilson at Harvard's Loeb Music Library, who retrieved countless items from the library's well-stocked vaults.

Although I have taken inspiration from classical improvisers such as Gabriela Monteiro, Robert Levin, and Michael Gees, I never heard them play free fantasies live. I have, however, had the good fortune to hear William Cheng's amazing, inspired improvisations on given themes in romantic style. I am likewise grateful to Hungarian virtuoso János Balázs for demonstrating with remarkable conviction what Lisztian improvisation might have sounded like. On Sunday evenings, over the past five years, I have been lucky to play with some of Boston's best jazz musicians at Wally's Cafe. Their musicianship and improvisational brilliance has kept me learning and searching.

This book incorporates, in reworked form, material from previously published articles. Chapter 2 incorporates material from "Saving Improvisation: Hummel and the Free Fantasia in the Early Nineteenth Century," in *The Oxford Handbook of Critical Improvisation Studies*, ed. George Lewis and Benjamin Piekut (Oxford: Oxford University Press, 2016), vol. 2, 185–205. Chapter 4 incorporates material from "Schumann and the Agencies of Improvisation," in *Rethinking Schumann*, ed. Roe-Min Kok and Laura Tunbridge (Oxford: Oxford University Press, 2011), 129–156. Chapter 5 incorporates material from "Liszt, Improvisation and the Idea of Italy," in *Liszt's Legacies*, ed. James Deaville and Michael Saffle (Stuyvesant, NY: Pendragon Press, 2014), 3–16. I thank all the editors of these projects and Bob Kessler at Pendragon Press for permission to re-work these articles.

Shortly after beginning this project I met Leah Segal, and we played "My Romance" at a jazz jam session. Our romance bloomed into a marriage, and has now blossomed into a family. I can't thank her enough for her support, intelligence, and humor throughout these years. This book is dedicated to her with love.

Abbreviations

NZM	*Neue Zeitschrift für Musik*
RGMP	*Revue et gazette musicale de Paris*
AMZ	(Leipziger) *Allgemeine musikalische Zeitung*
WAMZ	*Wiener allgemeine Musik-Zeitung (Allgemeine Wiener Musik-Zeitung)*
BAMZ	*Berliner allgemeine musikalische Zeitung*

A Note on Citations

OVER THE PAST decade there has been a vast expansion of online nineteenth-century newspapers and journals, both on open-source and subscription sites. The most voluminous include ANNO (Austria), GALLICA (France), British Newspapers 1800–1950 (UK), CIRPeM (Italy), Nineteenth Century U.S. Newspapers (US), Music in Gotham (US), and RIPM (Europe). These sites continue to add large quantities of content every year, and because most are keyword-searchable it is no longer difficult to find sources about targeted topics. The challenge now is filtering and selecting from the vast quantities of documents one can summon through a simple search.

To avoid an accumulation of notes, I have opted for a short-citation system for these periodical sources. They can easily be found using the year and page number, or the issue date. This system has the disadvantage of not identifying the author of the article cited, but a great many of these articles lack author identifications in the original sources. In cases where the authorship of the cited article seems relevant to the point being made, I discuss the author in the text. For periodicals that are not through-numbered, I cite the source by date.

FANTASIES OF IMPROVISATION

Prelude

THE VIRTUE OF IMPROVISATION

IN RECENT TIMES improvisation has made a significant comeback in classical music concerts, education, and scholarship. Pianist Robert Levin has injected fresh life into Mozart by improvising ornaments, lead-ins, and whole cadenzas to Mozart concertos. More impressively still, he plays free fantasies in Mozart style on themes given by the concert audience. Gabriela Monteiro has built a distinctive reputation among concert pianists by improvising at length on themes solicited from the audience, drawing on an eclectic range of styles from Bach-like baroque to modern jazz. Early music practitioners have long understood the importance of improvisation to historically informed practice, but artists such as violinist Andrew Manze and harpsichordist Richard Egarr have pressed it to new limits. Organist Thierry Escaich has been inventing entire four-movement symphonies on themes suggested by the audience, setting a new standard for a tradition already rich in improvisation. Students and fans of these elite musicians are showing signs that they intend to keep the flame burning by cultivating improvisational practice in various classical idioms.

The incentives for this revival are various. For Manze and Levin the impetus is clearly historical: by learning to improvise the way Mozart or Corelli did, they intend to arrive at some version of historical authenticity. For Monteiro the motive is more personal. By her own account she always followed her natural inclination to improvise, and her teachers encouraged it. Escaich, for his part, is an ambassador of the French organ school, which has taken deep pride in improvisational skill for well over a century. In all cases, the market conditions in which classical music circulates favor the revival, since improvisation can be marketed to audiences and consumers as something novel, attractive, and different. In a saturated and competitive field of professionals, the improvising performer can claim a mark of distinction setting one apart from the crowd. And in the ongoing project of giving classical music a more hip image, the risk and whimsy of improvisation seem to offer a helping hand.

With so much renewed interest in classical improvisation, the time is ripe for re-examining why it went out of practice in the first place. During the first two or three decades of the nineteenth century, improvisation was an integral part of the education of nearly every advanced keyboardist and composer, and a good many amateurs as well. Musicians were not equally inclined or gifted in improvisation, but no one was surprised to hear a keyboardist or violinist extemporizing in salons, concerts, and churches. It was practiced as a matter of course by musicians as diverse as Beethoven, Schubert, Hummel, Liszt, Paganini, Schumann, Baillot, Mendelssohn, Chopin, and Carl Loewe, not to mention most organists and illustrious amateurs such as John Stuart Mill and Franz Grillparzer. Around 1830 there was a steep decline in improvisation and the prestige it carried, but plenty of residual momentum kept it afloat. After 1850 there was a more sudden drop-off, and by the end of the century very few musicians still improvised outside the church. The broader causes of this decline have become relatively familiar: the growing authority of the "work" concept among composers and audiences, the emergence of a guilty conscience about improvisation among piano virtuosos, and the growth of a large, general listening audience insufficiently informed to understand the nuances of improvisation.[1]

The pressures that discouraged keyboardists from continuing to improvise will be given considerable attention here, particularly in the case studies of Schumann and Liszt. They issued from large-scale transformations in the music profession, in the expectations of concert audiences, and in the moral economy of the middle classes— transformations that did not always enter directly into the consciousness of improvising artists. Schumann, Liszt, and other keyboardists submitted to such reconstructive pressures while also resisting them varying degrees, indicating a tension between residual practices of free playing and emergent ideologies that opposed them.

If the story of improvisation in the nineteenth century were a straightforward narrative of decline, it would be little more than a sad and lifeless tale. But there is a curious counterplot: as improvisation declined in musical practice, there persisted a strong, unreconstructed desire to keep it alive. Most composers continued to improvise at the piano as a vital resource for generating and testing compositional ideas. Listeners and critics, though not hearing free fantasies as often as they had in earlier times, lost no capacity to marvel at extemporaneous skill, and continued to enjoy the feelings of surprise or inspirational elevation that often came with the best improvisation. Above all, literary romanticism ushered in a seductive new *idea* of improvisation that, as I will argue, gained traction precisely because of the waning of the practice. In the writings of romantic authors, improvisation accumulated a surcharge of positive associations—with freedom, spontaneity, and naturalness—that found expression in music criticism, poems, novels, and stage works. This cluster of representations and meanings, which I will call the "improvisation imaginary," expressed the discontents of a musical world that had left real improvisations behind, but wanted them back in some revised or reflected form. No one embodies this paradox better than Richard Wagner, who was profoundly unreceptive to extemporization in his own works, but sang the praises of improvisation in his essay "On the Destiny of Opera," and invented two troubadours for the stage whose improvised singing is a mode of heroic action.[2]

This book focuses on European classical music from about 1810 to 1880 to trace the process by which keyboard improvisation moved out of living practice, only to be reborn as an idea or representation. It takes impetus not only from recent developments in classical music performance, but also from lively discussions of improvisation as cultural practice that have attracted increasing academic attention in recent times. In 1974 ethnomusicologist Bruno Nettl published a remarkable article calling for the comparative study of improvisation in various musical traditions of the world, including western classical music.[3] Perhaps because the methods of his field were evolving away from such broad cross-cultural comparisons, no one picked up the ball right away. A quarter of a century later, however, Nettl edited the essay collection *In the Course of Performance: Studies in the World of Musical Improvisation* (1998), which fleshed out the comparative project and reached a wide audience.[4] Its success prompted the follow-up collection *Musical Improvisation: Art, Education, and Society* (2009), edited by Nettl and Gabriel Solis.[5]

There is no simple explanation why the topic started attracting so much scholarly interest in the 1990s and 2000s. But the growth of jazz studies, which followed the surge of enthusiasm greeting the creation of Jazz at Lincoln Center, seems to have played a decisive role. Prior to this moment, jazz was a well-established field but was still methodologically narrow and lacking in humanistic resonance. The situation changed swiftly in the 1990s as musicologists opened the floodgates of cultural, political, and anthropological theory and offered sweeping new perspectives on jazz improvisation.[6] The comparative project of *In the Course of Performance* seems to have been inspired, at least in part, by the prospect of achieving comparably rich interpretations of improvisation in other traditions. Its contents were clearly designed to represent as many different traditions as possible, but jazz and African American topics came out proportionally overrepresented.

In the past decade improvisation studies have continued to proliferate in new directions, attracting the attention of philosophers, cognitive scientists, music educators, and scholars of popular music. But the center of gravity once occupied by jazz scholars has now shifted toward a coalition of artists and intellectuals associated with the journal *Critical Studies in Improvisation*. The discourse of CSI is of course not univocal, but it advances a fairly explicit and circumscribed agenda.[7] It focuses mainly on those kinds of experimental collective improvisation that are rooted in progressive black jazz styles from bebop forward. John Coltrane, who evolved through bebop and modal jazz to free jazz, is its attendant spirit. CSI conceives of improvisation as something much larger than music. It is a metaphor for the process of social formation itself, working toward progressive, democratic, and cooperative goals in a pluralistic world: "improvisation is at its heart a democratic, humane, and emanci-patory practice . . . a generative yet largely unexamined model for political, cultural, and ethical dialogue and action."[8] Although this is phrased as a general statement about the nature of improvisation, most writings within the CSI group understand improvisation, implicitly or explicitly, as a creative response to the historical experi-ence of African Americans under conditions of violence, dispossession, and political oppression, and, because born out of these conditions, as essentially emancipatory, collective, anti-institutional, or politically resistive. In a characteristically circular formulation, the authors of *The Fierce Urgency of Now* ask: "How has the substantial body of cultural practices associated with improvised musics been marginalized as a function of their challenge to orthodoxies?"[9]

Given the thematic emphases and the historical boundaries of CSI, it is not sur-prising that European classical music is rarely discussed or even mentioned within it. Classical music may, indeed, be the musical tradition against which improvisational music is implicitly defined.[10] It is, after all, associated historically with white European elites and dominant social powers. In an essay that played a seminal role in the forma-tion of the field, George Lewis spoke of a "gap of nearly one hundred and fifty years" in European improvised music—the period between 1800, when the extemporaneous realization of figured bass ceased to be a normative practice, and 1950, when bebop players and avant-garde composers began re-engaging with it.[11] As a heuristic marker for large-scale historical trends, the 150-year gap might suffice. But as a setup for the *critical* study of improvisation—that is, an approach that probes its social, political, and philosophical dimensions—it is in many ways counterproductive, for improvi-sation did not truly "disappear" in nineteenth-century European music. In liturgical music, for example, it did not disappear at all. In most other places it was rechanneled and redistributed, pressed from the mainstream out into certain margins, and this marginalizing process, which is at once social and aesthetic, touches on the central concerns of CSI.

This history, then, does not start from the assumption that improvisation always challenges orthodoxies. It attempts, rather, to show how the interpretation of improv-isation as resistive or subversive emerged historically. At the beginning of the period considered here, around 1810, improvisation was widely practiced by musicians who wielded authority in the musical mainstream, and it was one of the most effective demonstrations of their authority as specialized professionals. When critics began censuring it in the 1820s and 1830s, they doubtless frightened some talented musicians away. But this prohibition had the unintended effect of giving it the allure of the for-bidden, and this incited romantic artists to reclaim it in a rebellious, innovative, some-times visionary spirit. Even where romantic musicians did not continue improvising per se, they often sympathized with the valorized idea of improvisation that literary romantics were promoting.[12] Representations of improvisers increasingly constructed them as figures on the margins of cultural power—shepherds, gypsies, troubadours, marketplace entertainers—and all these characters were represented as virtuous or attractive *because* of their outsider status.

A main contention of this book, then, is that the vision of musical improvisation as a repository of a social and ethical "good"—a vision central to critical improvisation studies—is ultimately the product of the early nineteenth century, and owes its initial discursive development to literary romanticism. This point has been made most explicitly in Angela Esterhammer's valuable book *Romanticism and Improvisation*.[13] Esterhammer demonstrates that the very notion of improvisation as a distinct mode of artistic production was shaped by two developments. First, in the later eighteenth century, a growing culture of tourism sent hordes of people to Italy, where they encountered performances of extemporaneous poetry unlike anything they had ever witnessed at home. For foreign travelers this was truly an encounter with a culturally "other" practice. They experienced a combination of emotion, astonishment, and phantasmic connection to the ancient Latin world. The second development was a consequence of the first: in the first three decades of the nineteenth century, improvisers of poetry were brought to European audiences en masse through a combination of live performances and literary representations. Entrepreneurial Italian poets, recognizing the market for their performances outside Italy, undertook European tours, and soon enough they found imitators improvising poems in French and German.

Print culture played an even more decisive role in disseminating the image and idea of the improviser. The single most influential work was Germaine de Staël's novel *Corinne*, an international bestseller of rare proportions whose heroine is an Italian improvising poet. De Staël's work influenced representations of improvisers in popular poetry, novels, music, and opera. When Stendhal, for example, celebrated the improvisational spirit of Italian music, opposing it to the reflective and intellectual character of German music, he was operating squarely within the premises of national-ethnic comparisons established by Staël.[14] Esterhammer demonstrates that the character-allegory Corinne became a deeply entrenched literary topos that condensed a number of fraught binary oppositions: Italian-English, southern-northern, oral-written, feminine-masculine, performed-written, spontaneous-reflective, etc. In these oppositions the second term is the privileged one, but the improviser's activity always suspends that privilege temporarily, destabilizing the opposition and exposing the force involved in the reassertion of the second term. From the beginning, then, the romantic image of the improviser had a disruptive potential, exerting tension against the privilege of writing, reason, and masculinity.[15]

These literary developments unfolded independently from music, which had its own, separate history and practice of improvisation. But discourse about music, as distinguished from musical practice, was deeply shaped by Stäel's novel and the aesthetics of romanticism. One reason is that Italian poetry improvisers were normally accompanied by a guitar, violin, or piano, and their performances had much in common with those of musicians, especially solo virtuosos. Regardless of the cause, literary culture gave the term "improvisation" a currency it had not previously possessed in musical parlance. For the first half of the nineteenth century, French musicians, theorists, and pedagogues used the term *préluder* far more often than *improviser*. The latter term only became standard among music professionals in the second half of the century. However, romantic authors such as George Sand were partial to the poetic implications of the word *improviser*, and eagerly drew it into their writings about music and art. In Germany the terms *fantasiren, präludiren, vom Stegreif spielen*, and *extemporiren* took even longer to get displaced by *improvisieren*. In all languages the noun "improvisation," as used to designate a single event or single production, was used even more rarely for music. The noun form "an improvisation" was used to designate a verbal effusion like Corinne's much-excerpted "Improvisation at the Capitol," or a notable parliamentary or political speech.[16] The details of the semantics matter less than the fact that, for the first half of the nineteenth century, the terms "improvise" and "improvisation" were by no means the dominant nomenclature for what we now call musical improvisation. The terminology was far more differentiated according to instrument, style, and genre. As we will see when considering Carl Loewe, the term "improvisation" moved more or less unidirectionally from literary discourse into musical discourse.

It is important to underline that the "construction" of improvisation in romantic literature was not purely the work of writers, words, and readers. It was also the work of musical and poetic improvisers, with whose performances writers engaged in a sort of symbiotic dialogue. One of the salutary aspects of Esterhammer's history of poetry improvisers is that it upholds an ontological distinction between performances and literary representations, while also showing their imbrication and mutual constitution in the early nineteenth century. The distinction should be maintained not for a priori philosophical reasons, but because romantic rhetoric often marks the gap between the event and its recollection, and thrives on the tension between them. It is typical of romantic rhetoric, for example, to evoke improvisation as a generative act that escapes the boundedness of linguistic signs and the materialities of communication. Taking a consciously ironic stance, it employs literary artifice to revive the magical intensity of an event that is already lost to language and reflection.[17]

In focusing on this interplay between musical improvisations, literary representations, and critical reception, this book marks a departure from much of the previous musicological literature. The majority of existing studies of improvisation in the nineteenth century have focused on its production—on what performers did and what pedagogues prescribed. They have typically concentrated on single artists, documenting practices of preluding and free extemporization among influential instrumental composers such as Beethoven, Schubert, Mendelssohn, Chopin, Schumann, Liszt, and lesser-known contemporaries.[18] Far less attention has been given to the values and ideas that adhered to improvisation—the meanings it acquired in different social contexts, and the reactions of audiences large and small.[19] In order to give due attention to these latter issues, I draw extensively on sources such as journals, newspapers, letters, diaries, and literary works, and I read them for their evaluative as well as descriptive content. By examining the meanings invested in improvisation by practitioners, audiences, and critics, we will see that even in the midst of its "decline" many continued to view it as a valued, indeed privileged, art. Whether it was classicists nostalgically calling up memories of the beautiful improvisations of

Mozart, Beethoven, and Hummel, or romantic authors spinning fantastic paragraphs around the playing of Liszt and Chopin, there was no shortage of positive, idealizing representations of improvisation. This positive perspective on improvisation coexisted with the mounting opposition to improvisation among professional musicians and critics, and it is not always clear which party was getting the upper hand.

The resurgence of interest in classical improvisation has had a measurable influence on the historiography of nineteenth-century music. The techniques and motivations for "preluding" on the keyboard and the violin, for example, have only recently received in-depth attention. Valerie Goertzen's pioneering studies of preluding remain indispensable for anyone interested in the topic. She demonstrates just how widespread preluding was through the first half of the nineteenth century, and sheds new light on Clara Schumann's preluding practices.[20] Jim Samson situates preluding within the practice of the postclassical virtuoso, unpacking its various social, economic, and aesthetic dimensions in a rich and multivalent account. One of his signal contributions is to detail how the stylized keyboard figures employed by keyboard improvisers became a sonic and musical vocabulary *à part*—a vocabulary later appropriated for composerly purposes as the authority of "composition" gradually displaced the authority of the "virtuoso."[21]

Kenneth Hamilton has further enriched our knowledge of preluding from the time of Liszt through the early twentieth century by mining evidence from master classes, anecdotage, memoirs, and recordings. He shows that preluding and other forms of improvisation were perpetuated in the practices of virtuosos well beyond the familiar heuristic cutoff point of 1850.[22] Studies of violin preluding, too, have recently appeared, revealing a set of principles and motivations quite similar to their pianistic counterparts.[23] These studies collectively furnish a glimpse into an orientation toward music that was more flexible and open-ended than the one prevailing in today's classical music world, where the law of the work is so deeply entrenched. They index a more performance-centered musical ontology, where audiences were attuned to immediate temporal, spatial, and material contingencies of performance. This is not to say that works, compositions, and melody-objects were not also relevant. Players very often improvised on fixed musical entities, and the listener's recognition of these entities was often a precondition for the performance's legibility. But in comparison with today, the balance was shifted more toward the transmissive elements of performance and the agency of the player. Improvisation, in other words, radicalized the performative by bracketing or weakening the influence of the object—the piece or given theme—within the experiential field.

This book concentrates on forms of improvisation that were considerably more free, extensive, and elaborate than improvised preludes, embellishments, introductions, and shorter cadenzas.[24] As a general designation for these relatively expansive and unconstrained improvisational practices I have chosen the term "free playing." This term is preferable not only for its emphasis on musical action, but also as a more neutral alternative to "improvisation," whose discursive emergence and evolution will be tracked carefully. Free playing includes practices that never consolidated as genres—for example, playing a liturgical postlude, working up an arrangement of a single tune by request in a salon, or inventing what Czerny called "preludes of a longer or more elaborate type"—as well as those practices represented in genres such as the free fantasy, the chorale prelude, the extemporaneous fugue, and the short piano prelude. For my purposes the adjective "free" is meant only in a relative sense: free from a score, from memorization, or from rigorous formal norms. It goes without saying that most of the improvisation discussed in this book observed tonal and modal harmonic frameworks and followed conventional principles of melodic motion and chord succession.

The question whether free playing, within those constraints, accesses some deeper existential freedom—a window of indetermination into which the performing subject can enter in order to seize aesthetic agency or self-determination—has been central to critical improvisation studies, but it cannot be answered in a general way for nineteenth-century classical practice. As will be seen in the chapters to follow, attuned listeners did sometimes make judgments about how freely a keyboardist was improvising. More often, however, they expressed a sense of frustration at not being able to determine whether an artist was "really" improvising or not. (The exceptions were romantics such as George Sand, who for philosophical reasons were inclined to exaggerate the claim to "freedom.") This indiscernibility became increasingly problematic in the nineteenth century, as the professional music guild lost its exclusive authority and was forced to confront the judgment of lay audiences.

The relative lack of scholarly attention to forms of free playing other than preluding is understandable in light of the sparse, fragmented trail of historical evidence. And this evidentiary problem is partially responsible for the emphatically documentary approach taken here. The source problem has motivated scholars to rely heavily on pedagogical treatises, written out variants, and printed compositions of an improvisational character.[25] Pedagogical treatises are indispensable sources, of course, but as historical evidence they are limited by their prescriptive approach: they delineate rules and principles for how to start making extemporaneous music, but say little about the details of elaborating freely, which must have been transmitted aurally through direct modeling and imitation. And curiously, the authors of such treatises were rarely recognized as outstanding improvisers themselves. Grétry, Czerny, and Kalkbrenner were esteemed pedagogues who left valuable treatises on the subject, yet none of them had a strong reputation as an improviser. Meanwhile the most admired improvisers— Vogler, Hummel, Moscheles, and Liszt—wrote about improvisation in only a cursory way, if at all. We can hypothesize that the motivation for publishing such treatises came less from a desire to transmit the author's own practice than from a pedagogical impulse or a publisher's opportunity.

Musicology's deep attachment to scores has presented a far greater methodological limitation than the reliance on treatises. Many studies of improvisation in the early nineteenth century prove, when looked at more closely, to be about reflected images of improvisation found in published works or composers' sketches. The best of these studies contextualize the printed work in relation to improvised activity, opening our ears to provisional, incidental, or emergent status of passages that we might otherwise imagine to be "fixed." They attune us to fluctuations between a looser and tighter sense of apparent authorial control in the discursive unfolding of a piece.[26] Studies of this kind are nonetheless fundamentally about compositions. Improvisation enters as a component of the work's aesthetic character, not as a live event or performed phenomenon, and not as a practice transmitted from performer to performer through listening and imitation. Scholars have gravitated toward pieces with the title "Fantasy" as a potentially more transparent window into past improvisational practice, without reflecting on the disjunctions—temporal, social, stylistic—that are formed when music is written down.[27] At a conference on classical improvisation that took place in 2014, a concert pianist with a scholarly bent claimed that Beethoven's *Fantasia*, op. 77 was "probably as close to Beethoven's actual improvisations as anything we have on paper." This point is backed up by memoirs of Czerny and Moscheles. But such comments are usually offered as a reason to "round up" the interpretation—that is, to treat a piece like op. 77 as a "close enough" representation of Beethoven's improvisation, and to forget about the implications of its conversion into a published piece.

To avoid the limitations of prescriptions (treatises) and stylizations (scores), and to maintain a focus on improvisation as performance, this history takes root in descriptive sources—press reviews, diaries, letters, archival sketches, and memoirs. Such sources are of course widely used already, but in improvisation studies they typically serve as anecdotal prefaces preceding score-focused analysis. With an accumulation of descriptive details, we can reconstruct at least in broad outlines how keyboardists chose their material and how they elaborated upon it, and importantly, in some cases, they convey information about improvisation that cannot be gleaned from scores or treatises. Descriptive sources such as periodicals also provide information about audience behavior and critical response, giving access to questions of public reception, critical debate, and social meaning that are thematically central to this book. Descriptive and journalistic sources have the further benefit of filling out the picture of the events to which improvisational performances belong, thus opening up some of the temporal and communicative aspects of improvisation that scores and treatises necessarily filter out. No history of improvisational practice in this period, however, can do entirely without scores. They identify the stylistic horizons from which we can begin to imagine how extemporaneous music might have sounded at all, and to some degree any reconstruction of free improvisation will be back-derived from them. This study will treat them skeptically, as a necessary but relatively indirect avenue to the historicization of improvisational practice.

The time period 1810–1880 serves to delineate a large-scale transition: from an era in which free playing was common but relatively unmarked, into an era where there was little free playing but the improvisation imaginary prevailed. In 1810 the genre of the free fantasia, strongly linked to keyboard improvisation, had already accrued a distinctive constellation of meanings gravitating around the sensitive delicacy of the clavichord, the experience of solitude, the expression of intense melancholy, and the capricious or playful workings of interior psychological experience. In her study of the free fantasia genre from C. P. E. Bach to Beethoven, Annette Richards shows how musicians, aestheticians, psychologists, critics, and authors of romantic fiction all contributed to this multilayered hermeneutic of the genre, which marked it off from other kinds of music as a distinctive experiential, emotive, and cognitive realm. The widely circulated image of Beethoven's improvisations as expressions of an intensely feeling soul—by turns quirky, passionate, dark, and exalted—is an outgrowth of this particular hermeneutic, and in many respects it marks a historical endpoint. By 1810 the older type of free fantasia had largely been converted into a rhetorical style or genre of composition.[28] As a genre, it was now developing with little direct interface with improvisational practice, and few players after Beethoven pursued the older free fantasia aesthetic when improvising.[29]

The other kinds of free playing that prevailed around 1810, in contrast to the free fantasia, had very little hermeneutic baggage attached. When a pianist improvised a slow, free introduction to a composed-out rondo or variation set, for example, no one considered it especially remarkable or "meaningful." The practice was familiar enough to count as a natural part of a good performer's repertoire of skills. While such improvised music might have distinctive stylistic markers—martial rhythms, free-flowing lyricism, unexpected modulations, or sudden turns of mood—it did not necessarily have any of them, and these particular stylistic markers were already so well absorbed into the rhetoric of composed music as to weaken their status as "improvisational." Yet around this time improvisation was changing in response to the growing aesthetic autonomy of the piano. In the later eighteenth century Clementi, Cramer, and Dussek had displaced the *galant* style with a more "idiomatic" piano vocabulary, breaking the instrument's close ties to improvised figured bass realization and "emancipating" the piano from its role as an accompanying instrument. Composers and players, released from responsibility to figured bass (though still versed in it), redirected their improvisational impulses toward freer methods of elaboration based on motives, arpeggio patterns, and harmonic modulation, all of them greatly facilitated by the pedal, which allowed them to linger on harmonies while plotting the next move.

The performance of free fantasies was also transformed by the hegemony of the *stile brillante* or "postclassical" style in the period 1815–1830. Hummel, Moscheles, and Kalkbrenner capitalized on technological advances in piano construction to develop a style that would make the piano viable as a solo instrument in large concert venues. Improvised fantasies in the *stile brillante* played before larger public audiences came to a peak in these years, and they turned many of the values of the earlier, C. P. E Bach–type free fantasia on their head. They showed off the bright, pearly sonorities of the piano, as against the soft, subtle, and delicate expressive values associated with the clavichord. They aspired not to private, intimate expression, but to efficacious communication with large listening audiences. They did not project the improvising performer as a man of intense inward feeling, but as a learned, accomplished artist who combined lively musical invention with technical discipline, leavened with a sense of elevation or seriousness. Inverting the esoteric style of earlier free fantasies, *stile brillante* pianists pitched their improvisations to the social character of the concert event, taking themes from the audience and incorporating overtly popular, pleasing elements.

The historical endpoint of this study, ca. 1880, is admittedly somewhat more arbitrary. Improvising pianists did occasionally appear beyond that date. But after the child prodigy Ferruccio Busoni burst on the scene with free improvisations in the late 1870s, one looks in vain for signs of improvisational life.[30] Already by 1870 most of the pianists who improvised easily and fluently—Moscheles, Ferdinand Hiller, Meyerbeer, and to a lesser degree Liszt—had recently passed away or had stopped improvising for audiences with any regularity. The improvisation imaginary, on the other hand, was reaching a peak in its development. It was in 1871 that Wagner praised the Shakespearean drama as "a fixed mimetic improvisation of the very highest poetic value," and reminded readers that Beethoven's improvisations, according to his contemporaries, were so brilliant as to have outstripped his composed music. By this point, too, it had become a critical cliché to praise a performance for being "like an improvisation"—a form of praise that never translated into a desire or demand for the real thing. More and more, compositions were appearing with the title *Improvisation*, and most sounded like simple character pieces. Improvisation had completed its evolution into the highly valued, but vaguely defined, aesthetic quality of "improvisatoriness."

The central chapters of this book are case studies of individuals—J. N. Hummel, Ignaz Moscheles, Carl Loewe, Robert Schumann, and Franz Liszt—who extensively practiced some form of free playing. The case-study approach naturally brings with it certain disadvantages. It makes less room for highly reputed improvisers such Beethoven, Schubert, Mendelssohn, and Chopin, whose eminence as composers naturally attracts greater interest. Fortunately, the high status of these figures as composers has already translated into rigorous, detailed studies of their improvising habits. But the main reason for focusing on musicians like Hummel, Moscheles, Loewe, and Abbé Vogler, whose compositions are barely known today, is that they all had a strong native inclination to improvise and sustained impressive international reputations as improvising performers—something that cannot really be said of Beethoven, Schubert, or Chopin. Indeed, the fact that so many of the best-known improvisers of the nineteenth century have gone down in history as second-rate composers (though always admired in their own day as composers) suggests that high-level improvisation could be maintained only at the expense of those energies and skills that favored the production of long-lasting works—a tension that will be dramatized in the chapter on Schumann.

Another advantage of the case studies chosen for this book is that their extemporaneous playing is exceptionally well documented. They therefore allow us to trace in a richly "networked" way the motives and values—institutional, personal, philosophical, aesthetic, and pragmatic—that made them want to improvise, to reinvent it in a new way, or to stop doing it altogether. Schumann and Liszt, who transitioned out of improvisation in different degrees, are particularly suitable for historicizing the onset of pressures discouraging or restraining improvisation. The case-study approach also reins in the production of general, "panoramic" claims about improvisation "as a whole." In researching this book I was surprised to discover just how dispersed and unevenly distributed the practices were. Even within a single institution there could be large differences. Church organists in big cities were generally far better improvisers

than those in small towns, and church music reformers anxiously discouraged players
from ruining services with poor improvisation. Amateur keyboardists probably played
from sheet music most of the time, but among them there were some enthusiastic free
players including John Stuart Mill, Franz Grillparzer, and Friedrich Nietzsche. Many
composers treated improvisation as an essential resource for composition (Meyerbeer,
Liszt), but others largely dispensed with it in their creative process (Berlioz, later
Schumann). The free fantasy genre had some standard formal procedures, but
Mendelssohn seems to have disregarded them, and developed his own proprietary
strategies such as using chorale tunes or devising imperceptible transitions between
different melodies.

Improvisational practices, then, were unruly with regard to genre, institution, and
individual player. It is difficult to find centers of gravity or demarcated "areas" within
which it can be analyzed. Historians have commonly considered it the special province
of a professional type that emerged in the early nineteenth century: the freelance instrumental virtuoso. But even here it seems that the dispositions and inclinations of
individuals distributed the practices unevenly. Liszt, Hummel, and Moscheles were
stellar representatives of modern virtuosity, and each garnered special mention for his
skill in improvisation. But Friedrich Kalkbrenner, Sigismond Thalberg, and Alexander
Dreyschock were also among the top pianistic celebrities of this period, and while they
might well have embellished here and there, none of them performed free fantasies in
public or had a comparable reputation for it.[31] Clara Wieck improvised a fantasy on a
pair of given themes at her public Paris debut of 1832, but as Robert Schumann proudly
reported somewhat later, "after this she never did this publicly and only rarely in very
small private circles, when unexpectedly demanded, thus unprepared in the strictest
sense of the word" (NZM 1838, 103). In fact Wieck did later on improvise transitions
between self-devised suites of short pieces, but only for a short time and with little
critical notice. Most virtuosos appear not to have improvised very often in private
either, though there is no reason to doubt they had the requisite training to do so.
Chopin improvised free fantasies in public before 1830 but never at his subsequent
public concerts, reserving it exclusively for private contexts and appearances before
royalty. Nor did audiences and critics complain as improvisation gradually ebbed from
concert programs. It was neither expected nor especially desired that a great pianist
should improvise at a concert unless he already had a stellar reputation for it (for example Hummel or Bocklet). From what we can tell, listeners were perfectly content to
hear superb keyboard execution, and if they heard a good improvisation on top of that,
so much the better.

I emphasize such unevenness in the distribution of free practices because many
partisans of the recent revival in classical improvisation, discovering that it was more
common than they had previously realized, sometimes leap to the claim that "everyone"
in the nineteenth century improvised, and this does not make a good starting point
for thinking about the practice historically. Although it may seem counterintuitive,
the institution of the concert virtuoso probably contributed more to the decline than
the survival of improvisation. As we will see many times in the chapters that follow,

the virtuoso's overriding need to communicate successfully with a large and socially heterogeneous audience presented major obstacles to improvisation, and no virtuoso successfully reconciled the free fantasy's elevated status with their public activities. Institutions that were free from the demands of public-sphere communication—such as the elite salon and the church-music profession—were far more favorable to the survival of improvisation.

If any institution kept improvisation vital in nineteenth-century musical life, it was not the modern, "emancipated" virtuoso, but the profession of the kapellmeister, whose education revolved around ideals of rigorous theoretical training, pragmatic skill, and stylistic flexibility. Nearly all the musicians who serve as case studies in this book—Vogler, Meyerbeer, Weber, Hummel, Moscheles, Loewe, Liszt, Schumann, Hiller—carried the official title "kapellmeister" at some point, if not their entire professional lives. Today the word has an archaic resonance associated with eighteenth-century courts and absolutism. But kapellmeisters, music directors, *maîtres de chapelle*, and *maestri di cappella* survived through the nineteenth century (and indeed into the twentieth), serving in churches, theaters, and orchestral societies as well as royal houses. Often working off the usual maps of music history, they were versatile generalists, called upon to fulfill a variety of functions as instrumentalist, composer, conductor, teacher, administrator, pedagogue, and sometimes theorist.[32] The balance of such responsibilities depended on the needs of the employer and the capacities of the individual musician, but the prerequisite of a broad, general musical education was everywhere the same. For the first half of the century especially, the kapellmeister had to be highly skilled on an instrument, thoroughly grounded in harmonic and contrapuntal theory, versed in a variety of compositional genres, and fluent in score-reading, notation, and transposition. This general, all-around musicianship could feed into less tangible requirements such as keeping polyphonic or concerted music in good coordination and balance, projecting a sense of authority over the band, and perhaps also a certain gift for leadership and management.[33] Very few musicians, of course, could fulfill all these requirements, but those who came closest, usually keyboardists, ascended most easily in the professional world. This model of musical education, feeding what I will call the "kapellmeister network," was the principal foundation for high-level improvisational skill, whether taking the form of preludes, interludes, and postludes on the church organ, or free fantasies on themes given by a concert audience.[34]

In Christian churches across Europe, organ improvisation in free and strict forms thrived throughout the entire nineteenth century, largely untouched by romantic ideology, by the philosophy of the "work," or by the development of public concert culture. General narratives of nineteenth-century music have been able to ignore organ music and practical liturgical music almost completely, leaving the organ in a ghetto of specialized organ scholarship. Improvisation was so integral to organ practice that, much of time, players did not even perceive it as "improvisation" at all. Only at inaugurations of new instruments, and at the occasional organ concert (still very rare in the early nineteenth century), was it marked as such. Organists thus had little impact on the public experience of improvisation and on the developing improvisation imaginary.

But they belonged squarely to the kapellmeister network and had the same harmonic and contrapuntal knowledge–base as did composers of opera, instrumental music, and church music. The difference was that organists had many more opportunities to develop and exercise this knowledge on their instrument, and they employed a wider range of idioms, including fugal and contrapuntal styles that transferred less easily to the piano. Organ improvisation is too vast a topic to treat in any comprehensive way for the nineteenth century, but the first three chapters will all show that it underpinned superior piano improvisation in the first decades of the nineteenth century, most notably with Vogler and Mendelssohn. Later in the century organ improvisation broke decisively into "mainstream" relevance as organists like Saint-Saëns, Bruckner, Franck, and Alexandre Guilmant attracted listening audiences, acting simultaneously as liturgical organists and composers of concert music, with some obvious cross-feeding of practices.[35] But this topic lies beyond the scope of my study.

The case studies in this book elaborate on the persona, aura, and visual presence of the musician as well as the more strictly musical-stylistic elements of their performances. This approach is intended, however quixotically, to reconstruct improvisation of the past in a more completely performative way—that is, with attention to all the factors, including the performer's look and gestures, that contribute to the meaning of the event. Ideally it will bring into sharper focus the temporally and spatially immanent aspects of improvisation. But the greater advantage, perhaps, is to show how musical improvisation intersected with other sorts of improvised cultural performance so that, in the spirit of CSI, the study of improvisation enriches our understanding of social relations more generally. Links between musical improvisation and poetry improvisation, supported by the cult of Corinne and conventions of artistic salons, were uncommonly intimate. The key visual codes central to the romantic image of poetry improvisers— the inspired countenance, the transported gaze, and energetic physical signs of mental labor—all worked their way into solo musical performance by the 1830s. But the field of improvisational performance extends wider still—into theater, political oratory, church sermons, painting, academic lectures, marketplace entertainments, and salon rituals such as toasts or spontaneous lyric poems—and all these connections will be found in the reception of the musicians studied most closely here. The story of musical improvisation in the early nineteenth century thus belongs to a larger story about intersecting, sometimes overlapping strains of performance culture, with a particular emphasis on the solo performer and his relation to larger audiences.

The first two chapters concentrate on the years 1810–1830 and on musicians in the kapellmeister network. Chapter 1, "The School of Abbé Vogler: Weber and Meyerbeer," tracks a line of improvisational influence that issued from the organ playing and theoretical teachings of Georg Joseph (Abbé) Vogler, whose most famous students were Carl Maria von Weber and Giacomo Meyerbeer. Although Vogler was in many respects a product of eighteenth-century aesthetic and theoretical dispositions, he also had a progressive, even experimental streak that manifested itself in his keyboard improvisations. He anticipated the figure of the modern virtuoso by touring and playing organ concerts that featured dramatic improvisations depicting biblical narratives. Most important, he made keyboard improvisation an integral part of his pedagogical method, requiring students to improvise simultaneously with him and with each other. It is clear that while Vogler instructed his students in thoroughbass methods, his improvisational teaching featured freer types of contrapuntal and figural elaboration that influenced their performances and compositions. Vogler's approach to improvisation encouraged harmonic experimentation that influenced Weber's and Meyerbeer's expanded use of tonality. Because the material of this chapter precedes the era of widespread music journalism, it has a more music-technical character than the remainder of the book, and readers with less technical knowledge may want to begin with Chapter 2.

Chapter 2, "The Kapellmeister Network and the Performance of Community: Hummel, Moscheles, and Mendelssohn," concerns the free fantasy and its relationship to the public concert life that emerged in the years after 1815. While giving significant attention to less well-known improvisers of the postclassical generation, its main protagonists are Johann Nepomuk Hummel, the undisputed master of the improvised free fantasy in this period, and his close rival Ignaz Moscheles. I argue that Hummel's free fantasies were admired for hybridizing the learned style of the kapellmeisters with the popular style associated with modern virtuosi, thereby modeling a solution to one of the major problems of this period: the gap between experts and laypersons, dilettantes and connoisseurs. A close look at Hummel's strategies shows that in private circumstances he improvised in a different way addressed to the values of connoisseurs alone, and that some critics objected to his more "popular" public fantasies on given themes. Moscheles's approach to free fantasies, while not fundamentally different from that of Hummel, accented the pleasurable, hedonistic values of the genre, and in his reception we find the first stirrings of the improvisation imaginary. This chapter considers how improvisation served as a performance of authority and learnedness rooted in the kapellmeister network, a network that includes Mendelssohn, the little-known Carl Maria von Bocklet, and Hummel's most celebrated student, Ferdinand Hiller.

Chapters 3–5 are case studies of musicians whose free playing was rooted in the postclassical pianism of the 1820s, but took improvisation in quite different directions under the influence of romanticism. Chapter 3, "Music-Poetry-Improvisation: Carl Loewe's Performative Romanticism," is about a little-known musician who undertook an unprecedented and remarkable task: improvising entire songs, both the melody and the accompaniment, on poems given to him by the audience. This chapter reconstructs Loewe's methods for performing this difficult feat and describes the cultural impetuses that motivated it. I propose that Loewe's improvisations, performed mainly on a series of concert tours he undertook in the 1830s, condensed a number of independent cultural strains: the kapellmeister's fluency in keyboard improvisation, the practice of touring virtuosos, the literary cult of poetic improvisers, and the genre theory of the ballad, which described it as a species of epic or bardic narration that was understood as improvisatory in character.

Chapter 4, "Schumann and the Economization of Musical Labor," details Robert Schumann's remarkable evolution from an eager and fluent improviser into a composer who advocated writing music away from the piano entirely. His evolution symptomat-ically demonstrates the growing tension or polarization between improvisation and composition—modes of music-making that were generally viewed as mutually benefi-cial up until the 1830s. His early, piano-centered output provides clues into how certain transitional and rhetorical strategies were rooted in keyboard improvisational practices, but consciously invested with a "depth" or "psychology" that gave them a romantic cast. Later in the chapter I broaden the interpretive lens to consider how Schumann's anxiety over improvisation was shaped by what I call an "ethos of economy" common to the edu-cated classes in this period. Improvisation thrived on certain anti-economic impulses—a dilated sense of temporal unfolding, a strenuous type of performer training, and a risk of inefficacious communication—that ran counter to bourgeois ethical codes such as the containment of excess or waste and the rational ordering of available resources.

Chapter 5, "Liszt and the Romantic Rhetoric of Improvisation," follows another mu-sician of strong improvisatory inclinations who modified his practice in response to rising criticisms. Unlike Schumann's more linear development, though, Liszt's rela-tionship with improvisation was up and down. Free improvisations were central to his reputation as a child prodigy, yet the more he sought recognition as a composer, the more compelled he felt to rein it in for fear of being judged as superficial. At the same time, romantic authors such as George Sand and Heinrich Heine were advancing a pos-itive new vision of improvisation as a privileged, elevated mode of artistic utterance, and Liszt was one of their main exhibits. To an extent matched only by Chopin and Paganini, Liszt gave the impression that he was blurring the line between playing a prepared piece and improvising. He thus played a key role in linking improvisational practice with the emerging imaginary ideal of improvisation, while submitting himself in less conscious ways to the new order of "works" and "interpreters."

Chapter 6, "Improvisatoriness: The Regime of the Improvisation Imaginary," is some-what different from the others in its focus on representations and discourses of im-provisation, which overtook practices in the period 1847–1880. The chapter begins with a discussion of pockets of improvisational activity that survived in the tributaries, in-cluding conservatory training in *accompagnement*, the ongoing interludes and preludes of concert pianists, and the uninterrupted practice of organists. The second part of the chapter discusses literary representations of improvisation, all of which present it in an aesthetically and ethically positive light, thereby exerting tension against mainstream or dominant values that were working against it. Wagner's essay "On the Destiny of Opera" praises improvisation as a model of perfect artistic creation, uniting inven-tion and execution in a single moment. His troubadour-heros Tannhäuser and Walther von Stolzing (from *Die Meistersinger von Nürnberg*) demonstrate virtue and genius by performing spontaneous, unpremeditated songs, to which Wagner attributes distinct social and political agencies. Improvisation also finds heavily idealized representation in the figure of the gypsy, about whom Liszt writes in a simultaneously idealizing and condescending manner. The *coup de grâce* of the improvisation imaginary, however, was the installation of a receptive disposition that defined the ideal performance as "improvisatory."

This study joins a broader field of recent musicological work that aspires to re-imagine the history of European music through improvised practices and processes of aural transmission. In two lengthy essays Leo Treitler endeavored to understand the role of improvisation in the creation of medieval chant and organum. He found that while medieval theorists did sometimes use terms like *ex improviso* to describe a certain kind of singing, scholars of medieval music often misinterpreted these texts by importing an anachronistic notion of "improvisation." In the nineteenth century, Treitler argued, improvisation came to be understood as the antipode of composition, of notated music, and of musical fixity, and this oppositional logic led to all kinds of conceptual errors on the part of twentieth-century scholars. Just as significant, he claimed, the term "improvisation" often carried pejorative connotations associated with a lack of discipline, rationality, or planning, thus feeding the misunderstandings and simultaneously twisting them in a moral direction. Even in Treitler's more pos-itivistic research, then, improvisation brought up ethical issues and seemed to need an "underdog" defense. As he traced the complex relationships between oral practice, memorization, and notation in medieval chant, Treitler found himself taking on the entire privilege his discipline accorded to notated sources and to interpretive stability. In his revisionist perspective, the practicing singer was as central to the music's on-tology as the written source: "Addressing medieval improvisation in terms of what it was . . . will bring primary attention to performance, not just as medium for the presentation of works, but as primary musical fact."[36]

Treitler's arguments resonated with the sustained critique of score- and work-centered methods that marked the "new musicology" of the 1990s. His interpreta-tion stressed the agency of medieval church singers and the close interplay between improvisational performance and composition, building an interpretation that pow-erfully opposed the reification of chant as a fixed, "work"-like repertoire. It gave me-dieval chant and organum the appearance of "musicking"—Christopher Small's term for music conceived as human activity, embodied practice, and social behavior. "The fundamental nature and meaning of music," Small wrote, "lie not in objects, not in musical works at all, but in action, in what people do."[37] Small's critique was motivated by a profound dissatisfaction with the behaviors and social relationships that had be-come sedimented in the culture of classical music, which he judged inimical to the music's potential for meaningful engagement and participation. The revival of interest in improvisation in scholarship and practice probably takes impetus, at some level, from a similar fatigue with the intellectual and experiential limitations of the "work" as the central organizing concept of classical music culture, and a desire to restore players, performances, and audience participation to a more central position within that culture.

Such an aspiration is also evident in Robert Gjerdingen's work on mid-eighteenth century *galant* style, which is one of the most ambitious attempts to recover and revive improvisation as a constituent element of classical music of the past. Sidestepping the conceptual baggage of "works" almost entirely, Gjerdingen reconceptualizes "galant style" as a repertoire of patterns and schemata that performers and composers of the

eighteenth century internalized through various short exercises (*solfeggi*), and which
they could freely draw upon to generate legible and stylistically idiomatic music. In the
practice of *partimento*, musicians trained in figured bass were encouraged to invent entire pieces over a given, through-composed bass line.[38] In this context, the improvising
musician or ensemble was not asked to invent music *ex nihilo*, but could assemble "a
string of well-learned musical schemata to form a seemingly spontaneous and continuous musical performance."[39] As with Treitler, this revisionist picture of *galant* style
draws improvisation and composition into close proximity: they appear to be different
extensions of the same basic skill set, and the musical language employed is in most
respects identical. Gjerdingen has made suggestive connections between the inventive
capacities of *galant* musicians and the ethos of courtly etiquette in the mid-eighteenth
century, and thereby opened windows for historical and hermeneutic elaboration, but
his main goal is a practical one: to excavate the *solfeggi* and schemata from historical
oblivion and present them in an orderly way for the use of practicing musicians. He
aims at educating classical players not as interpreters of works, but as players who take
active possession of the *galant* musical language and think of themselves as creators
in the fullest sense.

Annette Richards's book *The Free Fantasia and the Musical Picturesque*, likewise
written by a performer-scholar, has less of a pedagogical emphasis and represents
a breakthrough for the cultural archeology of free playing. It traces connections between the free fantasia and discourses of psychology, aesthetics, and selfhood in the
late eighteenth and early nineteenth centuries, offering insights into how improvised
music gathered up associations with melancholy, madness, non-representational sensory experience, and the quirky effects of "picturesque" landscape. Because the time
frame of Richards' study coincides with the early growth of musical journalism, she
is able to source these connections in ways that would be difficult for earlier periods.
My study in many respects picks up where hers leaves off, starting with keyboardist-
composers who emerged in the generation after Beethoven and tracing the meanings
co-engendered by instrumental practices and critical discourses. The historical territory covered here, however, is considerably different as it revolves around the
institutions of the sociable salon and the public concert, which are not as central to
Richards' perspective. The explosive development of music journalism in the 1820s,
furthermore, makes it possible to compare developments in different parts of Europe
and to follow the international peregrinations of performing improvisers. If the "first
wave" of improvisational hermeneutics appeared at the intersection of C. P. E. Bach's
fantasias and eighteenth-century philosophical literature and aesthetics, the "second
wave" departed from the convergence of the kapellmeister network with the cult of
Corinne.

NOTES

1. On the tension between improvisation and the "work," see Carl Dahlhaus, *Nineteenth-
Century Music*, trans. J. Bradford Robinson (Berkeley: University of California Press, 1989),

134–41. Jim Samson expands on the issue at greater length in *Virtuosity and the Musical Work: The Transcendental Studies of Liszt* (Cambridge: Cambridge University Press, 2004); see especially chapter 5 on Liszt's transition to an identity as a "composer." See also Lydia Goehr, *The Imaginary Museum of Musical Works: An Essay in the Philosophy of Music* (Oxford: Oxford University Press, 1992), especially 230–34 on *Werktreue* and improvisation. On the conscience of the "romantic virtuoso" see Robert Wangermée, "Conscience et inconscience du virtuose romantique: A propos des années parisiennes de Franz Liszt," in *Music in Paris in the 1830s*, ed. Peter Bloom (Stuyvesant NY: Pendragon Press, 1987), 553–74. On the question of audience comprehension, see Robin Dale Moore, "The Decline of Improvisation in Western Art Music: An Interpretation of Change," *International Review of the Aesthetics and Sociology of Music* 23, no. 1 (1992): 61–84. A more up-to-date general account of the causes of the decline of improvisation is found in Anna G. Piotrowska, "Expressing the Inexpressible: The Issue of Improvisation and the European Fascination with Gypsy Music in the 19th Century," *International Review of the Aesthetics and Sociology of Music* 43, no. 2 (2012): 325–41.

2. Richard Wagner, "On the Destiny of Opera" [1870], in *Richard Wagner's Prose Works*, ed. William Ashton Ellis, 8 vols. (New York: Broude Brothers, 1966), 5:142–43.

3. Bruno Nettl, "Thoughts on Improvisation: A Comparative Approach," *The Musical Quarterly* 60, no. 1 (1974): 1–19.

4. *In the Course of Performance: Studies in the World of Musical Improvisation*, ed. Bruno Nettl and Melinda Russell (Chicago: Chicago University Press, 1998).

5. *Musical Improvisation: Art, Education, and Society*, ed. Gabriel Solis and Bruno Nettl (Urbana and Chicago: University of Illinois Press, 2009).

6. A short list of such studies would include Gary Tomlinson, "Miles Davis: Musical Dialogician," *Black Music Research Journal* 11, no. 2 (1991): 249–64; Robert Walser, "Out of Notes: Signification, Interpretation, and the Problem of Miles Davis, *Musical Quarterly* 77, no. 2 (1993): 343–65; and Ingrid Monson, *Saying Something: Jazz Improvisation and Interaction* (Chicago: University of Chicago Press, 1996), especially chapter 4. All three of these authors made liberal use of Henry Louis Gates, Jr.'s theory of "signifyin(g)" from *The Signifying Monkey: A Theory of African-American Literary Criticism* (New York: Oxford University Press, 1989). Other influential paths rooted in anthropology and critical theory were forged by Paul Berliner, *Thinking in Jazz: The Infinite Art of Improvisation* (Chicago: University of Chicago Press, 1994); George Lewis, "Improvised Music after 1950: Afrological and Eurological Perspectives," *Black Music Research Journal* 16, no. 1 (1996): 91–122; David Ake, *Jazz Cultures* (Berkeley: University of California Press, 2002), especially chapter 4; and Gary Tomlinson, "Cultural Dialogics and Jazz: A White Historian Signifies," *Black Music Research Journal* 22 (2002): 71–105. An anthology of readings reflecting the renewed interest in jazz and cultural practice was *The Jazz Cadence of American Culture*, ed. Robert O'Meally (New York: Columbia University Press, 1998).

7. *Critical Studies in Improvisation* is an open-access journal and its entire run is available at www.criticalimprov.com. Many aspects of the CSI perspective were articulated in the editors' introductory chapter to *The Other Side of Nowhere: Jazz, Improvisation, and Communities in Dialogue*, ed. Daniel Fischlin and Ajay Heble (Middletown, CT: Wesleyan University Press, 2004), 1–44. This school of thought is sometimes referred to using the name of the scholarly project that launched it: Improvisation, Community, and Social Practice (ICASP).

8. Ajay Fischlin and George Lipsitz, *The Fierce Urgency of Now: Improvisation, Rights, and the Ethics of Cocreation* (Durham: Duke University Press, 2013), xi–xii. According to the program statement on the CSI website the project aims to "assess how innovative performance

practices play a role in developing new, socially responsive forms of community building across national, cultural and artistic boundaries" (http://www.criticalimprov.com/article/view/3082/3300).

9. *The Fierce Urgency of Now*, 191.

10. Thus Derek Bailey, in a typical formulation, writes: "There are . . . musicians who not only cannot improvise but to whom the whole activity is incomprehensible. As might be expected, the non-improvisor is usually to be found in classical music." Derek Bailey, *Improvisation: Its Nature and Practice in Music* (New York: Da Capo, 1992), 66. The statement is true for the context in which Bailey was writing, but it is highly polemical and ahistorical.

11. George Lewis, "Improvised Music after 1950," 215, 226. On p. 226 Lewis nuances the historical picture by discussing retentions of improvisation in nineteenth-century European music. Two other classic books on improvisation, Derek Bailey's *Improvisation: Its Nature and Practice in Music* and Denis Levaillant's *L'Improvisation musicale: essai sur la puissance de jeu* (Arles: Actes Sud, 1996 [1980]), share a primary concern with their present-day avant-garde or experimental practices, and their excursions into the history of improvisation in European music are strongly inflected by this perspective.

12. Robert Wangermée, "L'improvisation pianistique au début du XIXe siècle," In *Miscellanea musicologica Floris van der Mueren* (Ghent: L. van Melle, 1950), 229.

13. Angela Esterhammer, *Romanticism and Improvisation* (Cambridge: Cambridge University Press, 2008).

14. See Stendhal's *Vie de Rossini*, where he characterizes the typical "young Italian" in these terms: "I knew twenty young people in Naples who wrote a tune with as little pretention as one in England writes a letter or in Paris a couplet. Often when returning home in the evening, they sit at the piano and, in this delightful climate, spend a part of the night singing and improvising. . . . They give light of day to the emotion that animates them—that is their secret, that is their happiness." *Vie de Rossini*, ed. Henri Martineau (Paris: Lévy frères, 1854), 7.

15. These tensions come to the fore in Angela Esterhammer's article "The Improviser's Disorder: Spontaneity, Sickness, and Social Deviance in Late Romanticism," *European Romantic Review* 16, no. 2 (2005): 329–40.

16. Erik Simpson has carefully tracked the semantics of the word "improvisation," arguing that Germaine de Staël's 1807 novel "gave British readers a new theory of improvisation, with its modern vocabulary largely vistible in direct cognates" ("Germaine de Staël's *Corinne, or Italy* and the Early Usage of of Improvisation in English," in *The Oxford Handbook of Critical Improvisation Studies*, ed. George Lewis and Benjamin Piekut [New York: Oxford University Press, 2016], 2 vols., 1:3-4). Stephen Blum, too, discusses the semantic and conceptual shifts of improvisation-related terms, including European usages, in "Recognizing Improvisation," in *In the Course of Performance*, 27–46. Marc Perlman is writing a study of the history of the term within musicological discourse, giving particular attention to the late arrival of the abstract noun "improvisation." I thank Professor Perlman for sharing his paper with me.

17. Susan Bernstein argues that performance and improvisation enter romantic discourse as forces to be contained or suppressed, so that an ideology favoring self-present meaning and subjective authorial integrity—that is, "composition"—can be maintained. See *Virtuosity of the Nineteenth Century: Performing Music and Language in Heine, Liszt, and Baudelaire* (Stanford: Stanford University Press, 1998), 83–89. While she insightfully exposes the resistances to improvisation in romantic writing, Bernstein overstates the opposition between composition and improvisation by making Wagner its main antagonist.

18. For some general points on keyboard improvisation of this period see Derek Carew, *The Mechanical Muse: The Piano, Pianism and Piano Music, ca. 1760–1850* (Aldershot: Ashgate, 2007), 431–55. On Beethoven see William Kinderman, "Improvisation in Beethoven's Creative Process," in *Musical Improvisation: Art, Education, and Society*, ed. Gabriel Solis and Bruno Nettl (Urbana and Chicago: University of Illinois Press, 2009), 296–312, and Annette Richards, *The Free Fantasia and the Musical Picturesque* (Cambridge: Cambridge University Press, 2001), 183–231. On Schubert see Walburga Litschauer, "Franz Schuberts Tänze—zwischen Improvisation und Werk," *Musiktheorie* 10, no. 1 (1995): 3–9. On Chopin see Krystyna Kobylànska, "Les improvisations de Frédéric Chopin," in *Chopin Studies* 3 (Warsaw: Frederick Chopin Society, 1990), 77–104; John Rink, "Chopin in Transition," in *La note bleue: Mélanges offerts au Professeur Jean-Jacques Eigeldinger*, ed. Jacqueline Waeber (Bern: Peter Lang, 2006), 45–71; idem, "The Legacy of Improvisation in Chopin," in *Muzyka w kontekscie kultury*, ed. Malgorzata Janicka-Slysz, Teresa Malecka, and Krzysztof Szwajgier (Cracow: Akademia Muzyczne, 2001), 79–89; Jean-Jacques Eigeldinger, "Chopin and 'la note bleue': An Interpretation of the Prelude, op. 34," *Music & Letters* 78, no. 2 (1997): 233–53; idem, *Chopin as Pianist and Teacher*, trans. Naomi Shoet (Cambridge: Cambridge University Press, 1986), 282-89. On Mendelssohn see Wm. A. Little, *Mendelssohn and the Organ* (Oxford: Oxford University Press, 2010), 90–103; R. Larry Todd, "Mozart according to Mendelssohn: A Contribution to *Rezeptionsgeschichte*," in *Perspectives on Mozart Performance*, ed. R. Larry Todd and Peter Williams (Cambridge: Cambridge University Press, 1991), 158–203; Angela R. Mace, "Improvisational, Elaboration, Composition: The Mendelssohns and the Classical Cadenza," in *Mendelssohn Perspectives*, ed. Nicole Grimes and Angela Mace (Aldershot: Ashgate, 2012), 223–48. On Schumann see Dana Gooley, "Schumann and the Agencies of Improvisation," in *Rethinking Schumann*, ed. Laura Tunbridge and Roe-Min Kok (Oxford: Oxford University Press, 2011), 129–56. On Liszt, see the notes to Chapter 5.

19. A notable exception is Jeffrey Kallberg, "Chopin and the Aesthetic of the Sketch: A New Prelude in E♭ minor?" *Early Music* 29, no. 3 (2001): 408–22, which differentiates various aesthetic positions on improvisational painting, music, and literature within the French romantic circle.

20. Valerie Woodring Goertzen, "By Way of Introduction: Preluding by 18th- and Early 19th-Century Pianists," *Journal of Musicology* 14, no. 3 (1996): 299–337. Idem, "Setting the Stage: Clara Schumann's Preludes," in *In the Course of Performance: Studies in the World of Musical Improvisation* (Chicago: Chicago University Press, 1998), 237–60. Idem, "Clara Wieck Schumann's Improvisations and her 'Mosaics' of Small Forms," in *Beyond Notes: Improvisation in Western Music of the Eighteenth and Nineteenth Centuries*, ed. Rudolph Rasch (Lucca: Brepols, 2011), 153–62. For the early nineteenth century see also Nicholas Temperley, "Preluding at the Piano," in *Musical Improvisation: Art, Education and Society*, ed. Gabriel Solis and Bruno Nettl (Urbana: University of Illinois Press, 2009), 323–42. For an approach that similarly emphasizes formal models and social motives, see Claudio Bacciagaluppi, "Die Kunst des Präludirens," in *Zwischen schöpferischer Individualität und künstlerischer Selbstverleugnung: zur musikalischen Aufführungspraxis im 19. Jahrhundert*, ed. C. Bacciagaluppi, R. Brotbeck, and A. Gerhard (Schliengen: Argus, 2009), 169–188.

21. Jim Samson, *Virtuosity and the Musical Work: The Transcendental Studies of Liszt* (Cambridge: Cambridge University Press, 2003), especially chapter 2.

22. Kenneth Hamilton, *After the Golden Age: Romantic Pianism and Modern Performance* (Oxford: Oxford University Press, 2008), 101–38.

23. Renato Ricci, "Charles-Auguste de Bériot e l'improvvisazione virtuosistica per violin," in *Beyond Notes: Improvisation in Western Music*, 217–37. Pierre Baillot's 1834 treatise *The Art*

of the Violin, adopted by the Conservatoire de Paris, devotes an entire chapter to "Melodic and Harmonic Preludes" and is gaining increasingly attention from historians of performance practice. See Pierre Marie François de Sales Baillot, *The Art of the Violin*, ed. and trans. Louise Goldberg (Evanston, Illinois: Northwestern University Press, 1991), 329–45. On violin improvisation see also Dana Gooley, "Violin Improvisation in the Early Nineteenth Century: Between Practice and Illusion," in *Exploring Virtuosities: Heinrich Wilhelm Ernst, Nineteenth-Century Musical Practices and Beyond*, ed. Christine Hoppe, Mai Kawabata, and Melanie von Goldbeck (Hildesheim: Olms, 2018), 109–21.

24. Philip Whitmore has argued that the practice of improvising concerto cadenzas ended with Beethoven, particularly in his fifth piano concerto where the cadenza is not optional. See *Unpremeditated Art: The Cadenza in the Classical Keyboard Concerto* (Oxford: Oxford University Press, 1991), especially chapter 4. Mendelssohn is one of the few pianists we know improvised cadenzas to concertos after 1830, although many players still wrote or worked out cadenzas of various kinds. Martin Edin considers short cadenzas—fermata elaborations—and interprets them as historically residual in "Cadenza Improvisation in Nineteenth-Century Solo Piano Music According to Czerny, Liszt, and their Contemporaries," in *Beyond Notes: Improvisation in Western Music*, 163–84. Practices of improvised melodic embellishment post-Cramer have not yet been researched in detail, and are possibly too difficult to reconstruct. Czerny offers many models in his treatises *Ecole ou traité des embellissements pour le piano sur des thèmes anglais, allemands, français, et italiens*, op. 575, and *Die Schule der Verzierungen, Vorschläge, Mordenten, und Triller auf dem Piano-Forte in 70 Studien*, op. 355, but their relation to improvised practice is unclear. As early as 1804 Louis Adam, author of the piano manual for the Paris conservatory, suggested in the chapter on melodic ornaments that "modern composers ordinarily write them out, and it is up to the student to study carefully the different signs they use" (L. Adam, *Méthode de Piano du Conservatoire* [Paris: Magasin de musique, 1805], 157). Yet Antoine Marmontel identified Marie Pleyel, associated with the more modern pianism of the 1830s and 1840s, as "a very ingenious ornamenter, embroidering gracious arabesques on the singing phrase in fine and delicate counters . . . in this genre of ornamentation she considerably anticipated Chopin" (*Les Pianistes Célèbres* [Paris: Heugel, 1878], 77).

25. Classic studies taking this approach are Frederick Neumann, *Ornamentation and Improvisation in Mozart* (Princeton: Princeton University Press, 1986), and Clive Brown, *Classical & Romantic Performing Practice 1750–1900* (Oxford and New York: Oxford University Press, 1999), 415–454.

26. John Rink, "The Rhetoric of Improvisation: Beethoven's Fantasy Op. 77," in *Secondo Convegno Europeo di Analisi Musicale*, ed. Rossana Dalmonte and Mario Baroni (Trent: Università degli Studi di Trento, 1992), 303–17. Rohan H. Stewart-MacDonald, "Improvisation into Composition: The First Movement of Johann Nepomuk Hummel's Sonata in F-sharp Minor, op. 81," in *Beyond Notes: Improvisation in Western Music*, 129–52. Elaine R. Sisman, "After the Heroic Style: Fantasia and the 'Characteristic' Sonatas of 1809," *Beethoven Forum* 6 (1997): 67–96. James Webster, "The Rhetoric of Improvisation in Haydn's Keyboard Music," in *Haydn and the Performance of Rhetoric*, ed. Tom Beghin and Sander M. Goldberg (Chicago: University of Chicago Press, 2007), 172–212. Karen Leistra-Jones's article "Improvisational Idyll: Joachim's 'Presence' and Brahms's Violin Concerto, op. 77," *19th Century Music* 38, no. 3 (2015): 243–71, comes closer to finding a rapprochement between the status of work and that of its performer-advocate, Joseph Joachim. Yet as she shows, the improvisational qualities ascribed to Joachim's playing were mostly metaphorical; they were not rooted in any regular practice of improvisation on Joachim's part.

27. As Leonard Ratner noted long ago, "fantasia" was already a consolidated style or topos in the later eighteenth century. It had migrated from keyboard music into orchestral, choral, and string quartet settings. Its legibility as a style implies that it was already one step removed from the practice of improvisation, regardless of its historical genealogy. Leonard G. Ratner, *Classical Music: Expression, Form, and Style* (New York: Schirmer, 1980), 24–25.

28. The classic historical overview of the fantasy genre is Peter Schleuning, *Die Fantasie*, 2 vols. (Köln: A. Volk, 1971). In relation to the early nineteenth century his work has been expanded considerably by Jean-Pierre Bartoli, "L'esprit de fantaisie dans l'oeuvre de Jan Ladislav Dussek," in *Jan Ladislav Dussek (1760–1812): A Bohemian Composer en voyage through Europe*, ed. Roberto Illiano and Rohan H. Stewart-MacDonald (Bologna: Orpheus, 2012), and by Jean-Pierre Bartoli and Jeanne Roudet, *L'essor du romantisme: La fantaisie pour clavier* (Paris: Vrin, 2013). The term "écriture improvisatrice" is from *L'essor du romantisme*, 140–42. The older free fantasy style appears occasionally in printed compositions such as Mendelssohn's early Piano Sonata, op. 6, and the slow movement of Schubert's late Piano Sonata in A major.

29. The musician who most consciously emulated Beethoven's pianistic work, Ferdinand Ries, played free fantasies at some earlier concerts, but they were infrequent and he did not have a particular reputation for them. A review of his 1815 composition "Le songe" commented that its programmatic subject matter—"shadows and dream images"—was appropriately matched by its lack of regular form, "completely free fantasies" (AMZ 1815, 147). Thus Ries, too, was developing the free fantasia into a compositional style. Indeed his improvised free fantasies appear to have been in a rather different style. See the reviews in AMZ 1813, 321, and AMZ 1826, 857–58. Czerny, in his improvisation treatise, described the older free fantasia rhetoric in the following terms: "there is another very interesting style of preludizing which the performer has to assimilate, namely, completely unmeasured, almost like a recitative, with some sections in chords sounding simultaneously and others with broken chords, seemingly without a conscious plan, resembling wanderings into unknown regions. This distinctive style, especially of the older masters (Bach—Johann Sebastian and Carl Philipp Emanuel), leaves room for a great deal of expressiveness and striking harmonic changes." Carl Czerny, *A Systematic Introduction to Improvisation on the Pianoforte*, trans. and ed. Alice L. Mitchell (New York: Longman, 1983), 23. Czerny evidently considered the style somewhat dated and relatively marginal. He treats it as a subgenre of the extended prelude (an improvisation with no set form or procedure) rather than as a relative of the free concert fantasies. Czerny also says that this distinctive style should not carry on for long without returning to a regular metrical melody, as if there is some interference between the older style and the newer *stile brillante*. It is unlikely that any improvising performers of the 1820s made use of the Bach-derived style, although further studies might turn up remnants in northern German circles.

30. On Busoni's early concert improvisations see Edward Dent, *Ferruccio Busoni: A Biography* (Oxford: Clarendon, 1933), 20–41. Busoni does not appear to have improvised in concert during his mature years.

31. Kalkbrenner sometimes pretended that his *Effusio musica* was a free improvisation, leading to occasional remarks about his "improvisations." This has led some scholars to claim Kalkbrenner had a reputation for improvisation. See for example James Davies, *Romantic Anatomies of Performance* (Berkeley: University of California Press, 2014), 11, and Andrea Estero, "L'improvvisazione pianistica a Parigi intorno al 1830: Permanenze e innovazioni," in *Sull'improvvisazione*, ed. Claudio Toscani (Lucca: LIM Editrice, 1998), 95. But contemporary press reports almost never mention Kalkbrenner as a free improviser, especially as compared with coverage of Moscheles and Hummel. In a series of portraits of pianists of the past,

published in 1878, Antoine Marmontel (b. 1816), professor of piano at the Paris Conservatoire, remembered Hummel, Hiller, Marie Pleyel, Stephen Heller, Liszt, and Rosenhain as excellent improvisers, but did not mention improvisation at all in his portrait of Kalkbrenner. Antoine-François Marmontel, *Les pianistes célèbres* (Paris: Heugel, 1878).

32. The social profile and role of the nineteenth-century kapellmeister, as distinct from the celebrity conductor of the later nineteenth century, has yet to be studied in depth. In a recent book on the English "maestro al cembalo" and "Musical Director" Michael Costa, whose career took off around 1830, John Goulden notes that Costa, like "other early professional conductors on the Continent—Guhr, Habeneck, Chélard, Musard—felt a similar need to develop an autocratic image." *Michael Costa: England's First Conductor* (Surrey: Ashgate, 2015), 23.

33. The self-advertisement E. T. A. Hoffmann placed in a newspaper, which won him a kapellmeister position in Bamberg in 1808, can serve as an example: "Someone who is thoroughly instructed in the theoretical and practical aspects of music, and has himself produced significant compositions for the theater, and who has been applauded as director of a significant musical institution, seeks employment as a music director of a theater, no matter where. Apart from the mentioned knowledge, he is fully accustomed to the demands of the theater, including the décor and costumes, and is fluent in French and Italian languages as well as German." *Hundert Jahre Bamberger Theater: Festschrift zur E. T. A. Hoffmann-Feier*, ed. Karl Schmidt (Bamberg: Hepple, 1908), 11.

34. Roger Moseley, comparing eighteenth-century practices with jazz, suggests that improvisation knowledge is often transmitted "across temporal and spatial networks of pedagogues, performers, and audiences," and that "analogous networks must have existed wherever and whenever improvisation has flourished." See his *Keys to Play: Music as a Ludic Medium from Apollo to Nintendo* (Oakland, CA: University of California Press, 2016), 143.

35. William Peterson, "Saint-Saëns's Improvisations on the Organ (1862)," in *Camille Saint-Saëns and His World* (Princeton: Princeton University Press, 2012), 102–108. On Bruckner's improvisations see Erwin Horn, "Anton Bruckner—Genie an der Orgel," *Bruckner-Jahrbuch 1994/95/96* (Linz: Musikwissenschaftlicher Verlag, 1997), 211–19; and Thomas Leibniz, "Between Interpretation and Improvisation: Anton Bruckner as Organist," in *Bruckner-Symposion: Zum Schaffensprozess in den Künsten* (Vienna: Musikwissenschaftlicher Verlag, 1997), 111–39. Kurt Lueders has documented Guilmant's improvisation practice thoroughly in "Alexander Guilmant (1837–1911): Organiste et compositeur," doctoral thesis, Université de Paris-Sorbonne, 2002, 2 vols.

36. Leo Treitler, *With Voice and Pen: Coming to Know Medieval Song and How It Was Made* (Oxford: Oxford University Press, 2003), 33.

37. Christopher Small, *Musicking: The Meanings of Performing and Listening* (Middletown: Wesleyan University Press, 1998), 8.

38. Robert Gjerdingen, "Partimenti Written to Impart a Knowledge of Counterpoint and Composition," in *Partimento and Continuo Playing in Theory and in Practice*, ed. Thomas Christensen et al. (Leuven: Leuven University Press, 2010), 43–70.

39. Robert O. Gjerdingen, *Music in the Galant Style* (New York: Oxford University Press, 2007), 10.

1

The School of Abbé Vogler

WEBER AND MEYERBEER

THE COMPOSITION LESSONS of an aging eighteenth-century kapellmeister hardly sound like a promising place to look for new improvisational impulses in European music ca. 1810. But something new, or at least different and exciting, was brewing in the class of Georg Joseph Vogler in the years preceding his death in 1814. Vogler is usually remembered as an eccentric composer, performer, and abbot that many contemporaries—Forkel, Mozart, and Beethoven, among others—dismissed as a charlatan. His reputation is somewhat less tainted among music theorists, who recognize his ambitious treatises *Tonwissenschaft und Tonsezkunst* (1776) and *Betrachtungen der Mannheimer Tonschule* (1778–1781) as significant innovations in the theory of harmony. Connoisseurs of musical instruments know him as the designer and popularizer of a type of organ he called the "orchestrion," which diversified the organ's sonorous palette by emulating the sonorities of an orchestra. But to many people in the nineteenth century, the *abbé* was known above all as an inspiring and influential teacher who mentored two epoch-making composers, Carl Maria von Weber and Giacomo Meyerbeer, as well as the theorist Gottfried Weber and the Vienna kapellmeister Johann Gansbächer.

On weekdays these students composed in various styles on themes given by their master, submitting their pieces in the afternoon for performance and critique. On Sundays, however, the method of instruction changed:

> The students met at the church: Vogler played the organ, and his students piously absorbed the lessons of his inspirations. Often a sort of academic tournament established itself between the master and his disciples; the two organs of

the cathedral responded to each other; on one instrument the professor improvised a sacred motif; on the other the student, seizing it on the fly, developed
it in turn, until the moment where the master, having become a rival, picked it
back up. And so the noble motif soared from one arch to the other, carried by the
powerful wings of learning.

Sometimes it happened that the chosen theme accidentally yielded, in em-
bryo, out of its folds, a line or a rhythm whose developments could be treated
according to *a more independent and less scholastic system.* It was then a question
of which young disciple would be the first to dare break the fetters, pry open the
door to the ideal, and leave with his eyes blinded by such a brilliant light. When
these fiery improvisers, abandoning themselves without restraint to the ardor
of their imagination, took off this way in search of the unknown, juxtaposing
rhythms, lines, and modulations according to their caprice, the dear *abbé* interrupted himself in astonishment. He no longer recognized his well-instructed
students of the previous day; he did not sulk, but he became a bit melancholy;
perhaps his pride suffered: these bold gestures revealed to him rivers of inspiration from which he had not been permitted to drink; he admitted that he had
barely come halfway, and that the hour had come when he should stop in the road
while his students continued to travel on the most sunny and flowery stretch.[1]

This evocative passage, published in 1853 by the French opera critic (and friend of
Meyerbeer) Léon Kreutzer, is at once highly informative and richly imaginative. It
stages a scene in which improvisation mediates a transfer from the older generation to
the younger generation. Yet the direction of influence is not perfectly linear: the melodic motive devised by Vogler, after being transformed by the student, is sent back to
the teacher for further elaborations. Such circular exchanges inaugurate an intersubjective process in which the players not only follow one another sympathetically, but
also challenge one another antagonistically. In the "tournament" that unfolds, Vogler
acquires the role of a "rival," whose musical answers prod his students on to new ideas,
fueled by rising inspiration. Nor is Vogler the sole agent of invention. The theme, as
if by some autonomous agency, also plays a generative role, "accidentally" spawning
ideas and developmental implications that the students take in directions entirely beyond their teacher's imaginative capacities. At the end of the process the students have
landed in a place entirely different from where they began; Vogler's modest intent to
transmit the rules and craft traditions of sacred counterpoint has become a portal to
uncontainable inspiration, to rules infringed, to the bright light of the ideal. Out of the
chrysalis of the old, impersonal rules there emerges youthful romanticism.

The idealized tone of Kreutzer's story originates partly in nostalgia, partly in literary
tropes that ascribed particular meanings to improvisation. In the music criticism and
journalism of the 1830s and 1840s, writers habitually characterized improvisation as a
rhetoric of "bold gestures" and inspiration "without restraint." It was capable of freeing
musicians from a "scholastic system" or launching them "in search of the unknown."
By 1853, when Kreutzer was writing, true improvisation was a rare phenomenon

outside of churches, but the *concept* of improvisation had become linked with ideas of freedom, emancipation, and historical progress that have retained their currency into the present. This discourse was hardly in place in 1810–1813 when Vogler was meeting with his students, and so we might suspect that Kreutzer was entirely romanticizing the past. His spin on Vogler's lessons, however, seems better justified when we consider that two of his students, Carl Maria von Weber and Giacomo Meyerbeer, were among the most successful pianists and most adventurous harmonists of their generation, while another student, Gottfried Weber, elaborated an influential theory concerning the multiple harmonic implications of a single chord. It is no accident that Vogler's improvising students became self-conscious innovators in composition, harmony, and theory, for although his outlook generally belonged to a much earlier era, he had a taste for novelty and experimentation that manifested in his theory, composing, concertizing, instrumental building, and teaching. Intentionally or not, this experimental streak wore off on his students.

By focusing on improvisation in Vogler's school and particularly its influence on Carl Maria von Weber and Meyerbeer, this chapter offers an alternative to the previous historiography of improvisation for this period, which has nearly always revolved around Beethoven. It is well established that Beethoven, particularly in his younger years, was a phenomenal piano improviser and that his free playing distinguished him favorably from performers such as Wölfl and Steibelt. The originality of many of his piano works lies in the tension they establish between improvisational impulse and formal restraint, digression and structure. The historical importance of this compositional appropriation and stylization of the free fantasia style is inestimable, not only for future composers but also for performers such as Schumann and Liszt who viewed themselves as his successors. But the emphasis given to Beethoven on account of his music's influence has overshadowed other modes of free improvisation that thrived in the same period.

A rough map of such alternative approaches would include at least four different lines of practice, not including practices of extemporaneous gracing, ornamenting, and fermata-filling that were common in this period but do not constitute free playing in the more inventive and generative sense. Beethoven's improvising, and to an extent Haydn's, stood in the line of the north German free fantasy practice associated with C. P. E. Bach and the clavichord—an expressive, stirring style that mixed intense, melancholic feelings with capricious surprises and lively *bravura* flights. Another line stemmed from the practice of church organists trained in the improvisation of free preludes, postludes, interludes, fugues, and hymn accompaniment. A third line—emanating from the pianism of Mozart, Clementi, and others—was characterized by *galant* textures, patterned figuration idiomatic to the piano, variations on binary-phrase melodies, free-form adagios ("fantasy"), *cantilena* slow introductions, and capriccios. The fourth line of practice, "accompaniment" (in French *accompagnement*, in German *accompagniren*), involved both professionals and amateurs. It was a semi-improvised way of backing up singers and instrumentalists in elementary chord progressions, with or without a given bass.[2] We cannot attend to all these different branches of improvisation equally here, but Vogler's teaching and practice opens windows onto all of them and reveals what was happening in keyboard improvisation outside the stylistic orbit of the north German keyboard fantasy.

In Vogler's teachings improvisation—*phantasiren*—was valued as one component of all-around musicianship. It belonged to a whole system of musical production in which theoretical rules, instrumental realization, and compositional writing were interrelated and only loosely differentiated. It was recognized as a species of keyboard-playing different from score-reading (*vom Blatt spielen, exécution*), but otherwise it remained unmarked as a special practice or a particular expressive domain. The only consistent features of *phantasiren* on the piano, in Vogler's school, were that it concentrated on single theme, melody, or motive, and that it treated the material to "developmental" sorts of elaboration that will be discussed below. The ability to improvise was a pragmatic necessity for aspiring organists and pianists, who would eventually be called upon to extemporize in various circumstances, but it was considered equally valuable as a means of developing facility and flexibility in a variety of compositional languages and styles. In Chapter 2 we will see the coalescence around 1815–1820 of a concert practice—improvising "on given themes" before larger audiences—that represents a distinct genre of free playing specific to public contexts. In Vogler's school this genre received no particular emphasis. Improvisation was bundled together with theory and composition and was not specifically geared toward concert performance.

Gänsbacher, Weber, Meyerbeer, and Gottfried Weber all took what they learned from Vogler in different directions, but each of them profited from their teacher's approach to improvisation in some way. The entrepreneurial Carl Maria von Weber helped promote his compositions and pianistic reputation by giving concerts where free improvisations were a main attraction, while Meyerbeer made keyboard improvisation a key element of his compositional process. A focus on improvisation within Vogler's teaching is worthwhile not because he gave it undue emphasis, but because it gave rise to some of the progressive, experimental musical ideas that later made Weber and Meyerbeer famous. In the relatively free territory of keyboard improvisation his students were invited to test new combinations, find new harmonizations, and devise new methods of elaboration. Vogler based his lessons on institutionally conservative traditions of liturgical organ improvisation. But ironically, these same lessons incubated experimental ideas that Weber and Meyerbeer could seize upon and mobilize for their secular, dramatic innovations. Out of organ improvisation they developed what Kreutzer called "a more independent and less scholastic system."

ORGANS AND PIVOTS

It would be anachronistic to attribute to Vogler "progressive" motivations in the modern sense, as though he foreshadowed the modernist avant-garde or the New German avant-garde of the mid-nineteenth century. As Floyd Grave has noted, Vogler did not consider himself an initiator of progress himself, but a propagator of the rational, theoretical breakthroughs of Rameau, which he saw coming to life in the music of the "Mannheim school."[3] The "progressivism" he espoused was that of the Enlightenment—an optimistic progressivism proud of its liberation from the old prejudices, principles, and rules of composition. The conservative opposition was represented by the north German music scene, where J. N. Forkel and other writers were propagating rigid dogmas born of an unhealthy reverence for J. S. Bach and for the theory of Kirnberger.[4] To make progressive music meant engaging the powers of reason to question dated rules and bring a greater sense of logic and cohesion to procedures of musical creation. Even when teaching a topic as tradition-bound as fugue, Grave writes, Vogler's goal was "to avoid arbitrary and groundless rules, to relate all precepts to fundamental principles, and to promote that free play of the imagination normally stifled by existing pedagogical methods."[5]

Yet in his later years Vogler started adopting more modern ideas of "progress." In 1806 he published a set of 32 preludes intended to demonstrate a more modern approach to this genre of free playing. As Grave notes, several of the preludes include central passages featuring "the kinds of far-reaching tonal excursion that Vogler associated with progressive contemporary practice."[6] Moreover, the publication was intended to cancel the impression made by the recent unauthorized republication of his much older *112 petits preludes pour l'orgue ou fortepiano* (orig. 1776), which potentially compromised his self-construction as "an apostle of musical progress." Vogler's progressive voice was most forceful at the end of his revised *Choral-System*, published in the first year of the nineteenth century, where the reform of theory and organ playing was explicitly aligned with the French revolutionary quest for freedom and democracy:[7]

> Authority ruined thought and sought to reign over thinking people; it pensioned off the brain and exacted contributions from minds. In all nations and sciences, villages and trades, even in politics, there is freedom of the press; but in the realm of tones reason is supposed to remain suppressed. The church claimed infallibility, and organists granted it. No! Madame Authority, like the eighteenth century itself, must give up the ghost under convulsions. . . . Wake up, puppets and Lilliputian denizens, from your slumber . . . and think![8]

It is no accident that the organ takes central stage in Vogler's polemic, for the controversy that surrounded him concerned mainly his organ playing. His reputation as a charlatan stemmed from organ concerts he played all over Europe where he improvised programmatic concert fantasies with titles like "The Last Judgment," "The Battle of Jericho," "A Naval Battle," "The Excursion on the Rhine, interrupted by a Thunderstorm," and "The Death of Leopold [of Brunswick]." Surviving accounts of these narrative pieces are too brief to make conclusions about their style, with the exception of the storms, which are often described in detail. Vogler probably improvised a series of discrete representational sections using stereotyped topoi such as pastorals, storms, laments, military marches, and the like. One motive for playing such improvisations was that they allowed him to promote his colorful instrumental invention, the orchestrion. In order to show off its bells and whistles he assembled programs rich in representational variety:

First part

1 Overture: March, Allegro
2 Nocturno
3 Carillon
4 Swedish national music
5 The Siege of Jericho [improvised]

Second part

1 Flute concerto
2 Cossack national music
3 Portrayal of a naval battle
4 Grand fantasia and fugue[9]

It is possible that many or all of these pieces were improvised, but only the narrative fantasias were consistently framed and received as extemporaneous creations, possibly because Vogler had little reason to publish them. Dramatic fantasies of this kind became, for better or for worse, Vogler's claim to fame after his death. A concert fantasy played in Hamburg in 1848 by organ virtuoso J. M. Homeyer was described as being "in the style of Abt Vogler, with obbligato trombone calls, resurrections of the dead, and in accordance with this, laments of the cursed or victorious cheers of the absolved" (NZM 1848, 217).

Although Vogler's improvised epics fell squarely in line with certain mimetic conventions of eighteenth-century music, they provoked controversy with the north German musical establishment, which dismissed them as pure charlatanry. The main problem was not mimetic music itself, but its introduction into the sacred space of the church. Vogler himself regretted that he was compelled to play such pieces in churches, and looked forward to the day when the advanced, timbrally flexible organs of the best German churches would become more widespread and find their way into the public sphere: "the organ is moving out of the church into the world, as already seen in England and North America, and it will first prove its musical universality there."[10] Vogler's desire that organs should escape the confines of the church in order to realize their "universal" potential is typical of the enlightened progressivism that pervaded his thought. Refusing to acknowledge a strict sacred/secular boundary, he redeployed the highly developed improvisational capacities of the church organist toward modern and secular ends: the spontaneous creation of representational, dramatic music that could grip and delight the broader lay public with brilliant effects.

Even musicians who dismissed Vogler's representational experiments and his personal eccentricities recognized his eminence as a keyboard performer. The prominent keyboardist and writer Schubart was not a great admirer of Vogler's instrumental compositions and considered the keyboard improvisations a far better representation of his genius.[11] A report in the *Allgemeine musikalische Zeitung* (1806, 317) named him "the greatest organist of our time," and Carl Ludwig Junker, writing in 1788, ranked him "among the most outstanding German clavier players."[12] Already by 1796 Vogler had played nearly a thousand concerts, and he played another thousand before his death, making him far better known as a performer than Mozart or Beethoven had been in their respective lifetimes.[13] The popular response, moreover, was enormous. Eduard Hanslick, while researching his history of music in Vienna, discovered that Vogler's Vienna concerts of 1803–1804 "represented the equivalent for that period of the Liszt-craze of our times," and many subsequent historians described Vogler as the first concert organist in the modern sense.[14]

During this same 1803–1804 season Vogler and Beethoven faced off in a legendary keyboard duel, indicating that Vogler was hardly less inclined to improvise on the piano than on the organ. Beethoven gave Vogler a 4.5-measure theme, which the older musician treated first as an *adagio*, then as a fugue.[15] Vogler, in return, asked Beethoven to improvise on the C-major scale *alle breve*, a pattern he often recommended to students.[16] Gänsbacher was present at this event and found much to admire in Beethoven's playing, but claimed that Beethoven "could not stir up in me the enthusiasm that had been aroused by Vogler's learned playing, which was beyond parallel in respect of its harmonic and contrapuntal treatment."[17] Also in Vienna at this time was the young Carl Maria von Weber, who attended a grand concert celebrating Vogler's thirtieth year as a priest. He reported that Vogler played variations on a Norwegian folk song that aroused general applause "all the way up to the fugue, which Vogler always played off the cuff [*aus dem Stegreife*] and never the same way for as long as I heard him, which was greeted with enthusiasm; indeed it was so extremely well received that he had to sit down once again and improvise, which was received just as enthusiastically."[18] Evidently Vogler, like Hummel after him, preferred to conclude improvisations on both organ and piano with a fugue in the learned style, whether preceded by an adagio, a fantasia, or variations. From the indications given in Vogler's treatise on fugue, we can gather that his fugal playing proceeded by freely developing three types of material: the main subject (*Ausführung*), complementary non-subject ideas (*Fortführung*), and figures derived from the accompanying voices (*Durchführung*). Of these three sorts of elaboration, the one most relevant to his teaching of improvisation is the *Ausführung* of the main subject, a developmental procedure whose "diversity consists in keeping the relevant outline, but treating it to various new accompaniments, progressions and keys, changes of harmony, modulations, etc."[19] We will again encounter this diversification of initial motivic cell, through reharmonization and recombination, when we examine the improvisational practices of his student Meyerbeer.

Vogler used such combinatory procedures not only when playing polyphonic fugues on the organ but also when playing piano. His unpublished collection *Polymelos* offers an unusual glimpse of how this might have sounded. He put the collection together in 1806 to memorialize a concert he gave for the Queen of Bavaria after completing the renovation of her chapel organ. Vogler's subtitle describes it as "a national-characteristic organ concert in two parts with 16 different original-pieces," and his foreword emphasizes that it was fully improvised; the entire concert came "from his imagination" (*aus der Phantasie*), and "only the main ideas were fixed; everything else

was played off the cuff [*aus dem Stegreife*]."[20] The *Polymelos* pieces are not intended
to reproduce the concert literally, but rather to approximate what he had played as
adapted to the piano. Each piece takes up a short phrase or melody—African, Chinese,
Finnish, Swiss, Swedish, Bavarian, etc.—and fleshes it out in a light, pleasing *galant*
style. Some of the pieces elaborate the melodies as straightforward figural variations,
while others receive a freer fantasia-like treatment. The piece on a Swiss melody, for
example, interpolates wandering harmonic digressions between the otherwise normal
variations, always initiating the digression with the head-motive. The "Finnish
Melody" (Example 1.1) begins with an unadorned statement of the four-measure

EXAMPLE 1.1 Opening section of "Finnish Melody," from Vogler's *Polymelos*

EXAMPLE 1.1 Continued

theme, followed by a harmonization of the same theme, before initiating a section marked "Fantaisie," which freely develops the head-motive in "troubled" D-minor. The transition out of the "Fantaisie" sounds like an improvisation, with loose, meandering harmonies searching their way toward a new key (mm. 27-43). When the new key of D-major arrives, the Finnish theme is restated in the style of a classical minuet. Typical of Vogler's improvisatory explorations is his reinterpretation of the head-motive at the minuet. Whereas the first melodic tone had been treated as scale-degree 7 on its first appearance (m. 3), it is now harmonized as scale-degree 3 and the harmonic progression is entirely different (m. 44).

The pieces in *Polymelos* suggest that Vogler extemporized mainly on the terrain of *galant* and fugal styles. The Copenhagen-based keyboardist C. E. F. Weyse, whose reputation for free improvisation rivaled Vogler's, exhibited a similar duality, impressing listeners on both piano and organ in a diversity of styles. But Weyse was aligned with the north German school and his free playing reflected the influence of C. P. E. Bach's free fantasia style. In later years he even devised a way of playing tremolo melodies with the left hand, greatly impressing Ignaz Moscheles.[21] Vogler, in contrast, seems to have left the north German style out of his stylistic vocabulary. As a pianist, Carl Junker suggested, he excelled in the "virtuoso style" rather than the "pathetic style."[22] This is conspicuous because the free fantasy style was prestigious and "modern" and Vogler was ecumenical in the extreme. The style had been translated to the piano in pieces such as Mozart's keyboard fantasies or Dussek's *Fantasia and Fugue*, op. 55 (ca. 1804), and it exerted a powerful influence on Beethoven's improvisations as well as his published *Fantasia*, op. 77. It thus required a certain effort *not* to adopt it. Vogler's feud with the north German establishment must have played a role in this. But his obsession with logical procedure and rational justification made him temperamentally averse to the aesthetics of the free fantasia, which valorized expressive intensity, the unpredictable play of feelings, and irrational turns of discourse.

Vogler's resistance to the free fantasia style, combined with his reverence for fugue and counterpoint, can make him look conservative or resistant to the modern currents of his time. But his restless pursuit of methodical, reasoned procedures of production—whether for fugue, thoroughbass, or text-setting in opera—generated exploratory and expansive outcomes. As he wrote in his treatise on chorale-playing, he wanted to reverse the dry and reductive tendencies of previous music theory: "It has been known for 2000 years that music is founded on mathematical relationships. The goal of my investigations was exactly the opposite: I wanted to show how the most varied impression and aesthetic sensibility follow from mathematical foundations."[23] In his treatise on fugue he criticized old teachings for their "rigid, strict prescriptions," which hemmed in the "free flow of the imagination" and gave the impression that "learned music shouldn't sound good."[24] The priority Vogler gives to sensual beauty and imagination over abstract rules betrays the practicing performer behind the rationalizing theorist. In the same treatise, anticipating the link between improvisation and play, he pleads for a more flexible approach to voice-leading, claiming that "voice-leading should be less a studying than a playing [*wenig ein Studium als ein Spiel*]."[25]

The link between keyboard improvisation and theory is perhaps most evident in Vogler's teaching of modulation, as found in his books *Tonwissenschaft und Tonsezkunst* and *Betrachtungen der Mannheimer Tonschule*. Both treatises include his tabular "Summa of Harmony" listing all possible modulations between major and minor keys. Floyd Grave has proposed that this tabular demonstration "was likely inspired by Vogler's own experience as a master of improvisation," but the table vastly exceeds pragmatic origins by demonstrating no fewer than 528 possible modulations (Figure 1.1).[26] Some of the modulations link keys that presumably no liturgical organist would have needed to link, such as F♯ minor and D♭ major, and all the modulations proceed through two intermediate chords, no matter how distant the keys are. Many of the examples have an abrupt, foreshortened effect that would seem undesirable in a liturgical context. What appears to be most reflective of organ improvisation in them is the voice-leading: stepwise movement predominates in all four voices as the fingers "search out" the quickest route to the target key. In sharp contrast to the "rational" appearance of the table, these voice-leading patterns are positively anarchic, regulated only by a manual practice of nearest-note smoothness, and there are no rules whatsoever about the harmonic properties of the interme-diate chords. Vogler's drive to demonstrate the rational coherence of the modulation system, paradoxically, gives rise to untrammeled, antisystematic proliferation.

This duality of the ordered and the disordered, the rationally scripted system and the vagrant finger movements, is crucial to understanding how an institutionally con-servative practice can "flip over" into experimental practice. Vogler recommends that organists use the "Summa" to develop facility in modulating spontaneously between all keys so that they can become good liturgical players, but the method simultaneously

FIGURE 1.1 Excerpt from Vogler's "Summa of Harmony," demonstrating the twenty-two possible modulations starting from C-major. The continuation of the table lists all 528 possible modulations. Note the predominantly stepwise voice-leading.

encourages free, experimental harmonic explorations via nearest-note connections. As he specifies, the table is not a set of rules to be followed but an invitation to the musician's free exploration: "hundreds of sorts of passages, sequences, harmonies, simultaneities, inversions, etc. can etch into the mind a rich inventive faculty for the organist, the amateur accompanist, or the composer; they can make him agile in all situations with living practice, and *without noticing it* his mind will be filled with harmonic turns."[27] In other words, through diligent practice of the entire modulatory system, a player will more or less automatically develop the capacity for spontaneous and inventive improvisation and composition. Vogler also defines para-liturgical benefits of facility in modulation, for both the player and the listener. The listener who hears unusual or unexpected modulations "is surprised at every moment, without knowing the reason," and the performer therefore has a valuable resource at his disposal: "how useful it is when he, through this knowledge, gets the heart of the listener in his own hands and manipulates it at will with intentional surprises and deceptions."[28]

To constrain the anarchy implicit in his modulation system, Vogler underlines that regular compositions should normally modulate to closely related keys. But the exceptions he names are revealing. First, the more remote modulations may be used in dramatic music underlining liminal or transitional states:

> The distant modulations have their place in pieces that do not make up a whole, e.g. in ballets, where one passion transitions to another; where the scenery changes from one city to another; where occasionally the gods or people metamorphose into one another. Here unity need not rule: consequently one may modulate at will.[29]

This suspension of the law of unity is remarkable for Vogler, who perpetually asserted the importance of "diversity in unity," and indicates that he recognized a hermeneutic link between improvisation and transition or emergent states without any clear contact with romantic or proto-romantic ideas. Second, the distant modulations are allowed in certain forms of improvisation: "The same exception applies to the organ in fantasies [i.e., free improvisations], in preludes, which in certain ceremonies finish quickly and must finish in pre-given keys, and finally in interludes, which must gently lead the ear from one key to a distant one, e.g. into another church-song."[30] While the "preludes" and "interludes" mentioned here are closely tied to liturgical ritual, the "fantasies" seem to belong to the organist's more independent artisanal domain. Whatever the intention, Vogler's exceptions demonstrate that in improvisation church organists opened modulatory possibilities that could potentially be redeployed in instrumental and dramatic music, with specific uses for the representation of indeterminate or emergent phenomena.

The speculative, expansive ethos of Vogler's theoretical investigations is also evident in his most influential concept: *Mehrdeutigkeit*, best translated as "multiple-meaning" or "polysemy." This is the idea that a single tone can have multiple meanings depending upon the vertical interval to which it belongs, and by extension that a single chord can have multiple meanings depending on its harmonic context. Vogler used the concept to justify revisions to the older rules, notably the rule that a dissonant interval must be prepared by a consonant one. He proposed that a dissonance may also be prepared by a dissonance, as long as the preparatory dissonance is of a lower order. A harmonic interval of a thirteenth, for example, may be prepared by a seventh, a ninth, or an eleventh.[31] The range of allowable harmonizations of a tone or interval was thus considerably expanded. The polysemy of chords follows similar principles, and has become familiar today because Vogler's student Gottfried Weber, building off the *Mehrdeutigkeit* concept, devised a system of roman-numeral labeling still in use today.[32] The "Summa" systematically lays out the many possible keys to which a single chord, whether a triad or seventh chord, can belong. Conceptually, each chord is a field of possibility and multiple implication: "it remains undetermined [*unbestimmt*]."[33] The exceptional polysemy of the diminished-seventh chord, with its capacity for multiple resolutions, gets an especially strong endorsement, for "here a harmonist finds abundant material for many years of entertainment."[34]

Vogler's pedagogical ideas, in sum, were rooted in an enlightened, progressive ethos that stressed the student's rational engagement as a vehicle of emancipation from arbitrary, rule-bound restraints. In his teaching of harmony he sought to widen the field of combinatorial possibilities by allowing previously forbidden dissonances and encouraging the exploitation of the polysemic implications of chords. He promoted such liberties not in a spirit of transgression, but in the spirit of rationally regulated exploration and experiment that would nurture the student's curiosity, combine learning with play, and furnish listeners with novelties and surprises. Vogler attributed no special or privileged meaning to improvisation, but students consistently marveled at the mental and formative powers that his improvisations unfolded, and the lay public took a strong interest in his earth-shaking programmatic fantasies. The students in his school absorbed not only what he explicitly taught them, but also what he modeled in terms of attitude and completeness of musicianship. "Just being around him," Gänsbacher said, "was in itself a school."[35] In the organ lessons, though, it was mainly the free fugal playing, with its propensity for motivic elaboration and harmonic recombination, that proved most productive and generative. Through the improvised trading of passages, Vogler's lessons became an important transition point between older and younger musicians, between the organ and the piano, and between sacred and secular styles. During those lessons, the church organist's traditional facility in modulation and harmonic recombination released a latent potential that transformed itself into the secular composer's exploration of novel harmonic, developmental, and sonorous resources.

WEBER

Weber often affirmed that Vogler, in his fantasies and preludes, never drank more directly from the pure stream of the beautiful than when he sat before his three beloved apostles, as he liked to call them, and drew angelic voices and thundering phrases out of the organ.[36]

Carl Maria von Weber and Johann Gänsbacher had both heard Vogler play in Vienna during the 1803–1804 concert season, but the "school" comprising Weber, Gänsbacher, Gottfried Weber, and Meyerbeer first crystallized in Darmstadt in 1810 and held together for two or three years. There was a strong sense of camaraderie within the group. They treated Vogler with deep reverence, referred to him as "Papa," and even co-composed a cantata in his honor. They organized themselves into a secret circle, the "Harmonic Association," whose goal was to advance "the good" in music and literature through cooperative organization and the production of quality music criticism. Anticipating Schumann's "League of David" by two decades, this was a self-consciously intellectual collective, striving to advance music's position in the stream of cultural development more broadly conceived.[37] Some impetus came from the broad-minded vision of Vogler, which manifested in his dual identities as musician and ecclesiastic as well as his encyclopedic reading. Meyerbeer was instructed by Vogler not only in music, but was also given "a grounding in literature and foreign languages such as all artists should be given whose intentions are serious."[38]

For all three students, skill in improvisation was more than just the standard acquisition of a well-trained musician. It was a critical resource for showing exceptional skill and ambition, attracting patrons, making connections, and building a reputation. Having gathered support this way, the artist could then hope to mount a public concert in which he appeared as a solo performer while also featuring large-scale original compositions. Having proven his public worth through such concerts, he might eventually be rewarded with a commission for an opera or oratorio, or possibly a kapellmeister appointment. The main stage for free improvisation beyond the church, then, was the network of private concerts, informal salons, and court concerts under the patronage of local elites. The mutual obligation between patron and artist was expressed in the pianist's ritual of soliciting a theme from the host for improvisation—usually a familiar, widely liked tune—which he "returned" to the patron and assembled guests in a transformed state. In this way free playing was more conducive to the atmosphere of spontaneous and convivial exchange than fixed pieces were, and pianists gravitated toward it when they had the opportunity.

Gänsbacher's early activities can serve as an example of these social pragmatics. During his student years at Innsbruck (ca. 1794–1796) he played violin, cello, and organ, and proved himself an excellent singer, but he attracted attention in society mainly as a piano improviser. In his memoir he recalled practicing at the house of a local amateur who hosted frequent chamber music concerts: "I improvised [*phantasirte*] for hours and often even forgot about lunch, for which I had to be fetched. I thereby acquired great ability in improvisation, which subsequently recommended me so favorably when I became known in the home of Count Firmian."[39] When he moved to Vienna in 1801 to make a living as a music teacher, it was by means of "improvising on the fortepiano and accompanying on the violin" that he found entry into elite salons and secured the patronage of Firmian.[40] Under Vogler's tutelage Gänsbacher continued to improvise solos and duets on various instruments and in private society. At the Firmian household he often improvised for the Count, "a very attentive listener," for a short hour before going to sleep.[41] But Gänsbacher did not aspire to a career as a keyboard performer, and he was unable to match Weber or Meyerbeer in improvisational skill. When the apostles gathered in 1810 to celebrate their teacher's sixty-first birthday, for example, "Beer improvised first on the piano at Vogler's request, then Weber," but Gänsbacher himself opted not to play.[42] Gänsbacher sought instruction mainly in "ideal" composition, and spent the better part of his professional career in the church milieu conducting choirs and composing sacred works. Eventually, in 1824, he landed the kapellmeister post at St. Stephen's Cathedral in Vienna.

Although free playing often helped musicians build networks and find publicity, it was also valued by musicians "among themselves." Even at the famous encounter between Vogler and Beethoven, an event heavily laden with competitive undertones, improvisation was the privileged medium for testing, demonstrating, and appreciating skills among a small assembly of appreciative fellow musicians and connoisseurs. Such encounters became competitive precisely because the improvisational situation seemed to level the playing field and expose the musician's barren skill without the security of preparation. Vogler's students often extemporized among themselves in a blend of competitiveness and friendly play. Weber's friend Alexander von Dusch reported that

> Meyer-Beer occasionally came, though not often, to Mannheim. . . . Sometimes there would break out a competition in free improvisation [*freier Phantasie*] between the two of them [Weber and Meyerbeer] on a requested theme on two pianos, with all sorts of odd rules and conditions: e.g. when one person broke off unexpectedly and willfully, the other must quickly enter and continue, etc.[43]

At other times the teacher would simply play for the student's edification and inspiration: "Vogler played the organ for Gänsbacher; he improvised extraordinarily for two hours."[44] Although these performances were insulated from the public and from the demands of patronal exchange, they cemented the values of the musical guild and gave satisfaction through the presence of a maximally attentive and understanding audience.

Like Gänsbacher, Weber was improvising at the piano before joining the circle in Darmstadt, but the record reveals little about how he approached it. A reminiscence by tenor Julius Miller about gatherings of the musical club in Breslau in the years 1804–1806 sheds at least some light: "Hummel and Moscheles likewise improvised extremely well; but the way they reworked their themes and their transitional passages remained nearly always the same; with Weber and [F. W.] Berner that was not the case: their harmonic transformations were always new."[45] Miller's comparison of Weber and Berner to Moscheles and Hummel, whose free improvisations became widely known only later on (in the 1820s), sounds invidious and ideological, yet the stylistic difference he describes is credible. As will be seen in Chapter 2, Hummel and Moscheles played to large heterogeneous audiences and played parts of their free fantasies a relatively light, decorative variation style. In the smaller circle of the Breslau club, Weber and

Berner are likely to have foregrounded their contrapuntal and harmonic learning by steadily developing motives and themes in new harmonic combinations.[46]

Weber made his wider reputation as a free improviser precisely during the years he was studying with Vogler—a period he called "traveling years" because of the numerous concerts he arranged throughout the German-speaking realm.[47] Indeed, he became so adept at touring and setting up concerts that he wrote a handbook, never published, explaining how other virtuosos might do the same. These concerts were designed to spotlight his achievements as both composer and virtuoso, and the free improvisations contributed substantially to their overall impact. At an 1810 concert in Heidelberg, whose proceeds were intended to support his classmate Gottfried Weber, he programmed his own piano quartet and first symphony, after which he improvised.[48] At his first Munich benefit of 1811 the free fantasy "drew exceptional applause" and the concert was described in the press as a "double triumph" for the pianist and composer.[49] Following a common practice, this improvisation was part of a "free fantasy and variations," indicating that it served as the introduction to a composed-out variation set.[50] For the second Munich benefit, attended by the Queen of Bavaria, he programmed his newly composed dramatic scene *Atalia* and announced a completely free fantasy. The Queen gave Weber the *romance* "A peine au sortir de l'enfance" from Méhul's *Joseph*, a simple melody on which Meyerbeer also had improvised, and elaborated it "with rare agility to the pleasure of his audience."[51] In the aftermath he wrote and published a set of seven variations.

Weber also deployed improvisation to generate publicity for his public benefit concerts. When he arrived in Prague with clarinetist Heinrich Bärmann in 1811, for instance, his first step was to search for a piano to practice on, eventually landing at a banker's home "where he, improvising on a beautiful Streicher instrument, quickly and permanently won over everyone's sympathy, first through his playing, then through his personality."[52] Subsequent introductions by influential noblemen drew further attention to the traveling duo within high society, where "especially Weber's improvisations met with the greatest success."[53] When he paid a visit to the theater Intendant Liebich, he found out that rumors were circulating that he "plays the piano like the very devil."[54] After about two weeks of preparation of this kind, Weber and Bärmann were able to put on a public concert drawing a broader audience and making a substantial profit. On this occasion Weber showcased his virtuosity not in a free fantasy but in his first concerto, perhaps because he was sharing the spotlight with Bärmann. But at his own benefit concerts the free fantasy often sealed the public triumph. After a Berlin concert of 1814, which was likewise prepared by improvisations in salons, he wrote to Caroline Brandt: "After my fantasy, through which I threaded a favorite theme from the wonderful Himmel ["An Alexis"], the noise would not come to an end, and it kept recommencing as long as I was visible in the orchestra, so that I exited to the sound of loud cheering."[55]

Weber's reputation as a free improviser in these years was possibly stronger than that of any other pianist in the German milieu. Not only did he travel widely and promote himself assiduously, but he also impressed contemporaries with his literary intelligence, lively imagination, and commitment to the realization of a romantic and fantastical form of opera. The popular romantic author Friedrich de la Motte Fouqué, upon meeting him in 1814, was fascinated by the fusion of musical and personal aura: "In Berlin I heard Maria Weber improvise and spoke with him at length. What a man!"[56] Also in Berlin at this time was naturalist Hinrich Lichtenstein, who came under Weber's personal spell and left detailed accounts of his improvisations. Lichtenstein published his reminiscences of Weber in 1833, about twenty years after the events, and they are written in a highly idealizing tone. They are all the more revealing of a range of values associated with free improvisation. When accompanying a song he knew or liked well, Lichtenstein related, Weber would often launch into a "longer postlude" without any solicitation: "when he wanted to preserve and follow a musical thought, he gave himself over to free improvisation and then achieved—as a complete master of his instrument . . . always led by the clearest consciousness of rules—the most extraordinary things that the art of pianism was capable of bringing forth."[57] Lichtenstein evokes a summer soirée in the suburb of Pankow, where Weber accompanied Haydn's three-voice part-song "Betrachtung des Todes"—a severe, serious meditation on transience and death. As the song came to its end, Weber

> played on, as if deeply moved by the truth of the poetic idea, lightly modulating the theme, out of which there then emerged an artfully developed three-voice fugue, which, accompanied by frequent cries of increasing amazement from the connoisseurs, flowed forth in calm clarity for their relaxed mental pleasure [*unbefangen geniessenden Sinn*], and, riding the waves of the 6/8 meter, steadily preserved the character of the underlying poem despite the most audacious changes, turns, and rhythmic shifts.[58]

This passage from Lichtenstein is an early example of the "improvisation imaginary"—a fantastical mode of discourse that attributes to improvisation a sense of wholeness and perfection not to be found elsewhere. In this account, nothing is missing from Weber's performance. It is both learned and pleasing, satisfying connoisseurs and dilettantes alike. It is deeply unified by a central poetic idea yet richly varied in the rendering. It is full of turns and breaks but flows like a stream. The social scene of the improvisation, too, transcends the play of differences. It takes place outside the city, far away from the tensions and compromises of urban society and public life. In this private and implicitly homosocial context Weber's improvisations find their optimal realization: "the impression at such times was above all that he had found a means of revealing his deepest feelings to his closest friends, and that his whole being was concentrated on making himself understood."[59] Such perfect social and artistic community contrasts starkly with the feeling that prevailed at another elite Berlin soirée related by Lichtenstein, where Weber was in nervous spirits and was given a theme on which to improvise by "some dummy with no musical sense." When Weber failed to get anywhere with the theme, the person who had offered it left the room to continue a conversation elsewhere, prompting Weber to break off his performance. Just

as good improvisation, in the improvisation imaginary, is aligned with the achievement of community, so failed improvisation and failed community go hand-in-hand.
Lichtenstein further idealizes Weber's Pankow postlude by contrasting it with the
fantasies of the great concert improvisers of the 1820s: "His improvisations in this
vein differed greatly from that of greater (or rather, more accomplished) pianists like
Hummel and Kalkbrenner, with whom, however little they may have intended it, there
always seemed to be a will to please."[60]

To say that Lichtenstein idealized Weber's improvisations is not to say he was
writing pure fiction. The simple motivic and sequential organization of Haydn's
theme lends itself exceptionally well to improvisational elaboration (Example 1.2), and
Weber's studies with Vogler would have made him fluent in fugal or imitative styles.
Nor is Lichtenstein's the only account of Weber segueing into an improvised postlude
(AMZ 1820, 92). But as Lichtenstein points out, the Haydn postlude was an exceptional improvisation, lacking "the mischievous audacity in brilliant passages and the
fire in full-voiced chordal crescendos with which he normally drew applause."[61] Other
accounts confirm that Weber's free fantasies were full of expressive drama, indulging
generously in harmonic modulations, rhythmic shifts, and "modern" dynamic effects
such as sudden *pianissimos* or, in his trademark effect, a slow *crescendo* enhanced by
the use of full pedal.[62] A report on his Berlin concert of 1814 noted that "from his
free fantasy special mention should be made of a unique and extremely effective way
of performing the Crescendo" (AMZ 1814, 651). Such effects show the influence of
Vogler's fondness for sonic instrumental experiments, and perhaps less directly of the
Mannheim school's orchestral crescendos.

Weber's fantasy style may also have owed something to the north German free fantasy, but he had little tolerance for its irrational ethos. Around 1809 he wrote that
Beethoven's recent, improvisation-inflected compositions "seem to me hopeless chaos,

EXAMPLE 1.2 Haydn, "Betrachtung des Todes," opening

an incomparable struggle for novelty, out of which break a few heavenly flashes of genius proving how great he could be if he would tame his rich fantasy. . . . I do at least believe I can defend my own music from a logical and technical point of view."[63] The value he placed on logic and procedure, as a good student of Vogler, probably had the effect of making his improvisational rhetoric considerably less violent and disjointed than that of the north German tradition. He probably had C. P. E. Bach's fantasy style in mind when he penned an aphorism criticizing "the seemingly torn-away fantastical fragment, which appears to be more a fantasy-piece than a normally regulated music-piece."[64] Such a piece was insufficiently capable of communicating the emotions clearly to the listener.

Weber's free fantasy style was generally the same when he played in Vienna in 1822, nearly a decade after his performing peak and less than a year after the triumphant premiere of *Der Freischütz*. The influential critic F. A. Kanne left an uncommonly specific account of the fantasia:

> A free fantasia with a Rondo . . . was the closer. The improviser swam at length in arpeggios and tension-arousing modulations, whose piquant turns were often quite interesting, and many times the player introduced passages that placed the good sound of the Conrad Graf instrument in a clear light. The highest degree of attention was directed toward the course of ideas—or rather the expected course, for each was an artful development of a theme written by the famous composer. At a fermata Weber used the entire damper mechanism and the sound was so soft, even inaudible, that for a long time the silence was taken to be a musical joke or an intermission. . . . Eventually there appeared something like the first star in a sky of tones, and others gradually appeared, but the arpeggio lasted all too long before the sky was fully lit and, with dampers lifted, its full power emerged. And upon this he played one of his rondos. (WAMZ 1822, 204)

The only stylistic novelty here was Weber's decision to improvise on his own melodies, which were now widely known. But this novelty made all the difference to the critical response, for as will be seen in Chapter 2, free fantasies on familiar themes had only recently come into vogue, popularized by concert pianists like Johann Nepomuk Hummel and Ignaz Moscheles and imitated badly by many aspiring virtuosos. Kanne frankly admitted that Weber's discerning admirers were disappointed with the fantasy. The pianist seemed to sacrifice all learned style in favor of ingratiating lyricism: "Surely all elements of fugal art are at the disposition of Carl Maria v. Weber, so that . . . he could not only divert and inspire with his beautiful vocal music, but could also be in the position to surprise his audience with a truly free fantasy—i.e. invented by the creative mind [*Genius*] in the moment of performance and characterized by a satisfying unity" (WAMZ 1822, 204–205). The standard of comparison here is unquestionably Hummel, whose free fantasies contained many passages in fugal counterpoint alongside passages decorating popular tunes. Another reviewer reiterated the complaint, identifying Weber as "a thinking, truly solid pianist who clearly does not bother himself with modern neck-breaking buffoonery," a pianist capable of better things: "the free fantasy was rather too light a commodity [*Ware*], in fact nothing more and nothing less than a spun-out Präludium to the subsequent Rondo" (AMZ 1822, 306–307). In short, Weber's fantasy, bordering on a potpourri, violated the dignity of the "higher" free fantasy.

Weber's published oeuvre does little to illuminate the sound of his free improvisations. He often published variation sets shortly after improvising on the relevant theme at a concert. But all of these variation sets dispense with the slow introduction he normally improvised in concert, beginning instead with a plain statement of the theme. In addition, the variations are nearly always composed in a *bravura* style that rigorously follows the theme's harmonic and phraseological structure. There is, however, one formal juncture in these compositions where the music tends to proceed more freely: at the end of the final variation of a given set Weber sometimes expands upon the principal motive, leading it through a harmonic digression of an apparently improvisatory character.[65] Such digressions are relatively brief and normally lead to an equally brief coda. Example 1.3 shows such a transitional passage from his *Variations sur un thème original*, op. 9. From the home key of F-major it passes through A♭ major (m. 17) and arrives climactically on a C♯ major triad (m. 28), heard initially as the dominant of F♯ but then, after some lingering, reinterpreted as ♭VI of F-major. Vogler's teaching of *Mehrdeutigkeit* thus bears fruit here. But a stronger index of improvisational practice is the voice-leading, which stays rigorously stepwise in both soprano and bass voices (and the inner voices, too). The arpeggio figures keep both hands in a comfortable, natural and closed position, freeing the player from the burden of negotiating leaps, voice-crossings, or textural differentiation. The meandering harmonies seem to obey what David Sudnow described as the semi-autonomous "ways of the hand," as the fingers search out the next chord through incidental neighbor-note connections.[66]

It is important to underline that this digression is not a *representation* of Weber's free improvisation, but rather a *trace* of improvisational practice inscribed within a fixed composition. The distinction was of utmost importance to Weber, who drastically favored product over process. He praised his studies under Vogler as a process of clarification and rationalization that enabled him to inscribe and fix his intentions precisely and secure the intended effect upon the listener. By the end of this evolution he was deeply critical of isolated, local effects that are not integrated into a larger concept. In a miscellaneous jotting he mocked composers who delighted in short, abrupt modulations: "What an effect this transition has! Wow! Someone hears a modulation consisting of three or four, or indeed just one measure, and gets mentally inebriated. No one considers how it came about, why it is has this effect and not another."[67] Although Vogler is not mentioned here, such brief modulations are precisely what Vogler had offered in the "Summa," and at least some students of the Mannheim school were earning a reputation for overusing them.[68] There may even have been an element of self-critique here, for as Joachim Veit has argued, Weber's early variation sets have quick transitions bearing the imprint of Vogler's modulation teaching.[69] Nor could Weber affirm the semi-autonomous magic of the "ways of the hand." In his autobiographical novella *Tonkünstlerleben* the protagonist laments: "It is these very hands, these cursed piano fingers—which through constant practice and mastery finally acquire a kind of independence and self-willing mind, which are completely unthinking tyrants and despots of creative power. . . . How completely differently does he create whose inner ear is the judge of both invented and evaluated things."[70] Weber was thus sensitive to the wayward powers of keyboard playing and struggled to harness them with a sovereign, "interior" creative faculty. Indeed the brevity of the digression in Example 1.3, in comparison with similar digressions in the variation sets of Mozart and Beethoven, shows an exceptional degree of restraint on improvisatory impulses.

EXAMPLE 1.3 Weber, *Variations sur un thème original*, op. 9

EXAMPLE 1.3 Continued

Weber's concept of improvisation, then, bore no privileged relation with artistic progress or emancipation. From his perspective, progress was achieved only when new ideas and sounds were appropriated intelligently and purposefully and set within an integrated musical whole, whether by an improviser or a composer. He demonstrated this when he republished, in 1815, an edition of twelve chorale settings by Vogler (1784) in which Vogler purported to "improve" J. S. Bach's settings. For his edition Weber wrote a preface affirming Vogler's enlightened and progressive approach: "Vogler—who goes about his work purely systematically, and whose more liberal principles are generated and proven by the nature of the matter, thus offering to harmony an incomparably wider field of variety—is the first person not only to prohibit and mandate but also to explain and lay out his philosophical principles."[71] Vogler's harmonizations differ from Bach's mainly in the choice of cadential chords. Instead of arriving exclusively on tonics, dominants, and secondary dominants as in Bach's practice, Vogler cadences on medial degrees and sometimes tonicizes them. The chorale melodies are thus furnished with novel harmonic colorings, particularly in the middle phrases of a given chorale. Vogler's approach is clearly the outcome of an experimental process in which he tried out at the keyboard alternative harmonizations. And importantly, his chorale examples are not fixed, finished pieces to be played by rote. They are intended, like Vogler's organ classes, to stimulate a harmonically enriched practice of improvisation among church organists.

Weber, for his part, was little invested in the liturgical use of these chorale settings. He was inclined to underscore the value of Vogler's chorales as models of harmonically enhanced and formally rounded composition. A specific example of how he imported his study of chorale harmonization into his composed output is the *Variations sur "Vien' quà Dorina bella,"* op. 7. The first five variations in brilliant style are all harmonically tame, sticking closely in the diatonic orbit of the theme (Example 1.4). Variation 6, however, marked *A piacere, quasi corale*, introduces the church style, with the melody played in the soprano voice and contrapuntal movement in the lower voices (Example 1.5). The melody is slightly tweaked to add mournful, expressive dissonances, and for the final phrase Weber reharmonizes the tune with a sudden dramatic turn to minor, answered by an ironic "brushing off" of the serious tone. This, again, is not a representation of "how Weber improvised" but rather a trace of an unwritten practice—a practice of harmonic recombination and experimentation that Vogler encouraged in his improvisational pedagogy.

EXAMPLE 1.4 Weber, *Variations sur "Vien' quà Dorina bella,"* op. 7, theme (excerpt)

EXAMPLE 1.5 Weber, *Variations sur "Vien' quà Dorina bella,"* variation 6

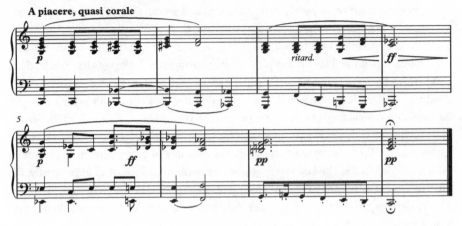

MEYERBEER

In July 1812 the *Morgenblatt für gebildete Stände,* a popular cultural paper based in Stuttgart, published an opera review by a little-known author and inserted a footnote to clarify his identity: "For a couple of months a young musician from Berlin, Hr. Meyer Beer, a student of the great Vogler, has been arousing admiration in various elegant private circles with his fantasies on the Forte-piano. He has also played at a court concert at the Nymphenburg [palace in Munich]."[72] Meyerbeer had been studying with Vogler for about two years, but only now was he beginning to garner public attention, and it was as a pianist, not as a composer. By a coincidence he started his diary in April 1812, allowing us to trace the "private circles" mentioned in the *Morgenblatt.* Between April and July the diary records approximately fifteen different events at which he improvised, sometimes more than once. The patrons were mostly men and women of the nobility, but he also improvised for musicians, teachers, travelers, and friends. He sometimes took themes from the assembly, most often winding up with comic opera melodies by composers such as Gyrowetz, Weigl, Méhul, Vogler, and Winter. At such events he also played compositions by Steibelt, Cramer, Vogler, and himself, very often supplementing the original piece with a newly worked-out cadenza, variation, or "fantasia" of his own.[73] But improvisation occupied a certain extra weight in his growing reputation. As an early biographer put it: "Meyerbeer appeared in various concerts in Munich and aroused astonishment, wonder and enthusiastic applause through his eminent pianism as well as through his rare and most remarkable talent for free improvisation, a shining inheritance of the Vogler school."[74]

    The immediate goal of Meyerbeer's entry into society was to drum up publicity for the performance of his first opera, *Jephtas Gelübte,* which was to be premiered at the Munich court opera before the end of the year. As seen in the cases of Gänsbacher and Weber, improvisation was a resource for building patronal networks and proving one's professional mettle. But Meyerbeer's pianistic talent was of another order and revealed itself at an early age. By the time he was fourteen the influential critic J. F. Rochlitz was expressing concern that the boy had outgrown his teachers and needed a greater challenge (*Berlinische musikalische Zeitung* 1805, 96). He practiced diligently and entertained the possibility of making his career as a pianist. Weber claimed that during the Vogler years Meyerbeer was "one of the leading pianists, if not the leading pianist, of the day."[75] When he first visited Vienna Moscheles heard him and was deeply impressed: "His bravura playing is unparalleled—it cannot be surpassed. His original manner of treating the instrument amazes me."[76] But soon Meyerbeer was wavering, unable to decide whether to pursue a career in composition or performance. From Paris in 1814 he wrote: "my energies for the small Italian operetta are slackening. Since yesterday, however, the pianistic spirit has started to glow again, but how soon will it be before it is extinguished? What terrible prospects for someone already twenty-three years old!"[77] The next year he visited London and took inspiration from the opportunity to hear Cramer play, but he was also daunted by heavy action of the English pianos and the powerful virtuosity of Kalkbrenner, concluding that "in my piano playing I have regressed by a year, rather than progressed."[78]

Evidently the choice had now tipped toward composition, but the seriousness of Meyerbeer's pianistic ambitions had a long-term impact on his compositional process, in which improvisation never ceased to play a significant role. He probably learned little about improvising from his childhood teacher Franz Lauska. Lichtenstein claimed that Lauska's free playing (*freier Vortrag*) bore "the stamp of a prepared and thought-out work," unlike the "truly immediate inspiration and variety of invention" of other improvisers like Weber.[79] For lack of brilliant improvisers in the milieu of Berlin, he probably took inspiration mainly from Vogler, whose improvisations he repeatedly described as "extraordinary." While working under Vogler in Darmstadt he was improvising regularly, almost daily, whether for an assembly of listeners or in the solitude of his practice room. It is likely he made a habit of practicing on those popular opera tunes that were most likely to be requested in society. It is also likely he practiced extemporizing on fugue subjects in various sorts of counterpoint, since this was the approach taken in the Sunday organ lessons. Otherwise we are largely in dark about how he learned and improved upon his improvisational skill.

The only specific technique we can identify—improvising in three tones—merits closer attention because it is not attested in pedagogical books and was possibly unique to the school of Vogler. On several occasions during the summer of 1812 Meyerbeer mentioned improvising this way: "I played for [Herr von Pappenheim] my new Sonata in E♭ and improvised on three notes he provided for me (E, D, G) to my complete satisfaction" (May 12); "I played the Variations in D Major, and improvised on three suggested notes: C, E, G" (May 25); "After lunch I played the Divertimento and improvised on three suggested notes: A♭, C, B" (June 11).[80] The value he placed on this approach is evident from a diary entry written about a month later, after the disruptions of his move to Munich: "From tomorrow I want to tackle seriously many outstanding tasks; I also want to improvise daily on three notes or on a given theme, as I used to do in Darmstadt. . . . Improvised on the three notes G, D, A."[81] The three-note strategem was not Meyerbeer's personal quirk; Carl Maria von Weber used it as well. While in Berlin in 1814, for example, Weber participated in a soirée hosted by the Prince Radziwill where "a great deal of music was made, and I improvised on 3 notes given to me by the Princess."[82] In other diary entries he mentioned improvisations on C-F♯-G (Prague, 1814) and F-D-E♭ (Dresden, 1817).[83]

As vehicles for improvisation, such three-note constellations differ significantly from fugue subjects, folk tunes, and opera melodies. They are not musical unities possessing a defined shape or internal coherence, but abstract, pre-compositional sets that are radically open-ended in their possible realizations. They are not even generative "schemata" in Gjerdingen's sense, since they define no linear-temporal structure.[84] Historically they are clearly related to the shorter subjects, perhaps especially *alla breve* ones, used in fugue improvisations. Both Gänsbacher and Weber, for example, heard an organ concert where Vogler was given the motive G-A-B-C "to fugue upon as a closing piece, wherein Vogler showed himself to be quite singularly the greatest master and organist."[85] This four-note motive is banal and insignificant on its own terms, but it does define a melodic gestalt and it suggests definite harmonic and rhythmic realizations. The arbitrary cells upon which Weber and Meyerbeer expounded were considerably more open-ended. They could be elaborated as a driving figural motive, a melody beneath which various chords are dropped, a bass upon which chords are built, a motive for sequential reiterations, a delicate accompaniment figure, a point of imitation in counterpoint, or a dramatic recurring motto in double octaves. Presumably pianists exploited many or all of these combinatorial and stylistic possibilities in this largely unconstrained but still thematically unified mode of improvisation.

Carl Czerny, in the chapter of his 1829 improvisation treatise concerning improvisation in a single theme, demonstrated how a three-note motive—A-B♭-C—can be varied and elaborated, asserting that "the more simple the subject, the more free, indeed more interesting the development, since the inventiveness of the artist will be guaranteed greater latitude." Most of his sample elaborations, however, simply iterate the motive to launch a passage in a recognizable style—scherzo, adagio, march, etc. They do not treat the motive to reharmonization, counterpoint, sequencing, or modulation.[86] Vogler's students are not likely to have followed Czerny's approach. Having been trained in Vogler's chorale-harmonization method, they might instinctively have begun by reharmonizing the motive in several ways, or, if they were preparing for a Sunday class, going straight for a fugal treatment. But as Léon Kreutzer implied in his vignette of the organ lessons, Vogler's students often summoned their own, more modern frames of reference to break away from their teacher's more traditional orientation. The crucial point is that the three-note cells issued a special sort of invitation to the improviser. Whereas fugue subjects invited elaborations in the learned style, and popular diatonic melodies invited *galant* style treatment, the three-note strategem invited the pianist to free development, to harmonic and contrapuntal recombination, and to stylistic heterogeneity. And in this sense the strategem best embodied the exploratory and experimental aspects of Vogler's pedagogy.

From the moment he traveled to Italy in 1816, Meyerbeer was devoted almost exclusively to opera composition. He did not maintain a balance between composition, conducting, and piano performance like Weber, and he only acquired a kapellmeister appointment much later, after becoming well established as a composer. Piano improvisation nevertheless remained a vital, integral part of his compositional process, as indicated by countless diary entries written during the composition of *Robert le Diable, Le Prophète, L'Etoile du Nord*, and *Vasco da Gama*. When he embarked on the commission for the never-completed *Le Portefaix* in 1831 (at which point he was simultaneously working on *Robert*), he wrote: "I stayed at home in the evening, reflecting and improvising on the introduction to *Le Portefaix*."[87] The locution "reflecting and improvising" is revealing: Meyerbeer did not extemporize with the intention of stumbling upon a sudden, inspired idea that could be captured immediately on paper, as if to preserve the heat of the moment. His main goal was to find the "right" disposition or formal layout for a dramatic and musical idea whose kernel he had already found. To this end he could spend long hours trying out different sequences, combinations, and harmonic realizations and judging their efficacy. While working on *Le Prophète* in 1839, over a span of ten days, he described himself as improvising "vaguely" on the conclusion of Act II for one hour and forty-five minutes; on Duprez's Act III aria, also for one hour forty-five minutes, during which time he "devised an original, happy start to the stretta 'Roi du ciel'"; and on the cavatina of another Duprez aria for two hours fifteen minutes, during which he arrived at the decision: "I will shape the piece into a *rondo agitato*."[88] The latter comment suggests he had worked out most of the piece at the piano but not yet written it down.[89] Even at the age of seventy-two, as he worked on *l'Africaine (Vasco da Gama)*, he often improvised at the piano for four hours.[90]

Although it can be difficult to draw the line between composition and improvisation in Meyerbeer's practice, he kept them somewhat distinct in his mind and we should not assume they were synonymous. He sometimes improvised in order to awaken his creative energies and prepare for the higher exertions of "composition." On an evening in 1841 he "improvised and tried to induce the mood for composing, but without success."[91] Numerous diary entries anxiously record such failures to compose, as if improvising did not lead him toward a final decision, but rather fed upon its own tail and postponed the arrival of any decision. He felt particularly blocked in the summer of 1844 while returning to the composition of *Le Prophète*: "The whole day passed in fruitless attempts, either by reading or by improvisation, to achieve the right mood for working on the Flute Scene or the closing march of the finale."[92] The parallel drawn here between reading literature and improvising indicates that he may have mulled over the dramatic idea he was trying to bring to fruition, or possibly ancillary ideas loosely connected with it, in order to suffuse his mind with a rich field of associational meanings that might eventually leave their mark on the composed work. For Meyerbeer, as for many other musicians, it seems that physical contact with the keyboard was an indispensable resource for opening up inventive pathways in improvisation. The composer and pianist Ferdinand Hiller, recalling lessons he took with Hummel, said that when improvising Hummel "placed himself at the piano and, disregarding everything around him, let himself get lost in thoughts on *that keyboard which means the world to the composer*."[93] On occasion, when working out a single dramatic scene or idea, Meyerbeer would let his improvisations carry him dreamily away from the task at hand: "While improvising on the piano in the evening I involuntarily began composing the trio in Act 3, even though I have not yet finished writing out the quintet."[94]

The compositions that resulted from Meyerbeer's creative process do not sound "improvisatory" in any significant way. On the contrary, as commentators have long observed, they give off a strong sense of reflection, intention, and calculation. Yet Vogler's improvisational pedagogy did leave indirect traces in the finished works. As Sabine Henze-Döhring has argued, Vogler taught both Weber and Meyerbeer to build contrasts between the independent voices of a fugue, contrasts that would give variety to the combinations and could eventually be united at a climax. These guidelines found translation in Meyerbeer's dramatic techniques of "thematic montage" and the "simultaneous representation of complex dramatic proceedings." Henze-Döhring further argues that Vogler prioritized "the linear unfolding of a theme consisting of a 'cell' consisting of only a few tones, thus conveying the impression of through-organization."[95] This compositional idea is clearly linked to the three-note improvising strategem, and it finds a compositional reflection in Meyerbeer's longer, more elaborate numbers, where motivic reprises bind together discrete patches of heterogeneous music. Meyerbeer's habit of interrupting diatonically stable passages with abrupt harmonic turns may also reflect Vogler's relatively liberal approach to harmony and modulation. The "Roi du ciel" scene, whose opening he devised in improvisation, draws together both motivic recurrences and harmonic turns of this kind.

The notion that Meyerbeer's brilliance as a composer might be related to his early pursuit of improvisation was barely heard in his time. But an obituary from 1864, taking an expansive view of his life and work, drew attention to the uninterrupted role of improvisation in his creative process, while also noting the little-known fact that Meyerbeer improvised often in private company:

Meyerbeer had preserved from the days of his piano studies a great command of technique that served him well in improvisation. In Chopin's house, where his visits were always welcome, discussions of fingering, rhythm, and phrasing almost always led to an improvised *étude*. He knew how to shape his fleeting ideas with such certainty and clarity that he seemed to be playing compositions that had been worked out and reflected upon for a long time, rather than momentary improvisations. Witnesses (G. Sand) report that he had a habit of reserving the theme whose motives formed the substance of the fantasy for the conclusion; one heard it bud, grow, and develop, until at the end it crowned and rounded off the entire thing. . . . These accounts of Meyerbeer's piano improvisations are not without interest. They show with what decisive drama and liveliness he was able to form ideas, and they illuminate a talent in him that had previously, at least for many years, retreated entirely into the background—a talent about which hardly anything else was known except that he had developed it with astonishing energy in the years of his youth.[96]

This passage draws attention to those benefits of improvisation that did not leave concrete traces in his completed works—namely, presence of mind and definiteness of formulation. They reveal a side of Meyerbeer—the unreconstructed piano virtuoso discussing fine points of technique with Chopin—that looks quite different from the stereotype of the "calculating" composer, and indexes the range and depth of musicianship he acquired under Vogler. In addition, the account of Meyerbeer's "cumulation" gambit points up the historical link between Vogler's improvisation of fugues—which developed the separate voices and channeled them toward a climactic unification—and the romantic aesthetics of George Sand, which celebrated Meyerbeer's *point de culmination* as a moment of sublime transcendence. That Meyerbeer's improvisations were available for romantic appropriation of this kind was already evident in Balzac's 1837 novel *Gambara*, whose composing and improvising protagonist is based partly on Meyerbeer, and whose musical consultant was George Sand.

In Vogler's school, improvisation was not invested with any particular virtue. It was one mode of music-making or "musicking" broadly conceived. Vogler modeled free playing at a high level on both piano and organ and expected his students to emulate him. Skill in improvisation could open doors to church positions, to the elite salons where professional reputations were built, and, as Vogler's popular concerts demonstrated, to success with larger public audiences. It was also a source of bonding, professional pride, and pleasurable play within the community of musicians and connoisseurs. As a display of learning, craft, and discipline, it allowed the teacher to impress students and inspire them toward higher achievements. In dual improvisations players challenged and prodded one another in a spirit of friendly competition. In the presence of musicians and connoisseurs, pianists had an audience that could appreciate the difficulty and originality of the best extemporaneous ideas—a circuit of sympathy and intimate understanding rarely found in their experiences elsewhere. For all of these advantages, though, improvisation had not yet been "invented" in the stronger sense. The noun "improvisation" hardly existed in musical discourse. The verb forms—"to fantasize," "to prelude," "to extemporize"—were far more common, indicating that it was conceived as a practice rather than an abstract category of musical production. With the exception of the north German free fantasia, which had already become an encoded style, there was no shared or widespread understanding that improvisation differed in some fundamental way from other modes of production. If there was a difference it was a difference of degree, not of kind: free playing was somewhat more difficult for the performer, demonstrating greater mastery of rules and craft. Neither Weber nor Meyerbeer had any incentive to cease improvising as they directed their ambitions toward the composition of dramatic works, and they remained in this respect "unreconstructed" improvisers. However, the weight they eventually placed on their identities as composers was a departure from Vogler, in whom the various branches of musical activity were more equalized.

What was novel and distinctive about the school of Vogler was not improvisation itself, but the ethos of progress, emancipation, and exploratory freedom in which it was embedded. The master's enlightened, progressive attitude made him hostile to the blind observance of old compositional rules and prohibitions. He encouraged students and readers of his treatises to use their independent rational judgment, rather than set prescriptions, to determine how to elaborate a fugue subject, accompany in thoroughbass, compose dramatic music, or harmonize an ascending C-major scale. Improvisation opened up an exceptionally wide field for such independent exploration, though not all students capitalized on its progressive potential. Gänsbacher wanted mainly to soak up the traditional church styles, and he defined his future horizons along conservative lines. Weber and Meyerbeer, however, were young lions of the piano and had read widely in contemporary literature and philosophy. As windows of opportunity seemed to be opening for German opera, they were more susceptible to Vogler's progressive vision and how it might be mobilized for the stage. In Vogler's organ class, in private practice, and elsewhere, they made improvisation an incubator of novel harmonic, developmental, and combinatorial ideas that would later, in acts of written composition, coalesce as progressive musical and dramatic ideas. The "years of entertainment" that Vogler had said were afforded by the diminished-seventh chord, for example, found a spectacular realization at the end of the famous scene in the Wolf's Glen in *Der Freischütz*, where the music suddenly lurches from C minor to F♯ minor by means of a reinterpretation of the diminished-seventh chord. In general, though, the link between the students' keyboard improvisations and their operatic compositions is at best indirect, since there are vast conceptual disjunctions between variations and combinations, on the one hand, and dramatic representation, on the other. Vogler had been pressing hard to make instrumental music "speak" representationally, not only in his *Hamlet* overture—an early experiment in program music—but also in his organ concerts directed toward lay listeners, where he represented entire epic stories in improvisation, simulating the effects of the orchestra on his newly devised instrument. He was too old to take such crossover experiments very far, but his students in many ways extended and completed his work.

It can seem paradoxical that a musician entering his sixties, deeply invested in religion and ecclesiastical identity, and acknowledged even by his detractors as a master of fugal improvisation on the organ, should become a source of musical progress and experimentation in the nineteenth century. This is the paradox that lends charm to Léon Kreuzer's story about Vogler's lessons with Meyerbeer and Weber. One would expect the conservative ideological profile of church institutions to act as a restraint on progressive musical thinking. But the organist's practice was not determined exclusively by the institution it was supposed to serve. Sometimes he performed for other musicians, or played a separate concert for the congregation—situations that set into play different values and priorities. Within the structure of the liturgy there were spaces for free elaboration—pockets of liberty inviting the player to summon his independent inventive craft such as the prelude, interludes, the Offertory, and especially the postlude. Moreover, church organists were liberated from a responsibility that weighs on nearly all other musicians: the responsibility to communicate with a listening audience or a public. As liturgical accompanists, their primary responsibility concerned ceremonial affect and control—guiding and affecting the assembled congregation rather than communicating something *to* it.

In several respects, then, the institutional conditions of organ practice opened up more space for experimental play than any other. An especially radical potency was lodged within the short, four-chord modulations Vogler modeled in his "Summa," though they ostensibly arose from a liturgical demand for short, improvised transitions. When divorced from their liturgical context, these progressions invited the curious musician into further explorations. Vogler specified that his realizations were only provisional, and that the modulations could be realized in various other ways. His disciple J. H. Knecht sought to demonstrate just how many "ways of the hand" were possible. A great admirer of the Vogler's system and a torchbearer for the Mannheim School, Knecht expanded the "Summa" to list 3,069 independent chords and 6,336 "essentially different modulations."[97] Vogler, in giving quasi-systematic presentation to an improvised practice based on nearest-note connections, had unleashed a ceaseless proliferation of possibilities. Over the succeeding generations, keyboardists, theorists, and composers continued to explore such alternate harmonic pathways through nearest-note connections. Schubert's music, as theorists have recently been noting, is full of such stepwise "sliding."[98] Felix Draeseke justified the "transgressive" harmonic practices of the New German School by appealing to treatises published by Carl Friedrich Weitzmann in the early 1850s, in which nearest-note voice-leading justified previously forbidden progressions. According to Draeseke, Weitzmann's theories contained the basic principles for "the building of a completely new system of harmonic instruction."[99] It only looked "completely new" if one ignored the dozens of modulation treatises, most of them directed at organists, in which nearest-note connections and short modulations retained the primacy they had held in Vogler's own work. To name just one example, an obscure "L. Schönfelder" published in 1850 a "Theoretical-practical Introduction to playing preludes correctly in improvisation [*nach eigener Fantasie*], even with little talent . . . A book for the self-teaching of pianists and practicing organists."[100] It lays out a "system" of modulation and borrows Gottfried Weber's term *Mehrdeutigkeit* to demonstrate how a soprano melody can be reharmonized. It further demonstrates how a three-chord progression can be reinterpreted as belonging to several keys.

The teaching and practice of church organists kept improvisation and theory vital throughout the nineteenth century. It was a subterranean undercurrent that had the potential to "break through" at any time to the mainstream of concert or opera music, while remaining in most respects quite separate from it. In this sense the improvisatory habits of organists constituted what Raymond Williams called an "alternative" form of culture—standing more or less completely apart from the dominant cultural paradigms as represented by opera and symphony. The power of such alternative forms is that, unlike "oppositional" forms, they are treated indifferently by the dominant culture. In Williams's words, they present "quite real alternatives [that] are at least left alone."[101] Although organ improvisation was "left alone" by the late-century regime of musical works, it was nonetheless available for reappropriation. Weber's and Meyerbeer's conversion of Voglerian practices into compositional and dramatic procedures began such a process. But the potential for organ practice to infiltrate mainstream music was realized on a greater scale only later in the century, when Bruckner and Franck, both of them brilliant organ improvisers with years of church practice behind them, came forth with symphonic works rich in enharmonic relations and modulations. Their innovations counted as "progressive" with respect to the direction of French or German music, but the source of this progress was to be found in the nominally "conservative" institution of the church, where organists had long been exploring harmonic modulation in improvisation.

NOTES

1. Léon Kreutzer, "Les Compositeurs contemporains: M. Meyerbeer," *Revue contemporaine* 2, tome 8 (July–August 1853), 636–37. Emphasis added. This essay was printed in slightly rewritten form in Arthur Pougin, *Meyerbeer: Notes biographiques* (Paris: J. Tresse, 1864), 13–14. It was excerpted in Eugène de Mirecourt, *Meyerbeer* (Paris; J.-P. Roret, 1854), 22.

2. On the north German free fantasy see Annette Richards, *The Free Fantasia and the Musical Picturesque* (Cambridge: Cambridge University Press, 2001). The organ traditions have a vast bibliography, but an overview for this period can be found in Karl Gustav Fellerer, *Beiträge zur Choralbegleitung und Choralverarbeitung in der Orgelmusik des ausgehenden 18. und beginnenden 19. Jahrhunderts* (Strassburg: Heitz, 1932). Next to Vogler, the most widely admired organist of this time period was probably Rinck. The only modern study of Rinck is *Johann Christian Heinrich Rinck: Dokumente zu Leben und Werk* (Köln: Dohr, 2003); more valuable as an indicator of improvisation is the much older *Züge aus dem Leben und Wirken des Dr. Christian Heinrich Rinck, gewesener Kantor, Hoforganist, und Kammermusikus zu Darmstadt*, ed. G. W. Körne (Erfurt: Körner, 1848). The literature on Mozart has focused mainly on ornamentation and concerto cadenzas. See Robert Levin, "Improvising Mozart," in *Musical Improvisation: Art, Education and Society* (Urbana-Champaign: University of Illinois Press, 2009), 143–49. Leon Plantinga's *Clementi: His Life and Music* (London and New York: Oxford University Press, 1977) gathers a number of testaments to Clementi's excellence in improvisation; see for example 151, 211, 313. In the same school we can place J. B. Cramer's fascinating, still underexplored *Pensieri Musicali: 36 Morceaux en forme de Préludes, Cadences et petites Improvisations*, op. 91. The term *accompagnement* (borrowed by contemporary German writers as *accompagnieren*) is often used in French harmony treatises of the early nineteenth century to mean playing chord progressions behind a soloist or singer or possibly a small ensemble. An early and important example is A. E. M. Grétry, *Méthode simple pour apprendre à préluder un peu de temps* (Paris: Imprimerie de la République, X [1802]).

3. Floyd Grave, *In Praise of Harmony: the Teachings of Abbé Georg Joseph Vogler* (Lincoln: University of Nebraska Press, 1987), 99–101. Graves's book is still the main study in English of Vogler's theoretical writings.

4. On the debates between Forkel and Vogler see Martin Stehelin, "Musikalische Wissenschaft und Praxis bei J. N. Forkel," in *Musikwissenschaft und Musikpflege an der*

Georg-August-Universität Göttingen: Beiträge zu ihrer Geschichte, ed. Martin Staehelin (Göttingen: Vandenhoeck und Ruprecht, 1987), 9–26.

5. Floyd Grave, "Abbé Vogler and the Study of Fugue," *Music Theory Spectrum* 1 (1979), 57.

6. See Floyd Grave's commentary in his edition of Georg Joseph Vogler, *Pièces de clavecin (1798); and Zwei und dreisig Präludien (1806)* (Madison, WI: A-R Editions, 1986), xi.

7. Ibid., x.

8. *Abt Vogler's Choral-System* (Copenhagen: Christensen, 1800), 104–105.

9. Program given in Grave, *In Praise of Harmony*, 229–30. For further details about his organ programs and concerts, as well as the political tension with north German musicians, see Jürgen Heidrich, "'. . . nicht eine Funken Genie': Vogler und die Norddeutschen," in *Abbé Vogler: Ein Mannheimer im europäischen Kontext*, ed. Thomas Betzwieser and Silke Leopold (Frankfurt: Peter Lang, 2003), 61–70.

10. Quoted in H. Kelletat, *Zur Geschichte der deutschen Orgelmusik in der Frühklassik* (Kassel: Bärenreiter, 1933), 55.

11. C. F. D. Schubart, *Ideen zu einer Ästhetik der Tonkunst* (Vienna, 1806), 133.

12. Quoted in Dr. Schaufhäutl, *Abt Georg Joseph Vogler* (Hildesheim: Olms, 1888), 18, from a letter in the *Musikalische Realzeitung* of 1788.

13. Kelletat, *Zur Geschichte der deutschen Orgelmusik*, 56–57.

14. AMZ 1866, 339, borrowing from Hanslick's feuilleton for the *Neue Freie Presse* of 1 September 1866. An early biographer of Meyerbeer, who was probably building off Hanslick, claimed that Vogler looked like an experimentalist *avant la lettre*: "with his strange works as well as his discoveries and inventions . . . [he] could justifiably be considered a musician of the future [*Zukunftsmusiker*] of that time, just like Franz Liszt today." Hermann Mendel, *Giacomo Meyerbeer: sein Leben und seine Werke* (Berlin: R. Lesser, 1869), 12.

15. Schaufhäutl, *Abt Georg Joseph Vogler*, 18.

16. Joachim Veit claims that Vogler made his students "compose out" both chromatic and diatonic scales as exercises. See *Der junge Carl Maria von Weber: Studien zum Einfluss Franz Danzis und Abbé Georg Joseph Voglers* (Mainz: Schott, 1990), 184–85. For an instantiation of the same paradigm close to Vogler's time, see Grétry, *Méthode simple*, 16–17 and 84–90. Kalkbrenner also gave scale-based harmonization exercises in Fréd. Kalkbrenner, *Traité d'harmonie du pianiste, principes rationnels de la modulation pour apprendre à préluder et à improviser, op. 185* (Amsterdam: Heuwekemeyer, [1849, repr. 1970]), 30–36.

17. J. Fröhlich, *Biographie des grossen Tonkünstlers Abt Georg Joseph Vogler* (Würzburg: F. E. Thein, 1845), 55. Translated into English with slight modifications in Alexander Wheelock Thayer, *Thayer's Life of Beethoven*, ed. Elliot Forbes, 2 vols. (Princeton: Princeton University Press, [1973]), 2:15–16. Gänsbacher related the event in his memoir in similar terms, saying that Vogler "wove in transformations and harmonic combinations never heard before, so that out of astonishment and delight I burned with enthusiasm for Vogler." Johann Gänsbacher, *Denkwürdigkeiten aus meinem Leben*, ed. Walter Senn (Tirol: Österreichischer Kulturverlag, 1986), 19.

18. Ludwig Nohl, *Musiker-Briefe* (Leipzig: Duncker and Humblot, 1867), 78. The review of this concert in the *Zeitung für die elegante Welt* (1804, 326) said that Vogler sat down again to improvise on a theme from his opera *Castor und Pollux*, first "varying" it then leading it into a fugue. See Joachim Veit, *Der junge Carl Maria von Weber: Studien zum Einfluss Franz Danzis und Abbé Georg Joseph Voglers* (Mainz: Schott, 1990), 69n.64.

19. Abt Vogler, *System für den Fugenbau, als Einleitung zur harmonischen Gesang-Verbindungs-Lehre* (Offenbach: Joh. André, 1811), 66–68.

20. See the editor's introduction to Abbé Georg Joseph Vogler, *Polymelos I*, ed. Eberhart Kraus (Regensburg: Eigenverlag Eberhard Kraus, 1999), n.p.

21. Heinrich W. Schwab, "'Plusieurs fois je me sentis ému jusqu'aux larmes en l'écoutant': Zur Improvisationskunst des Klavier- und Orgelspielers C. E. F. Weyse," *Danish Yearbook of Musicology* 31 (2003): 37–60.

22. Quoted in Schaufhäutl, *Abt Georg Joseph Vogler*, 18. The original source is "Brief an einen musikalischen Freund," *Musikalische Real-Zeitung für das Jahr 1788*, 60.

23. *Abt Vogler's Choral-System*, 5.

24. Vogler, *System für den Fugenbau*, 7.

25. Ibid.

26. Grave, *In Praise of Harmony*, 34. The "Summa" is an appendix to *Vogler's Tonschule, Tonwissenschaft, und Tonsezkunst, nebst Beyspielen* (Offenbach: Joh. André, 1778? [Mannheim, 1776]).

27. Georg Joseph Vogler, *Betrachtungen der Mannheimer Tonschule*, 4 vols. (reprint Hildesheim: Olms, 1974), 3:55. Emphasis added.

28. "Summe der Harmonik," III:5. Vogler was not the first author to affirm enharmonic modulation as a resource for the keyboardist's solitary inventive pleasure and for moving listeners with spontaneous turns of phrase and emotion. The ideas find a strong anticipation in Anton Bemetzrieder's *Leçons de clavecin* (published 1771), which were eagerly disseminated by Diderot and well received by Grétry. See Roger Moseley, *Keys to Play: Music as a Ludic Medium from Apollo to Nintendo* (Oakland, CA: University of California Press, 2016), 108, and Beverly Jerold, "Diderot (Part I)—Authorship and Illusion," *Music Theory and Analysis* 1, no. 1–2 (2014): 38–60. It is nonetheless unclear whether Vogler was familiar with this French discourse.

29. *Vogler's Tonschule*, 153–54.

30. Ibid., 154.

31. Grave, *In Praise of Harmony*, 32.

32. Gottfried Weber's harmonic theory and its debts to Vogler are explained in Janna Karen Saslaw, "Gottfried Weber and the Concept of *Mehrdeutigkeit*," PhD diss., Columbia University, 1992. See especially 47–62 and 93ff. Grave, in his edition of *Pièces de clavecin (1798); and Zwei und dreisig Präludien (1806)*, describes the final prelude of Vogler's *Zwei und dreisig Präludien* as "a study in harmonic ambiguity and changing function" (xiii).

33. *Betrachtungen* ("Summa") 3:5–6.

34. *Betrachtungen*, 3:13–14.

35. Fröhlich, *Biographie des grossen Tonkünstlers*, 55.

36. Max Maria von Weber, *Carl Maria v. Weber, ein Lebensbild*, 3 vols. (Leipzig: Ernst Keil, 1864), 1:199.

37. For Weber's letter constituting the association and its regulations, see Nohl, *Musiker-Briefe*, 189–92.

38. Carl Maria von Weber, *Writings on Music*, ed. John Warrack, trans. Martin Cooper (Cambridge: Cambridge University Press, 1981), 278.

39. Gänsbacher, *Denkwürdigkeiten aus meinem Leben*, 3; see also 152.

40. Ibid., 18.

41. Ibid., 41.

42. Ibid., 38.

43. Alexander von Dusch, *Flüchtige Augzeichnungen* (n. d.), cited from an unpublished archival source in Frank Ziegler, "Carl Maria von Weber als Klaviervirtuose," in *Weber-Studien*

9, ed. Markus Bundur, Manuel Gervink, and Frank Ziegler (Mainz: Schott, 2014), 39. Ziegler's article is the best study of Weber as pianist.

44. *The Diaries of Giacomo Meyerbeer*, ed. Robert Ignatius Letellier, 4 vols. (Madison, NJ: Fairleigh Dickinson University Press, 1999–2004), 1:188 (5 August 1812).

45. Ziegler, "Carl Maria von Weber als Klaviervirtuouse," 39, gives the dates at 1806–1808, but this is probably an error.

46. F. W. Berner's reputation for improvisation on both piano and organ stayed with him. The AMZ reported that his brilliant, clear playing, "combined with thoroughness and correct development of ideas in free fantasies, mark him as one of the best piano players of our time. What Mr. B. is capable of in free fantasies in the strict style and in extemporized fugues has already been acknowledged often enough" (1819, 783). A thorough biography from 1829 commented on the close bond between Weber and Berner: "They were very close in age and even more related in talent, inclination, and artistic aspiration. Consequently they soon developed an intimate friendship. . . . They diligently exchanged with one another their knowledge, thoughts, and ideas; a friendly rivalry hovered over them." "F. W. Berner," *Eutonia: eine hauptsächlich pädagogische Musik-Zeitschrift* 1 (1829), 279. The biography also made further comments on his improvisations at 299–300.

47. Ziegler, "Carl Maria von Weber als Klaviervirtuose," 28.

48. John Warrack, *Carl Maria von Weber* (London: John Hamilton, 1968), 84–85.

49. Robert Münster, "Zu Carl Maria von Webers Münchner Aufenthalt," in *Musik, Edition, Interpretation: Gedenkschrift Günter Henle* (Munich: Henle, 1980), 370.

50. Czerny, writing about "preludes of a longer and more elaborate type," indicated that "when the performer has to play a solo piece for which the composer himself has written no introduction, as, for example, in rondos or variations that begin directly with the theme, then it is not inappropriate if the improvised prelude is proportionately longer and more elaborate" (*Introduction*, 17).

51. Ibid., 378.

52. Max Maria von Weber, *Carl Maria v. Weber*, 1:311–12.

53. Warrack, *Carl Maria von Weber*, 136.

54. Ibid.

55. *Mein vielgeliebter Muks: Hundred Briefe Carl Maria von Webers an Caroline Brandt aus den Jahren 1814–1817*, ed. Eveline Bartlitz (München: C. H. Beck, 1987), 99 (27 August 1814).

56. Quoted in *Mein vielgeliebter Muks*, 577. Another celebrity, the poet and critic C. W. Wieland, heard Weber in Weimar and was "overwhelmed with his improvising" (Max Maria von Weber, *Carl Maria v. Weber*, 1:382–83).

57. *Briefe von Carl Maria von Weber an Hinrich Lichtenstein*, ed. Ernst Rudorff (Braunschweig: George Westermann, 1900), 3.

58. Ibid.

59. Warrack, *Carl Maria von Weber*, 141.

60. Ibid.

61. *Briefe von Carl Maria von Weber an Hinrich Lichtenstein*, 3.

62. See especially the accounts in Ziegler, "Carl Maria von Weber als Klavierviruose," 34, 41.

63. Letter to Hans-Georg Nägeli dated 21 May 1810, in Nohl, *Musiker-Briefe*, 178–79.

64. *Hinterlassene Schriften von Carl Maria von Weber*, ed. Theodor Hell, 2 vols. (Dresden und Leipzig: Arnold, 1828), 1:114–15 ("das scheinbar abgerissene Phantastische").

65. This convention, in which the final variation is extended into a kind of free elaboration with modulations, is found in Mozart's variation sets and elsewhere. On one occasion

Meyerbeer explicitly called this section a fantasia: on 9 July 1812 he played his Variations in E♭ major and emended it so that "in the fantasia section I counterpointed a new theme which I finally united with the principal theme." *Diaries of Giacomo Meyerbeer*, 1:296. Reviews of published variations in the AMZ often attribute an "improvisatory" quality to these expansions.

66. David Sudnow, *Ways of the Hand: the Organization of Improvised Conduct* (Cambridge, MA: Harvard University Press, 1978).

67. *Hinterlassene Schriften von Carl Maria von Weber*, 1:116.

68. J. P. Pixis, later known as a virtuoso in Paris, was associated with Vogler's school, and when his *Romantische Oper* "Almazinde" was premiered in 1820 a critic claimed that "Herr Pixis somewhat too often uses the enharmonic transformation of flats into sharps in the diminished-seventh chord in his transitions" (WAMZ 1820, 243). Another contemporary noted that "he understands very well the art of modulation." Lucian Schiewietz, *Johann Peter Pixis: Beiträge zu seiner Biographie, zur Rezeptionshistoriographie seiner Werke und Analyse seiner Sonatenformung* (Frankfurt a. M.: Peter Lang, 1994), 60.

69. Veit, *Der junge Carl Maria von Weber*, 184–85.

70. *Hinterlassene Schriften von Carl Maria von Weber*, 1:21–22. As will be seen in Chapter 4, Schumann later reprised this same theme. He might well have been familiar with Weber's writings, since they had been published in 1828.

71. *Zwölf Choräle von Sebastian Bach, umgearbeitet von Vogler, zergliedert von Carl Maria von Weber* (Leipzig: C. F. Peters, 1810), n.p. ("Einleitung").

72. *Giacomo Meyerbeer: Briefwechsel und Tagebücher*, ed. Heinz Becker, 6 vols. (Berlin: Walter de Gruyter & Co., 1960–2001), 1:623. The original source is *Morgenblatt für gebildete Stände*, 2 July 1812.

73. *Diaries of Giacomo Meyerbeer*, 1:258–96.

74. Mendel, *Giacomo Meyerbeer*, 31.

75. *Sämtliche Schriften von Carl Maria von Weber*, ed. Georg Kaiser (Berlin: Schuster & Loeffler, 1908), 307.

76. Charlotte Moscheles, *Recent Music and Musicians, as Described in the Diaries and Correspondence of Ignatz Moscheles* (New York: Holt and Co., 1873), 12.

77. *Diaries of Giacomo Meyerbeer*, 1:328.

78. *Diaries of Giacomo Meyerbeer*, 1:336.

79. *Briefe von Carl Maria von Weber an Hinrich Lichtenstein*, 4.

80. *Diaries of Giacomo Meyerbeer*, 1:269, 272, 276.

81. Ibid., 1:285.

82. *Mein vielgeliebter Muks*, 90.

83. Ziegler, "Carl Maria von Weber als Klaviervirtuose," 41.

84. Robert O. Gjerdingen, *Music in the Galant Style* (New York: Oxford University Press, 2007), 11–16.

85. Gänsbacher, *Denkwürdigkeiten*, 38.

86. Carl Czerny, *A Systematic Introduction to Improvisation on the Pianoforte*, trans. and ed. Alice L. Mitchell (New York: Longman, 1983), 46–47.

87. *Diaries of Giacomo Meyerbeer*, 2:407 (5 February 1831).

88. Ibid., 2:529–31.

89. The notion that he worked out many of his numbers at the piano, before writing them down, is strongly suggested by this entry: "In the evening I wanted to score the first two tempi

of the duet, but began improvising so that not much was completed—although plenty was prepared" (ibid., 2:46., 12 Oct 1841).

90. Ibid., 4:319, 320, 322, 326.

91. Ibid., 2:52 (17 November 1841).

92. Ibid., 2:97 (18 May 1844). For similar episodes around the same time see 98 (27 May) and 101 (13 June).

93. Ferdinand Hiller, *Künstlerleben* (Köln: DuMont-Schauberg, 1880), 10–11. Emphasis added.

94. *Diaries of Giacomo Meyerbeer*, 3:114.

95. Sabine Henze-Döhring, "Meyerbeers Unterricht bei Vogler," in *Abbé Vogler: Ein Mannheimer im europäischen Kontext* (Frankfurt: Peter Lang, 2003), 302, 296.

96. Maurice Cristal, "Des Mélodies de Meyerbeer et de ses oeuvres en général relativement au piano," in RGMP 1864, 227–28. This article was excerpted in AMZ 1864, 519.

97. Fritz Schröder, *Bernhard Molique und seine Instrumentalkompositionen* (Stuttgart: Berhold und Schwerdtner, 1923), 46. Knecht's principal treatise was *Vollständige Orgelschule, für Anfänger und Geübtere* (Leipzig: Breitkopf, 1795–98).

98. Frank Lehman, "Schubert's SLIDEs: Tonal (Non-) Integration of a Paradoxical Transformation," *Music Theory & Analysis* 1 (2014): 61–100. David Neumeyer uniquely explored the link between neighbor-note finger movements and Schubert's harmonic turns, interpreted in a neo-Riemannian framework—what he called Schubert's "Riemannian Hand." His findings are published online at http://hearingschubert.blogspot.com/search?q=riemannian.

99. Felix Draeseke, "Franz Liszt's Nine Symphonic Poems," ed. James Deaville, in *Franz Liszt and His World*, ed. Christopher H. Gibbs and Dana Gooley (Princeton: Princeton University Press, 2006), 499–500.

100. L. Schönfelder, *Theoretisch-praktische Anleitung nach eigener Fantasie regelrecht zu spielen, auch bei geringen Anlagen Vorspiele u. mit Leichtigkeit zu bilden und den Generalbass gründlich zu verstehen. Ein Buch zur Selbstbelehrung für Flügelspieler und für angehende Organisten* (Breslau: Selbstverlage des Verfassers, 1850).

101. Raymond Williams, "Base and Superstructure," in *The Raymond Williams Reader*, ed. John Higgins (Oxford: Blackwell, 2001), 170.

2

The Kapellmeister Network and the Performance of Community

HUMMEL, MOSCHELES, AND MENDELSSOHN

DURING HIS LIFETIME, Johann Nepomuk Hummel enjoyed a level of public esteem that can baffle anyone who hears his music today. Many of his compositions, when compared with those of his peer and rival, Beethoven, strike our ears as bland. They lack qualities of tension, dynamism, and brevity that modern listeners tend to expect or demand. Yet his most recent biographer does not exaggerate in claiming that Hummel was "the most popular composer of his era."[1] Pianists of the 1820s studied his piano concertos religiously as they climbed the Parnassus of piano virtuosity. Hummel was also an exceptionally popular and successful concert performer, touring all of Europe in the 1820s to constant critical acclaim. And he was by far the most famous improviser of his time, extemporizing at the conclusion of every concert. Audiences expected him to improvise not just preludes or cadenzas, but full-length, extended free fantasies on themes offered by the audience. Listeners and critics praised these fantasies for their instrumental virtuosity, their evident spontaneous inspiration, and their fluent handling of diverse musical vocabularies.[2] A critic at the *Allgemeine musikalische Zeitung* voiced a widely shared opinion when he asserted: "if you want to experience the power of music and learn to feel its magical effect, you must hear Hummel improvise" (AMZ 1834, 585).

These are not the words of a listener who wants to bury piano improvisation as a relic of the past or a superseded aesthetic. On the contrary, they suggest that Hummel's free fantasies delivered something to listeners that improvisation alone could offer. Although the regulative concept of the "work" was tightening its grip in this period, Hummel protected an unconquered space where improvisation could be experienced as both aesthetically ambitious and fully satisfying for listeners. What was it about

Hummel's improvised fantasies that made them so effective, and so different from the often-maligned improvisations of his peers? Hummel's raw talent, presence of mind, and native inclination undoubtedly contributed to the exceptional interest and fluidity of his free playing. But contemporary reports allow us to see that his fantasies mixed social and stylistic codes in a manner that made them uniquely attractive to audiences. His free fantasies achieved a unique reconciliation between older and newer institutions and values. They mediated the traditional authority of the kapellmeister, which was sanctioned by professional guilds and courtly patrons, while simultaneously channeling the authority of the modern *stile brillante* virtuoso, which was acquired and maintained through successful public performances in a commercially organized sphere of relations. While improvising at the piano, Hummel seemed to bridge some of the most troubling gaps—between elite and popular, connoisseurs and amateurs, professional guilds and the public sphere—that divided the terrain of European music in the early nineteenth century. In doing so his free fantasies produced, or at least allowed people to imagine, a listening community of an exceptionally heterogeneous and inclusive kind.

This chapter situates Hummel's improvisational practice in the context of the kapellmeister network by discussing several keyboardists who improvised during the apogee of the free fantasy on the piano from 1815 to 1830. Hummel's principal rival in the genre was the Bohemian virtuoso Ignaz Moscheles. Moscheles's improvisations were more popular and less severe in character than Hummel's, and he was more inclined to improvise for the sake of social conviviality in salons and small gatherings. Because of this popular orientation and his lack of a kapellmeister title, Moscheles projected a more modern image than Hummel, but in the 1820s the two pianists were often heard back-to-back and they generally shared the same range of improvisational practices. Their fantasies exerted some influence on the next generation of pianists. Hummel passed on his wisdom to two students, Ferdinand Hiller and Rudolf Willmers, who kept the free fantasy practice alive through the 1830s and 1840s. But Hummel had set a standard that few pianists of the younger generation could match, and his students lost the incentive to continue improvising publicly. Only Carl Maria von Bocklet, a relatively obscure Vienna-based pianist, continued to improvise publicly to strong critical acclaim. As Hummel tapered down his concert activities in the 1830s, critics began lamenting the decline of high-level concert improvisation. The aesthetic and social ideals associated with the free fantasy were losing their attainability. But the ideals were still alive, and they found one last shining representative in Moscheles's most talented student: Felix Mendelssohn.

THE KAPELLMEISTER AND THE PERFORMANCE OF AUTHORITY

Born in 1778, Hummel was a career kapellmeister in the eighteenth-century mold—an all-around musician who produced liturgical works alongside operas, concertos, piano sonatas, and chamber music, though curiously no symphonies. Unlike Vogler, he did not produce theory but kept his focus on keyboard playing, teaching, and composition. Before undertaking Europe-wide concert tours in the 1820s he held kapellmeister appointments in Esterházy and Stuttgart, and he was named principal kapellmeister in Weimar in 1818, where he remained until his death in 1837. His link with Mozart, with whom he had studied for two years as a child prodigy, figured largely in his reception, and was reinforced by the dissimilarity of his music to Beethoven's. Even after 1815, when Hummel infused his piano music with more Beethovenian weight and drama, the influence was sporadic and the stylistic dissimilarity clear. Hummel's "Mozartian" clarity, however, possibly obscured the modern dimension of his playing, which featured a brilliant, florid piano style of writing considerably more dense than the playing of Clementi, Cramer, and Dussek. Some contemporaries considered him *the* founder of the modern school of brilliant piano playing. As will be seen in later chapters, he had a measurable influence on the playing and compositions of Schumann, Chopin, and Liszt, and on all pianists who worked through his compendious 1828 treatise on piano playing.[3]

Hummel's duality as simultaneously "classic" and "modern" gave his reputation a layered quality unlike that of his peers. Friedrich Kalkbrenner, for example, was Hummel's contemporary but was perceived as a distinctly "modern" pianist on account of his steely power. Cramer was also roughly contemporary with Hummel but was perceived as a "classic" pianist-composer. In the balance the classic element may have slightly outweighed the modern. Critics praised the "purity" of his playing as though it had been uncontaminated by the "noise" of modern virtuosity. A writer at the *Harmonicon* contrasted Hummel's "free and easy style" with Kalkbrenner's "brilliant and elegant manner." By the standards of the 1820s his tempos sounded unhurried, and his sonority evaded the forced, metallic sound of the more modern instruments.[4] Hummel's persona, furthermore, carried an air of traditional authority and solidity. His unattractive physique, often noted by contemporaries, contributed to an impression of honest, no-nonsense musicianship. His persona distinguished him from Beethoven, who seemed introverted and misanthropic, and from Kalkbrenner, who was polished, cosmopolitan, and suave. The sense that Hummel's musicianship came out of earlier, simpler times shaped the reception of his improvisations. He seemed to extemporize with an ease and security that no pianist except Moscheles came even close to matching. In his piano treatise he made the remarkable assertion that he felt "less constrained improvising before two or three thousand listeners than playing a written composition to which I was slavishly subjected."[5]

Hummel's duality as simultaneously classic and modern can be attributed to an unusual wrinkle in his career. From 1804 to 1811 he was *Konzertmeister* to Prince Nikolaus Esterházy at Eisenstadt, where he diligently composed sacred works and operas and prepared their performance at court. While at Eisenstadt he maintained a parallel career in Vienna, and moved there in 1811 to promote and perform his compositions, performing only infrequently as pianist. He had arrived at a pinnacle of success: he held a prestigious court position and had acquired an audience eager to hear his concerts and purchase his published compositions. Yet around 1815, in a striking reversal of the normal trend, Hummel reawakened his pianistic career and began organizing concert tours. There were personal reasons behind the change: Hummel had long suffered from a sense of inferiority vis-à-vis Beethoven, and his wife, a singer, was encouraging him to play more concerts. But the strongest stimulus probably came from the Congress of Vienna (1814–1815). With the flood of diplomatic gatherings and social festivities that characterized the Congress, Hummel was given numerous opportunities to shine as a pianist, winning audiences in a manner that Beethoven, a pianist of a more specialized taste, could not. At the Congress he captured the attention of elites from various European nations who would be able to sponsor, organize, and host future concert tours. The relatively stable political situation that followed the Congress of Vienna, furthermore, made it easier to travel internationally, opening up the horizon for virtuosos who wanted to tour. It is not a coincidence that the other pianistic lion of the Congress of Vienna was the twenty-year-old Ignaz Moscheles. His concert career, too, was launched by the exposure he received during the events, and it unfolded in parallel with Hummel's career in the years 1815–1830.

Under the favorable social and political conditions of the Restoration, Hummel and Moscheles brought the *stile brillante* into its heyday, and with it came a relatively new or at least renovated genre: the improvised fantasy on given themes. They were certainly not the inventors or sole purveyors of the genre. In the years 1815–1820 many keyboardists working in the German-speaking milieu freely played or performed free fantasies (not yet called "improvisations") at the conclusion of concerts. There is very little we can say for sure about the style or formal models, since only a few sources report on them, and briefly. Most of the available information comes from the Leipzig *Allgemeine musikalische Zeitung*, the only journal that attempted to cover musical conditions in cities all over Europe. A survey of these reports suggests that keyboardists employed a wide diversity of styles and approaches, depending on whether he was playing organ or piano, using preexisting themes or not, or playing a free-standing piece versus a preface to a regular rondo or variation set. According to experience and inclination, keyboardists could draw on various styles: free fugue, Italianate *cantilena*, the north German free fantasia style, or the more modern genre of the potpourri, with its free, loose variative treatment of popular melodies. Reviews of newly published compositions in the AMZ sometimes point to specific passages as sounding "like a free fantasy"—typically when there are unexpected modulations, capricious shifts of tone, or exceptions to standard formal procedures. The final two variations of Kuhlau's variation-set on Cherubini's "Guide mes pas, ô providence"— which abandon the theme's chord progression to enter into free elaborations in *cantilena*, chromatic modulations, sequences, and tremolos—were judged "far more like free fantasies on that theme than actual variations" (AMZ 1816, 111–12). The extended introduction to Cramer's *Divertimento* on the song "Days of Yore" was described as "a capriccio . . . quite literally a free fantasy, full of original modulatory turns, and alternating between boldly attacking and very sweet expressions" (AMZ 1817, 734). And the first movement of Beethoven's Sonata in E-minor, op. 90—a compact elaboration of the two opening ideas, and exceptionally rich in rhetorical and harmonic surprises—was judged "more like a free fantasy" than a sonata proper (AMZ 1816, 61). These pieces by Kuhlau, Cramer, and Beethoven were composed in quite divergent styles, but all of them were correlated with the stylistic universe of the free fantasy.

In the period 1810–1820, many writers for the AMZ, channeling the values of the professional music guild, began worrying about the stylistic eclecticism of piano improvisations. As long as pianists gave evidence that they were familiar with the established styles—the fugal style associated with organ playing, or the free fantasia style associated with the north German school—critics had no objection. Trouble only came when pianists put their improvisational talents in service of lighter and more popular styles—variations and potpourris elaborated on simple, well-known songs and airs from comic opera—and called such performances by the honored name *freye Phantasie*. Variation-like modes of elaboration lacked the techniques of "development" or "leading-through"—*Durchführung*—that many professionals considered indispensable to any "good" improvisation based on a theme or a motive. When a pianist improvised on a popular tune, musicians and critics expected him to show professionalism by subjecting the tune to "leading-through" techniques, thus alienating it from its popular, commodified form. And if he wanted to improvise on many themes in the manner of a potpourri, the pianist needed somehow to unify the heterogeneous materials, even if this was not achieved by leading-through techniques.

This conflict between elite and popular styles came out in the reception of Vienna-based pianist and composer Hieronymous Payer. In 1814 Payer played a piano improvisation on "Gott erhalte den Kaiser" and earned applause for "the unbelievable agility and the steady adherence to his theme . . . which he lengthened, shortened, and at the end played fugally" (AMZ 1814, 286). Here was a "noble" theme treated in a suitably learned manner. A few years later Payer gave a public concert for his own benefit where he improvised on two popular tunes, Weber's "Schwertlied" and Rossini's "Di tanti palpiti," before proceeding *attacca* into a composed-out rondo for piano and orchestra (AMZ 1817, 295). This latter performance elicited no particular comment, but in the years that followed critics hardened their stance against Payer. At an 1818 performance he seems to have improvised in a potpourri style: "Mr. Payr worked up on the pianoforte several rhapsodic, loosely connected beloved themes, which he called improvising [*phantasiren*]; but it was no easier to find one's way around this than around the Cretan labyrinth without Ariadne's thread" (AMZ 1818, 70). Two years later, a concert reviewer denied Payer the right to call his performance a *freye Phantasie* because "he gave it a different meaning from the meaning attached to it by Mozart, Meyerbeer and Hummel. Mr. Payer would do better to play variations from a score or from memory" (*Wiener Zeitschrift* 1820, 1293). Payer was by no means the only pianist to provoke this protectionist attitude toward free fantasies. In Chapter 1 we saw that Carl Maria von Weber was criticized along similar lines when he played in Vienna in 1822. And in 1819 Mozart's son Franz Xaver, on a concert tour, elicited similar complaints: "A so-called free fantasy on a Russian and Polish theme made less of an impression, probably due to the inappropriate name, since it was more like free variations on two themes. But the performance of this piece was applauded just as well."[6] By 1828 the more severe critics were in a state of despair about the genre's popular transformation: "one has to deplore the practice of improvisation among pianists of the present. An improvisation was once a free fantasy of the imagination, a truly spontaneous creation of the artist; today it is a succession of more or less difficult decorations, most often on popular airs."[7] The tension here between critic's response and audience response, between professionals and public, between elite and popular values, organized many of the debates over improvisation for the next thirty years, and it is the backdrop for the particular significance of the improvising of Hummel and Moscheles.

KAPELLMEISTER AND PUBLIC

Although free fantasies were often played in intimate company, mingling musicians and appreciative connoisseurs, they also connected kapellmeisters to their local publics. Concerts of the post-Congress period did not have large audiences by today's standards. Most took place in medium-sized or larger venues that were sufficiently public in character to be considered worth reporting to the readers of the AMZ. The AMZ reports were not just giving information, but were *producing* the idea of "public" musical culture. Its foreign correspondence reports, in particular, created a simulacrum of a unified, international concert "scene" to which readers could imagine they belonged, even if they only went to local concerts. In this way the journal defined what was "of public interest" and thereby promoted the emergence of a musical public sphere.[8] To judge from these sources, most musicians who improvised concert fantasies were kapellmeisters or young aspirants to that title. From the period preceding 1820 alone, the list of noted improvisers includes, besides Weber and Meyerbeer, Hieronymous Payer, Ferdinand Ries, Friedrich Schneider (Leipzig), J. L. Böhner (Gotha), Haydn's protégé Sigismund Neukomm (former kapellmeister in St. Petersburg), C. E. F. Weyse (Copenhagen), Conradin Kreutzer (Fürstenberg), F. W. Berner (Breslau), Aloys Schmitt (Frankfurt), Joseph von Szalay (Vienna), and the young virtuoso Charles Arnold (Frankfurt).

With the possible exception of Arnold, none of these musicians was a concert pianist in the modern sense, and nearly every one of them held a kapellmeister title at some point. Normally the kapellmeister improvised at the conclusion of a so-called benefit performance—a concert for the artist's personal profit featuring compositions in various genres (vocal, orchestral, choral, or chamber), and played by a variety of distinguished professional associates.[9] The concert programs of keyboardists who concentrated mainly on the organ, like Weyse and Berner, were for pragmatic reasons considerably less diverse. But in all cases the beneficiary stepped out from the milieu of his service or employment—the theater, church, or court—to present himself to the public or the audience *as a musician*. Benefit concerts suspended the musician's institutional or patronal affiliations in order to demonstrate his identity as a professional—as a member of the music guild and, not least, as a person of interest to the local public conceived as an autonomous civic body. The placement of the improvised fantasy at the concert's conclusion served a ritual purpose. After a series of pieces that mediated the musician's talents through other performers, the concluding fantasy brought forth the artist "himself," making direct contact with the audience and displaying a type of knowledge and skill that the other performances, even his own within ensembles, could not convey. When keyboardists played free fantasies at the end of their concerts, in other words, they condensed the symbolic aspect of the event as a demonstration of an artist's independent merit and of the public's regard for him. Improvisations authorized their players to call themselves learned professionals, ready and able to produce music and communicate actively and directly with the public, rather than through the cultural capital of aristocratic patronage or institutional affiliation.

As a brief case study of these relations we can consider Ludwig Böhner, a keyboardist and composer best known as the real-life model for E. T. A. Hoffmann's kapellmeister Kreisler.[10] Born in 1787 and considered one of the most promising musicians of his generation, he was fluent on both the organ and the piano and concertized on both instruments. His inability to hold down a steady position kept him moving from city to city in a desperate attempt to find patronage, and at many of these concerts he played free fantasies. When Spohr invited him to play a court concert in Gotha, for example, Böhner chose to present himself in an overture and a piano concerto of his own composition, with a free fantasy at the conclusion—a model identical to that of Hummel's concerts at the Weimar court in the same period.[11] From 1812 to 1816, the only period when he was steadily employed, Böhner served as *Musikdirektor* at the theater in Nürnberg, and it was in this estimable role that he returned to his hometown to give a benefit concert featuring original music. The reviewer praised his pieces for displaying "novelty of invention and thoroughness of working-out [*Ausarbeitung*]," but these qualities were even more evident in the improvisation: "In a free, extemporized fantasy on the piano alone, with which Mr. B. concluded the entertainment, he displayed these advantages unmistakably; his playing here seemed to this reviewer even more decisive and expressive [than in the written compositions]" (AMZ 1815, 280).[12] This remark on the qualitative superiority of the free fantasy is a recurrent rhetorical trope in discussions of improvisation, not only in this period but also in later periods. It is as though the fantasy must be presented as the crowning achievement of the event.[13] The trope undoubtedly had a literary motive, furnishing the critic's account of the concert with a satisfying climax and conclusion. But the trope may also result from the shift of address—a sense of intimacy with the audience—that was established when the kapellmeister, after a series of larger-scale works, sat down alone at the keyboard and improvised. This moment, like the modern recital encore, was bound to carry a strong affective charge regardless of how well it was played.

The bond between kapellmeister and public that free fantasies cemented—especially when themes were solicited from the audience—reflects a broader shift in his political and social position in the early nineteenth century. As Horst Heussner has shown, the changing economic conditions of musical life in the German-speaking milieu raised the social status of kapellmeisters to the point where they were no longer "estimable protégés of the aristocracy" but generously remunerated employees with secure positions and considerable artistic independence.[14] The difference between Louis Spohr's subservient appointment at Gotha (1805–1812) and his later appointment at Kassel (1822–1859) was massive in this respect. In Kassel Spohr was paid generously and was given much more free initiative because his favor with the larger public was an extremely valuable asset to his royal patron. One reason is that Spohr had nurtured a relationship to the emerging musical public, first by making many concert tours as a freelance virtuoso, and second by conducting at numerous regional music festivals where large-scale choral and orchestral works were programmed. The latter events were exceptionally heterogeneous, uniting hundreds of instrumentalists, soloists, and amateurs from different places. They staged Spohr as a leader of musical and social communities simultaneously. With this newly acquired public prestige Spohr was able to leverage the advantages of his position in Kassel against the traditional subordination of court musicians. In the German states, anyway, the same power that emancipated the virtuoso soloist—the affection and admiration of large, heterogeneous, transregional public audiences—could contribute to the emancipation of kapellmeisters, since the latter now possessed cultural power extending beyond the territorial and municipal boundaries of their patrons.[15] Contrary to the viewpoint advanced so influentially by Liszt, who was borrowing rhetoric of French-revolutionary ideology, artistic emancipation did not require the total dissolution of courtly and ecclesiastical institutions.

The aura of authority that surrounded kapellmeisters was a compound of elements: the prestige of the church, court, or theatrical institution to which he belonged, the prestige of the musical guild with its specialized command of a difficult body of knowledge, and the prestige derived from being popular, as a performer and composer, with the musical public. In the eighteenth century the first of these three elements had been the most important, but in the early nineteenth century the emphasis was shifting toward the latter elements. Spohr's successor as first-call leader of music festivals, Friedrich Schneider, serves as a good example. In 1815 Schneider, a pianist, organist, composer, and central figure in Leipzig's musical life at the time, made a guest appearance at a grand gala concert that included choir, orchestra, and soloists and was distinguished by the presence of the king and queen. Following an orchestral overture and a choral hymn by Mozart, the correspondent reported, "our estimable master" Schneider played a free fantasy followed by a rondo: "we can hardly recall that any pianist since Mozart, in a solo, in public, and playing between full orchestra pieces, has so completely satisfied connoisseurs and amateurs at the same time" (AMZ 1815, 791). This somewhat odd appearance of a solo improvisation amid large-scale works, and its evident intention of channeling the memory of Mozart, attests to the authority that Schneider, and musical culture more generally, carried within Leipzig's civic life.

In 1880 Ferdinand Hiller, recollecting his years of study with Hummel, remembered the attitude of awe and reverence that leading musicians once inspired: "The type of unconditional reverence [*Hochachtung*] that followed Hummel everywhere is no longer to be found. . . . The respect with which one conveyed the news 'kapellmeister Hummel has arrived' is, as far as I know, accorded to no living person."[16] The historical moment Hiller is describing, or idealizing—the 1820s and early 1830s—was not yet filled with celebrity instrumental virtuosos, with scores of amateur concerts, and with an oversaturated press. In Hiller's eyes it was a less jaded era in which a musician of Hummel's stature commanded not just higher ticket prices but also a measure of honor and deference absent from the ethos of modern concert life. Such "unconditional reverence" was voiced by a German correspondent who, summarizing the Paris concert season of 1825, meted out praise to pianists Schuncke, Herz, Pixis, Moscheles, Kalkbrenner, Liszt, and Mendelssohn, and then turned his attention to Hummel, who had improvised free fantasies at every concert: "By speaking of the celebrated Hummel last, we wish to reserve a special place for treating of one who justly stands in the first rank of his profession. . . . Instead of charlatanism we found science and power" (QMMR 1825, 313). Hummel's French fans expressed their reverence by gathering a subscription and having a medal engraved and inscribed on the back with the words: "From French artists and amateurs to Hummel, 1825." The front side of the medal included not only the pianist's profile but also his date of birth, underlining his age as part of his claim to "classic" status.

HUMMEL'S STYLE SYNTHESIS

In his memoirs violinist Ludwig Spohr described a soirée that took place during the Congress of Vienna, where Hummel was asked by "some ladies" to play a waltz and he gladly assented, causing the young ladies in the adjoining room to begin dancing. Once the waltz had been played, "his playing transitioned into a free improvisation that nevertheless steadily preserved the waltz rhythm, so that the dancers were not interrupted." Hummel enriched it with contrapuntal motives drawn from other pieces heard that evening, eventually arriving at a fugue theme on which "he let loose all his contrapuntal arts, without impinging on the pleasure of the dancers." After the fugue Hummel "turned back to the galant style" to play a bravura finale. Spohr's account highlights not only the stylistic contrast between waltz and fugue but also the contrasting engagement of the soirée audience. While the young ladies were dancing in the other room, "I and some other artists, attracted by his playing, gathered around the instrument and listened attentively." Hummel simultaneously satisfied women and men, dancers and attentive listeners, social demands and artistic demands, popular and learned tastes.[17]

This delicate balancing act became a leading theme of Hummel's reception after the Congress, when he started playing free fantasies in public. His exalted reputation as an improviser established itself quickly in the years following the Congress, even though he was not yet playing extended tours. In summer 1816 he played two benefit concerts in Berlin featuring mainly original compositions. At the first he programmed an overture and a piano concerto, but the concluding improvisation was

judged the highlight: "what was most appealing was his long free fantasy play extemporaneously. It began by developing a main idea, then transitioned to a singing
Adagio, then touched in a most captivating manner upon some favorite themes from
Don Juan, Richard the Lionhearted, etc." (AMZ 1816, 425). This seems to be a potpourri-
style fantasy, geared toward popular taste through the choice of lighter comic-opera
melodies and the playful, pleasurable manner of treatment. If there was a learned
element, it would have been in the treatment of the "main idea," but the description
is too vague to be certain. At the second concert Hummel's free fantasy interwove a
learned, contrapuntal motive with popular, capricious passages: "[it] alternated fugal
phrases with free, surprising twists on well-known melodies" (AMZ 1816, 497). Over
the next few years his free fantasies continued to make a strong impression. At a concert in Prague he attempted a completely free fantasia together with violinist Franz
Clement, a rare experiment that Carl Maria von Weber, wearing his music-critic hat,
criticized as pushing things too far.[18] By 1818, the year of Hummel's appointment
at Weimar, improvisation was already the cornerstone of his reputation. As a correspondent wrote from Mannheim: "It is his free fantasy at the conclusion of every concert that most elevates him above so many of his contemporaries; the wealth of ideas
that he takes the happy occasion to unfold here, and the manner in which he once
again reworks each one of them, show him to be one of the greatest musical geniuses
in the world" (AMZ 1818, 380).

At the peak of Hummel's concert activity in the 1820s, critics left a few uncommonly
detailed accounts of improvisations, allowing us to reconstruct the style and sequence
of ideas to an extent not possible for earlier or later players. These accounts consistently mark distinctions of style and tone that were already well established in the discourse of the AMZ. The critical vocabulary distinguishes different sorts of thematic
work, from the more rigorous *Durchführen* and *Verarbeiten* (developing, transforming)
to the looser *Ausführen* and *Ausarbeiten* (elaborating, spinning out). They nearly always mention fugal and quasi-fugal styles when pianists used them, very often at the
improvisation's conclusion.[19] The discourse around Hummel's improvisations, however, included newer thematic strains:

> Mr. Hummel seemed even more interesting in the free fantasy, where he again
> revealed the mastery with which he commands figures of all kinds, and how the
> most varied idioms and passages his momentary mood leads him to stand at his
> disposal in an uninterrupted stream. One could not play a well-studied, notated
> piece with such precision and purity as Mr. H. plays everything while improvising.
> The worthiness of his playing and certain small melodic turns that are surely
> his own (I am tempted to call them Anacreontic) delighted everyone. The begin-
> ning of the fantasy spoke to me the most, corresponding completely and faith-
> fully to the idea of this genre, representing the various arbitrary expressions and
> movements of a poetic mood. But the applause of the public grew like the prog-
> ress of an avalanche as he interwove certain well-known themes and developed
> them in the most diversified shades. (AMZ 1820, 359)

New here is the attention to Hummel's desire to please, whether through charming "small melodic turns" or the incorporation of familiar themes. Also new is the attention to audience response and the designation of the audience as a "public." In these ways the discourse around improvisation was being inflected by the emergent practices of touring concert virtuosos, who needed to broaden their appeal to attract the widest possible audiences. This correspondent, while generally positive, comes across as skeptical of the more modern and popular elements. By declaring a preference for the fantasy's opening section he takes distance from its "Anacreontic" pleasures.

Hummel's benefit concerts fell into a standard format in which he played three times: two large-scale original compositions (one of them being a piano concerto) and an improvisation on given themes, always played at the close. These three numbers were relieved by vocal solos and instrumental pieces played by assisting artists. Although concert programs of touring artists were quite varied, the placement of the free fantasy at the end of the concert remained a stable convention. By placing the fantasy at the end, the pianist wound down the concert with a reaffirmation of performer-audience intimacy that had been suppressed during the more formal performances of written-out pieces. The free fantasy's open, indeterminate character loosened expectations and provoked audiences into a more intensively attuned, localized mode of listening. And by requesting themes from the audience, pianists plugged the audience into the circuit of communication. The audience could now see itself as a productive agent within the performance event, giving a phantasmal sensation of intimacy with the performer. As Liszt later noted about the practice of taking themes, "this way of improvising . . . establishes a more direct rapport between the public and the artist. . . . It becomes a communal work."[20]

Hummel's special gift for improvisation made him a key figure in the developing critique of improvisation in the 1820s. As early as 1820 there was already concern that "improvising could perhaps become an epidemic fashion among our concert public" (AMZ 1820, 214). The issues were aired with uncharacteristic vehemence in an article published at the peak of Hummel's fame as an improviser: "Thoughts on Free Fantasies, with a retrospective look at Hummel's Fantasy, published in the Museum for Piano Music, Vol. 6" (AMZ 1824, 314–15). The author attacks the current state of pianistic improvisation and urges young artists to reform their bad habits by taking Hummel's published *Fantasie*, op. 18 as a model. Improvisation has degenerated into the simplest and most repetitive form possible—plain variations on a theme: "A chain of variations is not yet a fantasy; it merely adds to their number." Pianists regress to banal variations when they lack sufficient musical training to do much else, or when they need to fill out a concert program without preparing another piece. This critique appears to be aimed at advanced pianist-composers—musicians who play free fantasies in imitation of the great Hummel. Over the next two decades, however, the target would broaden to include dilettantes, amateurs, and musical consumers everywhere. The Paris-based pedagogue François Stoepel, reviewing Czerny's improvisation treatise in 1834, articulated the standard gripes of the professional class: "It is unfortunately too often that so-called improvisations are only a mass of reminiscences, disfigured leftovers of beautiful ideas invented by other composers, or indeed litanies of variants without intelligence or contrary to those ideas" (RGMP 1834, 61). The editors of the journal *Le Pianiste*, in the face of such severe critiques, defended improvisation as a legitimate aspect of amateur music-making, while also recognizing the free playing of Hummel as belonging to a higher order of achievement.[21]

The author of "Thoughts on Free Fantasies," after lamenting the descent into simple variations, presents his positive ideal of the genre:

> Not only does it [the free fantasy] permit the combining of the most heterogeneous things into a pleasing whole, but the entire realm of romanticism is opened up quite specially in these pieces. Those endearing dallying sylphs called variations fearlessly form ranks against strict counterpoint, and pure melody can indeed be wedded [*vermählen*] with a canon, whether one- or many-voiced, forward- or backward-moving. The master remains unbounded in his creative power, and here true talent, copulating [*begattet*] with true art, can show itself in a beautiful light, quite apart from the delicious diversion the listener inevitably enjoys through the alternations. (AMZ 1824, 314–15)

Here light variations and learned counterpoint, sensual pleasure and intellectual severity, join together in a beautiful, quasi-sexual union. The masculine side (counterpoint) preserves its sovereign power, but it is softened and rendered more pleasing by the "dallying sylphs" (variations). Surprisingly, this idealized stylistic heterogeneity is poorly represented by Hummel's *Fantasie*, op. 18, the piece offered as an antidote. Op. 18 lacks melodic tunes and variations, and has only intermittent flashes of counterpoint. The critic has thus based his "ideal" free fantasy not on Hummel's published work, but on the concert improvisations. And this is what concert reviews most consistently describe in Hummel's concert fantasies: a particular aesthetic, not found in other musical genres, that unites the learned and pleasing styles.

Determining just what Hummel played when he improvised is of course a challenge. Carl Czerny's 1829 treatise on improvisation, the most important single source of information about improvisation in this period, gives guidelines for free fantasies and is therefore an indispensable reference point.[22] Yet the examples Czerny provides for extended free fantasies seem to be more regular, more rooted in classical forms, than what Hummel played. Because Hummel improvised so often in public, his fantasies are better documented than those of his contemporaries, and from such reviews we can gather some provisional outlines of how he achieved his unique combination of the popular and the learned.[23] The pleasing, popular side of his improvisations lay in the choice of tunes and in methods of elaboration that kept the familiar tunes clearly in the listener's ear. By asking the audience to suggest themes for improvisation, he looped the audience in while simultaneously claiming the artist's sovereign right to deconstruct the themes. He most often chose tuneful melodies from French and German comic operas, with clear and balanced phrases, simple harmonies, and clearly defined sub-phrases that lend themselves to sequencing and development. Florid Italianate melodies almost never appear, perhaps because they resist breakdown into subsidiary motives. He improvised so often on "Là ci darem la mano" and "Fin ch'han dal vino" from *Don Giovanni* that many suspected he knew what audiences would request and engineered the choice of melodies to suit his own strengths.[24] But Hummel could also work with the unexpected. At one concert he accepted two themes from the audience that he did not particularly like, and acquitted himself decently though he treated the second melody only briefly. Louis Moreau Gottschalk recalled a fantasy in which Hummel riffed off church bells ringing outside the hall, incorporating them seamlessly into his improvisation.[25] Hummel often based his fantasy on melodies from two different operas by the same composer, pairing, for example, themes from Mozart's *Don Giovanni* and *Entführung aus dem Serail*, or from Hérold's *Zampa* and *Pré aux clercs* (*Zweikampf*), or from Spohr's *Faust* and *Jessonda*. To these suggestions Hummel sometimes added a third, or a fragment thereof, as a kind of unifying head-motto for the entire fantasy. At an 1830 concert in Paris, for instance, he worked in a march-motive from *La Muette de Portici* in a fantasy based mainly on two themes from *Don Giovanni*. Czerny recommended the head-motto technique right at the beginning of his discourse on free fantasies: "The first subject selected for the opening . . . must occur frequently between the remaining themes (especially if it is comprised of only a short figure), and it must be heard again at the end also, for it is the pillar on which all else is constructed."[26]

Contemporary descriptions are too imprecise to determine exactly what techniques Hummel employed when elaborating on these themes. It is hard to imagine that he did not sometimes play decorative or brilliant variations based on the melody's harmonic structure, since this was such a familiar and comfortable procedure of elaboration. But overall he appears to have avoided this straightforward approach in favor of a more flexible, exploratory development or "spinning-out" of the theme and its motives. Perhaps he transformed melodies and motives by playing them in different styles or topoi—cantabile, march, polonaise, scherzando, etc.—as Czerny recommended in his treatise.[27] Hummel's brief words about improvisation at the conclusion of his piano treatise indicate that when he chose a "known theme" he did so "less in order to vary it than to *treat it freely* in many forms, with several turns of phrase and in several styles."[28] Even with this relatively sophisticated treatment, contemporary critics were consistently attuned to Hummel's preservation of a popular, less learned tone:

> In this fantasy we were able to give his talent the pure admiration that he earned to the highest degree, especially through the logical treatment of the theme that he first stated. For the rest of the public bonbons were also served up, and some lapped them from the stream, while others nibbled. But everyone was transported and showed their satisfaction with fiery applause. (AMZ 1820, 305–307)

In 1835, when Hummel was quite old and his playing had lost much of its power, he improvised at a charity concert on four popular themes in the manner of a potpourri, with each theme developed lightly, if at all. A critic described it as "directed more toward a mixed public, but nevertheless, even with its uncommon popularity, also fulfilling the higher demands of art."[29]

The learned side of Hummel's concert fantasies was rendered in fugal, imitative, and contrapuntal passages. These could appear at any transition point and even at the opening of the performance. But he tended to arrive at fugal playing after freely varying the "given" themes, so that the concentrated density of the fugal playing formed the culminating point of a linear process. This was clearly not his invention. We have already seen that Vogler and others did something similar. It was nonetheless recognized as a trademark of Hummel's improvisations, setting him apart from his contemporaries. In 1821 he played "a free fantasy on the fortepiano, where he eventually treated amazingly 'Dammi la cara mano' and another melody from Mozart's D. Giovanni, then transitioning into the fugal style, and using everything that the modern art of the piano allows, [he] won the loudest applause" (AMZ 1821, 455). An account of a London performance in 1830 likewise described a seamless transition from casual, pleasing treatment of the themes into a more learned fugal section: "he commenced with an introductory adagio, followed by some light and playful variations on the Swiss air; he modulated through a variety of keys into an elaborate fugue, in the progress of which he displayed all the enthusiasm and powerful genius, with the consummate art and refinement of the most profound musical science."[30]

In this instance, the progression to fugal playing took place *before* Hummel had moved to the second theme of his fantasy, an apparent anomaly that might account for his perfunctory treatment of the second theme. In the fantasy that Gottschalk heard, Hummel first treated his own Polonaise "La bella capricciosa," then treated the interfering church-bell tones with harmonizations, and, after combining this with motives from the Polonaise's slow introduction, "capp[ed] off the whole with a fugue improvised on the main theme of the Polacca."[31] Taken together, these accounts show a fairly consistent formal paradigm of free slow introduction, treatment of first theme, treatment of second theme, fugue, and brilliant finale—a pattern also typical of Hummel's contemporaries with the exception of the fugue. The accounts further suggest that Hummel liked to weave in a short motive unrelated to the fantasy's two "proper" themes as a kind of unifying device (the "Plough-Boy," the *Muette de Portici* march, the larghetto from the Polonaise).

In private contexts Hummel felt no need to furnish his fantasies with a popular tone. A Berlin critic indicated that "his improvisations in social circles are entirely different from those directed at a larger public and never resemble one another" (AMZ 1821, 332). This point was confirmed, and made more explicit, by the correspondent reporting on Hummel's Russian trip of 1823. After his arrival in St. Petersburg Hummel first played free fantasies at "private gatherings," and before long "everyone was calling him 'the famous improviser' [*Improvisateur*]." Yet the free fantasy he played at his first benefit "was not comparable with those wonderful ones with which he had delighted people in private gatherings, for this was more of a potpourri and seemed only concerned with displaying great agility of the fingers." Such a style could not please the connoisseurs, but on this occasion it did not please the public either. St. Petersburg listeners, the correspondent explained, were accustomed to hearing the piano as a "singing instru-ment," whereas Hummel had treated it "as a representative of the orchestra and as an organist." Perhaps realizing that he had gauged the style incorrectly at the first concert, Hummel redeemed himself at his second benefit: "the connoisseurs this time found his free fantasy completely outstanding and extraordinary" (AMZ 1823, 552–53).

Hummel's student Ferdinand Hiller affirmed that "in the concert hall the master adapted himself to the level of comprehension [*Fassungsvermögen*] of the listeners."[32] Some writers were able to see this as a sign of artistic maturity. A Vienna critic explained that Hummel's closing free fantasy "had the form of a Potpourri, which probably spoke mainly to the uncommonly numerous and thus mixed assembly, and demonstrated the artist's prudence, which carefully considers to whom he is directing his gifts" (AMZ 1827, 369). If Hummel did indeed have more diverse improvisational strategies in private, it may simply reflect the diversity of what we today call "pri-vate" circumstances. Some of these improvisations may have been light, off-the-cuff inventions of the sort that Czerny called "capriccio."[33] But when Hummel had the ear of a sophisticated private audience, he more likely improvised in the manner of his *Fantaisie*, op. 18. This is a long, complex, and sometimes quite dramatic piece in which all the motives are of Hummel's invention and the methods of elaboration are excep-tionally rich. In line with Czerny's general recommendations for the genre, it makes use of standard formal frameworks—first-movement form, cantabile slow movement, rondo—while treating these frameworks more freely than they would appear in a so-nata. (The involved, half-hour effusions Beethoven was known to play in private so-ciety may often have followed a model something like this.) This style, like the sonata genre, did not translate well to the public concert context in the 1820s. Czerny noted the great challenges faced by pianists who wanted to improvise an extended fantasy before "a larger gathering," and underlined the need "to avoid dullness and boredom" out of "consideration of his listeners' powers of concentration."[34] Indeed, he presented the potpourri genre as a more reliable model for public audiences:

> *A propos* of improvising before a large audience, as in a theater for example, the first two styles discussed hitherto [the free fantasy on a single theme, and the free fantasy on several themes] are not always felicitous and present the per-former with two kinds of difficulties. First, the natural embarrassment inherent in a public performance, and particularly the very destructive fear of boring the audience . . . In dealing with a largely heterogeneous public, surely the majority by far will be entertained only by pleasant, familiar tunes and will be sustained in spirit by piquant and glittering performances.[35]

Contemporary discourse about Hummel's free fantasies, in sum, engaged a series of binary oppositions organized around a core opposition between public and private. The "private" pole was aligned with connoisseur values, learned style, counterpoint, ex-tended forms, and intellectual satisfaction, while the "public" pole was aligned with mixed audiences, pleasing style, popular melodies, variation, and audience delight. Hummel was distinguished in his ability to unite the two tastes: "For connoisseurs and amateurs Capellmeister N. Hummel alternated between contrapuntally developed passages and pleasantly varied popular themes, satisfying and entertaining everyone" (AMZ 1821: 332). There was always a severe critical contingent of critics who found this compromise with popularity troubling, but many contemporary critics looked upon it favorably:

> He gained the greatest applause with his *Fantasias*, in which this great master knows how to mingle with admirable art the gay and the serious, the playful and the severe; at one moment he lets us hear what he is capable of effecting in the church style, then in that of the chamber and theatre. So varied are his powers that even those who had the least pretensions as connoisseurs were charmed, they knew not why, while the cognoscenti applauded with unfeigned admiration. He appears equally great both in the grand and the simple.[36]

Passages such as these show that in Hummel's free playing, the normal markers of aesthetic difference and their social correlates were temporarily suspended or broken down. They established a peaceful coexistence between styles normally separated out into different genres. Hummel's free fantasies did not merely juxtapose learned and pleasing styles in the spirit of mutual accommodation, but sometimes hovered imperceptibly between them. The free-variative modes of elaboration, in which popular motives were subjected to "developmental" techniques such as reharmonization, modulation, and recombination, were neither "popular" nor "learned," but some blend of the two. The same goes for a fugue generated from the opening motive of Mozart's "Là ci darem la mano." Such hybrids realized a virtual "fantasy-space" lying somewhere in between, as though the opposing styles belonged to one underlying substance rather than an order of discrete, hierarchized differences. This kind of music did not exist in formal compositions, but only in improvisation.

Insofar as Hummel's fantasies realized a combination of learned and popular not found in other genres, they modeled a utopian vision, a social "fantasy" in which people belonging to different social groups with unequal levels of knowledge and education co-existed in a mutually beneficial and harmonious alignment of interests. In this way they confirm one of the central theses informing critical improvisation studies in recent years: the idea that the free improvisational situations open up, through their indeterminacy and their invitation to individual agency, a space in which social differences—of ethnicity, gender, and class, for example—meet face to face, and move toward creative reconciliations in which new, unfamiliar social formations are posited or imagined.[37] Hummel's concert fantasies parallel this by preserving distinct signifiers of learned and popular style while simultaneously exploring middle grounds between them. Hummel certainly did not consciously intend his improvisations to function this way, but contemporary critics repeatedly returned to Hummel's successful mediation of stylistic and social difference in a tone of unreserved, almost breathless enthusiasm, suggesting that he aroused intense cultural desires unfulfilled by other modes of musical experience.

The special charge of Hummel's improvisations was related to transformations in musical life that were first being felt, often painfully, in the 1820s. Hummel's ability to satisfy both connoisseurs and amateurs was judged miraculous because the presumed gap between the two kinds of listener appeared to have widened. A conceptualization of the musical public as a mixture of connoisseurs (*Kenner*) and amateurs (*Liebhaber*) had been conventional since the mid-eighteenth century, and to an extent Hummel's admirers were simply reiterating it conventionally. However, the commercialization and democratization of musical life in the first two decades of the nineteenth century altered the social context of these two terms. For most of the mid-to-late eighteenth century, the *Kenner-und-Liebhaber* public was a numerically small, relatively elite group that carried on a "patronal" relationship with composers through subscriptions to their published compositions and concerts. Around 1800, commercial publishers began taking over these patronal functions and inserted composers and performers into a commercial marketplace in the modern sense.[38] Publishers took a leading role in stimulating the production not only of scores, but also of music periodicals, pianos, pedagogical books, and, acting as managers of publicity and ticket sales, public concerts. Virtuoso pianist-composers like Hummel, Kalkbrenner, Moscheles, and Herz were the most natural allies of publishers. All of them published large numbers of pieces whose sales would be augmented by public appearances. One result of musical commercialization was a massive increase in the size of the *Liebhaber* public— those who enjoyed listening to and practicing music without possessing knowledge of its theoretical underpinnings. With this increase in the size of the musical public came a greater diversification as well. Friedrich Rochlitz, writing in 1813, distinguished not two but *four* types of listener: connoisseurs, dilettantes, laymen and "the hopeless."[39] Rochlitz's "dilettante" is essentially equivalent to the *Liebhaber*, but his categories of "laymen" and "hopeless" are new to the field, and they recognize a new class of listeners—a more anonymous, nominally "mass" musical public—positioned at a greater distance from musical learning than the eighteenth century had known, or at least theorized.

With this diversification of competences and tastes came new anxieties. The late-eighteenth-century instrumentalist could presume a comparable level of interest from his *Kenner* and *Liebhaber*, but the public performer of the 1820s had to make choices about how to gauge the style. If he chose to target the dilettante-layman band of the spectrum, as most pianists ultimately did, he might court the wrath of serious critics and lose professional prestige. There was a risk that a long or complex concerto might bore less experienced audiences, while a potpourri of folk tunes might irritate connoisseurs. It is easy to imagine (though difficult to document) that audiences, too, experienced discomfort with the heterogeneous constitution of the audience. Listeners had the opportunity to applaud or hiss performers at will, but these opportunities were tinged with the possibility of embarrassment and of internal dissension: one might applaud something considered by others tasteless, or hiss something well-liked by the rest of the crowd. The mixed audiences that musical commercialization had generated, in short, inhibited the production of community at public concerts. It is against this background that Hummel's free fantasies, with their multi-layered appeal, were so effusively celebrated. Uniquely among living pianists, he successfully negotiated the transition from the world of *Kenner* and *Liebhaber* to the modern world of heterogeneous audiences, without sacrificing the virtues of either. His improvisations mitigated fears that connoisseurs and lay listeners had grown hopelessly apart and that musical community had become impossible in the public sphere.

BEYOND THE KAPELLMEISTER NETWORK: MOSCHELES

Hummel's closest rival in free improvisation was Ignaz Moscheles. In contrast to Hummel, who carried an aura of tradition and learnedness, Moscheles embodied the modern directions in pianism and concert virtuosity more completely. His *Variations on the Alexander March* marked the onset of a new, more powerful kind of bravura that Hummel never acquired, leading Ferdinand Hiller to describe him as the first of the modern virtuosos: "He was the first person who ever elicited that kind of sensational success that is these days almost indispensable, if success is even the right word."[40] Hiller also remarked upon the "facility of his extemporaneous playing, commanding all artistic means," which showed him to be "the fully-formed product of thorough schooling."[41] In spite of this education in the kapellmeister network, Moscheles placed little weight on the older traditions of learned counterpoint and never became a titled kapellmeister or *Musikdirektor*. (He held the title *Kapellmeister-Adjunct* briefly under Salieri, which meant little more than that he was a copyist and rehearsal keyboardist.) He made his living rather as a freelance composer, touring composer-pianist, and teacher. What he lacked in traditional forms of patronage was compensated by the flourishing musical commerce of London, where he spent the first part of his career, and by the establishment of a conservatory in Leipzig, where he spent his later decades. These factors, we will see, inflected the style in which he improvised. Biographies have taken note of Moscheles's exceptional reputation as an improviser, but they have never examined his free playing more closely.[42] His improvisational activities are exceptionally well documented for various reasons. He had a long and wide-ranging concert career, he was closely associated with the Mendelssohn family, and his wife Charlotte condensed his diaries and letters into a book—*Recent Music and Musicians* (hereafter RMM)—that mentions dozens of improvisations.

If the hallmark of Hummel's free fantasies was a reconciliation of the learned and the popular, Moscheles's free fantasies pivoted more decisively toward the popular and attractive. A report on his earliest concerts in Paris suggested that he aimed his fantasies at amateurs and the supposedly lighter tastes of the French audience: "he is capable of winning over artists and dilettantes, the former through the performance of his ingenious compositions, the latter mainly through his free fantasies, which he consciously addresses to Parisian taste to the extent that his German origin allows" (AMZ 1821, 194). Another Viennese writer corroborated this distinction, complaining that Moscheles's improvisations did not rise to the level of artistic inspiration that his compositions did:

> The fantasy should express freely and without inhibition what the heart feels and what burns inside; it should give shape to tones and should boldly emerge as born in the moment. But I did not find this in Moscheles' so-called fantasies. They were rather artificially assembled melodies, variations on known themes— in short, much more like musical potpourris than creations of the moment (fantasy). (*Wiener Zeitschrift* 1825, 260)

The hedonistic aesthetic we have already encountered in the reception of Hummel's potpourri-style improvisations was fully embraced by Moscheles, who could pick up given themes and "develop and intertwine them in the richest variety and the most luxurious colorations, furnishing the greatest pleasure" (AMZ 1823, 773).

From the beginning there was a strain of anxiety about the popular tone of Moscheles's improvisations, especially among the Viennese critics who followed him most closely. At stake was the elite status of the improvised fantasy and its problematic relation with the heterogeneous, musically less-educated public. Already in the Congress of Vienna days it was noted that "Mr. Moscheles is an uncommonly agile and also precise player on this instrument, but he is not yet able to dig deep in free fantasies" (AMZ 1814, 355). This writer assumed Moscheles had internalized the values of the musical guild, and wanted the improvisation to "dig deep" into psychologically dark territories, in line with the hermeneutic tradition of the north German keyboard fantasy.[43] But in the aftermath of the Congress, as concert conditions improved and Moscheles aroused major enthusiasm in various cities, it was no longer obvious that the goal was to please the guild. He was now making a habit of improvising on "given themes," a relatively novel practice that temporarily suspended the virtuoso's professional authority to give the audience a participatory voice. A reporter summarizing his recent concert improvisations tried to put this point diplomatically: "It gave us a special pleasure that Mr. Moscheles took into consideration the fact that the numerous assembled public would not consist exclusively of connoisseurs [*Kunstkennern*]. Among the connoisseurs present, everyone knew that a more artistic, deeper development of the main idea was within his powers" (*Wiener Zeitschrift* 1818, 666). For connoisseurs this was a reassuring thought, but also a resigned one: there was no way both connoisseurs and amateurs would equally enjoy the improvisation, and in the balance the amateurs were winning. It was possibly the same correspondent who claimed, two years later, that "[Moscheles's] virtuosity made an uncommon impression on connoisseurs and non-connoisseurs [*Kenner und Nichtkenner*]," but could not credit the improvisations with such a socially united response:

> If his free fantasy was not satisfying to all parties, this might be ascribed to the pressures of the day, to *the effort to be popular*, or to the circumstance that a true artist's genius cannot flow as freely when external circumstances are affecting

him. In this connection I would note that Mr. M. improvised in private circles, and indeed without prompting, in such a way that the strictest critics were astonished and delighted. (AMZ 1820, 431, emphasis added)

In the face of such a popular and publicly resonant improviser, Vienna's music elites needed to save him from "the effort to be popular" and the "prompting" of public audiences. They wanted to preserve Moscheles, and the free fantasy genre, for the connoisseurs.

During his concert tours of the 1820s, Moscheles's free improvisations were often described as "potpourris." A Berlin critic was following the tracks of the Vienna hardliners when he said that Moscheles's *Reminscences of Ireland* was much freer and bolder than his extempore fantasy, which was "more like a potpourri." This critic was bothered in particular by the improvisation's direct juxtaposition of the two extremely dissimilar tunes—one from Auber's comic opera *Le Maçon*, the other a "worthy Handel oratorio-melody." But the larger problem was that Moscheles devoted most of his elaborations, including the brilliant coda, to the Auber melody, leaving the Handel motive in the dark (BAMZ 1826, 390). If Moscheles chose these tunes to achieve a balance between learned and popular element à la Hummel, he was not convincing the serious critics. The combination of an antique, fugal motive with themes from comic opera was nevertheless a strategy he turned to more than once. Fugal motives appeared particularly often during a tour of Saxony and Prussia in 1824, as though adapting to a north German horizon of expectations. For an improvised fantasy in Dresden he played the "first theme" in strict style—"in four-voices and fugally"—before weaving it together with the gypsy march from Weber's *Preciosa* (*Wiener Zeitschrift* 1824, 1346). In Berlin around the same time he improvised on a "fugue-theme" by Handel combined with two themes from current comic operas (by Spontini and Marschner). In all likelihood the fugue-theme served as the fantasy's unifying head-motto, to be heard at the beginning, reprised at transitions to frame the opera melodies, and possibly brought back in counterpoint against those melodies. Yet one reviewer suggested Moscheles did nothing quite so advanced: "in the fantasy—or rather potpourri—at the concert's conclusion three amazingly heterogeneous themes were developed first separately, then combined with much art and great ability" (*Wiener Theater-Zeitung* 1824, 591). Perhaps Moscheles really did treat the Handel motive as just another melody to vary.[44]

Moscheles employed fugal topoi rarely, giving his free fantasies a distinctly different balance of elements from Hummel's. In the examples just mentioned he took a fugal subject from Handel but did not improvise a fugue as Hummel would have. This was clearly a choice and not a matter of ability. Moscheles was capable of turning on the counterpoint when necessary. When he first went to London in 1821, for example, he needed to impress those local connoisseurs who could recommend him to wider circles. At his first benefit he chose for improvisation "My Lodging is on the Cold Ground" and developed it "not in variation style, but in the most varied sorts of contrapuntal elaboration" (AMZ 1821, 552).[45] But this was an exception, not the rule. Moscheles's taste inclined him toward the virtues of lucidity and charm rather than learned combinations. In a rare proclamation of aesthetic principles he wrote: "I hold that the treatment of a melody, and clearness as well as unity and an interesting fusion of the leading subjects, are the most important ingredients in a composition, and I shall always strive to attain these goals" (RMM, 207). These ideals evidently concern his composed concert fantasies and concert improvisations. The contrapuntal art that most engaged him was not fugue but the ingenious combining and interweaving of already existing popular melodies.

In free fantasies, this fusion of themes was such a common gambit that audiences probably anticipated it from the beginning. Along the route to such a climax, the pianist would play thematic fragments off and against one another in an exploration of combinatorial possibilities. At an 1832 concert in Frankfurt, for instance, Moscheles improvised on the *Allegretto* from Beethoven's Seventh Symphony and "Escouto d'Jeannetto" from Dalayrac's 1789 comic opera *Les deux petits Savoyards* (*Harmonicon* 1832, 281). The pairing sounds strange until one compares the themes, which are strikingly similar harmonically, rhythmically, and phraseologically (Example 2.1a and 2.1b). Though radically different in style, genre, and historical location, the two themes— or more accurately, fragments of them—can be made to "speak to one another." Disaggregated from their native musical contexts, the melodies lose their discrete identities and unfold new relations with other melodies, motives, and harmonies. Starting as radically different types of music, they are "fantasized" into a virtual space where they become one kind of music. In Moscheles's practice improvisation was the privileged forum for explorations of this sort. The Beethoven/Dalayrac improvisation was a very rare instance where he did *not* take the themes from the audience. More exceptionally still, he again improvised on these themes in London shortly afterward.[46] Perhaps he was working up the themes with the intention of composing and publishing a fantasy, but if so, it never came to fruition. More likely he stumbled upon the striking correspondences of the two melodies, was drawn into improvising on them, and then decided they were worth sharing with the public in improvised form.

The branch of musical knowledge most fundamental to Moscheles's melodic-combinatorial thinking was not imitative counterpoint, but thoroughbass and chordal harmony. Like most musicians who went to Vienna for instruction in the early nineteenth century, he studied thoroughbass and counterpoint with Albrechtsberger, mastering them on both organ and piano and finishing the lessons at age fourteen.[47] He also studied with Salieri, who treated him like a protégé, steered him toward Italian opera composition, and hired him as an assistant for three years (*Harmonicon* 1823, 176). But because Moscheles did not write sacred music and was not seeking a church organ position, he had little practical use for active contrapuntal knowledge, and such knowledge was not on display in his improvisations. Thoroughbass practice however ran deeply in his system. In a sketchbook finished off in 1823, which included piano concertos he was writing and playing on tour, the left-hand piano parts are sometimes written as barren figured basses (the right hand parts are always written out).[48] Nourished by thoroughbass, Moscheles's phrasing was rooted in a classical ideal of directed, purposeful motion toward and away from cadences. In his published compositions he made restrained use of modulations, and in later years he spoke out against what he considered the outlandish harmonic turns of Chopin and other romantics. But in free playing he seems to have felt more liberty to show his harmonic

Example 2.1a "Escouto d'Jeannetto" from Dalayrac, *Les deux petits Savoyards* (1789)

Example 2.1b Beethoven, Symphony no. 7, theme of second movement

knowledge with sophisticated modulations. A critic writing specifically about his improvisation wrote: "it is known that in pieces of this genre Moscheles possesses the secret to uniting all styles without confusion, and makes use of the most learned modulations" (AMZ 1822, 226).

Without resorting to fugal playing, then, Moscheles's free fantasies projected a sense of solid knowledge and learning. Charlotte Moscheles scoffed at the pretensions of young English ladies who, after hearing him improvise, requested lessons in this practice: "of course they could not learn to improvise in a few finishing lessons, for this presupposed vast musical erudition" (RMM, 48). His improvisations demonstrated not only harmonic fluency but also exceptional stylistic range, as well as a more intangible sense of organic unity and formal completeness that many critics found lacking in the productions of younger musicians. The more serious critics at the *Revue musicale*, who normally took tough stances on improvisation, made an exception for Moscheles because "[his improvisation] does not at all resemble what we are used to hearing; there is a plan, an initial idea to which the others are related, and this is rare"

(*Revue musicale* 1830, 24). This particular remark seems to be based on the unifying head-motto strategy. Other critics, too, singled out Moscheles's free fantasies for the completeness of musicianship they conveyed. A dazzled Scottish journalist drew attention to the impression of cultivated instruction: "his extemporaneous powers are more wonderful than those of Kalkbrenner. . . . We see in Mr. Moscheles a person of a powerful and well-organised mind, the energies of which must have been judiciously directed and indefatigably exercised in the acquirement of the art" (*Caledonian Mercury*, 28 Jan 1828). And in a similar spirit a Paris correspondent reported: "the several visits made to Paris by this admirable artist had given ample opportunity for all the amateurs and connoisseurs of music to appreciate the brilliancy of his talents, and the solid, rich, and scientific powers with which nature seems to have almost exclusively endowed him for extemporaneous playing" (QMMR 1825, 311). The "popular" side of Moscheles's improvisations, then, was balanced by an understated sense of deep learning that helped ward off the familiar accusations of superficiality.

Although Moscheles clearly had some standard techniques for elaborating on given materials—head-mottos, the fusion of themes—his approach was exceptionally flexible, spontaneous, and non-formulaic, especially in comparison with Hummel. Like other improvisers, including performers of poetry, he spent some time collecting his thoughts on how to shape the given materials into a coherent improvisational statement. This ritual had the potential to intensify the audience's anticipation. At his Leipzig debut of 1816 he performed his compositions for larger ensembles and then made "a pause of a few moments, after which I began my Improvisation. The public, feeling more and more interested, came nearer to me, and ended by regularly hemming me in, so that I became the centre of a great and admiring circle" (RMM 21). Here the improvisation opened up a more informal, intimate mode of communication that licensed the audience to approach the stage. Later, at a private gathering of musicians and connoisseurs in Copenhagen, which included the city's two most admired kapellmeisters, Moscheles found himself "fenced in by a wall of listeners, who were silent as death, while I was collecting my thoughts; I would try to be learned as Kuhlau and Weyse, interesting in harmony, plaintive and sentimental, and I would wind up with a storm of bravura passages" (RMM 155). He paused, in other words, to develop a game plan before launching into the fantasy, and adapted the style to the learned taste of his audience. At the Copenhagen performance, however, the social intimacy occasioned by the improvisation bordered on the embarrassing, as Kuhlau and Weyse "besieged me till I gasped for breath" and "old Professor Schall fell on my neck and kissed me ('for shame!' the English would say)" (RMM 155).

Moscheles was as flexible and spontaneous in the choice of subjects as he was in his methods of elaboration. In contrast to Hummel, Liszt, and others, he did not gravitate toward a relatively small repertoire of tunes and motives. He kept the field of possibilities wide open based on the demands of the audience and the social occasion. It was such flexibility, and a readiness to treat any materials, "however various in style—whether florid or strict," that he admired in the improvisations of Copenhagen master C. E. F. Weyse.[49] A phrase from his diary could have served as his motto: "I was obliged to extemporize. This I did in a way to humor the particular kind of audience" (RMM 158). He had all the standard tunes at his disposition but often stretched out into the less familiar territory, picking up songs and choral numbers from comic operas, Handel choruses, French *vaudeville* tunes, and the florid melodies of Rossini, the latter mostly avoided by improvisers. In Berlin he improvised an unusual tribute to German opera with a free fantasy on Gluck's "Che faro," Mozart's "Voi che sapete," and Beethoven's "Namenlose Freude"—none of them standard tunes for improvisation, and none of them conducive to motivic treatment (RMM 183). Passing through Rouen on a tour, he was asked to play a "concert spirituel" on Easter Sunday, and selected a church chorale suited to the holiday for his improvisation (RMM 43). Moscheles was equally as willing to improvise on very unfamiliar songs. At the height of the London concert season he was so busy with appearances at various benefit concerts that he did not have time to practice, and chose simply to improvise on something he heard at that concert, whether familiar to him or not (RMM 86). Melodies even sprung into his mind unexpectedly in mid-performance: "I had intended to-day to introduce no extraneous subject into my Improvisation, when coming to a pause, the melody, 'Das klinget so herrlich' (*Zauberflöte*), involuntarily forced itself upon me. Two rounds of applause rewarded my treatment of this subject" (RMM 21). In comparative perspective, Moscheles may not have been the most varied or colorful of improvisers, but he was unquestionably the readiest and most adaptable. Only in the piano treatise he compiled with Fétis in the 1830s, the *Méthode des méthodes*, did he articulate the independent value he placed on improvisation's irreducible immediacy:

No matter how great the talent of the improviser, there will always be some disorder, some redundancy in the premature fruit of his mind, and sometimes his sleepy imagination will let him wander into the indefinite: but these faults will be redeemed by a certain boldness of invention that taste may disapprove of, but which gains in power precisely from its unusual attraction. This boldness is precisely the characteristic mark of improvisation.[50]

Although Moscheles's choice of materials for improvisation was based on the specific occasion, he had an unusually strong penchant for improvising on folk songs. This was another way to establish an intimate connection with audiences during his wide-ranging concert tours. At a private soirée in Gothenburg he improvised on Swedish airs that were written down for him (RMM 158), and when asked to play at the Duchess of Kent's palace in Kensington, he decided to improvise on Tyrolese melodies simply because the guests of honor were from the Tyrol (RMM 128–29). Recalling a command performance before the Danish royal court, he explained how his call-out to the audience fed his own inspiration: "first I Rossinified a little, for I knew that Rossini fever rages at Court here. Then I was a Dane, and worked up some national melodies. The shouts of applause made me desperately confident, and I wound up with the Danish 'God Save the King'" (RMM 155). There are countless examples of Moscheles "playing to the locals" in this manner, but he was also drawn to folk tunes when they were not of immediate local relevance. At a Leipzig recital he received several themes from the audience and chose for the free fantasy only "Marlborough" and a "Russian folk song" (AMZ 1824, 860). At a London concert he chose a pair of Swiss-Valais melodies out of the eight different subjects offered (*Wiener Theater-Zeitung* 1830, 344).

Moscheles's penchant for folk materials aligns his improvisational aesthetic with his original bravura compositions, such as *Recollections of Ireland, Anticipations of Scotland,* and *Souvenirs de Danemarc,* which were based on folk tunes or popular materials. To an extent this reflected the success of national-characteristic pieces in Britain's amateur music market. Ferdinand Hiller was stating a fact, not a criticism, when he observed that "in London, where Moscheles lived many years, the pianos and pianists, the public and the publishers exercised a wide-ranging influence over him."[51] The fashion for national-characteristic music was closely linked to early romanticism in Britain, which, stimulated by the popularity of Ossian, Thomas Moore, and Walter Scott, celebrated folk songs and imagined scenes of bardic narration. It is thus not surprising to find in Moscheles's reception the first stirrings of what I call the "improvisation imaginary"— the idealized representation of improvisation in romantic literature and journalism. A colorful story that made its way around periodicals and biographies recounted the pianist's encounter with Sir Walter Scott during his Scottish tour of 1828. On this occasion, the story went, Moscheles was given opportunity to display "the extraordinary talents of this great musician as an improvisatore in his art."[52] The choice of the word "improvisatore"—derived unambiguously from the figure of the Italian poetry improviser—makes a link between musical extemporization and Italian poetry improvisation that will be important in the future of the improvisation imaginary. At Walter Scott's soirée the conversation turned to the martial songs of the Scottish Highlands. The famous author asked someone to sing for Moscheles the melody "Pibroch o' Donald Dhu" using the text of Scott's "Tyrtaean verses." As the company retired to the drawing room, Moscheles went to the piano and began improvising:

> The soul-stirring Highland melody burst forth in all its wild force and fury! It was perhaps never played, at the head of the clan before battle, with more passionate energy ... The musician, who had never heard the melody but once, and who was previously almost a stranger to the very existence of the bold race whose energies it spoke, exhibited the whole soul of the Highland melody, throughout all its varying struggles and emotions, as if he had learned from infancy to sweep the harp with Ossian, and burnt and wept all his life with the children of the mist and the desert. (*Caledonian Mercury,* 26 January 1828)

In this fanciful recounting, the improviser Moscheles is transformed into an ancient bardic narrator, singing the songs of an ancient nation, sympathizing intimately with their national spirit, and reliving the violent delirium of past battles.

After this performance Scott turned the discussion toward real-life, present-day martial airs, and recalled a poetic impression he had experienced at St. Cloud after the battle of Waterloo: "amidst the calm of a French summer's night, he described the mingling sounds, in the distance, of the instruments of almost all the nations in the world, rising in strange and wild harmony around." Scott prompted the pianist to materialize this vision by playing martial airs from the continent, and Moscheles was happy to oblige with another improvisation:

> He sat down again, accordingly, to his instrument, and produced the most ad-mirable melange of every sort of military music that can be conceived . . . the wonderful facility and grace with which he arranged and combined them—passing through more than imaginable variety of keys and measures, yet ever maintaining one uniform tone of high martial feeling—excited the profoundest admiration. They all agreed, that though they had often heard before what were termed extempore fantasias, yet the real bard-like spirit, which alone gives value to such efforts of improvisation, they then listened to for the first time. (*Caledonian Mercury*, 26 January 1828)

Such an explicit layering of romantic fantasy with musical improvisation was by no means the norm in the discourse around Moscheles. But his frequent recourse to folk materials when playing freely opened itself to bardic fantasies to an extent that opera melodies or national anthems could not. And as the Walter Scott anecdote suggests, Moscheles was willing to "play along" with the illusion. As mentioned earlier, while improvising on Danish national airs in Copenhagen, he had imagined himself as a native: "I was a Dane."

The entry of keyboard improvisers into the improvisation imaginary was catalyzed by the fact that Moscheles's celebrity coincided with the peak of interest in Italian po-etry improvisers among British romantic writers and their readers. In the period 1815–1830, authors in the Shelley-Byron circle were quite preoccupied with the figure of the *improvvisatore*, especially the prodigiously gifted Tommasso Sgricci. Madame de Staël's novel *Corinne*, too, had inspired a number of British female writers to create Corinne-like spin-offs.[53] A handful of Italian improvisers had recently settled in London and were giving regular performances there. Moscheles became a fan of one of them: Filippo Pistrucci.[54] Charlotte Moscheles, summarizing her husband's life in 1823, wrote:

> In London he had perfected himself still more [in the Italian language], and never failed to attend the Pistrucci evenings, where he listened with great delight to the "Improvisatore," as he enlarged, in well-sounding harmonious verses, on a chance theme suggested by the public. "It gives me food for thought in my own improvisations," he adds [in his diary]. "I must constantly make comparisons be-tween the sister arts: they are all closely allied." (RMM 53)

At Pistrucci's recitals, the sisterhood of music and poetry was underlined by the structure of the program, which broke up the poetry recitations with arias and songs by Mozart and Rossini, all of them sung by Italian singers. Moreover, Pistrucci performed, as most poetry improvisers did, to musical accompaniment (Sgricci was an exception). As a writer for the *Musical World* fancifully put it: "the improvisator, like his predecessors the Troubadours, is accustomed to deliver his thoughts to an instrumental accompaniment" (*Musical World* 1837, 154). As a guide to British readers who were still unfamiliar with this practice, the *Harmonicon* explained: "Those who possess this talent are called *Improvvisatore*, from the verb *improvvisare*, which signifies to sing, or recite verses, extemporaneously. . . . This art is so connected with music,— indeed, music almost invariably constitutes a part of it,—that we consider Signor Pistrucci . . . entitled to some notice in our work" (*Harmonicon* 1823, 87).[55]

The convergence of Italian poets, German musicians, and Scottish romanticism made London exceptionally fertile ground for the emergence of the improvisation imaginary. The novelty and exoticism of Italian *improvvisatore* found an echo in the response to Moscheles's piano improvisations. Both were relatively unfamiliar forms of artistic production that registered as continental imports. The *Morning Chronicle* reported in 1822 that Moscheles's "extemporaneous effusion was quite wonderful, and so far as our experience enables us to affirm, has never been paralleled in this country" (AMZ 1822, 659). The point was reiterated a year later by London's AMZ correspondent: "here the free fantasy is a complete new genre of playing, and a path to fame not attempted by anyone before Moscheles. This is quite completely his own territory, since only in this manner can the passion of his creative mind flow in unimpeded streams. . . . Germany can indeed be proud of such a man" (AMZ 1823, 598). The claim is not strictly accurate, since Moscheles had improvised at London concerts at least as early as 1821, but it is true that London audiences were less accustomed to keyboard improvisation than elsewhere. Hummel and Liszt had not yet traveled to the British Isles. Clementi, though a capable improviser, had ceased playing concerts, and Cramer, though well known as a melodic embellisher, did not improvise freely with any frequency. Apart from Clementi, the only musician in England with an exceptional reputation as an improviser was the organist Samuel Wesley, but his public impact was limited by his focus on religious music.[56] One loyal admirer felt obliged to stress the difference between Wesley's compositions and his improvisations: "the published works of this master can give not the faintest idea of his powers when he sits down unpremeditatedly to his instrument, and of the effective original combinations of harmony, in which he delights so much to indulge" (QMMR 1823, 292).

Friedrich Kalkbrenner was based in England at this time as well, but he did not improvise free fantasies. His concert fantasy *Effusio musica*, composed in 1823 and played often on tour in the following years, is stylized as an improvisation and was occasionally mistaken for one. It is not based on familiar tunes or themes but is entirely original, meaning it did not originate in a concert where he solicited themes from the audience. By corollary, its "improvised" status was a matter of faith. A scandalous anecdote that got around musical circles told of Kalkbrenner's visit to the Mendelssohn house in Berlin, where he announced he would play a "Freie Phantasie" but in fact played his composed-out *Effusio musica*.[57] Chorley's observation that the *Effusio* was "sometimes played as an improvisation" by Kalkbrenner is an index of the confusion.[58] We can be similarly skeptical about the "free fantasy" Kalkbrenner supposedly played at his Vienna debut concert of 1824.[59] The three themes on which he claimed to be improvising—"Heil Dir im Siegerkranz" and two themes from *Der Freischütz*—are identical to the three themes of his "free fantasy" in Berlin a few weeks earlier. The Berlin performance, moreover, was described in two reviews as a potpourri—that is, in style quite different from that of the *Effusio*.[60] At Kalkbrenner's second and last Vienna concert of 1824 he did not offer a free fantasy at all—an odd choice if he was really prepared to play one. Eduard Hanslick, looking back on the year 1824 in his history of concert life in Vienna, added that "Moscheles' free fantasies stood decidedly above *the one* by Kalkbrenner."[61] Kalkbrenner was probably faking free fantasies in order to keep up with the popularity of the genre, which had reached its peak in the early 1820s through the efforts of Hummel and Moscheles. This is not to deny that Kalkbrenner had the capacity to improvise, but to suggest that he probably did not play truly free fantasies in public.[62]

DUAL IMPROVISATIONS: MOSCHELES, MENDELSSOHN, AND HILLER

Moscheles's improvisational talent found a very different outlet while playing together with his close friend and colleague Felix Mendelssohn.[63] Around 1830, while Moscheles was visiting the Mendelssohn family in Berlin, they engaged a novel form of musical recreation:

> We often extemporize together, each of us trying to dart quick as lightning on the suggestions implied by each other's harmonies, and to construct others upon them. Then Felix, whenever I introduce any motive out of his own works, breaks in and cuts me short by playing a subject from one of my compositions, on which I retort, and then he, and so on *ad infinitum*. It's a sort of musical blindman's bluff, where the blindfolded now and then run against each other's heads. (RMM 182)

Moscheles's son had vivid memories of the game-like spirit in which these improvisations were carried out: "Like a ball thrown out the motive was picked up, boldly hurled into the air or held tenderly in suspense by one of them, by the other reclaimed, artfully broken down, dried out in learned style, and then perhaps triumphing in a new form, drawn into other worlds triumphantly by four hands."[64] This fascinating exercise in intersubjective communication comes closer to the "dialogic" ideals of jazz improvisation than do most forms of classical improvisation. It demands strenuous attention to the immediate thought-pathways of the other player, and provokes instantaneous elaboration on the implications and affordances of the other player's ideas. It requires, in others, the player's entry, or attempted entry, into the "other space" of the opposing improviser's mind: "Four hands and one soul, that's how it sounded sometimes."[65] Moscheles's description underlines the situational risks and the ethos of agonistic confrontation (interruption, collision) that emerge within the play-frame of the improvisation—qualities celebrated by the CSI school as "discrepant engagement" within collectively improvising ensembles.[66]

After discovering the delights of such dual improvisations, Mendelssohn and Moscheles rarely missed an opportunity to indulge in them. It was a pleasurable game and challenge "among artists," as well as a ritual of friendship liberated from the exigencies of public communication. As an insider's art, the pleasure experienced by the players was not likely to reach spectators and listeners to its full extent. But because it took place in the home it was shaped by, and in turn contributed to, the ethos of domestic play and leisure. Their joint improvisations unleashed the ludic potential of improvisation to a rare degree, and the humorous dimension—underlined by laughter and verbal comments to one another in mid-performance—did transmit itself to the spectators. Charlotte Moscheles, relating events around 1833 and 1834, reported that "they often play to one another Beethoven's Sonatas, which not infrequently diverge into joint improvisations of the maddest kind, and musical caricatures. On one occasion the nursery song, 'Polly put the kettle on,' is chosen as a subject on purpose to please the two little girls" (RMM 197).

The satirical character of such games needed to be set aside when Mendelssohn and Moscheles took their dual improvisation public. At an 1833 Moscheles benefit in London, Mendelssohn joined for one number that had been announced as a "duet on two of Erard's grand pianofortes by Moscheles and his friend Mendelssohn, composed expressly for the occasion by them" (*Morning Post*, 2 May 1833). A lack of time and preparation, however, forced them to work out a plan for a duet on Weber's gypsy march (from *La Preciosa*). Mendelssohn would play the introduction and first two variations, while Moscheles would take responsibility for two more variations and a coda-finale (*verbindendem Tutti*). The formal model, in other words, was that of brilliant concert variation set, not that of a free fantasy. In practice, though, the two pianists broke with convention and treated the finale in their unique dual-improvisation style. Mendelssohn led off with an Allegro-phrase that Moscheles broke off with a *più lento*, and a few cadence points were scribbled down to organize their solo hand-offs: "Not a soul observed that the duet had been merely sketched, and that each of us was allowed to improvise in his own solo, until at certain passages agreed upon we met again in due harmony. The scheme, which seemed to be very hazardous, ended triumphantly, and was received with applause" (RMM, 194). The one published review of this concert took note of the "friendly conflict" that obtained between the players as they traded variations and "cadenzas" (*Harmonicon* 1833, 155).

Insight into how Moscheles and Mendelssohn might have carried out their dual improvisation comes from a later concert where Hiller and Mendelssohn performed Mozart's concerto in E♭ for two pianos. Hiller recalled that

Mendelssohn and I . . . had prepared the cadenza for the first movement thus: I was to begin extemporizing and make a pause on some chord of the 7th. Mendelssohn was then to continue and pause on another chord that we had settled on, and for the finish Mendelssohn had written a few pages for both instruments, now separately, now together, till the return of the Tutti. The thing came off perfectly and the audience, few of whom could make out how we had managed it, applauded enthusiastically.[67]

What is interesting about this plan is its deliberate linear progression. Starting from a relatively loose and open mode of elaboration between dominant-seventh cadence points, it gradually accelerates the shuttling between instruments, creating an effect in which the performers' two "voices" converge upon a single point, which is then greeted by an orchestral release. The scheme deliberately obscures the transition point between improvisation and composition, challenging spectators to figure out "how they managed it." It stages a mysteriously unified thought process emerging from the apparently separate, individuated utterances of the improvisers. And as described in an eloquent review, this "coming together" of the soloists resolved the agonistic and communicative tension hovering over the entire duet:

> Both cadenzas, up to their conclusions and transitional lead-ins, were performed by the esteemed artists in a totally free manner; one heard, so to speak, a free double fantasy. The one lay in wait for the other, in order to follow him, direct him, or procure terrain for some freely independent excursion. Each found and took the opportunity to perform various motives of the concerto plainly and to develop them. It was extremely interesting how, in the first cadenza, Mr. Hiller played at some length several themes and reworked them in an excellent fashion, and how immediately and artfully Mendelssohn caused those themes to be taken up, pursued further, and rewoven with new motives, thereby producing a veritable contest, so to speak, which in itself formed a unified whole, though performed independently by two different artists. . . . The applause of the public was immense; both artists celebrated a true triumph.[68]

This description reminds us that, for all of the importance of cadence points in giving coherence and structure to the improvisation, it was the motives from Mozart's concerto—the "thing in common"—that served as key site of intersubjective action. Mendelssohn's effort *not* to develop the motives in the same manner as Hiller was not an attempt put his own "personal spin" on the materials. It was rather an attempt to absorb and react to Hiller's elaborations so that he could complement and enrich them—an intersubjective dialogue geared toward "a unified whole, yet . . . performed independently."

Dual improvisations of this kind were extremely rare in public concerts, but Moscheles and Mendelssohn made them a regular feature of private or semi-private soirees. Charlotte Moscheles recalled the balance of artistic ambition and humorous play that characterized their at-home improvisations of the 1840s:

> When time came for serious music, then were the two M.'s in their real element; then did they give us their very best, winding up as usual with a grand improvisa-tion *à quatre mains*. Then followed such remarks as these: "How insane of you to

bring in my madcap Scherzo while I was just fairly launched in your A flat major study, which I wanted to do ever so sentimentally;" or, "Isn't it a wonder it went at all? Upon my word, we have been too reckless to-day!" (RMM, 291)

Such bonding through improvisation was exceptionally strong between Mendelssohn and Moscheles on account of their familial ties, and was possibly enhanced by domesticity and intimate ideals characteristic of Biedermeier culture. But it also extended a form of inter-artist sociability already known from earlier times. While Dussek was in the service of Prince Louis Ferdinand of Prussia, the two often improvised *in alternatim* at two pianos.[69] The young Carl Maria von Weber and his friend Friedrich Wilhelm Berner (the latter revered by Mendelssohn as a great organist and improviser) sometimes traded turns improvising on a single theme, using the arrival on a diminished seventh chord as a hand-off point.[70] When Meyerbeer first arrived in Vienna in 1813, Moscheles was profoundly impressed with his playing and it led to a close association: "for hours together they sat extemporizing and improvising on one piano; hence arose the 'Invitation to a Bowl of Punch,' and other duets" (RMM 12). In 1832 Moscheles was the featured guest artist at one of Hummel's court concerts in Weimar. In a scene emblematic of the cultural ambitions of Weimar's royalty, the Grand Duchess sat on one side of the piano while Hummel sat on the other side and gave him the theme for his free fantasy. At the post-concert dinner Moscheles and Hummel had the opportunity, perhaps the first since the Congress of Vienna, to play together "extemporaneously on one piano-forte" (*Harmonicon* 1832, 281). The shared competences subtending all of these dual improvisations demonstrate the unity of the kapellmeister network and the desire to reaffirm that unity through dialogic performance when opportunities arose.

HUMMEL'S STUDENTS

The pianist who most directly inherited Hummel's improvisational wisdom was Ferdinand Hiller. For a period of just under two years, from 1825 to 1826, the precocious teenager from Frankfurt went to Weimar to become Hummel's protégé. Hiller might already have been trained in improvisation by his childhood teacher Aloys Schmitt, a highly accomplished pianist and prominent musician on the Frankfurt scene. At the time Hiller studied with him, Schmitt was acquiring a reputation as a free improviser. Inspired directly by Hummel's example, Schmitt "applied himself to improvising often in public and in private circles" and even published a piece entitled "Freie Fantasie über Themen von Hummel."[71] An AMZ correspondent passing through Frankfurt in 1820 attended a Schmitt benefit at whose conclusion the pianist

played by himself, in improvisation, a storm scene: self-evidently a joke, but brilliant and depicted with remarkable skill. . . . Since he is at both a brilliant and a well-grounded artist and composer he shows his greatest powers in free improvisation. So claim the connoisseurs here, anyway, who have heard him play in private circles; and anyone who, like myself, heard him that evening will be very inclined to grant it is true. (AMZ 1820, 348)

Six years later the journal reviewed Schmitt's *Rhapsodieen in Uebungen für das Pianoforte* and commended them for helping develop superior bravura technique, "which at the same time greatly facilitates free improvisation," an art in which "Hr. Schm. is himself so distinguished" (AMZ 1826, 847). Each etude in this collection focuses on a single idiomatic figure that fits comfortably under the hand, with almost no traces of the more modern bravura techniques. Although somewhat dated in his aesthetic horizons and little known outside the German milieu, Schmitt continued to make occasional tours through the 1830s and 1840s where he promoted new symphonic compositions—including a dramatic composition entitled *Improvisation: Fantasia for Large Orchestra*—and played free fantasies on given themes. We have little indication of how the improvisations sounded. The serious critic F. A. Kanne, reviewing Schmitt's 1831 benefit in Vienna, was exasperated by the light tone of the free fantasy, which seems to have been a potpourri of Mozart melodies: "it was nowhere rigorous [*gebunden*], neither the handling of a theme, nor in contrapuntal things, nor even in an imitation thereof. . . . [he is] merely a player of *galant* things" (WATZ 1831, 35). In private contexts, as already indicated, their style may have been different.

Besides training Hiller in idiomatic figures for improvisation, Schmitt often made his young protégé work out modulations in his head during walks they took together.[72] With such a rigorous theoretical foundation and the apprenticeship under Hummel, Hiller became a fluent improviser who continued to play free fantasies in public well into the second half of the nineteenth century, even after his activities were overtaken by composing and fulfilling the duties of a busy kapellmeister. Hiller was ready to improvise in a variety of situations. After playing to Goethe for the first time (1826) he wrote a letter reporting: "I improvised—where I got the courage to do this in that moment I cannot imagine. G. sat across from the piano and listened very attentively. I worked in a theme from *Don Juan*."[73] With Mendelssohn he improvised not only the dual cadenzas discussed above, but also accompaniments to poetry recitations, as will be described further in Chapter 3. And as the occasion demanded, he might improvise a fantasy on given themes or pick up a melody just sung and work it up into an *impromptu*.

For all of Hiller's talent in the genre, improvisation did not play a proportionally large part in his reputation. His identity as a prolific composer of serious works and as an influential kapellmeister overwhelmed his very considerable skills as a pianist. When he gave concerts and concluded with improvisations they did not receive much special attention, but rather filled out his image as a thoroughly trained and broadly educated kapellmeister. Critics and friends rarely described his extemporaneous playing in any detail, and he did not give the subject much attention in his voluminous letters and memoirs. The evidence trail for Hiller's improvisations is thus uncommonly thin, making it difficult to establish even general patterns in his approach.

There are signs his contemporaries did not consider them very interesting or original. French critic Henri Blanchard, a partisan of piano improvisation and normally generous to a fault, found Hiller's improvisations rather dry: "Though he is logical in the rendering of his instantaneous thoughts, he is not sufficiently poetic or capricious in the episodes, where he is obliged to combine the two or three subjects he treats simultaneously" (RGMP 1854, 77). At a Paris recital of 1852, Blanchard recognized Hiller as "a true disciple of Hummel, who improvised so well" when he played a fantasy on solicited themes. The audience offered the *Allegretto* from Beethoven's Seventh Symphony (requested by Meyerbeer, who was in the audience), the Austrian national hymn, and the aria "Grâce" from *Robert le Diable*. As if these themes were not heterogeneous enough, Hiller threw in the minuet from *Don Giovanni* (RGMP 1852, 387). (This could well be the melody on which he had improvised before Goethe, used as connective tissue between the tune elaborations.) Blanchard's description tells us little more—only that Hummel played each of the themes separately and then began to intercalate them "with novel harmonic effects and picturesque pedal-tones."

Although we know little about the sound of Hiller's own improvisations, his memoir *Künstlerleben* (1880) provides a unique insider's portrait of Hummel's playing. Hiller's memoir is a complex source because it was written fifty-five years after his studies in Weimar and it was inflected by the ideological battles in which he was embroiled. As he "remembered" the Hummel of the 1820s, he had a chance to refurbish the image of his old master, whose music and reputation had fallen out of favor. Hiller was particularly keen to reconstruct Hummel as a dignified, serious "artist" by dissociating him from the figure of the modern concert virtuoso. Instead of calling Hummel's performances "free fantasies," for example, he anachronistically called them "improvisations, which I would rather call intimate effusions."[74] The ideological weight is carried not so much by the word "improvisation" as by "intimate effusions," since the fundamental point Hiller wanted to make was that Hummel's private improvisations were superior to his public ones:

> It was marvelous, overtaking the ear, mind and soul, when the master, giving in to my earnest request or to a fleeting inner motivation, placed himself at the piano and, disregarding everything around him, let himself get lost in thoughts on that keyboard which means the world to the composer. What a wealth of motives, whose distinctiveness occasionally bordered on the strange! What power over all means of harmony, of polyphony, of rhythm! And how agile were those otherwise stubby fingers! No matter how long it went on, nor how diversified it was— the listener never lost the prospect of a harmoniously arranged whole—never did freedom lose itself in abandon [*Zugellosigkeit*]. When I then gave voice to my amazement, the master would hear nothing of it and would say he just wanted to try something out.[75]

When describing Hummel's famous improvisations in public, however, Hiller took an extremely defensive posture. Hummel only improvised on well-known melodies, he asserted, because the general public would have been unable to follow him, or unable to believe him, if he invented his own motives on the spot. Hummel often chose the same familiar themes, Hiller continued, not to avoid confronting the unfamiliar, but "in order to treat them with the most intelligent and graceful naturalness of which he was capable."[76] Hiller went so far as to claim, against all the known evidence, that Hummel normally selected his own themes rather than soliciting them from the public: "It is difficult for me to imagine him in the attitude of a Minister, taking favorite melodies like parliamentary motions, or in that of a conjurer who begins to empty out a mystical vessel (full of musical motives)."[77] With comments such as these Hiller was striving to differentiate his hero and mentor from those pianists, Liszt among them, who did pick themes out of a vase, and to construct Hummel as a "higher" artist, with a status well above that of a minor minister or popular entertainer. To do this Hiller had to suppress the obvious: that Hummel, like himself, took his themes orally rather than on slips of paper.

Other high-profile virtuosos who studied with Hummel, such as Sigismond Thalberg and Adolf von Henselt, improvised rarely if at all.[78] However the Danish pianist Rudolf Willmers did improvise, and his little-known story illustrates how the changing professional and critical climate of the 1830s and 1840s reconstructed the inclination to improvise. A precocious talent, though not quite a prodigy, Willmers (b. 1821) studied with Hummel for a year and half between 1834 and 1836. The lessons were focused on mastering a few of Hummel's difficult large-scale works and learning how to improvise freely. Willmers made his concert debut in Berlin at the age of fourteen, and the motives he took for the free fantasy happened to be his teacher's favorites from *Don Giovanni* (AMZ 1836, 291). Moving straight on to Leipzig, Willmers impressed Robert Schumann, who considered Willmers' improvisations superior to his other performances. Schumann had an opportunity to offer the subject for improvisation: the E♭-major horn motive from Beethoven's Fifth Symphony. At first Willmers, not knowing the piece, fumbled around to determine its correct harmonization, but once he found its tonal identity "flowers, flashes, and pearls flowed smoothly from his fingers" (NZM 1836, 49).

After these attention-grabbing debut concerts Willmers went into a "three-year course in theory" with the Dessau kapellmeister Friedrich Schneider, and displayed the fruits of his study in a concert tour of 1838 (WAMZ 1845, 94). Observers in Leipzig opined that "his free fantasies do not yet belong in public" and worried that his activities as a virtuoso might be impeding his artistic development. But they also admitted their standard of comparison might be inappropriate, since quality free fantasies would only be expected of an "experienced master" (NZM 1838, 190 and 202). At a subsequent concert in Dresden, however, Willmers's improvisation seems to have hit the target:

> The crowning achievement of the whole thing was a free fantasy with which the concert-giver pleased us at the conclusion. . . . Kapellmeister Reissiger took out two [melodies from the vase], namely Mozart's "Reich mir die Hand mein

Leben" and Méhul's "Ich war [ein] Jünglich noch an Jahren." Mr. Willmers immediately played the first of these and led it through several extremely charming variations, then suddenly broke off to make the second theme the opponent of the first and to display them fighting for the prize. The variations gradually increased in intensity, jumping from the one melody to the other; the competing waves of sound welled up louder and louder until finally both themes reconciled, combined in a single great celebratory hymn, with which the loud applause of the enraptured listeners united. (AMZ 1838, 839)

These words give the impression of a quite dramatic and dialectical process played out over the course of the fantasy. But the absence of any reference to a prelude, or to transitions, modulations, and counterpoint, suggests that the improvisation may have been quite simple and schematic in approach. There was evidently little of Hummel's fugue-tinged free fantasy practice on display here. Mozart's and Méhul's melodies are so close in terms of rhythm, harmony, phrasing, and melodic character that there is little to "reconcile" by combining them. The review, then, probably exaggerates the progressive dynamism of the improvisation; it is a deliberately evocative, "literary" description. It is nevertheless important to acknowledge what the discursive trope aspires to convey: heterogeneous musical materials in tension with one another, working out their differences, eventually uniting with one another in a higher synthesis—and from this point initiating a higher synthesis between the "great celebratory hymn" and the applause of the audience, so that a community of artist and audience has been achieved under a metaphorically "choral" sound.[79] The familiarity of this literary trope from other descriptions of improvising artists is one indication of how the improvisation imaginary was gradually lodging itself in conventions of journalistic description and music criticism.

Following these debut appearances, in which free fantasies played a conspicuous role, Willmers apparently ceased improvising publicly altogether. As if heeding the warnings of the Leipzig critics, he turned his attention toward the production of compositions and the attainment of superior virtuosity. Within a few years he had ascended to the upper echelons of traveling virtuosos, playing fantasies composed in the style of Liszt and Thalberg. During the 1845 season in Vienna he played no fewer than fifteen concerts as principal artist, and eight more as assisting artist, and he kept a steady stream of new concert fantasies coming off the press. In his short maturation, then, Willmers had transitioned decisively out of the kapellmeister circuit, as represented by his teachers Hummel and Schneider, and the improvisations had dropped away. When he debuted in Paris in 1843 the critics had no inkling of his auspicious early talent for improvisation. Henri Blanchard even saw Willmers as a symbol of a modern virtuosity completely devoid of the virtues of improvisation:

Along with slow, patient study of counterpoint and fugue there has disappeared piano improvisation, an artistic phenomenon through which musicians showed they knew how to combine boldness and method, that they had or didn't have ideas, invention, or in a word, genius. Mozart, Beethoven, Hummel, and Moscheles improvised delightfully: it is then that you saw the individuality of a great artist. Today, the *nec plus ultra* of audacity for our executant pianists is to play three or four fantasies without music on the stand, which can be equated more or less with a discourse memorized by a lawyer or a deputy. (RGMP 1843, 95)

CARL MARIA VON BOCKLET

The void that opened up when Hummel retreated from concert life in the 1830s was temporarily filled by a little-known pianist named Carl Maria von Bocklet. A product of the Prague conservatory, Bocklet first advanced himself as a violinist, but by the 1820s he was playing concerts in Vienna as a double virtuoso on piano and violin, and the violin soon ceded to the piano.[80] Throughout the decade he was a first-call chamber musician, appearing at benefit concerts of the city's leading instrumentalists. He clearly possessed a superior piano technique enabling him to handle the more difficult pieces by Beethoven, Schubert, Weber, and Hummel, and he sacrificed compositional ambitions in order to offer polished performances of these composers, whose works were already being called "classic." Like his colleague on the violin, Ignaz Schuppanzigh, he is an early example of a trend that would eventually lead to the "interpreter" identity in musical performance. In the later 1820s and early 1830s he seems to have devoted himself mainly to teaching at the conservatory of the *Gesellschaft der Musikfreunde*. His top students were making public debuts and his name was mentioned with a tone of reverence.[81] Although audiences knew him mainly as an interpreter of difficult works, he had already established a reputation as an improviser in 1822: "people who have heard him play in private circles unanimously praise his manner of improvising" (AMZ 1822, 206). Impressed by Bocklet's free fantasy, the author of this report made an optimistic prediction: "to improvise on a given theme in a private gathering [*in einer Gesellschaft*] and arouse the admiration of the world—few are capable of this! And with the advanced state of musical education today, a great artist in this domain could attract widespread interest." The author was clearly unaware of Hummel's track record of success, but the point was still valid: the free fantasy was fundamentally a private genre that could eventually, in the right hands, acquire greater public interest.

Several years later Bocklet followed through on this promise. In 1835 he made a phenomenal comeback to Vienna's concert scene with a series of benefit concerts that were followed closely in the press. Each of the first two concerts featured a Beethoven overture, a Hummel piano concerto, and a Mozart aria—a solidly "classic" framework—with a free fantasy at the conclusion. New in the press reception of these concerts was an emphasis on the brilliance of his free fantasies, which was now Bocklet's distinguishing mark. The most conspicuous article appeared in the cultural journal *Wiener Zeitschrift*, which crowned him king of improvisers in an article worth quoting at some length:

Among all the musical events of this winter, the concert of Mr. Carl von Bocklet is being called the most appealing and memorable by that part of our public we would call music-patrons [*Musikfreunde*] in the narrower sense of the word. As unforgettable as these achievements are in and of themselves, they are a greater gain for all through the added circumstance that after a long retreat, more than ten years, with regard to improvisation, they have drawn an artist toward the path of the public world to which he belongs by virtue of his outlook [*Standpunkt*], and in which he is called to shine as the best of his kind. Bocklet unquestionably occupies this honorable position in his double specialization as improviser and piano virtuoso. . . . Among the art-patrons [*Kunstfreunde*] of Vienna Bocklet has always been called the best, unsurpassed improviser; yet publicly he had not yet been heard in this quality for a number of years; now the general public, too, knows that this claim has its truth. (*Wiener Zeitschrift* 1835, 403–404)

The celebratory tone of this passage is inspired by the same social idealism that had inspired the reception of Hummel. Bocklet is credited with making the improvised fantasy a publicly viable genre and thereby bridging the gap between connoisseurs (*Kunstfreunde, Musikfreunde*) and the general public.

The conspicuous celebration of Bocklet as improviser by critics of a more serious stripe took place exactly at the moment Sigismond Thalberg was emerging as the pianistic lion of Vienna. Thalberg's profile in the 1820s was much like that of Bocklet: he was in demand for chamber music concerts and as a soloist in classic concertos by Beethoven and Hummel. But by 1835, when the above passage was written, he had developed a new, lush, and distinctly modern approach to the concert fantasy. Classic works and concertos disappeared from his repertoire as he paved the way toward an international solo career playing his own concert fantasies for solo piano. Though probably versed in improvisation, he had no reputation for playing free fantasies or improvised preludes. His sound and approach represented a new musical generation that was moving beyond the parameters of postclassical pianism, shedding in particular the lingering traces of thoroughbass practice. Critics thus began comparing Bocklet and Thalberg as representatives of different directions or styles. In 1834 a Vienna correspondent observed that when compared with Thalberg, Bocklet did not make a big enough sound for modern concert spaces (RGMP 1834, 147).

In the spring of 1835, as Bocklet made his breakthrough return, Thalberg published two new "Grandes Fantaisies" on Bellini operas, and a reviewer noted that Thalberg was considered the best pianist in Vienna "next to Carl Maria von Bocket, who remains preeminent specifically in the free fantasy" (AMZ 1835, 469–70). A few lines later this critic was fretting about the vulgarization of the title "Phantasie" in recent bravura compositions, which "failed to do justice to the word 'Phantasie' in the highest sense." Thalberg's fantasies, however, got a pass because they found a blend of popular and learned taste: "This young man has been meanly criticized for openly striving to make his works enjoyable for experts and non-experts [*Kenner und Nichtkenner*]. But in such pieces that is not criticism, but praise."

Bocklet's free fantasies, like those of other pianists examined here, raised issues about the relationship between the traditional and modern, between the learned and the popular, and between connoisseurs and dilettantes. They were recognized and cele-brated as manifestations of elite, "classic" musical values that were perceptibly eroding from pianistic tradition because older pianists were fading and younger virtuosos were gaining audiences with newer, more attractive music. In the *Theater-Zeitung* Heinrich Adami even named Bocklet the heir-apparent to Hummel: "Hummel's improvised fantasies [*Stegreif-Fantasien*] have achieved a European reputation, but in terms of wor-thiness of style, boldness of ideas, and bravura in performance, we have to award pref-erence to Bocklet's improvising," in part because it "is never limited to mere variations on the main idea" (*Wiener Theater-Zeitung* 1835, 291). Bocklet's competitive advantage vis-à-vis Hummel had something to do with his choice of materials for elaboration.

Whereas Hummel had modulated his approach to the perceived taste of his au-dience, and therefore sometimes played potpourris, Bocklet remained more severe and elevated in style. This was especially true of his season debuts. At the first 1835 concert he improvised on the *Allegretto* from Beethoven's Seventh Symphony, with no admixture of other themes, and so successfully that the *Wiener Zeitschrift* published a poem entitled "Bocklet's Phantasie" (*Wiener Zeitschrift* 1835, 360). At the second concert he improvised on a motive from a Beethoven sonata that one critic judged less conducive to free elaboration. These thematic choices suggest that Bocklet was avoiding the more typical choice of popular arias and folk tunes. At his first concert of the following season (December 1835) he also played a free fantasy but did not solicit themes from the audience, choosing instead to play on a self-devised theme that was unannounced. According to one reviewer, the unfamiliarity of the motto made it dif-ficult for ordinary listeners to follow: "This circumstance probably detracted from the effect of the first improvisation, though it perhaps even raised its value in the eyes of the connoisseurs [*Kenner*]" (*Wiener Zeitschrift* 1835, 1268). At his first benefit of 1838, too, Bocklet chose or invented his own theme for the fantasy, earning admiration for staying in an "artistically appropriate and elevated" style, so that "the listener did not one single time encounter a familiar motive, and no prosaic idea was heard" (*Adler* 1838, 1236).

For his second benefit concert of a given season, however, Bocklet lightened the tone. Here he would solicit themes from the audience, choose two or three of them, and develop a fantasy in which they were combined at the end. Even when taking this less severe, conventional approach, he kept it within "classic" boundaries by sticking to recognized composers. Thus at an 1846 concert he chose motives from Schubert's "Wanderer" Fantasy and Weber's *Jubelouverture*. Another free fantasy from this season took a motive from a Hummel composition that had just been played and, pivoting slightly toward the popular, Rossini's "Sorte secondami." At his second concert of the 1836 season he began the improvisation with Don Ottavio's aria "Il mio tesoro intanto" from *Don Giovanni*, a rare melodic choice that was probably delivered in a "straighter" manner, since its melody is spun-out and lacks motivic content. It continued with two C-major motives—from the rondo of Mozart's four-hand piano sonata, and the theme of Beethoven's choral fantasy—which he combined at the fantasy's conclusion. The admiring critic of the AMZ noted that this Mozart-tinged fantasy spoke especially to the tastes and memories of the older audience members: "silver-haired veterans, feeling rejuvenated, confirmed unanimously that, with the intensified technique, nothing similar had been heard since Mozart, the unforgettable one in this genre" (AMZ 1836, 77).

In methods of elaboration, too, Bocklet steered clear of the more popular, decorative styles such as variation and potpourri, which were in any case more suited to symmetrically phrased and periodic melodies. Heinrich Adami, commenting on the fantasy on Beethoven's *Allegretto*, praised him for "never confining himself to mere variations on the main idea" (*Wiener Theater-Zeitung* 1835, 291).[82] The most informative single description we have of Bocklet's improvisation style likewise highlighted the use of developmental techniques in treating Beethoven's *Allegretto*:

> The main idea stayed clearly perceptible and predominant in the foreground, yet always differently formed and shaped, now rejuvenated with surprising modulations and adorned with a wealth of figures and bravura passages, never honoring the beaten track of the routine variation-type; a steady fluctuation of novelty and originality, all in the purest flow, pleasantly ordered and connected, as if pouring out of a horn of plenty, so rounded and blended into an intelligent whole, as if the inventions of the moment were the ripened fruit of well-considered art-study. (AMZ 1835, 706)

A further aspect of Bocklet's fantasy style that emerges clearly in contemporary reception is a tendency to improvise at great length. Adami described a free fantasy on a single theme that lasted a full half-hour (*Wiener Theater-Zeitung* 1835, 1015). A sense of perpetual discursive unfolding distinguished him from figures who, like Hummel, were more likely to build a linear trajectory toward a culminating point: "[he] varies, modulates and figurates so fluently and easily that he would, if it were physically possible, continue improvising all day" (*Humorist* 1846, 267). A less generous critic judged that "it was spun out a bit too far" (WAMZ 1846, 135).

Though Bocklet's improvisations were strongly aligned with conservative and "classic" musical values, there are hardly any references to the fugal, contrapuntal, and imitative styles so often noted in Hummel. Where his playing projected "learnedness," it was more a matter of fluency, inner organic connection, and distance from popular material than of contrapuntal signifiers.[83] He was not a kapellmeister with a significant reputation as a composer, and he did not carry an aura of traditional authority or learnedness. Because of this more modest persona and the "heavenly length" of his extensions, his improvisations submitted more easily to the literary tropes of romantic criticism stressing inspiration, flights of spirit, and exalted moods. As he improvised on Beethoven's *Allegretto*, one critic wrote, "Bocklet, seized by the creating spirit, disjoined from the present moment, and sunk in the images of his bold imagination, improvised unusually long; but for the enchanted listeners it seemed like only blessed minutes" (AMZ 1835, 568). An exceptionally "literary" music journalist went so far as to note a difference in Bocklet's persona when playing classic works and when improvising: "there is a distinctive, artistic measuredness in his expressions that seems to ward off the poetic powers. . . . On the other hand he rises to creative potency in improvisation: his unrestrained playing gets more fiery, more accented, more ideal, and masterfully directs our feelings and thoughts. He shifts his magical throne to the ocean of imagination" (*Wiener Zeitschrift* 1839, 127).

Bocklet, in sum, forms an exception to two tendencies. First, his remarkable flexibility of invention in free playing was not joined to significant achievements or even aspirations in the realm of composition. His professional identity derived mostly from his status as a teacher and as a performer of classic works written in a noble or elevated style. Second, Bocklet's reception indicates that the values associated with classic works were fully compatible with those of improvisation, so long as improvisation did employ popular material or use decorative styles of elaboration to the exclusion of learned developmental and modulatory techniques. His brief, celebrated resurgence as an improviser in 1835 demonstrates that there was no *a priori* conflict between the reverence for works and composers, on the one hand, and free fantasies on the other. Indeed, his pivotal improvisation on the Beethoven *Allegretto* combined improvisation with reverence for the great composer. For Bocklet as for Hummel, free fantasies formed part of the artist's "elevated" standing.

POINT OF CULMINATION: MENDELSSOHN

> What this little man can do in extemporizing and playing at sight borders on the miraculous, and I could not have believed it possible at so early an age.
> GOETHE, 1821

Although trends of the 1830s and 1840s militated against the survival of free keyboard improvisation, the kapellmeister network gave forth one last, sterling example in Felix Mendelssohn. Mendelssohn was the most versatile of all keyboard improvisers, demonstrating equal fluency in the invention of fugues, chorale preludes, concert fantasies on two or three given themes, fantasias that introduce a composed rondo, cadenzas to concertos by Mozart and Beethoven, continuo accompaniments, melodrama accompaniments, variations, and other less conventionalized effusions, as demanded by the occasion.[84] He improvised on the widest possible range of subjects: motives from Handel choruses, fugues by Bach and Mozart, opera tunes, drinking songs, chorales, folk songs, national hymns, opera overtures—even, curiously, the opening of Beethoven's Ninth Symphony—and he had an unusual knack for adapting the style of the improvisation to the material at hand. Mendelssohn was also the least controversial of all improvisers. There is not a hint of dissatisfaction found in any accounts of his playing, and writers never exploited the occasion to make gratuitous criticisms of improvisation as a decadent or dilettantish practice.[85] This may simply reflect Mendelssohn's uncanny ability to defuse all forms of resistance. As one contemporary observed, "this was a personality who won love and respect from everyone coming into contact with him."[86] But there is little reason to doubt that his improvisations possessed a perfection, fluency, and charm setting him apart from his contemporaries. The specific virtues of his improvisations were already evident when Hiller heard him in 1825:

> Choruses from "Judas Maccabaeus" had been sung.—Felix took some of the principal melodies—namely "See the Conquering Hero"—and improvised [*phantasirte*]. I hardly know what was more amazing—the skillful counterpoint, the fluidity and calm with which the waves of sound streamed forth, or the fire, expression, and extraordinary technique that characterized his playing. He must have been deep in Handel around that time, for the figures in which he situated himself were thoroughly Handelian; the power and clarity of his passages in thirds, sixths, and octaves were truly great—and yet it emerged purely from the theme, with no pretention to virtuosity, all music, true, living, organic music. It swept me away. As often as I heard his wonderful playing in later years, it can hardly have had such a ravishing effect on me as the sixteen-year-old boy had on me on that occasion.[87]

Mendelssohn's childhood piano teacher Ludwig Berger probably did little to cultivate his improvisation skills. Berger had been a pupil of Clementi, in whose pedagogy improvisation played no significant part, and who was not an improviser of any note. Rigorous theoretical studies with Zelter in counterpoint and harmony must have enhanced Mendelssohn's extemporaneous skills, but this training took the form of written exercises rather than practical modeling at an instrument. Zelter was mainly a conductor and composer working in the realms and song and choral music—a rare example of a *Musikdirektor* with minimal instrumental skill. Nor is it obvious that the young Mendelssohn took cues from touring virtuosos. According to R. Larry Todd he was "oblivious to the music of virtuosi such as Hummel, Kalkbrenner, or Weber, all of whom were appearing in Berlin during the 1820s."[88] Young Mendelssohn's exposure to free improvisation was probably limited to his teacher August Wilhelm Bach, organist at the Marienkirche, who had been accompanying Lutheran services since his childhood. We do not know much about A. W. Bach as an improviser, but the impact of extemporaneous organ traditions on Mendelssohn's future as an improviser was profound, since he continued to improvise brilliantly on both organ and piano, in equal measure, for the rest of his life. Indeed his dual expertise on piano and organ ensured that his free fantasies preserved Hummel's learned-popular amalgam at a historical moment when other pianists were dropping the learned style altogether.

Although the combined influences of Zelter and A. W. Bach made Mendelssohn a product of the kapellmeister network, he did not have a clear role model prescribing a specific method or approach. More than any other keyboardist discussed here, his improvisations arose from raw talent, opportunity, and inner inclination. Like his fellow improvising child prodigy Franz Liszt, he had a phenomenal memory and assimilated new musical information instantly and permanently. Unlike Liszt, however, Mendelssohn was already in childhood composing prolifically in a variety of genres, and his improvisations seem to extend from this general productive exuberance rather than from some external pressure or public demand. The disjunction between Mendelssohn's kapellmeister-like theory training and his inclinations as a pianist came to the fore when Zelter took him to Weimar to play for Goethe in 1821. The first test was to improvise on a simple song by Zelter. According to Ludwig Rellstab, who was present, Mendelssohn replayed the song by ear, picked up the rolling triplet figure in the accompaniment, and immediately launched "the wildest Allegro" full of tumult and dramatic contrasts, apparently leaving Zelter's melody in the dust.[89] Zelter greeted this pianistic display coolly, as if somewhat embarrassed. This was not what he had taught his student to do! Such stormy, romantic music reflected the more modern styles Mendelssohn was experimenting with in his free compositions.

Mendelssohn looked askance at the vogue for free fantasies that Hummel and Moscheles had created, and when he returned to Weimar in 1825 to play for Goethe's circle a second time he saw to it that his improvisations made a better impression.[90] During a Paris sojourn of the same year he witnessed Liszt enrapturing audiences with "wretched" improvisations—the effusions of a musician "with lots in the finger but little in the head."[91] As serious critics like Kanne and Fétis became more vocal about modern virtuosity and its degradation of improvisation, Mendelssohn began developing a bad conscience. Yet he needed more than ever to impress audiences in the expected ways. Outside of Berlin he had acquired a reputation as a "dilettante" or "gentleman" composer, and he was making efforts to establish a solid professional identity. He therefore went to Munich in 1831 with the intention of making his compositions known and landing an opera commission.[92] Making rounds through salons and high society, he chafed at pressures to improvise at the concert he was about to give: "I must unfortunately improvise, which, believe me, I don't enjoy, but the people are counting on it."[93] After the concert, which drew an audience of 1,100, he expressed great frustration with the closing improvisation, for which the king had given "Non più andrai":

> I have become quite firm in my opinion that it is nonsense to improvise in public. Rarely has anything gotten me so down as the way I sat down there to play my fantasy for the public. The people were very satisfied and would not stop clapping—they called me back—the queen said everything courteous; but I was annoyed, for it had displeased me, and I will never again do it in public; it is abuse and nonsense simultaneously.[94]

The vehement tone of this resolution makes it a remarkable historical document. Two decades earlier, Carl Maria von Weber and Meyerbeer had gladly improvised for private circles, royal patrons, and the public of Munich in order to establish themselves and promote their forthcoming operas (see Chapter 1). But now, in Mendelssohn's eyes, piano improvisation had become a toxic site, exposing the public's lack of good artistic judgment, or a lack of true understanding between artist and audience. Pragmatically, however, he got what he wanted. The opera commission came through, and it was soon followed by a kapellmeister appointment in Düsseldorf. In this sense, at least, he was replicating the trajectory of Weber and Meyerbeer.

Mendelssohn did not keep his resolution to stop improvising. Once established as a kapellmeister, he seems to have lost many of his qualms. His deepening personal and artistic relationship with Moscheles, which included the dual improvisations described earlier, may have made him more open to free fantasies in public. Moscheles may also have modeled the technique of uniting and counterpointing disparate themes, which is rare in Mendelssohn's earlier improvisations and is more typical of the more popular, public free fantasies. But Mendelssohn's change in social status was probably the main cause of his more flexible attitude. He was no longer in the role of the freelance virtuoso-composer, playing for his own profit to an unfamiliar audience, but had become a kapellmeister—a conductor and concert-leader serving a civic community that knew and respected him, mostly in performances of other people's music. With this new social identity his free fantasies took on a different social meaning. At an 1834 concert in Düsseldorf where he conducted the *Zauberflöte* overture and parts of Handel's *Israel in Egypt*, he concluded with a "freie Fantasie" drawing on salient motives from those works.[95] He thus seized the event of improvisation to tie together the event's constituent threads—not only the works on the program but also the community of performers and listeners, which now found condensed representation in the person who had overseen, coordinated, and directed the concert. Mendelssohn's solo performance projected him as a hero, but a hero constituted in mutual relation with the community he served.

This ritual of leader-audience community became the hallmark of Mendelssohn's public improvisations, especially after becoming *Musikdirektor* at the Leipzig Gewanddhaus in 1835. His growing association with England, too, led to especially frequent organ performances where he played classic works and free improvisations in roughly equal measure.[96] As his celebrity magnified itself, he appeared at a Gewandhaus concert playing Beethoven's "Emperor" concerto and conducting the optimistic, inspiring third-act finale of Beethoven's *Leonore*. After the latter piece, while spirits were still running high, he returned to the piano for an unannounced encore: "A free fantasy on the themes of finale that had just been performed so well [*Leonore*] was greeted with resounding joy from the moment the artist appeared on stage, and after the themes were delivered in artful, complex interweavings to the attentive and crowded audience, thunderous gratitude resounded through the hall and closed off the first half" (AMZ 1837, 12–13). Mendelssohn did not treat Leipzig audiences to such improvisations very often. When he did it again in 1839 it was by public demand:

He responded to a request—expressed publicly the day of the concert, and urgently repeated by the aroused public through loud acclamations—and he shared with us, as he already did two years ago, the genius of his free improvisation on the pianoforte. His fecund mind, his deep harmonic knowledge, the agile ease with which he commands all artistic forms, posing and solving the most complex contrapuntal problems in the moment, manifests itself here in the most remarkable manner. He took the main motive of the fantasy from Beethoven's "Adelaide"; after developing this in a varied and interesting manner he continued with a strict figural phrase on a theme of his own invention, which he artfully wove with the first principal theme and eventually treated to a crescendo so brilliant that the effect on the listeners could only be extraordinary. It was a delightful, rare pleasure that only a pure artist like Mendelssohn is capable of offering, and for which we cannot thank him enough. (AMZ 1839, 175)

These descriptions suggest that Mendelssohn was now working from Hummel's basic model, evolving from the elaboration of attractive melodies toward a fugal culmination point, thus combining pleasing and learned musical styles.[97] Mendelssohn, however, inflected the tone "higher" by choosing melodies from Beethoven, the local deity of the Gewandhaus, rather than from the storehouse of folk tunes and comic opera melodies other virtuosos tended to use. The writer's emphasis on the warm reciprocity between kapellmeister and public is also different from the discourse around Hummel, in which admiration for the kapellmeister's artisanal mastery outweighed sentiments of love and sympathy.

In the 1840s Mendelssohn made a habit of incorporating his *Songs without Words* into his free fantasies as the main lyrical material. At an 1843 Gewandhaus concert conducted by Hiller, Mendelssohn appeared after the orchestra had played overtures and opera scenes in order to play a handful of his *Songs*. When the applause would not end,

he sat down again at the instrument and improvised on some of his Songs and the head-motive of the just-performed overture to *Euryanthe*, as well as the aria from *Oberon*; we know quite well that to improvise the way he does is a credit to heaven no less than to the artist; only a few people have ever been so richly gifted as him in this. . . . We have never seen our restrained Gewandhaus concert public in so enthusiastic a state as after this brilliant improvisation of Mendelssohn. In equal measure as this lively sympathy honors the minds and education of our public, may it also be a sign to Mendelssohn that, in us, his artistic effort has found a fertile ground for ripe fruits. (AMZ 1843, 741–42)

By incorporating music of a private or domestic character, Mendelssohn gave his fantasy an intimate spin uncharacteristic of the genre and inscribed it with his authorial signature. Figuratively, the improvisation was "about" Mendelssohn's status as a modern German artist, in dialogue with the deceased Weber—each composer represented by two motives. Yet as the critic's latter words indicate, it was also about the community to which Mendelssohn belonged and the sense of beneficent reciprocity between artist and public. This reciprocity could be recognized any number of ways, but the improvisations, by condensing public and private, classical and modern, and by tying together the pieces just played, performed forth this relationship in a heightened, concentrated expression. At the apex of his celebrity, Mendelssohn's public had widened far beyond that of Leipzig to include the German nation as an imagined whole. On the third and final day of the Lower Rhine Music Festival of 1842 he "played the E-flat major concerto of Beethoven and some of his *Songs without Words*, and after that made the principal themes of the entire festival heard once again in a free fantasy" (AMZ 1847, 902). Thus did he extend his "résumé" fantasy model to encompass the entire festival and project himself as its prime mover—a performance of community united under its kapellmeister.

CONCLUSION: SOLOIST AND SOCIETY

The rapturous written accounts of improvisations by Hummel, Moscheles, Mendelssohn, and others have an air of the unreal about them. The performances they describe lack nothing in terms of instrumental technique, stylistic flexibility, smoothness of connection, decisiveness of delivery, or listener satisfaction. This fictive sense of completeness and wholeness, which the writer has the privilege to conjure without contradiction since the phenomenon has already passed, was beginning to congeal into a literary trope. It was becoming a standard, widely imitated way of writing about improvisation in the vastly expanding field of music journalism in the 1820s—a field occupied not only by music experts but also by theater critics and freelance writers of diverse backgrounds. Music journalism was in this respect the principal medium of the musical improvisation imaginary—that is, the representational rhetoric that constructs improvisation as a "perfect" performance. This rhetoric peels itself away from music as phenomenon, event, or experience, but loops itself back into listener experience when it generates expectations, beliefs, and ideas that filter or frame their perceptions of what is happening in improvisation. Rumors and reports about Hummel's brilliance in free fantasies, in other words, ensured that listeners would be predisposed to perceive them as masterpieces, regardless of how well they were actually played. And as seen in reception of Moscheles, perceptions of musical improvisation were also being fed by romantic conceptions about folk bards and of Italian *improvvisatore* of poetry.

But the improvisation imaginary forming around Hummel and Moscheles was still in its infancy. Their free fantasies were in little need of literary supplementation because living practices of improvisation were still relatively vital, supported by the traditional training methods of the kapellmeister network and newly energized by the emergent public concert life of the post-1815 period, which opened new fields of opportunity and entrepreneurship for piano virtuosos. What critics wrote about improvisation in this period was, in comparison to later periods, relatively concrete and transparent to the phenomena of improvisational performance. It conveyed a relatively differentiated sense of the styles, situations, and comparative merits of the free fantasies under discussion. When this discourse idealized improvisation, it highlighted the pianist's learned mastery of musical languages and the successful communication between audience and player. Ethically and socially, improvisation was valued as a performance of worthy authority and inspired community. Driving this idealization was the anxious recognition, mostly on the part of the musicians' guild, of divisive forces in modern concert life that were widening the gap between connoisseurs and dilettantes, between educated and lay listeners, and between the professional sphere and the public sphere. The free fantasies of Hummel, Bocklet, and Mendelssohn promised that these social divisions might be transcended and healed.

Many of the keyboard improvisers discussed here successfully transitioned from the kapellmeister network into the public concert sphere with the use of styles and practices that made solo improvisation a discourse of community. Theorizations of improvisation in the CSI school have generally taken collective, group improvisation as a default norm.[98] They tend to interpret improvising musical ensembles as a microcosm of participatory and democratic processes through the flexible adaptation of individuals to one another's "voices" and to the shifting dynamics of the performance event. If group interaction is treated as the core of all socially meaningful improvisation, solo improvisation can easily be made to look like the epitome of the western individualism, supporting anti-dialogic values through an exaggerated investment in subjective autonomy. Although there have been extraordinary solo improvisers within the jazz and experimental traditions CSI concentrates upon—Art Tatum, Cecil Taylor, Eric Dolphy, Han Bennink, Evan Parker—it is difficult to see how, by this criterion, their improvisations can be construed as socially engaged in any sense. Is solo improvisation, by virtue of its format, always a performance of sovereign and heroic individuality—that is, of a "closed" subject that has foreclosed dialogue as part of the creative process? This position would essentially deny that solo improvisation is possible at all, since it would deny that a solo person can open the self to the alterity of the spontaneous impulse or the countersubjective agent.

The apparent difference between solo and group improvisation, as paradigms of social and political behavior, can be challenged by calling into question the literal analogy between performing group and social group. The theory of group improvisation as democratic social process privileges the format of musical performance to the near exclusion of music's linguistic or symbolic dimension. Jazz scholar David Horn has identified this problem in relation to one of jazz history's most celebrated soloists, Art Tatum: "Tatum performed most frequently as a soloist and has been judged as such, complete with all the trappings of a monological individualist, insufficiently interested in understanding others."[99] Horn's solution is to identify the multiple languages and styles, "dialogues" and "intertexts," that Tatum plays off against one another within a single improvised performance. The solo improviser does not impose his "self," but gathers up a multiplicity of voices and adopts a range of discursive positions. His subjectivity is already split, already distended, already opened out to the social, and the interest generated by the improvisation depends upon this circumstance. The principle of dialogue, in other words, can be located at the level of the musical utterance—the melange of languages and styles—rather than at the level of the performing group's physical constitution.

Hummel produced such dialogues and intertexts by making free fantasies into a meeting and reconciliation of pleasant and learned styles, with their distinct social coordinates. He also opened himself out to audiences by adapting his playing to their listening level according to the needs of the occasion. Hiller quoted a remarkable statement that Hummel made about his compositional process: "when I sit at the piano, I stand simultaneously over in that corner as a listener, and whatever does not speak to me, I do not write out."[100] Here Hummel claims to open his inventing self to an external agency—an "ear" not exactly his own—that might oppose or critique his inclinations, tastes, and intentions. Hummel furthermore labored to ensure that his free fantasies, formerly played mainly in private circumstances, would succeed in the public realm. In his piano treatise he testified to improvising assiduously "for several years in my room," testing out ideas on a few chosen friends, before "hazarding it in public."[101] An obituary from 1837 went further and claimed that the pleasure and creative interest of improvising motivated Hummel to resume his performing career after the Congress of Vienna:

A talent had developed in him that put him above all other virtuosos: that of musical improvisation. In his evening hours he sat down and let his imagination stream forth, reworking sometimes original ideas in varied characters, sometimes pre-existing themes in free, strict, and fugal forms; he tried presenting these in all manner of forms and styles and wove them together with striking, harmonic combinations, and he developed this with a dexterity and security that earned him his greatest successes. (NZM 1837, 154)

The performance of authority that Hummel achieved while playing freely was not that of a heroic individual imposing his distinctive genius upon an audience, but of an artist striving to give the kapellmeister's traditional skills renewed expression and communicative power in the emergent sphere of public music.

NOTES

1. Mark Kroll, *Johann Nepomuk Hummel: A Musician's Life and Work* (Lanham, MD: Scarecrow Press, 2007), xii.

2. Aside from Kroll's biography, the only significant study of Hummel's concert tours is Joel Sachs, *Kapellmeister Hummel in England and France* (Detroit: Information Coordinators, 1977), which gives many extracts from press reports.

3. Kroll, *Johann Nepomuk Hummel*, 275–94 and 309–30. The first edition of the three-volume treatise is *Ausführliche theoretisch-practische Anweisung zum Piano-Forte-Spiel* (Vienna: Haslinger, 1828), though citations are often made to the later French edition: *Méthode complète théorique et pratique pour le piano-forte* (Paris: A. Farrenc, 1838). For a recent interpretation of Hummel's pedagogy see J. Q. Davies, *Romantic Anatomies of Performance* (Berkeley and Los Angeles: University of California Press, 2014), 51–55.

4. In his diaries Moscheles said Hummel excelled in legato touch and a "soft velvety" sound. See Charlotte Moscheles, *Recent Music and Musicians, as Described in the Diaries and*

Correspondence of Ignatz Moscheles (New York: Holt and Co., 1873), 32–33. An anonymous critic noted Hummel's difference from the modern school in 1825: "It was expected that there would be found in his execution not only the highest degree of brilliancy, but the very excess of those difficulties which modern style so much affects. These expectations, however, were ill founded" ("Assemblage of Piano-forte Players in Paris in the Spring of 1825," QMMR 1825, 313). A *Harmonicon* article (1830, 264) clarified the contrast with modern pianists by saying that Hummel's sound was not particularly powerful, and that "his allegro movements were considerably slower than most of the pianists of the present day would have taken them."

5. Hummel, *Méthode complète théorique et pratique*, 468. Hummel's Article 7 is entitled "De l'improvisation," and it closes the third part of his three-part treatise.

6. AMZ 1819, 605. Cited in Franz Xaver Mozart, *Reisetagebuch 1819–1821*, ed. Rudolph Angermüller (Bad Honnef: K. H. Bock, 1994), 67.

7. "Nouvelles étrangères. Berlin, 29 mars," *Revue musicale* 1828, 262.

8. On the role of journalism and periodicals in the formation of a "musical public sphere" see Celia Applegate, *Bach in Berlin: Nation and Culture in Mendelssohn's Revival of the St. Matthew Passion* (Ithaca, NY: Cornell University Press, 2005), 90–113, and Ulrich Tadday, *Die Anfänge des Musikfeuilletons: Der kommunikative Gebrauchswert musikalischer Bildung in Deutschland um 1800* (Stuttgart: Metzler, 1993).

9. On this type of concert see William Weber, *The Great Transformation of Musical Taste* (Cambridge, UK: Cambridge University Press, 2008), 141–49.

10. Christian Sümmerer-Erlangen, "Das Modell des Kapellmeisters Kreisler," in *Hundert Jahre Bamberger Theater: Festschrift zur E. T. A. Hoffmann-Feier*, ed. Karl Schmidt (Bamberg: Hepple, 1908), 40–41. He claims that Böhner "believed his astonishing artistic genius would open all doors for him" (41).

11. NZM 1834, 258. This article comprises reminiscences Böhner wrote for the journal, published in two installments from 1834, 257–59 and 261–63. In these reminiscences he also mentions improvising, in 1818, at the court in Oldenburg on themes given to him by the Princess (262).

12. Böhner lived all the way until 1860, but was mentally unstable and impoverished after experiencing a breakdown in 1820. Schumann met him in 1834 and wrote in a letter: "old Ludwig Böhner gave a concert here yesterday. . . . But he looked so poverty-stricken that it quite depressed me. . . . The day before yesterday, he improvised at my house for a few hours; the old fire flashed out now and again, but on the whole it was very gloomy and dull." *Early Letters of Robert Schumann*, trans. May Herbert (London: George Bell, 1888), 241. The AMZ (1842, 100) reported him playing a free fantasy on a concert in Erfurt as late as 1842.

13. When the Berlin kapellmeister F. H. Himmel put on a concert of his works, his free fantasy was judged "unquestionably the most beautiful [piece]" (AMZ 1814, 156).

14. Horst Heussner, "Der Hofkapellmeister Ludwig Spohr—ein sozialgeschichtliches Porträt," in *Festschrift Hans Engel zum siebzigsten Geburtstag*, ed. Horst Heussner (Kassel: Bärenreiter, 1964), 142.

15. Spohr's peer Friedrich Schneider is another example of the newly empowered kapellmeister. A reputed pianist, organist, and composer in all genres, Schneider in the 1810s held positions in Leipzig as organist at the Thomaskirche and as conductor of the Singakademie and the Staatstheater. After the huge success of his oratorio *Das Weltgericht* (1820) made him a celebrity, he was sought after by the court in Dessau and accepted an appointment there as *Hofkapellmeister*. His main responsibility was to oversee opera productions at court, but the royal house supported his many initiatives to develop the city's musical life with new

educational, choral, and concert institutions, and he became the most sought—after conductor of choral music festivals for about thirty years. His identity as a nationally active conductor and civic musical leader, in other words, quite eclipsed his identity as a representative of the Dessau court. Officially he had to obey court commands, but in practice they had to obey his cultural directives. See William Neumann, *Friedrich Schneider. Eine Biographie* (Cassel: Ernst Balde, 1854), 4–16, 46–47.

16. Ferdinand Hiller, *Künstlerleben* (Köln: DuMont-Schauberg, 1880), 16.

17. *Louis Spohr's Selbstbiographie*, 2 vols. (Cassel and Göttingen: Wigand, 1860-–1861), 2:206.

18. *Hinterlassene Schriften von Carl Maria von Weber*, ed. Theodor Hell, 3 vols. (Dresden and Leipzig: Arnold, 1828), 2:195–96.

19. Ferdinand Ries closed a concert of his compositions with a free fantasy on given themes, among which was the motive B-A-C-H, "out of which he created a beautiful, though brief, fugue" (AMZ 1813, 321).

20. *Franz Liszt, Artiste et société* (Paris: Flammarion, 1995), 125–26. The essay is an 1838 installment of his series *Lettres d'un bachelier ès musique*. For the English language version see Franz Liszt, *An Artist's Journey*, ed. Charles Suttoni (Chicago: University of Chicago Press, 1989), 90. The social values Liszt invokes here are closely related to communitarian and socialist philosophies that he strongly advocated in the 1830s. His association with Saint-Simonism and the ideas of Ballanche led him to see art as a vehicle of social regeneration and a significant antidote to the divisive forces of modern industrial society, and the modern virtuoso as a figure who could contribute to these ends through his priest-like role.

21. Shaena B. Weitz, "*Le Pianiste*: Parisian Music Journalism and the Politics of the Piano, 1833–35" (PhD diss., City University of New York Graduate Center, 2016), 101–103. I am grateful to Shaena for also sharing with me her unpublished paper "'Monochromatic' and 'Polychromatic' Performance: Improvisatory Alteration in Early Nineteenth-Century French Pianism," which elaborates on *Le Pianiste*'s defense of free ornamentation.

22. Carl Czerny, *A Systematic Introduction to Improvisation on the Pianoforte*, ed. and trans. Alice L. Mitchell (New York and London: Longman, 1983 [1829]).

23. Joel Sachs has suggested that Hummel's "typical improvisation included a fantasy-like introduction, themes from popular operas or from the evening's concert or party and a series of free variations, sometimes ending with a paraphrase of the finale of an opera such as *Don Giovanni*" (New Grove). Besides being unclear how an opera finale of such distinct character could be part of a "typical strategy," this description outlines only one among many possible modes of elaboration, and it is not clear enough what "free variations" are. For lack of clear evidence, music historians have generally been forced to imagine an ideal-type of the free fantasy based on the "typical" published concert fantasy of the period 1820–1850, which is assumed to reflect improvisational practice. My approach here does not presume an ideal-type and gathers as much specific information as possible from contemporary descriptions.

24. Hummel was once taken to task by a Berlin critic for improvising on the same melody ("duet of the godmothers from *Maçon*") at appearances in Berlin separated by two years. *Revue musicale* 1828, 262.

25. Robert Stevenson, "Gottschalk in Western South America," *Inter-American Music Bulletin* no. 74 (Washington, DC: Organization of American States, Division of Cultural Relations, November 1969), 13.

26. Czerny, *A Systematic Introduction to Improvisation*, 73.

27. Czerny, *A Systematic Introduction to Improvisation*, 44–47 and 108–12.

28. Hummel, *Méthode complète*, 468. Emphasis added.

29. NZM 1835, 167. On the genre of the improvised potpourri see Czerny, *A Systematic Introduction to Improvisation*, 86–105.

30. *Athenaeum*, 15 May 1830, cited in Kroll, *Johann Nepomuk Hummel*, 131.

31. Cited in Kroll, *Johann Nepomuk Hummel*, 273.

32. Hiller, *Künstlerleben*, 10.

33. Ignaz Moscheles recalled summer-night gatherings at a house outside Vienna involving Salieri, Hummel, and Meyerbeer, where "walks were taken, tableaux arranged, all sorts of musical trifles composed and performed on the spot." See *Recent Music and Musicians, as Described in the Diaries and Correspondence of Ignatz Moscheles*, 9–10. On the genre of the improvised capriccio, see Czerny, *A Systematic Introduction to Improvisation*, 121–26.

34. Czerny, *A Systematic Introduction to Improvisation*, 42–43.

35. Ibid., 86.

36. Foreign musical report from St. Petersburg in *Harmonicon* 1823, 201. The *Harmonicon* report is actually a redaction of the AMZ's report.

37. See the introductory chapter in *The Other Side of Nowhere: Jazz, Improvisation, and Communities in Dialogue*, ed. Daniel Fischlin and Ajay Heble (Middletown, CT: Wesleyan University Press, 2004), 1–44.

38. Hans Erich Bödeker, "Mäzene, Kenner, Liebhaber: Strukturwandel des musikalischen Publikums in Deutchland im ausgehenden 18. Jahrhundert. Ein Entwurf," in *Europa im Zeitalter Mozarts*, ed. Moritz Csáky and Walter Pass (Vienna: Böhlau, 1995), 159–66. On definitions and relationships between the terms Kenner, Liebhaber, Dilettante, Künstler, see Erich Reimer, "Kenner-Liebhaber-Dilettante," in *Handwörterbuch der musikalischen Terminologie*, ed. H. H. Eggebrecht (Wiesbaden: F. Steiner, 1972-). Matthew Riley shows the emerging tension between the two groups in "Johann Nikolaus Forkel on the Listening Habits of 'Kenner' and 'Liebhaber'," *Music & Letters* 84, no. 3 (2003): 414–33.

39. "Kenner," "Dilettanten," "Laien," and "Nichtige." Friedrich Rochlitz, "Die Fuge. Zunächst an Dilettanten und Layen," in AMZ 1813, 309–17.

40. Ferdinand Hiller, *Erinnerungsblätter* (Köln: DuMont-Schauberg, 1884), 103.

41. Ibid., 105.

42. In the definitive biography by Mark Kroll, *Ignaz Moscheles and the Changing World of Musical Europe* (Woodbridge, Suffolk: Boydell Press, 2014), the improvisations are discussed briefly on 164–66.

43. Annette Richards, *The Free Fantasia and the Musical Picturesque* (Cambridge: Cambridge University Press, 2001).

44. Unambiguous examples of potpourri improvisations are rare in Moscheles's reception. At a Leipzig concert he gave his free fantasy on four themes from Mozart, all of them offered by the audience. The reviewer claimed they were elaborated "not in that combinatory development and melting-together wherein Hummel's mastery shines, but in that imposing, controlled unfolding, in which the quieter force of artistic combinations and the full force of the sentimental and lyrical sound forth" (AMZ 1832, 764).

45. The fact that this improvisation was based on a single tune, rather than two or three, might have played a role in directing Moscheles away from variation style. At a later concert where he improvised only on "Carnival of Venice" he treated it "in the most scientific and master-like way; it was sometimes played by the right hand, then by the left, and lastly by both, most ingeniously and in a variety of keys" (*Morning Post*, 2 May 1835). Another of his single-themed improvisations, played at Covent Garden, was singled out for its learning: "Mr. Moscheles performed a Fantasia on the grand Pianoforte. It is quite impossible to give an

adequate idea of his rapid and brilliant execution. . . . He selected a very simple theme for his fantasia, but he pursued it through all the compass of the notes, and introduced so many extraordinary combinations and amazing involutions" (AMZ 1822, 658, quoting the London *Times* of 27 May 1822). This description, with its emphasis on modulations and the migration of the motive, closely resembles those of the young Liszt who, as we will see in Chapter 5, usually improvised on a single theme.

46. Meyerbeer was at this concert and reported it in his diaries, noting that Moscheles "fused the two themes." *The Diaries of Giacomo Meyerbeer*, ed. Robert Ignatius Letellier, 4 vols. (Madison, NJ: Fairleigh Dickinson University Press, 1999), 1:445. Meyerbeer also said that in the *Recollections of Ireland*, also played at this concert, "the two themes were very delicately counterpointed one against the other."

47. Kroll, *Ignaz Moscheles*, 8.

48. Moscheles Skizzenbuch 1823. Gesellschaft der Musikfreunde (Vienna).

49. Quoted in Heinrich W. Schwab, "'Plusieurs fois je me sentis ému jusqu'aux larmes en l'écoutant': Zur Improvisationskunst des Klavier- und Orgelspielers C. E. F. Weyse," *Danish Yearbook of Musicology* 31 (2003), 44–45.

50. F.-J. Fétis and J. Moscheles, *Méthode des méthodes de piano* (Paris: Schlesinger, 1840), 73.

51. Hiller, *Erinnerungsblätter*, 106.

52. My source for this entire account is *Caledonian Mercury*, 26 January 1828, which was itself reproduced from the London *Observer*. An account of this event also appeared in AMZ 1828, 299–300. See also RMM, 135.

53. Angela Esterhammer, *Romanticism and Improvisation* (Cambridge: Cambridge University Press, 2008), 110–28, 78–103. Esterhammer calls 1824 "a banner year for the popularisation of poetic improvisation in England" (73), adding that "Sgricci's pan-European fame in post-Napoleonic Europe left its mark on English Romantic conceptions of spontaneity and performance" (127).

54. On Pistrucci and other Italian *improvvisatore* ca. 1824, see Frances Williams Wynn, *Diaries of a Lady of Quality, from 1797 to 1844* (London: Longman, 1864), 108–110, 124–27.

55. For all his interest in Pistrucci, Moscheles harbored a conventional disdain for popular Italian performing artists, including those who came to London during the entertainment season to make large sums of money. Exasperated by the busy London concert season, he wrote to Edward Speyer: "When an Improvisatore, an unfortunate Carbonara, or a fallen macaroni merchant comes here, he is immediately rewarded." Edward Speyer, *Wihelm Speyer der Liederkomponist 1790–1878* (Munich: Drei Masken Verlag, 1925), 218.

56. Wesley's improvisations are difficult to track down in any detail. Philip Olleson, in his biography *Samuel Wesley: The Man and His Music* (Woodbridge: Boydell Press, 2003), makes only a few scattered remarks about them (137, 205, 301). Nor do Wesley's published letters turn up anything on the topic. A foreign report on London musical conditions from 1819 mentioned that Wesley played fugues "extemporaneously [*auf dem Stegreife*] on any subject given to him" (AMZ 1819, 850). Composer and organist R. J. S. Stevens remembered an 1806 meeting of a musicians' club where Wesley "played upon the Piano Forte, some of the most ingenious and astonishing Combination *of Harmony*, that I ever heard. By way of Finale, *to his Extemporary*, he took the burthen of, *O strike the harp*, and made as simple and pleasing a movement on its subject, that we are all delighted. A rare instance of his *wonderful abilities!*" *Recollections of R. J. S. Stevens*, ed. Mark Argent (Carbondale and Edwardsville: Southern Illinois University Press, 1992), 150.

57. See for example Hiller, *Erinnerungsblätter*, 117–18.

58. Henry F. Chorley, *Modern German Music* (London: Smith, Elder & Co., 1854), 231. For more on this issue see Prelude, n. 31.

59. Hanslick, *Geschichte des Concertwesens in Wien*, 2 vols. (Wien: Braumüller, 1839), 1:221.

60. Compare BAMZ 1824, 14, and *Wiener Theater-Zeitung* 1824, 27. After the Berlin concert Kalkbrenner published a piece, *Les Charmes de Berlin*, op. 71, based on these themes. He also later published variations on "Heil Dir im Siegerkranz" (as "God Save the King," op. 99), and also variations on chosen themes from *Der Freischütz* (op. 77).

61. Hanslick, *Geschichte des Concertwesens*, 1:221. Emphasis added.

62. In Hans Nautsch's study of Kalkbrenner there are very few references to improvisation. One is from an AMZ report on a concert Kalkbrenner played in Frankfurt on 30 November 1804: "at the conclusion Mr. Kalkbrenner played some variations in the pianoforte. The short introduction—a sort of fantasia [*Phantasie*] or whatever you want to call it—was a colorful caricature of chords, passages, leaps and capriolas that I could not enjoy." AMZ 1804, 206; quoted in Hans Nautsch, *Friedrich Kalkbrenner: Wirkung und Werk* (Hamburg: Karl Dieter Wagner, 1983), 14. Henri Herz mentioned in a memoir that he "knew certain improvisers who learned all of their improvisations by heart" in order to avoid the embarrassment of a poor improvisation in public. One wonders if he had Kalkbrenner in mind. See Henri Herz, *Mes voyages en Amérique* (Paris: Achille Faure, 1866), 170–71.

63. For an overview of this quite distinctive friendship see Thomas Schmidt-Beste, "Felix Mendelssohn Bartholdy and Ignaz Moscheles," in *Felix und seine Freunde: Vortragsreihe Frühjahr 2006*, ed. Veronika Leggewie (Lahnstein: Rudolf Kring, 2006), 69–91.

64. *Briefe von Felix Mendelssohn-Bartholdy an Ignaz und Charlotte Moscheles*, ed. Felix Moscheles (Leipzig: Duncker & Humblot, 1888), x.

65. Ibid.

66. On this term and its relation to jazz see Nathaniel Mackey, "Paracritical Hinge," in *The Other Side of Nowhere*, 67–72.

67. Quoted in R. Larry Todd, *Mendelssohn: A Life in Music* (Oxford: Oxford University Press, 2003), 197–98.

68. AMZ 1840, 117–18; as quoted in Todd, *Mendelssohn*, 197.

69. Jean-Pierre Bartoli, "L'esprit de fantaisie dans l'oeuvre de Jan Ladislav Dussek," in *Jan Ladislav Dussek (1760–1812): A Bohemian Composer en voyage through Europe*, ed. Roberto Illiano and Rohan H. Stewart-MacDonald (Bologna: Orpheus, 2012), 439.

70. Reminiscence by tenor Julius Muller from the period 1804–1806, cited from an archival source in Frank Ziegler, "Carl Maria von Weber als Klaviervirtuose," in *Weber-Studien 9*, ed. Markus Bundur, Manuel Gervink, and Frank Ziegler (Mainz: Schott, 2014), 39.

71. Heinrich Henkel, *Leben und Wirken von Dr. Aloys Schmitt* (Frankfurt a. M.: Saarländer, 1873), 20. I have been unable to locate a copy of this composition, which was published by Trautwein in Berlin.

72. Hiller, *Erinnerungsblätter*, 93–94.

73. Ferdinand Hiller, *Briefe an eine Ungenannte* (Köln: DuMont-Schauberg, 1877), 21.

74. Hiller, *Künstlerleben*, 10 ("Improvisationen, die ich intime Auslassungen nennen möchte").

75. Ibid., 10–11.

76. Ibid.

77. Ferdinand Hiller, *Aus dem Tonleben unserer Zeit* (Leipzig: Leuckart, 1871), 62–63.

78. Franz Schoberlechner was another Hummel student who concertized extensively, but perhaps because he was extremely itinerant, his improvisations are difficult to track down.

In his autobiography he discussed an 1823 tour through Russia, the Baltic states, Prussia, and Saxony, where "in each of these concerts I improvised on the piano with especially great applause." See "Franz Schoberlechner: Ein Kosmopolit aus Wien in seiner Autobiographie," in *Figaro là, Figaro quà: Gedenkschrift Leopold M. Kantner (1932–2004)* (Wien: Verlag der Apfel, 2006), 111–26. The AMZ occasionally mentions him playing free fantasies in later years (e.g., 1827, 23; 1833, 618) but never provides any further detail. An obituary in AMZ 1839, 437–40, gives his life itinerary but does not make any special mention of improvisations.

79. Willmers played a second concert in Dresden where the free fantasy was frankly described as a failure, further suggesting that the first concert review was a "puff." See AMZ 1838, 876.

80. In its earliest years the Prague conservatory did not formally teach piano or keyboard, but only orchestral instruments. This may explain the peculiar circumstance that Bocklet, shortly after moving to Vienna, gravitated increasingly toward the piano as his main instrument. See Johann Branberger, *Das Konservatorium für Musik in Prag* (Prague: Verlag des Vereins zur Beförderung der Tonknust in Böhmen, 1911), 41–44.

81. There is almost no secondary literature on Bocklet. A brief discussion can be found in Elizabeth Norman McKay, "'Zur Eiche' (The Oak Tree) shrouded in Mist," in *Schubert und seine Freunde*, ed. Eva Badura-Skoda, Gerold W. Gruber, Walburga Litschauer, and Carmen Ottner (Vienna: Böhlau, 1999), especially 269–70.

82. The rhythmic motive subtending Beethoven's theme makes it exceptionally flexible and adaptable to harmonic and melodic developments and digressions, and it was a favorite basis for both composed fantasies and free fantasies for about twenty years. Hummel had improvised on it at a concert ten days after Beethoven's death, "obviously in a very elevated mood" (Hiller, *Künstlerleben*, 59).

83. A report in AWMZ, 19 March 1846, claimed his improvisation lacked "contrapuntal richness, depth and significance."

84. Mendelssohn's cadenzas have been the subject of two specialized studies: R. Larry Todd, "Mozart According to Mendelssohn: A Contribution to *Rezeptionsgeschichte*," in *Perspectives on Mozart Performance*, ed. R. Larry Todd and Peter Williams (Cambridge: Cambridge University Press, 1991), 158–203; Angela R. Mace, "Improvisational, Elaboration, Composition: The Mendelssohns and the Classical Cadenza," in *Mendelssohn Perspectives*, ed. Nicole Grimes and Angela Mace (Aldershot: Ashgate, 2012), 223–48.

85. For a survey of Mendelssohn's improvisational activities, see R. Larry Todd's exhaustive biography *Mendelssohn: A Life in Music*. The index entry for Mendelssohn as improviser is found on 671.

86. Karl Schorn, *Lebenserinnerungen: Ein Beitrag zur Geschichte des Rheinlands im neunzehnten Jahrhundert*, 2 vols. (Bonn: P. Hanstein, 1898), 1:150.

87. Ferdinand Hiller, *Felix Mendelssohn-Bartholdy. Briefe und Erinnerungen*, 2nd ed. (Cologne: DuMont-Schauberg, 1878), 4.

88. Todd, *Mendelssohn*, 57.

89. Ludwig Rellstab, *Aus meinem Leben* (Berlin: J. Guttentag, 1861), vol. 2, 140–41. Hummel was not present at this audience even though he was based in Weimar. In his description of Mendelssohn's improvisation Rellstab claimed that the young musician "might have had in mind Hummel's style and manner of executing such tasks" (140), but in fact Mendelssohn had probably not yet heard Hummel play.

90. *Goethes Gespräche*, ed. F. von Beidermann and Wolfgang Herwig (Zürich: Artemis, 1971), vol. 3/1, 755.

91. Cited in Todd, *Mendelssohn*, 144.

92. Ibid., 150.

93. Letter of 6 October, 1831, in Felix Mendelssohn, *Sämtliche Briefe*, vol. 2, ed. Anja Morgenstern and Uta Wald (Kassel: Bärenreiter, 2009), 403.

94. Felix Mendelssohn Bartholdy, *Briefe aus den Jahren 1830 bis 1847*, ed. Paul Mendelssohn Bartholdy and Carl Mendelssohn Bartholdy (Leipzig: Hermann Mendelssohn, 1889), 214–15. Letter dated 18 October 1831.

95. Todd, *Mendelssohn*, 296.

96. Wm. A. Little, *Mendelssohn and the Organ* (Oxford: Oxford University Press, 2010), 90–103. Another valuable study of Mendelssohn's organ improvisation, based on fragments written down apparently in preparation for a free fantasy, is R. Larry Todd, "New Light on Mendelssohn's *Freie Phantasie* (1840)," in *Literary and Musical Notes: A Festschrift for Wm. A. Little*, ed. Geoffrey C. Orth (Bern: Peter Lang, 1995), 205–18.

97. The learned component was also remarked upon at his first 1835 Gewandhaus concert: "The conclusion of the richly satisfying concert was a free fantasy by the celebrated master, which came off so well and was developed in such sturdy, complex combinations, that we never heard him improvise better" (AMZ 1835, 706).

98. In his classic book in *Improvisation: Its Nature and Practice in Music* (New York: Da Capo Press, 1993 [1980]), Derek Bailey gives solo improvisation separate attention and takes a relatively generous stance toward it. His comments nevertheless tend to reinscribe group improvisation as a norm: "For most people improvisation, although a vehicle for self expression, is about playing with other people and some of the greaest opportunities provided by free improvisation are in the exploration of relationships between players. In this respect solo improvisation makes no sense at all" (105). He further claims that although solo improvisation affords "greater cohesiveness and easier control," these qualities "are not, in improvisation, necessarily advantages and an even greater loss, of course, is the unpredictable elements usually provided by other players" (106).

99. David Horn, "The Sound World of Art Tatum," *Black Music Research Journal* 20, no. 2 (2000), 256.

100. Hiller, *Künstlerleben*, 6.

101. Hummel, *Méthode complète*, 468. Emphasis added.

3

Carl Loewe's Performative Romanticism

IN EARLY-NINETEENTH-CENTURY GERMANY, composers of songs faced a formidable challenge in the genre of the ballad (*Ballade*). How could one set to music a long narrative poem that unfolded its story in dozens of identically structured strophes? A strophic setting would risk becoming too repetitive, but a through-composed setting, if it aimed to capture the story's turns and character-voices, might sound like an opera scene and thereby violate the lyric boundaries of song. In the midst of this dilemma there emerged Carl Loewe (1796–1869), who made his name as an exponent of the musical ballad. Loewe thoroughly explored the narrative and dramatic potential of the genre and earned nicknames such as "the north-German Schubert" or "Germany's ballad-singer." His reputation as a song composer made him a strong seller in the mid-century sheet-music market, and he published a voluminous output of vocal works. Studies of Loewe have focused on his contributions to the history of the Lied, detailing the thoughtful strategies for setting the poems of classic and romantic authors.

The focus on his published output, however, has obscured his activities as an adventurous performer who pushed the boundaries of improvisation in an unexpected new direction. In the 1830s and 1840s he gained international attention by taking his ballads on recital tours and performing them solo, taking both the vocal and piano parts simultaneously. This was already a rare and remarkable feat, but the *pièce de resistance* arrived at the conclusion of the "ballad evenings," when he invited audience members to send poems forward. After selecting a poem he would place it on the keyboard stand, pause a few moments to reflect upon it, and proceed to improvise an entire setting—both vocal part and piano part—on the spot. This remarkable display of skill, invention, and musicianship had virtually no predecent. What prompted Loewe to attempt this phenomenally difficult and risky task? What musical techniques did he draw upon? How did audiences react to these performances? And why did Loewe, though greatly admired as performer and teacher, fail to produce imitators or successors?

Loewe's motivation to improvise songs grew from an ambition, shared by many German artists of his generation, to establish a higher status for music within the already prestigious literary culture of Goethe and Schiller. Like many of his peers he revered Goethe, and was fortunate enough to be granted an audience with the famous poet in Weimar in 1820. On that memorable occasion Loewe was bold enough to start with his own setting of Goethe's "Erlkönig," and the poet responded by encouraging him to continue refining his drama-inflected approach to the Lied. As Loewe continued to search for the inner affiliations of music and poetry, the *Ballade* genre was the most appealing because it had a built-in conception of performative and narrative presence. Its "voice" was that of a narrating poet, who occasionally switched out of narration into the voice of the story's characters, and by shifting the enunciating voice in this way the genre simulated, on a small scale, the storytelling art of epic bards. It was this dimension of the ballad genre that spoke to Loewe's special talents as a performer and prompted him to experiment with song improvisation. But that is only the literary side of the story. Loewe's capacity to improvise was rooted in the educational principles of the kapellmeister network, which nourished competence and facility in extemporaneous music-making. As a practicing church organist Loewe was improvising on a nearly daily basis, and without this skill set it is difficult to imagine he would ever have been able to improvise entire songs. Loewe's bold experiment with song improvisation thus represents a redeployment of traditional practices of improvisation, putting those practices in service of the literary ideals of Weimar classicism and romanticism and reinforcing improvisation's "poetic" associations in the ongoing development of the improvisation imaginary.

"WALLHAIDE" AND THE ORIGIN OF SONG

Loewe's career as a concertizing singer-pianist and improviser began with a carefully prepared and much celebrated debut in Berlin in 1832. There exists, however, an account of Loewe improvising fifteen years earlier, during his student years, and a careful consideration of this account will shed light on the complex relationship between musical practice and the improvisation imaginary. The unique source relating this youthful improvisation was written by Loewe's daughter Julie in a "Life Portrait" of her father. Her story concerns the origin of his composed setting of Theodor Körner's ballad "Wallhaide." In the year 1817 (Julie relates) Loewe took a long walk with his intimate friend Dessmann through the Thuringian forest, where the shadowy atmosphere and half-fallen castles awakened his fantasy. As evening approached the two men stopped at a parsonage to request hospitality, and the parson, who happened to be a music-lover, asked Loewe to play something: "Loewe picked up a book of Körner's poems, chose 'Wallhaide,' which suited his mood perfectly, and improvised it. In the year 1819 he wrote out the ballad."[1] Julie's story sounds romanticized. Indeed its opening events are spun out from the opening of Körner's poem ("Where yonder crumbling ruins descend/Where the evening light lies gleaming"). Loewe's improvisation takes place as if in a vacuum of human agency. His mood is induced by the sheer presence of nature, and by a happy accident he finds a poem that "suits his mood." The performance takes place in an enclosed shelter, deep within the forest, at maximal distance from the transactions of civilization and society. Apart from the parson's solicitation to play, there is no obligation to an audience or a "public." The circuit of communication is kept within the house and among the three men.

Julie's story, presumably learned from Loewe himself, conveniently situates improvisation at the origin of Loewe's entire career with the ballad genre. The date she gives for the "Wallhaide" improvisation, 1817, immediately precedes the composition of the two ballads—on Herder's "Edward" and Goethe's "Erlkönig"—that made Loewe's reputation. Before he began writing out ballads, the story implies, Loewe freely invented song in unmediated response to romantic poems. The specificity of the dates in Julie's story is conspicuous, and the editor of Loewe's collected ballads took care to inscribe them on the title page: "Improvised and sketched 1817, composed 1819, published 1826."[2] The urge to place improvisation before writing might seem to be a straightforward manifestation of the value romanticism invested in autopoiesis—pure poetic emanation, unmediated by the externalities of social exchange, technology, and learning. But the story also advances a "performa-poesis"—an image of poetry and music coming into being through the medium of the composer-singer-pianist. It aspires to reattach Loewe's published ballads—"dead" sheet music—to the living, performative moment in which they originated. As Angela Esterhammer has argued, early romantic discourse of improvisation, shaped by poetry improvisers, consistently accented this performative, anti-metaphysical "other side" of autopoiesis. The performative element was bound to come to the foreground in Loewe's thinking because the genre's distinguishing feature was its emphasis on the narrator as agent and persona.

A close link between Loewe's ballads and their performance is also suggested by the fact that he waited until 1824 to publish his *Drei Balladen*, op. 1. They had been composed several years earlier, and it appears he wanted to reserve them for his own performance before releasing them to the public. He might well have felt they could not succeed on their own. A reviewer of *Drei Balladen* sensed that Loewe's novel approach to the ballad placed different, unusual demands on the performer:

We would urge all singers who undertake to perform these pieces to renounce any ambition to show off his voice, his style, indeed his dexterity, and give himself over entirely to the composer's influence. But it is also important to keep in mind, that the score is always only dead signs and that it is the singer's task to bring them to life by trying to grasp what the composer wanted through feeling and reflection, and to express what he could never fully express through such signs. (AMZ 1824, 119)[3]

Throughout the nineteenth century, writers described Loewe's ballads using images of singing and performing. The first review of his "Edward" setting asserted that "this poem . . . has been *sung* by the composer with a possibly unprecedented power" (BAMZ 1824, 119), and it was not uncommon for critics to refer to him affectionately as a "ballad singer." Such tropes did not belong to Loewe alone. They formed part of a broader romantic rhetoric that militated against the "dead letter" of the printed word or printed score. Yet the ballad genre called forth this performative supplement more forcefully than other genres, and the image of the improvising singer, which bracketed the mediating score, served it especially well.

Although the "Wallhaide" story seems to be idealized and embellished, it is difficult to imagine Loewe concocting it out of nowhere. Assuming that there is a grain of truth in the story, how might he have improvised such a ballad? A strophic approach seems unlikely because Körner's ballad is thirty-one stanzas in length. A more likely model is the once well-known setting of Bürger's classic ballad "Lenore" by composer J. R. Zumsteeg, a composer of many ballads for solo voice and piano and a major influence on Loewe. Zumsteeg's setting is through-composed, employing a wide variety of styles and topoi to match the immediate dramatic content the poem. Loewe's published "Wallhaide" does the same, and there are many similarities between "Lenore" and "Wallhaide" at the levels of content and form alike.[4] The idea of improvising in a through-composed style may sound extremely difficult in comparison with a strophic approach. But this judgment may only reflect the prestige that through-composition has long enjoyed as somehow higher or more complex than strophic text-setting. Pragmatically speaking, it may actually be more difficult to come up with a satisfying, rounded melody for an eight-line stanza, and to remember it beyond the first iteration, than to invent a through-composed piece. Zumsteeg's through-composed approach in "Lenore" was well within reach of the improvising musician. Its disjointed, mosaic-like approach (already considered a formal weakness by Zumsteeg's contemporaries) releases the improviser from the requirement of having to devise a unifying formal scenario, allowing him to focus on the immediate images and shifts in the poem.

In hypothesizing how Loewe might have come up with musical ideas on the spot, two possibilities come to mind. First, a through-composed approach permits the performer to launch freely into recitative, a style easily invented without preparation and often found in Loewe's longer settings. Second, many German composers and pianists, including Loewe, were able to accompany poetry declamations extemporaneously in the style of the melodrama, using a conventional repertoire of moods and topoi that could be summoned *ad libitum*. Little seems to be known about this practice, but it was quite common at informal gatherings. Giacomo Meyerbeer, in a diary entry from his early years, mentioned attending a dinner where the host "declaimed Bürger's [ballad] 'Lied vom braven Mann' while Vogler improvised on it outstandingly."[5] A few months later Carl Maria von Weber spent a short time in service of a Duke who "had discovered a new pleasure in sitting by Weber's side at the piano and describing fanciful scenes in his mind's eye to an improvised accompaniment."[6] Weber was familiar enough with the practice that he included it in an outline for his novel about a wandering musician: "Makes various connections in a circle, meets a touring declamator, he declaims, accompanies him."[7] The year of the supposed "Wallhaide" improvisation, 1817, an anonymous critic at the AMZ broached the question how composers should approach settings of ballad poetry. He rejected the strophic approach as too redundant, and the through-composed approach as too fragmented. The ideal solution, he proposed, was melodramatic improvisation at the keyboard: "In my opinion and my experience the best way will always be to leave Schiller's ballads entirely to the speaker and, if he is prepared to do so, extemporize [*extemporirt*] music on the pianoforte to the declamation, freely supporting it and filling in the longer pauses" (AMZ 1817, 790). Assuming Loewe was versed in the basic tropes of melodrama accompaniment, it is entirely plausible that he would be able to improvise a setting of Körner's "Wallhaide" in through-composed style. Certain key ideas from the improvisation are likely to have found their way into the worked-out composition he completed two years later, but we can only speculate what they were.

THE KAPELLMEISTER'S TOOLKIT

By any standard, the task of improvising both a melody and an accompaniment simultaneously, while singing and playing, on a poem just offered, is extraordinarily difficult. What skills and forms of training gave Loewe the ability to pull it off? Like most exceptional improvisers, Loewe showed an early aptitude for picking out tunes and harmonies on the piano. An early biographer wrote of his childhood: "once, when he started giving free rein to his imagination at the piano, preluding and postluding, his father muttered to his mother under his breath . . . 'the kid already plays better than me'."[8] Loewe was also a gifted singer, and it was his beautiful and agile voice that earned him an invitation to Halle to study with Daniel Gottlob Türk. Like Vogler in Darmstadt, Türk was the *éminence grise* of the city's music scene—a figure from an older generation who had served as cantor, organist, teacher, and director of performances of large-scale works. Türk trained Loewe in Italianate singing methods and often featured his protégé in arias at oratorio concerts.[9] Loewe was also gifted with a solid musical memory. The songs by Zelter and Zumsteeg that he loved and often played lodged themselves in his fingers, accumulating a storehouse of figures, burned into muscle-memory, from which his improvisations could draw. After a concert in Dresden where he improvised a setting of Tieck's poem "Im Windsgeräusch," he noted that the improvisation "went well . . . the song by Reichardt that I often sung in my youth did not distract me."[10] The comment implies that the first thing entering his mind during a song improvisation was the previous settings he knew, and that he was lucky when those preexisting settings did not impede the invention of new ideas.

Loewe's capacity to improvise was nourished above all by training in harmony, counterpoint, and organ preluding under the guidance of Türk, which furnished him with his rare double-capacity as singer and keyboardist. Türk associated himself with the north German keyboard school and wrote several keyboard-centered treatises. In the treatises on thoroughbass and on piano-playing, he encouraged capable players to improvise cadenzas in order to sustain the attention and interest of listeners. Such training in singing, playing, and improvising laid the foundation for Loewe's future career as a kapellmeister. From 1820 to the end of his life in 1865 he was organist at the Saint-Jacobi church in the Prussian city of Stettin, a position that included duties teaching at the associated school. Although his reputation as an organist did not match his reputation as composer, singer, and pianist, he improvised for services on a nearly daily basis.[11] He was heard improvising outside of church services as well. On a visit to Münster in 1837 he was taken to the city's famous cathedral, together with a few musical admirers, and he found "a beautiful instrument, but out of tune; I found the well-tuned voices and then improvised a half hour. People were pleased with my style of playing."[12] In 1851, shortly after the death of his daughter Adele, Loewe was playing a church service where he was supposed to lead the congregation by preluding on the hymn "Alle Menschen müssen sterben." Instead, a student related, he improvised on the hymn as an expression of his private sorrow: "I have never again heard such organ playing, and indeed it was improvised, but the entire soul of the mourning father gushed forth in a true sea of tones, full of lamentations and sighs."[13] In later years Loewe further made sure his organ students were trained to improvise "interludes to the individual verses of the chorale, which were then still in use, and if necessary to be able to extemporize simple preludes."[14]

Loewe's ideas on organ playing were probably shaped significantly by Türk's teaching, in particular the treatise *On the Most Important Duty of an Organist*, originally published in 1787. This highly pragmatic text focuses on the accompaniment of the liturgical chorales and the freer practices of preluding and postluding. Concerning the free types of improvisation—namely, those not tied to a chorale melody—Türk writes: "The general prelude or free fantasy has the fewest complications because it is less accountable to a beat, modulation, rhythm, etc. than other genres; yet here, too, the organist can show his skill by playing in a serious and considered manner, *appropriate to the content of the song*."[15] Türk demands that the organist's improvisational elaboration support textual content and never exceed it. The playing must remain pious, always respecting the religious character of the rite and never degenerating into "wild and wandering ideas that border on the lascivious."[16] Like other reformers of liturgical organ playing in the early nineteenth century, he requires that the organist create improvisational elaborations supporting the affect appropriate to the chorale text.[17] This simultaneous concentration on textual idea, chorale melody, and embellishment figures—all in the context of liturgical real time—must have helped develop Loewe's capacity to improvise "secular" songs, for his song improvisations demanded a rare kind of mental concentration, requiring him to think about the content of the poem while simultaneously inventing new melodies and devising characteristic figures.

Another trace of Loewe's training in the kapellmeister network was his tendency to make light melodic embellishments. Julie Bothwell described cadential passages where Loewe was inclined, when moved, to add *Praller* or trills.[18] Türk, in the section of his piano treatise devoted to "ornamented fermatas," recommended similar light ornaments in the soprano line, clearly inspired by vocal models.[19] Careful studies of singing practices in Schubert's circle, too, have shown that simpler melodic additions of this kind were normal if not expected.[20] By gracing in this manner Loewe perpetuated performance habits of his late-eighteenth-century predecessors that were quickly becoming archaic. At the same time, Loewe was capable of validating such small alterations with reference to the romantic ideology of inspiration. When an early biographer asked him why he sometimes sang notes not present in the score in "Heinrich der Vogler," the composer retorted: "One does not write such things down; such things are felt!"[21]

Loewe engaged in one further form of song improvisation unrelated to his formal music training. Bothwell claimed that her father composed the song "Prinz Eugen" "in memory of his soldier period, when he himself wrote doggerel rhymes and adapted them to various Tyrtaean melodies."[22] These "Tyrtaean melodies," already encountered in Chapter 2 in connection with Sir Walter Scott, take their name from the ancient Spartan poet Tyrtaeus, who was known for his rousing battle songs. They were simple folk melodies with march-like rhythms that could easily be attached to standard poetic rhymes. Soldiers and university students apparently cultivated these extemporaneous songs as a form of play and social distinction well into the nineteenth century. In 1838 the AMZ reviewed a humoristic novel subtitled "three years at the university" whose hero "improvises the prettiest songs and duels masterfully" (AMZ 1838, 42). As an antique poet, Tyrtaeus also carried associations with the formulaic improvisational style associated with the romantic interpretation of Homer. Thus Hector Berlioz, while traveling through the Abruzzi mountains on his Italian tour, took a particular fascination with a song improviser he called "the Tyrtée companion" because of the poet's repetitions of the same melodic strains. Tyrtaeic singing thus blended with the popular, folkish forms of improvisation found in public squares, inns, and places of popular entertainment.[23] Loewe's "Prinz Eugen," though carefully worked out, stylizes the soldier's improvisation by means of an extremely simple accompaniment without regular meter, and a pattery style of declamation. Loewe furthermore gives the song an antique sheen by borrowing a seventeenth-century folk tune he had found in a collection, and peppering it with march rhythms for military accent.[24] The song documents a "popular" thread of the improvisation imaginary—the mindlessly crooning simpleton—that was elaborated extensively in nineteenth-century comic opera.

THE BERLIN DEBUT

Loewe took song improvisation into the public sphere in 1832, when he traveled to Berlin and mounted a large-scale concert of his own works. For over a decade he had been a dutiful kapellmeister in Stettin as well as a schoolteacher covering subjects as diverse as Greek, Natural History, and Universal History.[25] His reputation as a ballad composer was already established, and he now wanted to establish himself as a composer in larger-scale genres and build a receptive audience for projects in opera and oratorio. Since 1825 he had been waiting in vain for the General Intendant of the Berlin Royal Opera to perform his opera *Rudolph*, which the official court composer Spontini had already approved. He had also composed an oratorio, *Die Zerstörung Jerusalems*, which he hoped to see performed at Zelter's Singakademie. Loewe's campaign for attention in Berlin began in 1830, when he undertook a truly radical performance experiment. The former music director of the *Nationaltheater* in Berlin, Bernard Anselm Weber (d. 1820), had composed a much-discussed melodrama on Schiller's ballad "Der Gang nach den Eisenhammer." Loewe converted this lengthy piece, originally written for declamator and orchestra, into a monodrama by setting the unaccompanied spoken parts for voice and piano, while keeping Weber's orchestral music for interludes. He in essence converted the theatrical declamator of Weber's original piece into a self-accompanying singer.[26] Loewe performed this version of "Der Gang nach den Eisenhammer" with orchestra in Berlin in 1832, not long before his own debut concert. There were many bemused reactions to the novel performance concept, which resembled nothing so much as a concerto for singer-pianist and orchestra. One reviewer found the shuttling between orchestral drama and Lied-like narration too jarring, and suggested that a simple quartet accompaniment would have been preferable (AMZ 1832, 319). Other reporters marveled at the sheer difficulty of playing the piano and vocal parts simultaneously (AMZ 1833, 170).

Shortly after this concert Loewe prepared a new version by transcribing the orchestral parts for piano, thus making it a full monodrama for a single performer. In this form he played it at his 1832 debut, and subsequently offered it to publishers. With this publication Loewe was collapsing the boundaries of between the genres of melodrama, opera, and Lied. His performance condensed multiple modes of performance and enunciation that were usually kept separate: soloistic virtuosity, ballad narration, and stage acting. Such exchanges between theatrical performance and poetic declamation were common in Berlin in this period, though not always at such a high level. At the Potsdam court Loewe witnessed a command performance of the English ballad "Des Bettlers Tochter von Bednall-Green," which had been translated from English into German and set to music by Prince Carl von Mecklenburg:

> The piece was brought to performance in a completely new form. [Eduard] Devrient, accompanied by [Wilhelm] Taubert, stood sideways on the stage and sang the narrating parts of the ballad. Across from him stood other persons who performed their respective solos whenever a speaking character was introduced.[27]

These experiments all shared a desire to reinvent "classic" literary ballads as live performance, rescuing them from their printed condition and restoring to them phenomenal vitality.

It was in a similar spirit that Loewe decided to improvise in public in 1832. He initially planned the Berlin debut as a "grand instrumental and vocal" concert with a varied, mixed program that would draw in connoisseurs, laypersons, and royalty. The logistics proved extraordinarily difficult, but in the end he was able to secure violinist and kapellmeister Carl Möser to lead the orchestra at the Singakademie. He had to forego the participation of the city's leading opera singers, who were required at Potsdam for a royal birthday celebration: "I am thus confined to my own devices. But that is just as well; I would rather stand by myself before the public."[28] Although he described this decision to perform solo as a concession to necessity, he had earlier expressed to Zelter "my intention to present myself as ballad-singer and pianist," as though he ultimately did not want guest singers involved.[29] Loewe seems to have conceived the event, then, as a standard virtuoso concert with an unusual new twist: the virtuoso was both a singer and a pianist (see concert program in Table 3.1). The announced improvisation was an enticement to the public: "Everyone [here in Berlin] is amazed that I want to be up there completely alone at a concert; it is unheard of.—People are excited about my promised improvisation of a Lied or a ballad."[30] Even for audiences familiar with free fantasies on the keyboard, this was a bold move: "Mr. Löwe posed for himself an extremely difficult task by announcing the improvised composition and singing recitative of a lyrical poem lying before him" (AMZ 1832, 235).

As with "Wallhaide," we can only speculate how Loewe went about improvising the song at the concert. Fortunately he left some clues. In the immediate aftermath of the concert he wrote with rare explicitness:

In the second part I had promised an improvised composition. Many poetry books, indeed manuscripts, awaited me. Zelter was about to offer Goethe's "Kennst du das Land" when Duke Anton Radziwill sent me "Die Zauberlehrling" [Goethe's "The Sorcerer's Apprentice"] by way of Dr. Foerster.—The task was indeed very difficult; any mediocre solution would have caused laughter, at the least; for example at the words "welch' entsetzliches Gewässer"; or "Heer, die

TABLE 3.1

Concert of Carl Loewe	
March 10, 1832	
Berlin, Singakademie	
Part I	
Overture to *Rudolph* (Loewe)	Orchestra
Goldschmieds Töchterlein (Uhland/Loewe)	Loewe vc/pf
Herr Oluf (trad. Danish/Loewe)	Loewe vc/pf
Piano Concerto in A-major (Loewe)	Loewe pf w/orch
Part II	
Der Gang nach dem Eisenhammer (Schiller/B. A. Weber/Loewe)	
	Loewe vc/pf w/orch
Improvisation	Loewe vc/pf

Noth is gross."—My courage grew accordingly; I invented a melody that I could use for all strophes with increasing performative intensity, as well as an *obbligato* figure in the accompaniment, and launched an attack on the dragon that I had earlier conquered only in my imagination.[31]

The approach boils down to three elements: a melody devised to be used strophically, an *obbligato* figure in the piano for atmosphere and characterization, and a gradual crescendo by means of vocal and pianistic intensification. Before getting too comfortable with this model, however, we should linger over the first component: the invented melodic strain. Whatever melodic idea Loewe came up with for Goethe's strophes, it cannot have been simple and symmetrical. Each of Goethe's strophes consists of fourteen lines, subdivided into verse and refrain (eight and six lines, respectively) and articulated with metrical shifts (see Figure 3.1). Moreover, the sharp contrast Goethe draws between verse and refrain—it changes both meter and "voice"—cry out for some sort of musical response. Loewe's fear that the poem's climactic lines ("What

Verse	Hat der alte Hexenmeister	Good! The sorcerer, my old master
	sich doch einmal wegbegeben!	Left me here alone today!
	Und nun sollen seine Geister	Now his spirits, for a change,
	auch nach meinem Willen leben!	my own wishes shall obey!
	Seine Wort' und Werke	Having memorized
	merkt' ich, und den Brauch,	what to say and do,
	und mit Geistesstärke	with my powers of will I can
	tu ich Wunder auch.	do some witching, too!
Refrain	Walle, walle,	Go, I say,
	manche Strecke,	Go on your way,
	dass zum Zweke	do not tarry,
	Wasser fliesse,	water carry,
	Und mit reichem, vollem Schwalle	let it flow abundantly,
	Zu dem Bade sich ergiesse!	and prepare a bath for me!
	Und nun komm, du alter Besen!	Come on now, old broom, get dressed,
	Nimm die schlechten Lumpenhüllen	these old rags will do just fine!
	Bist schon lange Knecht gewesen:	You're a slave in any case,
	nun erfülle meinen Willen!	and today you will be mine!
	Auf zwei Beinen stehe,	May you have two legs,
	oben sei der Kopf,	and a head on top,
	eile nun, und gehe	take the bucket, quick
	mit dem Wassertopf!	hurry, do not stop!
	Walle, walle,	Go, I say,
	manche Strecke,	Go on your way,
	dass zum Zwecke	do not tarry,
	Wasser fliesse,	water carry,
	und mit reichem, vollem Schwalle	let it flow abundantly,
	zu dem Bade sich ergiesse.	and prepare a bath for me.

FIGURE 3.1 First two strophes of Goethe's "Die Zauberlehrling" (The Sorcerer's Apprentice, 1797).

a horrible watery mess," "Lord, help me") might become embarrassing suggests that, although his general approach was strophic, he was not holding to a strictly strophic approach. He must have planned to break out into a declamatory utterance at these lines. For these reasons we can safely exclude the possibility that Loewe was inventing or borrowing a simple tune with symmetrical, balanced phrases. Perhaps he would have taken such an approach if he had accepted Zelter's "Kennst du das Land," a lyric poem in three strophes. But he rejected that poem, choosing instead Goethe's lengthier and more dramatically conceived seven-strophe ballad, in which two speaking voices appear alongside the narrator's voice. Loewe was not looking for an easy or formulaic solution to the challenge of ballad improvisation: "The task was indeed difficult."

EXAMPLE 3.1 First strophe of Loewe's setting of "Die Zauberlehrling"

EXAMPLE 3.1 Continued

Loewe published a setting of "Die Zauberlehrling" just months after his concert improvisation, as one of the *Drei Balladen*, op. 20. Aside from "Wallhaide," this is the only published composition that can be linked to one of his known improvisations. We cannot of course presume a direct relation between the improvisation and the published piece, yet a close connection seems likely for many reasons. The published version (Example 3.1) correlates quite closely with Loewe's three-element model. The setting is basically strophic, making some adjustments for the specific content of individual stanzas. There is a sixteenth-note "obbligato" figure in the piano representing the increasingly copious flow of water. And Loewe's third component, the crescendo of intensity, materializes in the score as a gradually thickening accompaniment and a rising vocal tessitura. A relation to improvisation is further suggested by the uncomplicated, formulaic quality of the strophic melody. Harmonically it is elementary, implying plain diatonic harmonies in C-major for the verses. The melodic lines run up and down diatonic scales, outlining simple, iterative sequences, and the piano accompaniment does nothing but double the vocal part. The music of the refrain (at the key change to D♭ major) is even more basic, lingering on a single harmony while the singer bellows out the apprentice's exaltation. The song's phrasing is absolutely foursquare from beginning to end. Indeed, with the exception of the line "Walle! Walle!" Loewe sets each line of text to one measure of music. This may well have been his strategy for handling the poem's irregular line lengths without committing to any particular phrase model or cadence structure. These formulaic musical qualities distinguish Loewe's "Zauberlehrling" from his other composed ballads, which are normally much more complex and variegated in terms of harmony, phrasing, and form. We can thus speculate that Loewe's published "Zauberlehrling" represents a finessed version of the main ideas of his concert improvisation.

FIGURE 3.2 First full strophe of Zelter's setting of "Die Zauberlehrling," from *Sammlung kleiner Balladen und Lieder* (Hamburg: Böhme, ca. 1802).

The AMZ's sole press review of the concert provides a further revealing clue: Loewe's improvised song was "reminiscent of Zelter's own exquisite composition, but nevertheless entirely original" (AMZ 1832, 235). There are in fact many close rhythmic and melodic correspondences between Loewe's printed setting and Zelter's (Figure 3.2). The steady syllabic patter, the scalar melodic outlines, and the refrain's pivot between tonic and dominant pitches are just some parallels. The most conspicuous borrowing takes place at the transition from verse to refrain, where Loewe adopts Zelter's strategy of moving from steady eighth notes to running sixteenth notes. Although Loewe borrows bits and pieces from Zelter's setting, he scrambles and recombines these components, rendering them more modern, more chromatic, and more operatic, especially in the refrain. Zelter's version, then—lodged within Loewe's fingers and memory through repeated play—was probably the musical starting point for his improvised performance. One striking departure from Zelter's model is the final refrain, where the sorcerer's stern voice enters for the first time (starting at "In die Ecke" in

EXAMPLE 3.2 Final measures of Loewe's setting of "Die Zauberlehrling"

Example 3.2). In the published version Loewe sets it off as recitative—a style easily improvised in performance—and it furnishes an appropriately cold, sobering tone for the conclusion. These are the kinds of things that Loewe, when scanning a ballad to plan the improvisation, was likely to notice and mark for special treatment.

THE WANDERING BALLADEER

Contemporary accounts of Loewe's debut improvisation all agreed that it was a resounding success. Zelter himself wrote to Goethe expressing surprise at how well it came off: "The improviser acquitted himself of the task well, for it is no small thing to read away that poem in public without preparation."[32] Encouraged by the positive response, Loewe began taking his unique solo show on the road. During the summer months, when free from his official kapellmeister responsibilities, he made tours to various German, Austrian, and Danish cities and played concerts he called "ballad evenings" or "ballad cycles." Lasting up to two hours, these concerts consisted exclusively of his own compositions—mostly settings of classic texts by the three poets most closely associated with the ballad genre: Goethe, Schiller, and Uhland. For variety he occasionally threw in a piano piece, such as his narrative tone-poem for piano, *Mazeppa*, and he normally concluded with an improvisation on subjects given by the audience.

As seen in Table 3.2, the poems offered to or chosen by Loewe for the concluding improvisations ran the gamut in terms of style and genre. Some were by older poets such as Goethe, Matthison, and Uhland, and some by newer poets such as Ludwig Tieck, Emmanuel Geibel, Ludwig Giesebrecht, or the Jena professor Gessheim. Some were relatively ephemeral poems, such as the one he solicited from the hostess of a lunch or the one culled from the Frankfurt "Almanach of the Muses." Some were *volksthümlich* poems such as "Der Maikäfer" from *Des Knaben Wunderhorn*. A number of the poems suggested were in fact ballads: Uhland's "Das Schloss am Meer," a Danish naval tale "Van Spyk," Tieck's "Im Windsgeräusch," Emmanuel Geibel's "Der letzte Skalde" [The Last Bard], and of course "Der Zauberlehrling." The sheer diversity of these poems in terms of meter, stanza structure, and length indicates that Loewe did not rely heavily on preset melodic or phraseological schemes to achieve his improvisations. In cases where the meter and stanza structure were symmetrical or foursquare, he might well have fallen back on simple lyrical phrases and periodic phraseology—perhaps even preexisting tunes. But Loewe was clearly ready on all occasions to develop more elaborate songs with recitatives and contrasting sections in them. More often than not he judged the performances to be a success. From Breslau he reported that "the improvisation on the poem given by Dr. Kahlert, in particular, went wonderfully," and from Münster: "the improvisation too was favored . . . it went uncommonly well."[33]

The process of choosing a poem for Loewe's improvisations was not entirely arbitrary. Instrumentalists like Hummel and Liszt let their audience suggest subjects from a repertoire of familiar folk songs, opera arias, and national hymns, turning the process into an equalizing exchange with the public, or at least a simulacrum thereof. Loewe, however, was normally "offered" his poem by a member of the artistic or bureaucratic elite. At the Berlin debut of 1832, for example, he was on the edge of accepting Zelter's suggestion, but then turned to the subject offered by Prince Anton Radziwill, a prominent aristocrat, musical dilettante, and composer. Loewe's diaries and contemporary reports typically name the author, public official, or salon hostess who offered the poem. In Dresden it was Ludwig Tieck; in Jena the wife of the President Zigesar; in Köln the "Staatsprocurator Simon." Loewe's improvisations thus had less of a "democratic" social inflection than those of other virtuosos. Indeed the Prussian royals were among his most enthusiastic patrons. Yet his improvisations did not always obey the protocols of such top-down protectorship. A curious dissonance emerged the summer of 1859, long after his touring days had ended, when he found himself giving a concert in Danzig in the presence of Princess Marie von Hohenzollern:

TABLE 3.2

Table of known improvisations by Loewe, based mainly on *Carl Loewe's Selbstbiographie* (ed. C. H. Bitter). Blanks are left where no information is available.

Year	Location	Poet	Poem	Poem given by	Notes
1817	Thüringer Wald	Theodor Körner	Wallhaide	[Loewe]	Anecdote told by Julie Bothwell
1832	Berlin	Goethe	Die Zauberlehrling	Anton von Radziwill, via Dr. Foerster	*Selbstbiographie*, 133-34
1835	Dresden	Ludwig Tieck	Im Windsgeräusch ("Nacht")	Reissiger	"went well . . . the song by Reichardt that I often sung in my youth did not distract me." *Selbstbiographie*, 188
1835	Jena	O.L.B. Wolff	Van Spyk	Fräulein Zigesar	Poems were improvised and immediately written down on two pages. "The improvisation came off quite remarkably well . . . I played it with inspiration. The applause was beyond measure." *Selbstbiographie*, 214-15
1835	Jena	Hofrath Reinhold	Two sonnets	Reinhold	Post-recital dinner at the home of Reinhold. *Selbstbiographie*, 215
1835	Leipzig	Unknown (not one of the standard poems of this title)	Die Nonne		Two-hundred people in the audience. *Selbstbiographie*, 195
1835	Jena	O. L. B. Wolff	Three improvisations	Audience	Wolff improvised three poems, one on Jephtha Daughter, one a "picture of Mary in the Abruzzo mountains." Private soiree, melodrama-style performance. Loewe used an Ave Maria Stellis piece to accompany the "picture of Mary." *Selbstbiographie*, 213

(continued)

TABLE 3.2

Continued

Year	Location	Poet	Poem	Poem given by	Notes
1837	Elbersfeld		Volksverbesserung (from the Rheinische Musenalmanach)	Staatsprocurator Simon	*Selbstbiographie*, 251
1837	Mainz	Ludwig Uhland	Das Schloss am Meere	Prinzessin Wilhelm	"generous applause cheered me up." *Selbstbiographie*, 270
1837	Greifswald			Frau Ziemssen (wife of the Hochgerichtsrath)	Unidentified poem given to Loewe at lunch the day of performance. *Selbstbiographie*, 228
1837	Münster	Matthison	Wenn in des Abends letztem Schein ("Lied aus der Ferne")		"I also had luck in the improvisation . . . it went just right." *Selbstbiographie*, 248
1837	Jena	Dual improvisation with O. L. B. Wolff			Dinner soiree at Keferstein's; melodrama accompaniment; "so gut nicht wie voriges Mal gelang, obschon der Beifall rauschend war." *Selbstbiographie*, 272
1839	Breslau	August Kahlert	Der finstere König		"Especially the improvisation of the poem by Dr. Kahlert went superbly." *Selbstbiographie*, 302-3
1839	Breslau	Prof. Gessheim	Schön Dank, Sänger		*Selbstbiographie*, 308
1846	Erfurt	Schulrat Grafunder	"ein reizendes Lied," probably "Maikäfer"		*Selbstbiographie*, 390

1846	Coburg	Emanuel Geibel	Der letzte Skalde	"Auf die Improvisation spitzt sich Alles. Der Herzog [of Coburg] hat bereits geäussert, er habe doch davon keine Vorstellung, wie so etwas menschenmöglich sein könnte." *Selbstbiographie*, 404; "[es] gelang mir recht gut." *Selbstbiographie*, 406
1846	Jena	O. L. B. Wolff improvisation	Savanarola	Audience *Selbstbiographie*, 384
1846	Weimar			Court concert. *Selbstbiographie*, 396

Loewe had already finished the first half of his program when her majesty approached the song-master with a request that he immediately sing for her a song for which there was not yet any composition. He took the book and read through the text thoughtfully, sat down at the piano and right away sang what his genius offered him. The singer was rewarded with great applause; but as the princess requested he set the tune on paper as he had sung it, the modest man said: "Your majesty, I can't promise that what I write down will come out as it did when given to me in the moment."[34]

Loewe phrases this in the language of deferential humility, but it has mildly subversive tone as well. As the princess tries to make a "claim" on his performance with a souvenir-score, he underlines the ephemerality of improvisation in order to refuse her request, and by extension her protection. Although this improvisation had begun through a gesture of royal protection, it ended as a gesture of artistic defense against royal appropriation.

Loewe's ballad evenings hybridized the conventions of two types of event: the virtuoso concert and the literary salon. They were advertised to the general public and adopted the convention of soliciting themes from the audience, and they possessed a certain formality characteristic of public concerts. Yet they were not as commercial in tone as the "musical-declamatory academies," "evenings," and "entertainments" found all over German-speaking countries from the 1820s through the 1850s, where readings of poetry and drama were mixed with musical performances. Loewe sought audiences of 100–400 people, many of them invited from the educated social circles in which he circulated, and this gave the events a more intimate tone typical of a salon. At a performance in Münster the audience did not even clap, but merely shouted the occasional "bravo!" after each piece, as though clapping might be inappropriate for so intimate a setting. His highly acclaimed cycles in Vienna (1844) were exclusive, private events in the Viennese tradition of the connoisseur concert, and were not reviewed in the main newspapers.

The musical-literary hybridity of Loewe's concerts helps explain his motivation to improvise, for improvisation was enjoying renewed prestige in the literary and philosophical climate of romanticism. As Angela Esterhammer has shown, writers from various European countries celebrated the famous poetry improvisers of Italy, several of whom were actively touring European cities. Improvisers also figured prominently as the central characters of poems, novels, and theater works. Germaine de Staël's 1807 novel *Corinne* had a massive impact beyond the literary world alone. The fictional *improvvisatrice* was familiar to most major musicians. Rossini's 1825 opera *Il viaggio a Reims* has a scene for an improvising character named Corilla who is certainly based on the Corinne-type, and one of his successors, Pacini, did the same with the heroine of his 1840 opera *Saffo*. Hans Christian Andersen entitled his autobiographical debut novel *The Improvisatore*, and with it he launched his international fame in the early 1830s. Women of letters who made their reputations in the 1830s and 1840s were often compared with Staël's heroine. Saint-Beuve dubbed Liszt's partner

Marie d'Agoult "The Corinne of the Quai Malaquai."[35] In Germany, lyric poet Karoline Leonhardt-Lyser made appearances in the early 1840s as an improviser and aroused the admiration of Friedrich Rückert, who called her "Germany's Corinna." Schumann, in one of his literary fantasias, mentioned "Corinna" and "Desdemona" as "names of beauty and youth."[36]

The cult of *Corinne* also had a decisive influence on Loewe. During his student years in Halle, when the city was still under French administrative control, he sang before a select audience that included Madame de Staël herself. After the performance she congratulated him, handed him an eight-Groschen coin, and intervened with local authorities to get him a stipend to study at the university of Halle. Loewe remembered this encounter with irony, since Staël spoke so volubly he could barely get in a word, but his debt to the novel was meant in earnest. In a letter to Prince Radziwill shortly after the Berlin debut he wrote:

> I owe the idea of improvisation in general to my having read *Corinna* by the brilliant Fr. v. Staël, who awakened me to many new things in the region of art, not only concerning feeling but also true spontaneity and the noblest conception of life; without reading Fr. v. Staël I would not at all have had the idea of appearing in Berlin as singer and virtuoso.[37]

Here Loewe downplays the character of Staël's heroine (Italian, feminine, beautiful), accenting instead the "higher" philosophical and ethical principles that Staël allegorically identifies with the *improvvisatrice*. While making a link between improvisation and "feeling," Loewe links it to a more philosophical, noble, and elevated "conception of life." Most important, Loewe considers Corinne, the performer who earns the love of the entire Roman populace with poetry improvisations, a stimulus to his own goals as a performer. Precisely at the historical moment when musical improvisation was losing critical prestige and suffering critical fire as superficial or ephemeral, here was a new, positive validation of the practice and an assertion of its "higher" meaning.

Attention to poetry improvisation in Germany surged when the prodigiously gifted improviser O. L. B. Wolff appeared on the scene. In 1825 and 1826 Wolff undertook a highly publicized concert tour through Germany and other countries, claiming to have validated German as a viable language for mellifluous improvisation on a par with Italian. A young Ferdinand Hiller, studying with Hummel in Weimar, heard Wolff on this tour and recalled the impression: "Wolff was a very beautiful, slim, elegant young man, a predecessor of the modern virtuoso, which at that time had not yet been invented—his face in particular was grand and soulful."[38] Hiller's comparison to modern virtuosos stems not only from the "poetic" looks of figures like Thalberg and Liszt, but also from the practice of accompanying poetry improvisers on guitar, piano, or violin. The instrument's role was to support the ebb and flow of the performance and to provide an aura of exalted, otherworldly utterance. During the period of Wolff's greatest celebrity, writer Wilhelm Waiblinger published for German readers a series of essays romanticizing the Italian poetry improvisers, complete with transcriptions of the melodies used either by the accompanying instrumentalist or by the improvising poet.[39] The image of the *improvvisatore*, whether in novels or poems, Germany or Italy, was bathed in a halo of music.

However popular poetic improvisers were with the public, they had a difficult time satisfying critics and establishment figures. In the late 1820s Wolff published several volumes of original poetry supposedly spun out from his improvisations, but his career took a downward turn when he performed before Goethe and the master faulted him for a too "subjective" mode of delivery. Wolff soon realized that his status as celebrity improviser was working against him in higher literary circles, and that true prestige was to be found in finished, printed poetic works. He gave up his performing career to establish scholarly credentials and eventually became a professor at the University of Jena. Around 1830 another German improviser, Maximilian Langenschwarz, began making tours through Germany carrying out similar feats of free improvisation in diverse meters and rhyme schemes, often performing alongside his wife, who was a singer. But nearly everywhere he went Langenschwarz was suspected of charlatanism and nobody dared compare him with Wolff. The one German improviser who seemed capable of holding his own with Wolff was the lyric poet Emanuel Geibel, who had an extraordinary reputation for the extempore invention of verses though he never showed it in public.

In 1835 O. L. B. Wolff and Loewe crossed paths at a soirée in Jena, and the two became a dynamic duo of poetry-music improvisation in the salons of Jena and Weimar. Loewe in fact took direct credit for coaxing Wolff back to improvisation at one particular soirée: "since [Wolff] became professor here he has no longer improvised. My productions however awakened his desire to improvise so strongly that he caved in to the general wish of the assembly, and three times he recited the most beautiful poems in the most mellifluous verses and strophes with rhymes on given themes."[40] The theme for Wolff's first improvisation—Jephtha's daughter— was given by the poet and historian Ludwig Giesebrecht, and Wolff delivered it while sitting next to Loewe, who improvised accompaniments at the piano in melodrama style. The two teamed up again when Loewe returned to Jena later the same year and the audience proposed a Dutch naval ballad called "Van Spyk." Loewe was not familiar with the subject, so Wolff took five minutes to write up a version on two sheets of paper, which were placed on the piano for Loewe to improvise from. Loewe's perception that "the improvisation went quite especially well . . . I played it with inspiration . . . the applause was beyond measure," was confirmed by another witness, who said he "aroused the greatest enthusiasm through the thoroughly well-executed improvisation of a poem first dictated by Herr Prof. Wolf [*sic*] on a topic that was given to him."[41] In 1846 Wolff and Loewe, again meeting in Jena, improvised simultaneously in melodrama style on "Savanarola."[42] One spectator described the bond between poet and musician as a kind of erotic fusion, praising Loewe's capacity to find "the appropriate musical dress following immediately upon the naked words flowing from the naked hearts and lips of the poet, which then stimulates the poet to ever new and inspired creation."[43]

Melodrama accompaniment of this kind was not rare in German salons. The young Robert Schumann, during a rural adventure, mounted a "musico-dramatic soirée" with his friend at a pub where he "improvised freely upon [Schiller's] 'Fridolin'" and impressed the peasant audience by "flourishing about on the keys in a quite crazy manner."[44] Ferdinand Hiller recalled intimate gatherings with Mendelssohn where music and literature were brought together:

> When our life had become a little quieter so that we often spent the evenings at home, Mendelssohn proposed that we should improvise on given poems. We read and played in turn, each declaiming for the other, and found it a most amusing and stimulating pastime. Heaven only knows how many poems of Schiller, Goethe, and Uhland had to serve us for musical illustrations. After one of my improvisations Mendelssohn said to me, "I can't imagine how you can ever for a moment feel any doubt about your musical gifts."[45]

Hiller's reputation for poetry accompaniment followed him when he moved to Dresden in 1847, where he was often summoned to the court to accompany the ballad recitations of famous actor and singer Eduard Devrient.[46] In 1844 Liszt passed through Weimar and found himself in the company of Prince Radziwill, who expressed a desire to hear a reading of Goethe's *Faust*. O. L. B. Wolff was called in from Jena to read the poem aloud in an intimate circle of friends while, according to one report, "Liszt accompanied the appropriate scenes and situations melodramatically in free improvisation" (NZM 1844, 76). Liszt and Hiller were among the few pianists who played free fantasies in this period, and it is not surprising to find them fluent in melodrama accompaniment as well.

IMPROVISATION AND BALLAD AESTHETICS

Loewe's impulse to improvise songs in public was heavily influenced by German literary culture of the 1820s and particularly its fascination with Italian poetry improvisers. At the same time, his improvisation "project" was a natural extension of his commitment to the ballad genre, for the ballad was widely understood as a performative and improvisatory species of poetry. The theory established by Goethe and Schiller, and disseminated in many popular forms, distinguished the ballad from "lyric" and "dramatic" genres by its irreducibly recitational, performative character. Unlike lyric poetry, which was purely inward, and dramatic poetry, which fully externalized the feelings, the ballad conjured the image of the narrating poet in the process of narration. Goethe explained:

> The mysterious aspect of the ballad originates *in its manner of delivery*. The singer holds his potential subject, its related figures, and the deeds and movements, so deeply in his mind that he doesn't know how to bring them to the light of day.

Thus he makes use of all three types of poetry to express immediately whatever arouses his imagination or occupies his mind; he can begin lyric, epic, or dramatic, and continue as he wishes switching between forms.[47]

Described this way, the art of the ballad-poet resembles that of musical improviser: he employs his capacity to summon a variety of styles at whim according to the exigencies of the moment, and he perceptibly externalizes his effort to overcome the difficulty of forming ideas on the spot. In this same period, as Esterhammer explains, romantic philologists were advancing a reinterpretation of Homeric epics as improvisations: the *Illiad* and *Odyssey*, they claimed, were not written works by a single author, but extemporaneous formulaic compositions by bards belonging to the people.[48] Herder was particularly influential in countering the aesthetics of French classicism, which had interpreted epic poetry in terms of formal Aristotelian categories. He promoted the idea that epics were the "natural" expression of an entire nation or people, and that they gained in liveliness through their oral or preliterate form of circulation.[49]

These ideas about the ballad and narrative poetry were sometimes directly invoked in reviews of Loewe's concerts. A writer at the AMZ claimed that "the whole [of Loewe's performance] makes a strong impression and one is tempted to believe that the Homeric songs might have been accompanied in this way by the singers on zither or harp" (AMZ 1835, 536). Fanciful as this comparison is, it is rooted in a concrete and distinctive feature of Loewe's performances: his condensation of singer, pianist, and composer into a single body. In 1835 the Liszt-style solo recital had not yet been "invented," and Loewe's solo concerts had a far better claim on the term "recital." Robert Schumann, after hearing Loewe play a ballad cycle in 1835, marveled at "the rare combination that here unites composer, singer, and virtuoso into one person."[50] A Vienna critic parsed the roles somewhat more explicitly:

> What Loewe unites, with his unusually exact, intelligent, and soulful performances, into a single person, can only be understood by a capable, superior pianist, a superior, thoroughly trained singer, and perhaps also a superior third quality, which comments a little on the sublimer nuances of the composer; admittedly these three things are rarely found together. (*Wiener Zeitschrift* 1844, 1235)

The range of styles employed in the ballads, combined with the relative difficulty of the piano parts, gave the impression that Loewe, like other concert instrumentalists, was playing pieces tailored to his performance strengths:

> Surely no one is in a position to perform his wonderful songs and ballads with such refined declamatory, intellectual, and emotional delivery as Löwe himself, with his pleasing and varied tenor voice and his virtuoso piano playing. (AWMZ 1844, 361)

It is natural that his ballads have the greatest effect when sung by himself. No singer can perform them so intensely absorbed in the object of his contemplation, so innerly sympathetic and engaged. (*Wanderer* 1844, 748)

Loewe's "absorbed" delivery, combined with the narrative tension of the ballad poems, could also project him as a modern rhapsode. In the aftermath of a performance for an audience of Prussian compatriots he imagined an antique scene of bardic narration: "Most endearing of all is the pure enthusiasm of the wonderful Breslauers. This intense attention, this generosity of the listeners, this respect of every single person, as if it were Homer among the Greeks!"[51] In keeping with the tendency of the improvisation imaginary, he celebrates the communion of storyteller and national community.

Critics who praised Loewe's achievements in the ballad genre did not always single out his manner of performance, but they generally understood the genre's performative aesthetics. An anonymous essay in the *Neue Zeitschrift* complimented Loewe for achieving the distinctive narrative tone of the ballad: "It is often said that music . . . can only be combined with lyric poetry, and that epic poetry, which predominates in the ballad, is straight out uncomposable. But that is to forget that epic poetry, which does not express the feeling behind the thought, but *the mood in which the declaiming singer finds himself*, is composable" (NZM 1835, 98, emphasis added). In other words, vocal music naturally gravitates toward an inward, lyrical mode of expression, and some special effort is required of the composer if he wants to conjure up the ballad's requisite narrator. It is possible to find indexes of this narrative function composed into Loewe's settings, yet the real source of such comments was probably Loewe's performance manner itself. When teaching his ballads to students, he obsessively reminded them to preserve their distinctive mode of enunciation. Detailed notes on his lessons, compiled by his daughter Julie, are filled with exhortations not to lapse into a lyric tone or into a dramatic/operatic tone: "This is a ballad and not a Lied"; "Always keep the ballad tone!"; "Never forget that a singer is performing. Do not make a scene out of it; stay in the ballad tone." In relation to his setting of Herder's ballad "Edward," which is a dialogue between son and mother, he urged students: "do not make a duet scene out of it by employing tragic excess."[52] Evidently Loewe cultivated a precise register of performance address in which the ballad singer keeps himself positioned at the transition point between exterior and interior expression. The performer should become transparent to the story only partially or intermittently.

Several aspects of Loewe's performances, not all of them intentional, conspired to foreground the transmissive act and highlight narrative presence. The sheer physical coordination required to sing and play simultaneously prevented him from fully "acting out" the characters and thus spilling over into drama. With both hands occupied by the piano, his posture was necessarily fixed, thus externalizing what the Loewe scholar Karl Anton called "the objective performing style necessary for the reproduction of ballads."[53] Philipp Spitta, in an extended essay on Loewe and the ballad, did not over-look these indispensable performative conditions:

> [Loewe's] advancement of the ballad reached a point where the ballad singer accompanied himself at the piano, which is not wholly inessential to their performance. Through this the singer is brought to a state of confinement [*Gebundenheit*] that forces him to hold his expression in moderation, and specifically to not exaggerate the speaking characters.[54]

Loewe also focused attention on the medial channel with occasional gestures and facial expressions mimicking the narrative content. When playing his setting of "Die nächtliche Heerschau," at the moment when a spectral army first appears in array, he "changed his entire attitude" as though witnessing the very spectacle he was narrating.[55] When playing "Wallhaide," at the pivotal midnight assignation between the young lovers, he drew special attention to the twelve strokes of the bell by lifting his arm high in the air after each stroke. Following this dramatic pause, his daughter noted, "the ghostly feeling that he spread among the listeners doubled back upon the singer, who then recommenced and epically continued the ballad the same way as previously."[56] The ideal ballad performance, then, oscillated between narrative absorption and narrative distance—telling a story about the past and affectively responding to it in the present.[57] According to Spitta, a limited amount of dramatic acting was permissible as long as it did not overtake the narrative mode: "Characterization ought to be there; even Loewe, I have heard from his student Kurth in Bremen, did not shy away from mimetic means when playing. But it should all remain confined to hints and suggestions."[58]

This carefully balanced ideal of ballad performance, borrowed from literary aesthetics and adapted to musical practice, was not unique to Loewe's improvisations. But in many respects his improvisations epitomized the ideal by foregrounding the transmissive medium, the act of poeticizing, the apparatus of performance. When improvising songs he not only sang and played piano simultaneously, a difficult enough feat itself, but also read the words off a page sitting in front of him, further cluttering the media channel, and this had the potential to reconfigure the perceptions of his listeners. Their attention was claimed not only by his musical discourse, but also by the improvisational task—its difficulty, impressiveness, instability, and risk. Improvisational performance, like ballad performance, splits the listener's attention between the act of rendering and the thing rendered, and its fascination lies in the unresolved tension between the two. The ballad singer, Goethe had written, "does not know how to bring [his thoughts] to the light of day." The poet's struggle to enunciate, in other words, is an integral part of the ballad's total meaning, though not identical with the textual content. This was the situational crisis in which Loewe voluntarily placed himself when he took poems from audiences and offered to improvise musical settings. There was always a risk that the strenuousness of delivery might obscure the narrative content: "because he presupposes the same imaginative flight and expects the same emotional intensity and level of aesthetic education from the listener, he often came across as rhapsodic [*rapsodisch*] and the inner thread of his poem became opaque to his audience" (AMZ 1844, 383).

GERMANY'S CORINNA

Loewe improvised songs less frequently in the 1840s than he had earlier, but musical and poetry improvisation again joined hands in the performances of Karoline Leonhardt-Lyser, "Deutschlands Corinna," who toured the German-speaking lands widely in the years 1840–1843. She sometimes entitled her concerts "musical-improvisational academy"—a variant of the more familiar "musical-declamatory academy"—because her programs alternated poetic improvisations with musical numbers. When Leonhardt-Lyser began touring, improvisers in the German language had not been heard for some time. Both O. L. B. Wolff and Maximilian Langenschwarz had long ceased making regular public appearances, and many writers in the literary establishment still maintained that the character of the German language was inimical to poetic improvisation.[59] Critical response to her performances was thus tinged with the same ambivalences that had long surrounded poetry improvisation, but Leonhardt-Lyser was nonetheless warmly received and managed to convince even some of the skeptics. In notable contrast with Langenschwarz, she was rarely accused of charlatanry. Her remarkable flexibility with various rhymes and meters, combined with the quality and vitality of the verses that flowed forth in a steady stream, drew praise for "restoring honor to an art that had been discredited" (*Wiener Zeitschrift* 1842, 413).

Before going public with improvisation, Leonhardt-Lyser had established a reputation as a lyric poetic, storyteller, and author of short novels, publishing in literary and cultural journals and occasionally collecting her pieces into books. Like the portraits and literary sketches of her first husband Johann Peter Lyser, and like some of Loewe's published collections, her work belonged to the sphere of popular romanticism. It fed a surging consumer demand for fanciful fictions, travelogues, and biographical anecdotes about painters, musicians, and poets that could be read in the home. This "Biedermeier" network of cultural production impacted her choice of themes and her style of delivery. She steered clear of the classical, historical, and elegaic topics on which other poetry improvisers staked their fame, choosing instead lyrical, romantic, and humoristic forms. The program of her 9 March 1842 "musikalisch-improvisatorische Akademie" is representative:

1) Improvised sonnet on given rhymes
2) Song
3) Improvisation of a Lied [i.e., a lyric poem] on a given theme
4) Instrumental production
5) Improvisation of a fairy tale or saga on a given theme
6) Written improvisation of a commentary [*Glosse*] on a given refrain
7) Improvisation of a sonnet on given rhymes (Humorist 1842, 196)

In the small town of Reichenberg she improvised the Lied on "a child's first smile," and she based her "commentary" on the refrain "work is the ornament of the citizen" (*Ost und West* 1842, 642). At a Vienna performance she invented a fairy tale on "the origin of spring" and her Lied on the motive "all is quite lovely in my homeland" (*Adler* 1842, 349).

Leonhardt-Lyser's delivery, too, departed from the sublime, exalted tone of other improvisers, including that of Madame Staël's Corinne in her "Improvisation at the Capitol." Far less concerned with projecting "nobility," Leonhardt-Lyser recited in an emotive, warm, and appealing tone gauged to the more modest, quotidian topics of her improvisations. She adopted a natural and unpretentious stage demeanor, sometimes becoming so absorbed with the object of her imagination that she visibly wept. Her difference from other improvisers was probably exaggerated by conventional assumptions about gender difference. One critic described "the agreeable element, tender femininity, and charming childlike poetry that forms the prototype of her improvisations," and contrasted this with "improvised poems of entraining power, using deep or high-reaching images or metaphors, bold and fiery thoughts" (*Humorist* 1842, 270). Though the contrast is overdrawn, other descriptions confirm that Leonhardt-Lyser's improvisations accentuated the intimate and sentimental. A closely attuned critic noted that she improvised more slowly and deliberately than Langenschwarz, as though taking distance from the latter's flashy virtuosity and demonstrative learnedness.

Leonhardt-Lyser appears not to have improvised to musical accompaniment, but she often staged a winning combination of musical and poetic improvisation. She would take a theme from the audience and write out a Lied based upon it. She would then hand the text over to a composer—usually a local kapellmeister familiar to the audience—who would compose out a musical setting on the spot and hand it to a singer and pianist for immediate performance.[60] At a concert in Budapest she improvised on the given subject "gypsy darling in the starry night," which was set by kapellmeister Schindelmeisser (*Adler* 1843, 3), and at a performance in Brunn her improvisation on the motto "the first rain after a long dry spell" was composed out by a kapellmeister Schmidt (*Humorist* 1842, 868). One of these jointly produced improvisations, against all odds, made its way into print. At her Vienna appearance of 29 November 1842, when the Lied improvisation came around, the audience suggested Schiller's aphorism "Whatever lives immortally in song/Must perish in life." Riffing off this idea, Leonhardt-Lyser wrote out two eight-line strophes with alternating rhymes and a common two-line refrain. She then handed it to Adolf Müller Sr., a prolific kapellmeister working in Vienna's suburban theaters, who set it to music and immediately performed it, covering both vocal and piano parts. Within two weeks of the concert Müller had published a Schubertian Lied with the title "Der Sänger" and had memorialized the event on the sheet music cover (Figure 3.3).

Remarkably, the sheet on which Müller composed his song on 29 November 1842 has survived.[61] It suggests that he decided in advance on a fairly conventional four-phrase outline—one melodic phrase for each pair of lines (Figure 3.4). The first phrase is harmonically closed; the second begins in parallel to the first but moves to V; the third modulates to ♭III, and the fourth takes it back home with a cadential formula. There is

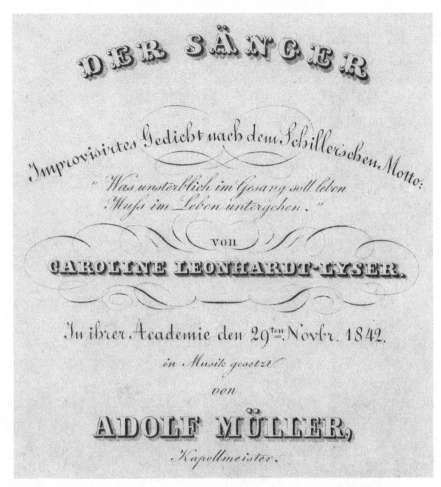

FIGURE 3.3 Cover page of Adolf Müller's song "Der Sänger" (1842). Reproduced with permission of the Österreichische Nationalbibliothek.

a short extension on the second phrase and a longer extension on the fourth. These formal articulations of the structural cadences, which require textual repetitions, show that Müller did not want to take the easy way out and simply compose a series of four-bar phrases; he was going for something slightly more "artful" within the boundaries of a prevailing naïve, charming tone. In Müller's sketch the keyboard part is almost entirely blank. Chords are only jotted in occasionally to mark non-standard harmonic turns and short modulations. This was obviously called for by the situation, which left no time to write out a full piano accompaniment. Nor was it necessary, since the style was meant to be light and simple. The published version of the song does not alter the basic four-phrase model, but it is slightly enlarged and more "finished" than the improvised sketch. It adds a four-bar, Schubert-style ritornello that punctuates and rounds off the form. And the refrain, repeated just once in the original version, is reiterated a second time with a climactic high note added in.[62]

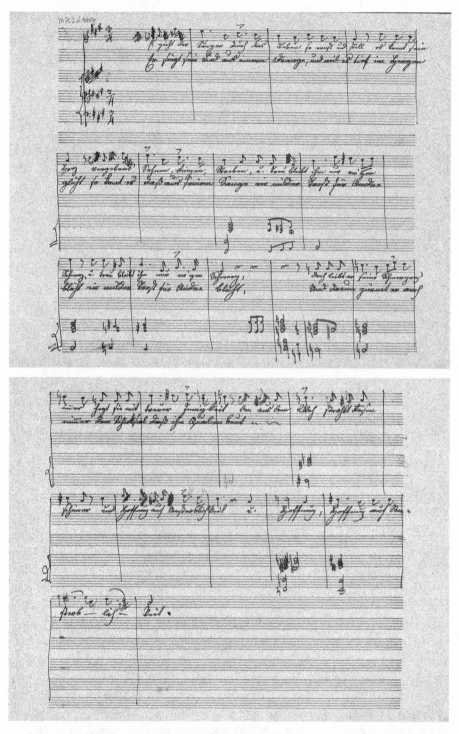

FIGURE 3.4 Adolf Müller's working sheet for his dual poetry-song improvisation with Karoline Leonhardt-Lyser (1842). Reproduced with permission of the Wienbibliothek im Rathaus (Vienna).

Both Loewe and Leonhardt-Lyser, then, were inspired by the romantic cult of Corinne to forge original convergences of improvised music and poetry. Their improvisational projects, however, inflected different cultural values. Loewe wanted to honor classic German poems and revive the distinctive aesthetics of ballad narration in an elite, top-down fashion. Leonhardt-Lyser's approach was far more sociable, accessible, and audience-oriented. Her audience furnished the topics and rhymes for every single improvisation, in a casual atmosphere that sometimes bordered on chaos as people shouted out their suggestions. And by giving a spotlight to the local kapellmeister, she gave the local community a presence or surrogate onstage. In these ways her musical-improvisational academies had the feeling of a Biedermeier salon writ large.

Yet Leonhardt-Lyser's incentive to appear as a public performer was born precisely of a desire to complicate the dominant hierarchy of cultural values, which had positioned elite literature "above" popular literature, writing above performance, and not least, male writers above female writers. Her motivations are evident in two novellas she published just before beginning her public tours. The first, *Louise Karschin: A Character Picture from an Eighteenth-Century Woman's Life*, fictionalizes the life of Germany's most famous *improvvisatrice*, who began as a humble peasant but eventually rose to become a darling of Berlin's high society. The narrative stresses Karsch's confrontations with intransigent male powers, which limit her potential for literary success and ruin her prospects for happiness in love. These tragic limitations are only partially redeemed by the recognition she acquires through her poetic talent and her ascent into elite society.[63] The second novella, *Rosa Taddei: The Improvisatrice*, takes its name from one of the most famous Italian poetry improvisers of the early nineteenth century. Modeled after Corinne, the character Rosa Taddei is a free and easy poetic genius—modest, virtuous, and fully appreciated by the Italian people wherever she goes. In the novella she is an entirely idealized, unreal character—a foil to the story's real protagonist Agathe, a German poet with a melancholic temperament who can't reach an audience and fails to find love. Agathe possesses the extraordinary talent of being able to invent and instantly write down poems on any given topic. Her friend Heinrich, also a poet, is deeply impressed and tries to convince her to perform improvisations à la Taddei. But cultural differences between Germany and Italy (the novel implies) prevent Agathe from attaining Taddei's beautiful freedom-in-art. She is too inhibited or awkward to speak her poems; she can only write them down. Agathe offers many explanations as to why her improvisational talent could never succeed in Germany. The German audience is too widely read and too accustomed to printed poetry to appreciate the style of extemporaneous verses on its own terms. The German literary establishment produces celebrity only through connections and protectors. Agathe dies unrecognized, and German conditions are taken directly to task for limiting the prospects of female authors. "It is true that Italy has lost its political freedom," Agathe says, "but in a certain sense there exists more freedom of thought there than in enlightened Germany, even the Protestant part."[64] Improvisation signifies a freedom of thought that Germany has yet to attain.

In real life, of course, Leonhardt-Lyser overcame Agathe's resignation and made herself a celebrity improviser. Her performance career even became a pathway to conjugal happiness, as she left her unhappy marriage to be with composer Hugo Pierson (1844). Her performances at least partly succeeded in challenging dominant literary values. A supportive critic at the *Wiener Zeitschrift*, wrestling with questions of valuation, staunchly defended her work against the anti-improvisation parties: "Caroline Lyser is a poet and her improvisations are true poems, better than many printed and admired ones, not on account of the speed of their creation alone, but for the deep significance of the thoughts and the beautiful inwardness of feeling" (*Wiener Zeitschrift* 1842, 414). And he suggested that her improvisations required somewhat different standards of evaluation:

> I know quite well, as the modest poet herself would admit, that creations of this kind have no pretension to shine as permanent monuments of the highest poetry for the "end of time" . . . but receptive, cultivated, discerning people are happy to give their minds a satisfying if ephemeral diversion [*Beschäftigung*], and their hearts a beautiful, refreshing pleasure. (*Wiener Zeitschrift* 1842, 414)

In the novella *Rosa Taddei*, the same opinion is offered by the poet Heinrich as he tries to persuade Agathe to perform public improvisations. When Agathe says that authors like Goethe and Tieck set a standard of storytelling too high for any improviser to compete with, Heinrich counters: "even if the critic is not sold on such poems, he will still praise the lightness of the writing and the inwardness of feeling. He will still sympathize with such distinctiveness."[65] Poetry improvisation, in other words, offers some irreducible poetic value that even the best written works cannot provide.

The parallels between Loewe's performances and those of improvising poets like Leonhardt-Lyser are unusually close. But there were other, less familiar domains of oral performance with which Loewe's improvisations intersected. After a ballad cycle performed in Magdeburg in 1845 he reported: "My manner of performance is being compared with that of bishop Draeseke, whom no one can forget as a speaker."[66] At the time Loewe wrote this Bernhard Draeseke (grandfather of the composer Felix Draeseke) was seventy-one years old, and his charismatic speeches at Magdeburg's ancient cathedral had made him a highly revered figure in church politics. He preached sermons asserting the unity of the church and advocating for religious tolerance among Protestant factions. His call to religious unity in the aftermath of the Napoleonic wars made him a favorite of the Prussian monarchs. It is difficult to say what aspects of Loewe's performance manner reminded people of Draeseke, but in Magdeburg he had done something uncommon: "Here I explained each ballad and its textual content before I sang them, and these explanations bore wonderful fruit; the attention was as lively in the last piece as in the first."[67] The didactic commentaries on the poems he was about to deliver in song might have sounded like Draeseke's commentaries on biblical texts. Universities, too, were sites of brilliant oratory, achieving particular fame in the post-Napoleonic era when Hegel was lecturing at the university in Berlin. Loewe's experiences at the university of Halle and elsewhere prompted him to a relevant reflection: "An academic lecture brings to the listener a whole new world, a refreshing, one might even say 'artistic' breath. A certain freedom of thought [*Denkfreiheit*] liberates one in such a beneficent way [*wohltätig*] from the compulsion to think in the manner required at school that one feels as if mentally reborn."[68] Loewe did not link this idea with musical improvisation, but his celebration of the free elaboration of ideas, and of the liberating effect of a flexible intellect unfolding thoughts in real time, does suggest an analogy with musical improvisation. His phrase "one might even say 'artistic'" stops just short of characterizing the academic lecture as an aesthetic experience.

CONCLUSION: THE ANTI-METAPHYSICS OF THE BALLAD

Loewe's ballad performances and improvisations countered the tendency within romantic music aesthetics to construct music as absolute, ineffable, or purely "inward." They did not present music as an object detached from the world, but channeled it through the performative aesthetics of the ballad and epic narration, in which the communicative process—the oscillating enunciatory stance of the poet and the rapt attention of the auditors—is framed as an object of attention. As Esterhammer has shown, and as Karoline Leonhardt-Lyser's career confirms, this focus on communicative materiality and temporality was central to the romantic cult of poetic improvisers, without ever becoming fully "legitimate." Improvisation exerted pressure on the values of romantic idealism and challenged the privilege of durable, printed works, but in the long run it could not compete with them. Both music and poetry submitted, broadly speaking, to the regime of the written. Loewe had laboriously worked out a method for improvising songs in a complex, through-composed style, and audiences clearly enjoyed them, but he found no imitators. Very few people even expressed regret that he tapered his improvisational performances after the tours of the 1830s. The popularity of Loewe's songs and ballads, too, declined after 1850. His great admirer Philip Spitta suggested that without a fully committed and comprehending performer these ballads could not survive: "The artistic tours on which he performed his ballads did not suffice to keep him in steadily arousing traffic with the music world. . . . The interest in [his ballads] quickly fell off in the second half of our century."[69]

The note of nostalgia in Spitta's voice is unmistakable. Loewe's performances had materialized a desire for a tightly knit community of artists and audiences, where "modern-classic" poems by Goethe, Herder, Uhland, and Körner came vividly to life through in-the-moment retelling and musical reinvention. In the realm of poetry, the German cultural nation had been built primarily through print culture and practices of private reading. Already by the 1820s, as Peter Seibert has shown, the democratization of literary culture through print was generating nostalgia for the elite salon culture it was displacing—the milieu in which Goethe, de la Motte Fouqué, and Theodor Körner were said to have improvised tales, stories, and poems.[70] Loewe's performances addressed similar desires, restoring what was left behind when poems were divorced from their authors and their audiences. He contributed to the fantasy that art might return to a state where production and reception were simultaneous, where genius and *communitas* were joined. His live song improvisations were designed to project him as a musical improviser *and* poetry improviser simultaneously. In reality he was only inventing music to poems that had already become "classic." Music supplied the "liveness" that the printed poem lacked. Ironically, then, Loewe's restoration of poetry to oral performance through improvisation thrived on the hegemony of print circulation, which had generated the "classic" status of the poem to begin with.

The revival of Loewe's music in the 1880s and 1890s laid emphasis on the specific performative aesthetics of the ballad.[71] Its recurring theme was that the ballad genre, as established by Loewe, contained something of great value that was on the verge of extinction. Critic and singer Martin Plüddemann, who eventually earned a reputation as a composer of ballads in Wagnerian style, founded ballad-schools in Berlin (1886) and Graz (1890) to address the special performance demands of the genre and to encourage composers to continue writing them. Plüddemann's advocate Richard Batka, in a defense of the ballad genre, expressed regret that modern audiences had lost sensitivity to the genre's unique mode of address. Modern listening habits had become polarized into lyric absorption and dramatic explicitness:

> Through the influence of concerts and theater it has become customary to perceive music as a direct outpouring; it wants to be followed with the eyes shut [i.e., at concerts] or in connection with tangible events [i.e., at operas]: the transmissive, narrative epic music style, which puts demands on the imaginative engagement of the listener, has become foreign. Indeed the once blooming art of epic poetry has almost completely retreated to the novel and novella, and these latter are, from my perspective, not for public performance, but are intended for quiet reading at home.[72]

The mass culture of silent reading, in other words, had destroyed the taste for performed narrative, for declaimed poetry, and for stories read aloud and heard attentively. Ideas of "absolute music" had defeated the ballad's transmissive aesthetics as Lied composers reverted almost exclusively to the lyrical approach. Batka's point finds support in the arguments of historian William A. Graham concerning the balance of oral and written practices in nineteenth-century Europe. Silent, private reading on a mass scale, according to Graham, appeared only in the second half of the nineteenth century. The majority of people "can only have known books or any other writings as vocal texts read aloud for them to hear . . . the latter half of the nineteenth century was the period in Europe in which mass literacy replaced the restricted, elite literacy of previous eras."[73]

Batka's nostalgia for an earlier, more communal era of storytelling found an echo in Walter Benjamin's essay "The Storyteller":

> The earliest symptom of a process whose end is the decline of storytelling is the rise of the novel at the beginning of modern times. . . . What can be handed

on orally, the wealth of epic, is of a different kind from what constitutes the stock in trade of the novel. What differentiates the novel from all other forms of prose literature . . . is that it neither comes from oral tradition nor goes into it.[74]

Benjamin associated the novel squarely with modern, industrial, and urban conditions that eroded communal bonds. He contrasted these conditions with a communal scene of narration in which storyteller and audience stand in lively contact, mutually expressing and realizing the community's wisdom: "the art of storytelling is reaching its end because the epic side of truth, wisdom, is dying out."[75] Although Benjamin dealt only with the work of published writers, his reflections compelled him to underline the real-time event as central to "the true nature of storytelling": "the value of information does not survive the moment in which it was new; it lives only at that moment . . . it does not aim to convey the pure sense of the thing, like information or a report. It sinks the thing into the life of the storyteller."[76] He moreover regretted the loss of the storyteller's corporeal presence, which guaranteed its authenticity and communal efficacy. In the storyteller's art "words, soul, eye and hand are brought into connection. Interacting with one another, they determine a practice. We are no longer familiar with this practice."[77]

Those people who expressed nostalgia for the musical ballad, then, mourned the loss not only of a genre but also of a past era in which performance-centered aesthetics had thrived and literature had taken the form of a meaningful communal practice. Some epistemic shift in art's mediation had stamped out the ethos of transmissive performance. Scenes of ballad narration and improvised storytelling conjured a vision of intense, attentive communication and performer-audience community that were missing from the culture of the modern, mass-mediated world. This form of nostalgia had already begun to form around Loewe and his romantic colleagues in the 1810s, as they constructed an idealized past in which storytellers and audiences bonded in epic narration. Loewe's bold experiment in song improvisation was meant to recover some of what had been lost. Later-century advocates of the ballad, for their part, imagined Loewe's era as a golden age of "oralized" musico-poetic culture. It was from this later, disenchanted period that Loewe and his daughter told the story of his youthful song improvisation on "Wallhaide." It had begun in the small cabin of a religious hermit, deep in the forest, at twilight, after a long, expansive walk with an intimate friend. . . .

NOTES

1. Commentary to *Carl Loewes Werke*, vol. 8: *Geisterballaden*, ed. Max Runze (Leipzig: Breitkopf & Härtel, 1900), xii. Runze describes the source as an unpublished "Lebensbild" written by Julie.

2. Ibid., 20.

3. This advice corresponds broadly with the philosophy of performance being advocated by numerous writers in the early nineteenth century, in which the performer is required to invest his or her own subjectivity into the interpretation of the objective signs. See Mary Hunter,

"'To Play as if from the Soul of the Composer': The Idea of the Performer in Early Romantic Aesthetics," *Journal of the American Musicological Society* 58, no. 2 (2005): 357–98.

4. Julie Bothwell noted that Loewe's "Wallhaide" was written in "Zumsteeg's style." *Carl Loewe-Balladenschule: Carl Loewes Sing- und Vortragslehre,* ed. Robert Hanzlik (Lobejün: Carl Loewe-Gesellschaft, 2007), 84. Hereafter cited as *Balladenschule*. This volume republishes a miscellaneous compilation of notes and commentaries that Julie Bothwell, Loewe's daughter, assembled after studying Loewe's ballads with him. It was originally compiled by Karl Anton, author of the first doctoral dissertation on Loewe.

5. *The Diaries of Giacomo Meyerbeer,* ed. Robert Ignatius Letellier, 4 vols. (Madison, NJ: Fairleigh Dickinson University Press, 1999), 1:270 (diary entry dated 26 June 1812). Perhaps Vogler could not resist accompanying this recitation, since the poem's recurring motto reads: "Nobly sounds the song of the brave man/Like organ tones and ringing bells."

6. Quoted from a letter of Weber to Caroline Brandt in John Warrack, *Carl Maria von Weber* (London: John Hamilton, 1968), 163.

7. *Hinterlassene Schriften von Carl Maria von Weber,* ed. Theodor Hell (Dresden und Leipzig: Arnold, 1828), 1:9.

8. Heinrich Bulthaupt, *Carl Loewe: Deutschlands Balladenkomponist* (Berlin: Harmonie, 1898), 18.

9. Konstanze Musketa, "Carl Loewe und seine Ausbildungszeit in Halle," *Musikkonzepte— Konzepte der Musikwissenschaft* (Kassel: Bärenreiter, 2000), 107–13.

10. C. H. Bitter, *Dr. Carl Loewe's Selbstbiographie. Für die Öffentlichkeit bearbeitet* (Berlin: Liebheit & Thiesen, 1870), 188. Hereafter *Selbstbiographie*.

11. Matthias Schneider, "Carl Loewe als Organist," in *Carl Loewe (1796–1869): Beiträge zu Leben, Werk, und Wirkung,* ed. Ekkehard Ochs and Lutz Winkler (Frankfurt am Main: Peter Lang, 1998), 83–97.

12. *Selbstbiographie,* 247.

13. F. W. Lüpke, "Persönliche Erinnerungen an Dr. Karl Löwe," *Musikpädagogische Blätter* 1, no. 2 (1896–1897): 19–22. This event took place in 1851.

14. Georg Wandel, *Studien und Charakteristiken aus Pommerns ältester und neuester Zeit* ([no city]: Anklam Verlag, 1888), 222. Loewe's 1851 *Orgelschule* appears to be aimed at lower-level students and makes no mention of free improvisation.

15. Daniel Gottlob Türk, *Von den wichtigsten Pflichten eines Organisten: Ein Beitrag zur Verbesserung der musikalischen Liturgie,* ed. Joh. Fr. Naue (Halle: Schwetschke und Sohn, 1849 [1787]), 112. Emphasis added.

16. Ibid.

17. In a typical formulation of this idea, Friedrich Schneider, the Dessau kapellmeister and former organist in Leipzig, stipulated that in free preludes the organist should "bring forth his skills in their complete range, but always in consideration of the worthiness of the situation and the special goal of the celebration." Quoted from Schneider's *Orgelschule* (1830) in K. G. Fellerer, *Studien zur Orgelmusik des ausgehenden 18. und frühen 19. Jahrhunderts* (Kassel: Bärenreiter, 1932), 32.

18. Julie Bothwell gives examples of embellishments Loewe made in performances of his Lieder "Frediricus Rex" and "Der Schatzgräber," in the *Balladenschule,* 35 and 77.

19. Daniel Gottlob Türk, *Clavierschule, oder Anweisung zum Klavierspielen* (Halle: Hemmerde und Schwetschke, 1789), 301–303.

20. Walter Dürr, "Schubert and Johann Michael Vogl: A Reappraisal," *19th Century Music* 3, no. 2 (1979): 126–40.

21. See the critical notes by Max Runze to *Carl Loewes Werke*, vol. 4: *Die deutschen Kaiserballaden*, iv–v.

22. *Balladenschule*, 75.

23. On popular improvisers and entertainers, see chapter 10 in Angela Esterhammer, *Romanticism and Improvisation, 1750–1850* (Cambridge: Cambridge University Press, 2008).

24. See Max Runze's commentary in *Carl Loewes Werke*, vol. 5: *Hohenzollern-Balladen und -Lieder*, xxvii.

25. Jean Chantavoine, "La ballade allemande de Carl Loewe," in his essay collection *Musiciens et poètes* (Paris: F. Alcan, 1912), 95.

26. A thorough study of the relation between Loewe's work and B. A. Weber's original is found in Till Gerrit Waidelich, "'Auf einen höheren Standpunct der Kunst gestellt': B. A. Webers Melodram *Der Gang nach dem Eisenhammer* und seine kompositorische Aneignung durch Carl Loewe in der zeitgenössischen Rezeption," in *Schubert und das Biedermeier: Beiträge zur Musik des frühen 19. Jahrhunderts*, ed. M. Kube, W. Aderhold and W. Litschauer (Kassel: Bärenreiter, 2002), 185–207.

27. *Selbstbiographie*, 176.

28. *Selbstbiographie*, 129.

29. *Selbstbiographie*, 124.

30. *Selbstbiographie*, 132.

31. *Selbstbiographie*, 133–34.

32. *Der Briefwechsel zwischen Goethe und Zelter*, ed. Max Hecker, vol. 3 (Leipzig: Insel, 1918), 566.

33. *Selbstbiographie*, 302–303, 248.

34. *Carl Loewe (1796–1869): Beiträge zu Leben, Werk, und Wirkung*, 21.

35. *Correspondance Franz Liszt Mme. D'Agoult*, ed. Serge Gut and Jacqueline Bellas (Paris: Fayard, 2001), 69.

36. Robert Schumann, *Gesammelte Schriften über Musik und Musiker*, 2 vols. (Leipzig: Breitkopf & Härtel, 1914), 2:313. "Die glücklichen Tasten, die diese Fingern tragen dürfen, Gräfin! Wahrhaftig, wär' ich ein Klavier, mit jedem Tone würde ich der Spielerin einem andern Namen der Schönheit und der Jugend entgegenrufen, bei C, Corinna, bei D, Desdemona."

37. *Selbstbiographie*, 133–34.

38. Ferdinand Hiller, *Künstlerleben* (Köln: DuMont-Schauberg, 1880), 30. Loewe reported on his first encounter with Wolff with a remarkably similar emphasis on appearance: "Visit to Prof. Wolff, whom you may know as the most famous German improviser. Wolff is a beautiful man; elegant and attractive in his appearance, unpretentious and most natural" (*Selbstbiographie*, 212).

39. See Melina Esse, "Encountering the *improvvisatrice* in Italian Opera," *Journal of the American Musicological Society* 66, no. 3 (2013), 751–57. Carl Ludwig Fernow's lengthy essay "Improvisatori" for the *Neue Teutsche Merkur* (1801), later published as a pamphlet *Über die Improvisatoren* (1806), helped stimulate interest in the Italian *improvvisatore* among German readers. Perhaps responding to Fernow's essay, Heinrich Christoph Koch included an entry in his compendious treatise of 1802: "*Improvisatori* are a kind of poet encountered only in Italy, who, when given a subject, as long it is minimally capable of poetic performance, declaim 50, 60, or even 100 verses immediately on the spot, or, as it usually happens, sing them

in recitative style while accompanying themselves on guitar." Koch, *Musikalisches Lexicon* (Frankfurt a. M.: August Hermann der Jüngere, 1802), 777.

40. *Selbstbiographie*, 213–14.

41. *Selbstbiographie*, 215, and AMZ 1835, 866.

42. *Selbstbiographie*, 384, and AMZ 1846, 888.

43. Wandel, *Studien und Charakteristiken*, 187.

44. *Early Letters of Robert Schumann*, trans. May Herbert (London: George Bell, 1888), 12. The letter is from 1827.

45. Ferdinand Hiller, *Mendelssohn, Letters and Recollections*, trans. M. E. von Glehn, 2nd ed. (London: Macmillan and Co., 1874), 174.

46. *Aus Ferdinand Hillers Briefwechsel (1826–1861)*, ed. Reinhold Sietz, 7 vols. (Köln: Arno, 1958), 1:60.

47. "Ballade: Betrachtung und Auslegung," in *Johann Wolfgang von Goethe: Berliner Ausgabe*, 21 vols. (Berlin and Weimar: Aufbau, 1960–), 17:590–91. Emphasis added.

48. On romantic interpretations of epic poetry and improvisation see Esterhammer, *Romanticism and Improvisation, 1750–1850*, 59–77.

49. On Herder's ideas concerning epic see Charlton Payne, *The Epic Imaginary: Political Power and Its Legitimations in Eighteenth-Century German Literature* (Berlin: De Gruyter, 2012), 164–66.

50. Quoted from the *Leipziger Tageblatt* in Klaus-Peter Koch, "Robert Schumann und ein Carl-Loewe-Konzert in Leipzig," in *Carl Loewe (1796–1869): Beiträge zu Leben, Werk, und Wirkung*, 111.

51. *Selbstbiographie*, 303.

52. *Balladenschule*, 21, 80, 80, 26.

53. *Balladenschule*, 33.

54. Philipp Spitta, *Musikgeschichtliche Aufsätze* (Berlin: Paetel, 1894), 454.

55. *Balladenschule*, 47.

56. *Balladenschule*, 84–85.

57. Carolyn Abbate has discussed the dramaturgical implications for opera of the ballad genre's distinctive mode of narrative enunciation. Composers of romantic opera often included ballads narrating past events. In an employment typical of the genre, the narrator-singer would get involved in the story he or she was narrating, so that the pastness of the events "broke through" to the immediate present. Carolyn Abbate, *Unsung Voices: Opera and Musical Narrative in the Nineteenth Century* (Princeton: Princeton University Press, 1991), 69–98. Thus in Wagner's *Flying Dutchman* "[Senta's] ballad is reflexive not only of an utterance, structure, or text-object (the plot of the opera), but also of acts of enunciation, structuring, and making—the acts of singer, composer, and, not least, the listener" (97).

58. Spitta, *Musikgeschichtliche Aufsätze*, 454.

59. See for example the review of the male improviser Beermann in the Vienna *Sonntagsblätter*, 4 May 1845, 425–26. This review mentions obscure poetry improvisers from other cities in the German lands.

60. The only other example of this practice I have found is from an 1840 benefit in Milan given by a soprano named Cavenago. After singing a barcarolle by Donizetti, she asked one of her assisting artists, the violin virtuoso Bazzini, to play the melody again phrasing it the way she did. Later in the concert she had the poet G. B. Pezzi improvise a poem, which was written down and set to music immediately "like in a salon." This piece was published by the

publisher of *Glissons, n'appuyons pas*. See Claudio Sartori, *L'avventura del violin: l'Italia musicale dell'Ottocento nella biografia e nei carteggi di Antonio Bazzini* (Torino: ERI, 1978).

61. This document is held in Vienna at the Wienbibliothek im Rathaus, Musikhandschriften, catalogued under the title "Der Sänger" and author "Müller, Adolf." The document was evidently produce in haste, as indicated by the bare minimum of musical information and the bar lines drawn through the words. The corrections on this sheet correspond to the printed version of "Der Sänger."

62. Adolf Müller (Sr.), *Der Sänger, op. 52. Improvisirtes Gedicht nach dem Schillerschen Motto: "Was unsterblich im Gesang soll leben, muss im Leben untergehen" von Carlotte [sic!] Leonhardt-Lyser* (Vienna: E. Mollo & A. O. Witzendorf, n.d.).

63. Caroline Leonhardt-Lyser, *Zehn Novellen*, 3 vols. (Meissen: F. W. Goedsche, 1842), 1:3–92.

64. Leonhardt-Lyser, *Zehn Novellen*, 2:267.

65. Ibid., 299.

66. *Selbstbiographie*, 363.

67. See also the comments on the "Rhetor" in *Balladenschule*, 43.

68. Maximilian Runze, *Biographie Carl Loewes* (Leipzig: Philipp Reclam, 1905), 20.

69. Spitta, *Musikalische Aufsätze*, 452.

70. Peter Seibert, *Der literarische Salon* (Stuttgart: Metzler, 1993), 266.

71. Scholarly interest began in 1869, shortly after Loewe's death, when Bach scholar C. H. Bitter published a collection of diaries and letters. Hugo Wolf and Richard Wagner began pushing singers to perform Loewe's works in orchestral transcription, and in 1882 a Loewe-Verein was established in Berlin. The revival gained steam with Maximilian Runze's 1888 book *Loewe Reborn [Loewe redivivus]* 1888, in whose wake Philip Spitta published a sixty-page, laudatory essay on Loewe and the ballad genre. Loewe's reputation also spread internationally. In 1890 the British writer Albert Bach wrote a book on the musical ballad, treating only Loewe and Schubert, and in France Jean Chantavoine published an essay to make Loewe better known to the French public. Chantavoine's essay appeared in 1912, the same year as the first doctoral dissertation on him, and the year Schoenberg arranged Loewe's setting of *Der Nöck* for orchestra.

72. Richard Batka, *Martin Plüddemann und seine Balladen: eine kritische Studie* (Prague: F. Ehrlich, 1896), 12.

73. William A. Graham, *Beyond the Written Word: Oral Aspects of Scripture in the History of Religion* (Cambridge: Cambridge University Press, 1987), 42–43. Around 1850 the estimated literacy of adults in Europe was only about 50 percent, as compared with 90 percent around 1930 (43).

74. Walter Benjamin, *Illuminations: Essays and Reflections*, trans. Harry Zohn (New York: Schocken, 1968), 87.

75. Ibid.

76. Ibid., 90, 91.

77. Ibid., 108.

4

Schumann and the Economization of Musical Labor

ONE OF THE paradoxes of improvisation in the nineteenth century is that it perceptibly lost credibility in some places, while in other places it persisted without any signs
of "reconstruction." Chopin, for example, submitted to the trends of the early nineteenth century when he renounced his ambitions to a career as a public virtuoso and
concentrated his energies on teaching and composition. But he apparently never lost
his motivation to improvise and did so often in his largely private performing career.
Similar to Chopin in this respect was his peer and colleague Stephen Heller, who had
a strong reputation as an improviser. Heller had studied in Vienna with both Czerny
and Carl Maria von Bocklet, giving him a double dose of improvisational influence,
and from about 1828 to 1830 he had a promising concert career that included free
fantasies.[1] At his second concert in Cracow in 1829 the program even announced *two*
separate improvisations on given themes.[2] His concert ambitions, however, were undone by a nervous, anxious temperament that was even more debilitating than those
of Chopin and Schumann, and although he continued to play improvisations in private
society he focused his energies mainly on composition.[3] Meanwhile, Ignaz Moscheles
and Ferdinand Hiller continued to improvise without compunction, both in public
and in private, even after they had evolved into establishment figures known for their
large-scale "public" compositions. For musicians like them, improvising felt like a
natural thing to do even when they were not practicing or performing much. Others
started to develop a bad conscience, due in no small measure to the aggressive stance
taken by serious professional critics against the practice. In 1831 Mendelssohn had a
crisis of faith about improvising publicly, although it turned out to be only a temporary

doubt.[4] Liszt, too, became less inclined to play free fantasies at the end of his concerts. He knew the public would be satisfied, but was not so easily satisfied himself.[5]

Of all the musicians whose perspective on improvisation changed, Robert Schumann is in many respects the most illustrative. In his youth he was obsessed with the piano and the advantages of improvisation. Like most composers in the early nineteenth century, he had learned to treat playing and composing as allies on a music-making continuum. For much of his youth in the 1820s he improvised to get inspired, to explore variations and combinations, and to cast about for sudden, unexpected ideas that could serve as a foundation for compositions. Yet in the course of artistic evolution, which he documented in diaries, letters, and published music criticism, he felt compelled to renounce the piano and improvisation as a valid creative outlet. In a diary entry from 1845 he proudly wrote that he had acquired "a completely new manner of composing." The main advantage of the "new manner" was that "I started to work out everything in my head," as opposed to his earlier years when "I used to compose almost all of my shorter pieces in the heat of inspiration."[6] He viewed the new manner, which followed a phase of intensive counterpoint studies, as a sign of maturity—a refinement of concentration, compositional oversight, and contemplative depth. He also advised young students and aspiring composers to liberate themselves from the piano in this manner.

Because the later Schumann was so uncompromising in his rejection of the keyboard and improvisation, his evolution demonstrates the tension between improvisation and composition as their valuation fluctuated in the 1830s and 1840s. His mentors and early heroes included postclassical pianist-composers such as Hummel and Moscheles, who clearly regarded improvisation and composition as complementary, mutually beneficial forms of music-making. Under what influences, then, did he come to view them as opposed or antagonistic? The most direct cause would appear to be the philosophical idealism that occupied so much space in romantic aesthetics. If music is understood as part of an ethereal, immaterial realm of fantasy lying "beyond," then any material mediation of music, whether by instruments, bodies, or scores, threatens to drag it back down to earth and negate its ideality. From this perspective, getting away from the piano is a gain because it removes the material obstacle standing between the mind and the musically realized idea. Schumann did not just absorb this aesthetic disposition from poetry and aesthetics, but actively disseminated it in his journal, the *Neue Zeitschrift*. The first part of this chapter unfolds the story of Schumann's experiences in improvisation and shows their gradual submission to this new aesthetic regime, culminating in the new manner of 1845. The second part zooms out and places Schumann's transcendence of the piano in a broader, less exclusively artistic context—that of "economy" or "economization." The ideal of head-generated music is a vision of streamlined compositional labor that intersects in literal and metaphorical ways with ethical, monetary, domestic, and capitalistic economies, and Schumann's habits of meticulous self-documentation offer a rare opportunity to track interconnections between them.

PLAYING AND FANTASIZING

When Schumann was coming of age in the 1820s, free improvisation was a familiar practice among the pianist-composers he most admired, especially Hummel and Moscheles. He was musically less precocious than his improvising peers Liszt and Mendelssohn, and he had less of the theoretical and systematic pianistic training that provided improvisational facility. His early relationship with the piano was relatively intuitive, amateurish, and free from didacticism. He became a pianist before he had even learned to read music fluently. As he later confided to his first teacher, Friedrich Wieck, in the early years he "improvised a great deal and rarely played from music."[7] Although Schumann attributed his improvising to a "complete lack of training, in listening, technique, and especially theory," it was evidently at the same time a source of intense pleasure and imaginative play. Diaries from his late teens and early twenties are filled with short, clipped summaries of his quotidian activities, and improvisation (*fantasieren*) comes up over and over again, sometimes on a nearly daily basis.

This period, from about 1827 to 1831, was a transitional phase. Schumann's erratic student life in Leipzig and Heidelberg was gradually giving way to a phase of discipline marked by serious piano studies, intensive exercises in counterpoint, and ultimately, a resolution to pursue a musical career. While moving in this direction he played the piano avidly, formulating and reformulating musical ideas at the instrument and reveling in the unimpeded flow. He improvised most often in the evening hours, and sometimes at great length: "When I get home about 6 o'clock I improvise till nearly 8, then usually go to supper with [Kömpel] and Wolff, and then come home."[8] On one occasion he logged six solid hours of extemporaneous bliss. Even after his finger injury forced him to play less, he could describe himself as improvising "at length and overflowingly" (TB 1:411). An early diary entry, written after an evening of improvisation, records his quasi-animistic sense of the piano as a repository of sentiments and memories:

> When I think of my childhood or the year 1826 I fall upon A-minor tonalities etc.; when I think of last September harsh dissonances in pp. pp. are automatically unleashed. Whatever thoughts come in the moment will seek expression in tones. The heart has already felt each tone on its keys, just as the keys on the piano must first be touched before they sound. In the moments when one thinks of nothing or of trivial things, the imagination becomes flatter and the playing paler; when one thinks of music itself, contrapuntal phrases and fugues come forth easily. (TB 1:112)

Schumann here privileges the affective immediacy of extemporaneous playing, and by equating "heart" with "keys" he celebrates the instrument as an extension of his subjectivity.

Schumann's youthful improvisations were intense, rhapsodic, and passionate, providing an outlet for inchoate adolescent energies and desires. Friedrich Wieck at first considered him an "enragé auf dem Piano," implying an undisciplined, dramatically compelling manner out of line with postclassical ideals.[9] When Schumann sketched memories of his teen years for a potential autobiography, he emphasized a dominating urge to emote at the piano: "Free improvisation [many hours daily] . . . Overwhelming desire to play piano when I have not played for a long time . . . At my best in free improvisation . . . entraining fire of my playing."[10] Several examples from his teenage diaries link erotic desires with the sense of exaltation and self-expansion he felt when improvising. On July 13, 1828, returning from the home of his first *amour*, Agnes Carus, he noted: "She is probably sleeping now; I improvised well; for she lives in my fantasies together with the entire universe of tones" (TB 1:94). On a trip to Milan, his playing attracted the attention of other travelers at the same lodge, and before long he was socializing and flirting with them: "the Englishwoman—the beautiful woman— the husband—smiles—enquiries about me—piano-enthusiasm—improvisation— the other woman livelier, always looking round, red, like Agnes in Gera" (TB 1:258). After a soirée spent at the Wieck residence in 1832 he went home and "sat myself down at the piano, and for me it was as though flowers and gods came out of my fingers, the thought so streamed out of me" (TB 1:400). The source of inspiration in this case was the memory of a kiss he had just given a Dutch sweetheart, and the diary tells us his spontaneous bass line was C-F-G-C. A few years later he superimposed one of Clara's melodies upon the C-F-G-C bass to produce his opus 4. In contrast to earlier improvisers such as Hummel and Moscheles, Schumann experienced improvisation as an intense, spontaneous outpouring of his emotional and psychic life.

Beyond these personal and creative benefits, Schumann's improvisations gave him the opportunity to demonstrate prowess in the university milieu of Heidelberg, where young men competed for social distinction and were more likely to demonstrate their masculine virtue through heavy drinking and swashbuckling *Mensur* contests. Although he had not yet settled on a concert career, he was reaping the social advantages of his talent in the salons and emerging as a local hero. As he reported to Friedrich Wieck, "I feel modestly conscious of my superiority over all the other Heidelberg pianists" (EL, 78). Anton Töpken, a close companion during this period, left the most complete testimony of his impact in salons:

> After social conversation there normally followed on his part free improvisa-
> tion on the piano, in which he unleashed all the spirits. I will admit that these
> direct musical effusions of Schumann gave me a pleasure unmatched by any other
> great artist I heard. Ideas flowed to him in inexhaustible richness. Out of a single
> thought, which he made appear in all different guises, everything streamed and
> poured forth as if from within itself and thereby drew characteristic feeling to its
> depth, and with all poetic magic while at the same time with the clearly recogniz-
> able marks of his musical personality, both the energetic and powerful side and his
> softly-sweet, reflective-dreamy thoughts. . . . He had already charmed everyone in
> larger circles, who really counted on his appearing, with his free improvisations,
> and would then have an opportunity to appear before the larger public.[11]

These performances clearly impressed audiences and opened up possibilities that Schumann's compositional achievements to date could not. Töpken was always "astounded by this self-confidence in playing, this consciously artistic performance" (TB 1:203), and Schumann monitored his effect upon listeners. Sometimes he reported a "good fantasy and little attention on the part of the listeners," or "little applause after a good fantasia." In better circumstances he might produce a "good fantasia and internal and external praise" (TB 1:209, 297, 217).

Even before the transformative experience of Paganini's virtuosity in 1830, Schumann's experiences at the piano made him acutely conscious of the performer's power over listeners. He once mused that "passionate [physical] movements during piano playing inspire the audience just like the expressions and gestures of an orator" (TB 1:110). A couple of weeks later he argued for the ethical advantages of music as a performed, event-oriented art:

> That is just the advantage of music and of acting: we can enjoy them collectively and are entranced or moved in the same moment; the other arts do not have this . . . not even poetry when it lacks its midwife, acting, which brings it to public life. (TB 1:154)

Considering that Schumann was still undecided about whether he should become a poet or a musician, these are significant words, and they remind us that his earliest known improvisations at the piano were accompaniments to "musical-declamatory" theater skits at his school. Paganini had brought the magnetic, self-aware element of performance to new heights, and when Schumann heard him he strengthened his resolve to acquire such entraining power. When his finger injury made a virtuoso career unattainable, Schumann turned these impulses inward. He sublimated his relatively extroverted history as piano improviser into the musical and literary persona of "Florestan," described by John Daverio as "the rambunctious improviser, his persona a mixture of Paganinian virtuosity and Schumann's inclinations in the same direction."[12]

In spite of the deep and absorbing pleasure Schumann took in improvisation, he did not throw himself into it without reservation or self-censure. He felt some guilt that he was improvising because he lacked more rigorous keyboard training. He was improvising with a minimum of theoretical knowledge, and this made him insecure. In diaries he frequently congratulated himself on "good" or "beautiful" improvisations but sometimes judged them merely "conventional," "decent," or worse: "at home very lame improvisation and frustration over my piano playing" (TB 1:201). Extemporaneous playing, no matter how "free" and expansive, still called for monitoring and judgment. And even though he enjoyed impressing people, he was bothered when "external praise" was out of sync with "inner praise." He waxed ironic about Töpken's rapturous compliments: "[he] rants and raves 'how I improvise' and praises me and 'just can't believe it'" (TB 1:203). This skepticism about the reliability and sincerity of improvisation gained the upper hand in his future development. Around 1831 he started to address his deficiencies by pursuing lessons in music theory, but it proved difficult to integrate the "objectivity" of counterpoint into his highly subjective experience of improvisation. To a greater extent than his peers, he came to view inspiration and craft, improvisation and composition, *schaffen* and *bilden*, as incompatible or even opposed. As he began to cast his lot more deeply with composition and "objectivity," it seemed necessary to take increasing distance from the piano and from the unrestrained subjectivity of improvisation.

Materials and Figures

However intimately Schumann aligned his improvisations with an interior life, their musical language was necessarily derived from the prevailing piano idioms of the day. The extent to which his early ideals were indebted to postclassical pianism is rarely observed by scholars, who have generally preferred to demonstrate how completely he "transcended" them. Schumann inhabited his interior life with such intensity, and documented it with such verbal flair, that we are perpetually lured into his imaginative field, making it difficult to establish any other perspective from which to view his oeuvre. The postclassical horizon of influence becomes even more difficult to access if we uncritically affirm his mission to "poeticize" music, for he explicitly waged this battle against the supposedly prosaic, blasé character of the postclassical *stile brillante*. Observing the postclassical influences on Schumann's improvisations thus requires reading somewhat against the grain of his own perceptions. It also demands some resistance to the habit of framing his improvisations as temporary milestones on the way to finished compositions. To take one example, in a diary entry from the early 1830s he reported a striking improvisational moment: "The fandango idea came upon me at the piano—that made me uncommonly happy" (TB 2:38). Scholars normally treat this as part of the *Entstehungsgeschichte* of his Sonata in F♯ minor, op. 11, which devotes an entire episode to a "Spanish" motive. But Schumann's epiphany might alternatively be understood as part of the history of postclassical improvisation, which unfolded a panoply of topoi and styles to the extemporizing musician. Weber, Chopin, and indeed Schumann had all used the fandango topos in recent piano works, and this "exterior" origin to the improvisational idea matters as much as the subjective impulse. By attending to Schumann's sincere debt to the postclassical aesthetic, complete with its iterable topoi and its accent on performative ontology, we will better understand just how forceful his later rejection of piano-based composition was.

Biographer John Worthen has rightly highlighted Schumann's taste for improvising and persuasively argued that "what he wanted to be was a virtuoso, an improvising pianist who (incidentally) composed. And this was the ambition that Wieck had supported him in."[13] One of his most enduring childhood memories, from 1816, was sitting in front of the great Ignaz Moscheles at a concert, and he later considered going to Vienna to study with Moscheles.[14] Before encountering Beethoven's piano works, he learned key pieces from the postclassical repertoire by composers such as Ries, Czerny, Field, Kalkbrenner, Cramer, and Weber. His growing dissatisfaction with the tutelage of Friedrich Wieck provoked him to seek out the Weimar kapellmeister Hummel as a potential alternative teacher. Hummel's playing was no longer at its peak, but his star had recently risen through the publication of his thorough and long-awaited treatise on pianism, whose final chapter is devoted to the free fantasy. Thus while Schumann was discovering the compositions of the recently deceased Schubert and Beethoven and feeding on the riches of their style, his living heroes were two keyboard masters, Moscheles and Hummel, who were famous for their brilliance in extemporaneous playing.[15] As he developed his keyboard chops Schumann spent enormous time and effort learning Hummel's Concerto in A Minor and Moscheles' *Variations on the Alexander March*, two touchstones of the modern *stile brillante* bravura style, and each adaptable to solo performance. By 1830, after a period of indecision concerning his future, he became convinced that "with patience and perseverance, and a good master, I should in six years be as good as any pianist" (EL 114). On a good day he was pleased to find himself approximating the clean, "notey" timbre of the postclassical pianists: "Up early—my sobriety rewarded; played extremely well—soft pearly touch and pearl-like improvisation" (TB 1:300).

It is nonetheless difficult to imagine Schumann as a typical postclassical pianist. Plenty of evidence, including the indiscipline Wieck observed, suggests that he played in a dramatic, *Sturm-und-Drang* manner. Unlike the *stile brillante* pianists, for example, he seems to have used the pedal heavily. Friedrich Wieck found his playing a little heavy, muddy, and monotonous, and hoped to compensate by pushing for more Paganinian zip and sparkle. A revealing moment in the formation of his pianistic ideals is from the year 1833, when pianist Wilhelm Taubert arrived in Leipzig. Taubert was the kind of musician Schumann might have considered a serious rival. Born one year later than Schumann, Taubert matured early under the tutelage of the revered Berlin pedagogue Ludwig Berger, who also taught Mendelssohn. Taubert was basically classical in orientation but did not entirely avoid the pull of modern romantic pianism and was occasionally faulted for "modern eccentricity." He was never arrayed with the lions of modern bravura such as Liszt and Thalberg, and he apparently lacked some imagination in free improvisation. When he appeared at an instrumental concert by Carl Möser in 1832, his free fantasy was judged "not interesting enough in invention or sufficiently varied" (AMZ 1832, 319). When he started his pianistic tours in 1830s he nevertheless staked his reputation on free fantasies and on his playing of Beethoven's concertos. In both capacities he promoted himself as a serious or learned musician, and he landed a kapellmeister position in Berlin, becoming known mainly as a conductor and composer of large-scale pieces. A biography from 1857, when Taubert was still alive, claimed "his virtuosity in piano playing rises to an elevated level through rare powers of memory, exceptional facility in score-reading, as well as the now less frequently encountered talent in the performance of free fantasias."[16]

When Schumann first heard Taubert in Leipzig in 1833, he was not too impressed with his performance of Beethoven's Third Piano Concerto. The free fantasia that followed the concerto was somewhat better, but he was still not satisfied:

His elegance and agility reveal themselves here more significantly than in the concerto. I did not hear beautiful ideas; nor that rapture that seems oblivious to itself, nor that genius that seems to work without a body—plenty of good and capable things, ripe and articulate things. It did not seem prepared, at most contrapuntal details.[17]

Schumann was clearly impressed by Taubert's competence, but his comment on the lack of genius or performative rapture reveals that he had other expectations of improvisation: free fantasies should ideally manifest poetic inspiration or unselfconscious rapture, unfettered by learning and rules. Schumann's comments might give the impression that Taubert was a "cold" performer, but a report on his Leipzig appearances suggests otherwise:

He still storms and blusters too much, notably in his free fantasias, the first of which (in the subscription concert) seemed better carried out than the second. We are generally of the opinion that young people should not improvise in public at all; they cannot stand on their own; not rarely a trivial thing will put them in a mood quite unfavorable to free improvisation. Hummel and a few other experienced masters can still improvise; the rest [can do it] at home and in friendly salons. (AMZ 1833, 835)

Though unsigned, these words were probably penned by Schumann, who had not yet founded his own music journal and occasionally wrote for the AMZ.[18] The comparison between the first and second free fantasia indicates a sharp, seasoned critic. The author appears to know from experience how a performer's mood influences his capacity to improvise; indeed there is a strong hint of frustration with the challenge of keeping concentration while publicly improvising. Moreover, Taubert is faulted with precisely the same "storm and bluster" that Schumann was trying to reform in his own playing, in response to Wieck's criticisms. If the passage is indeed Schumann's, it provides unusually direct evidence of his change of heart about improvisation. Free fantasies do not belong in public concerts, and young musicians should stay away from them if they cannot rise to the standards of the older masters.[19] And most significant, the genre lacks aesthetic self-sufficiency: "it can't stand on its own." This is the beginning of the trajectory that would gradually lead Schumann away from the piano toward the advocacy of "head"-based music.

In the same journal entry where Schumann commented on Taubert, he implicitly traced his own performative genealogy back to Beethoven, whose fiery improvisations were already the stuff of legend. Taubert's approach to the thematic reprises of Beethoven's concerto finale—playing them the same every time—was in his opinion "certainly contrary to *Beethoven's fantastic performing manner.*"[20] In this "Kreislerized" vision of Beethoven's playing, returns and repetitions never sound the same but should perpetually unfold new "poetic" dimensions of the theme. Schumann's markings for the repetition of the second strain of the "Abegg" theme

(Example 4.1) demonstrate his drive to vary repetitions in this manner. The spirit of
Beethoven, imagined as an improvising pianist, also hovers over the first movement
of Schumann's *Fantasie*, op. 17. This movement's rhetorical breaks and sudden emotive
surges place it in the free fantasia tradition extending back through Beethoven and
C. P. E. Bach. Schumann's performance indication, "To be played fantastically and pas-
sionately throughout" (*Durchaus phantastisch und leidenschaftlich vorzutragen*), echoes
Beethoven's wordy indication for the first movement of the opus 90 sonata: "With ani-
mation and throughout with feeling and expression" (*Mit Lebhaftigkeit und durchaus mit
Empfindung und Ausdruck*). The original marking Schumann gave for this movement,
"Allegretto," lacked all poetic implication, apparently assuming the performer would
figure out how to manage its fragmented rhetoric. This was first replaced with "To be
played completely freely and with strong feeling throughout" (*Mit durchaus heftiger
Empfindung und ganz frei vorzutragen*), a phrasing that makes more explicit the aspiration to improvisatory liberty at the levels of both time and expression. The final
revision of this marking replaces "completely free" with *phantastisch*.[21] Although these
words are essentially synonyms, *phantastisch* has an aesthetic or poetic implication
indicating the composer's imagination rather than the performer's interpretative role.
Schumann's shifting tempo indications, in sum, crystallize a shift from performance-
oriented thought to composerly thought.

　　Schumann's interest in the dramatic free fantasia style is also indicated by his great
admiration for Hummel's Sonate in F♯ minor (1819), which he called "a truly grand,
epic titan-creation."[22] The first movement of Hummel's sonata opens with a dramatically intense musical paragraph marked by dynamic and registral contrasts, harmonic

EXAMPLE 4.1 Schumann, *Variationen über den Namen "Abegg,"* op. 1

surprises, and an alternation of hesitant and bold gestures—all suggesting the free fantasia style (Example 4.2). It is not surprising that Schumann gravitated toward such music. Its phrasing and atmosphere are far less regular or predictable than most of Hummel's music, and it seems to emulate the "improvisatory," stop-and-start rhetoric of Beethoven's middle-period sonatas. At the opening of his *Allegro*, op. 8, Schumann was clearly borrowing from Hummel's opening, though he reconfigured its rhythmic, motivic, and gestural elements. He pushed the model even further in the improvisatory direction by dispensing with barlines and indicating *senza tempo* (Example 4.3). This unbarred music is recapitulated and extended later in the movement, producing

EXAMPLE 4.2 Hummel, *Sonate* [in F♯ minor], op. 81, 1st mvmt

EXAMPLE 4.3 Schumann, *Allegro*, op. 8

a striking anomaly to its overall sonata-allegro design (though it shares this anomaly with Hummel's piece).[23] Unbarred music was becoming extremely rare in this period, but it did appear in collections of preludes, such as those by Moscheles and Hummel, that modeled short improvised introductions. By invoking this tempo-less, improvisation horizon at key framing points, Schumann in essence produces his version of a *sonata quasi fantasia*.

The dramatic free fantasia style, with its characteristic oscillation between depressive and excited states, is not the only improvisation-based layer of postclassical pianism. A deeper and more constitutive layer lies in its repertoire of idiomatic keyboard figures. Such figures are often overlooked by musicologists because they do not participate in thematic, harmonic, or formal processes, and are thus sometimes deemed "inessential" surface features. But as Jim Samson has argued, they are central to the inventive and improvisatory practices of postclassical pianism: "The story of keyboard virtuosity is partly the story of such idiomatic figures. They are among the most transparent embodiments of instrumental thought available to us, and as such they document a medium-sensitive approach to composition. . . . For obvious reasons they involve the ancient craft of improvisation."[24] Postclassical pianists differed from earlier pianists in devising figures that fit comfortably within the span of the hand and could be executed without awkward positional shifts or finger crossings. They also made extensive use of the pedal to facilitate gentle stretches of the hand or to blend individual tones into washes of pianistic sonority, thus expanding the variety of possible figures. Such figures, when practiced sufficiently in several keys, facilitated the immediate recall so indispensable to fluent improvisation. The universe of figures belonged to a broader orientation—a bodily, tactile sensibility that James Davies calls "handedness"—that characterized keyboard playing in the years around 1830, due in no small part to Hummel's pedagogy and its emphasis on the "naturalness" of the hands on the keys.[25]

Idiomatic keyboard figures had an aesthetic purpose as well, giving the music a main "idea" that was not melodic or even motivic in character, thus liberating the improviser from the difficulty of having to invent melodies or develop motives. With the repertoire of idiomatic figures, textural and harmonic invention came to the center of the improvisational process. Two genres of composition—the etude and the prelude—catalogued the invention and elaboration of such figures, and postclassical pianist-composers published them in droves. Some prelude collections presented very short examples intended to model an improvised prelude. Other preludes were longer and stylistically indistinguishable from etudes that explored a single figure from beginning to end.

Most consumers of published preludes and etudes intended to use them as technical exercises that would help them climb the stepladder toward more difficult pieces or improve their sight-reading. For an advanced pianist like Schumann, however, they were encyclopedias of invention, offering a world of possibilities for the elaboration of idiomatic figures through improvisation and composition. Two works demonstrating this type of exploration are the *Studien für das Pianoforte, nach Capricen von Paganini bearbeitet*, op. 3, and the *Toccata*, op. 7. In the pedagogical preface to the *Studien*, Schumann states that students need not play the pieces from beginning to end, but can choose bits and sections according to the specific technical problem they want to address. Schumann even offers some exercises serving as preparation for the etudes—literally etudes for etudes.[26] One shows him experimenting with a figure that harmonizes a descending chromatic scale with iterative voice-leading patterns (Example 4.4). These patterns are tricky to play but they require practice more than dexterity. Once burned into muscle-memory, they are enormously practical for the improviser. As the "et cetera" (u.s.w., *und so weiter*) indication at the lower-right of the example suggests, they can be extended infinitely through the chromatic space, having no beginning or end. They can be summoned or abandoned by the improviser at will in virtually any harmonic context. Because these particular figures are harmonically unmoored, they were most likely to come in handy for improvised cadenzas and modulating transitions. However they were employed, Schumann's exercises and etudes point toward a performance- and piano-immanent ontology of music-making—an idea of music as a free, fluent spinning-out of practiced figures, without a "theme," without any aspiration to organic unity, and devoid of the metaphysics of the "work."

EXAMPLE 4.4 From pedagogical "Preface" to *Studien für das Pianoforte, nach Capricen von Paganini bearbeitet*, op. 3

EXAMPLE 4.5 Schumann, *Toccata*, op. 7, main figure

Schumann's *Toccata* can be seen, at one level, as an extensive exploration of the tritone-to-minor-6th figure found in Example 4.4. Apparently born of an 1828 improvisation, its principal "theme" is the alternating double-note figure seen in the right hand in Example 4.5, which dominates the entire first period.[27] Aside from its piquant sonority and its enticing possibilities for harmonization, this figure has one distinct practical advantage over the classic double-note figures—parallel thirds and sixths—familiar from Clementi and his successors. It fits under the hand more comfortably and naturally, and prevents fatigue by pivoting between outer and inner fingers. It is thus not surprising that Schumann wanted to master this resource thoroughly, and that he initially labeled the *Toccata* using the French words *étude* and *exercise fantastique en double-sons*. Before it was a work, it was a practice—an improvisatory exploration of a figure at the keyboard in the spirit of "study" and "exercise," with all the self-sufficiency implied by those terms. He discovered chromatic deployments of the figure that sounded dissimilar to the music of his postclassical forebears and radiated a *fantastique* tone (Example 4.6). But the figure itself came from the repertoire of postclassical pianism and can be found in contemporary examples of improvised music. Czerny's treatise on preluding (not to be confused with his treatise on improvisation) includes a short prelude "in connected chords" that is nearly identical to a segment of Schumann's *Toccata* (Examples 4.7 and 4.8). Kalkbrenner, in his improvisation treatise, took elementary voice-leading patterns through chromatic sequences in a manner similar to Schumann's exercises (compare Example 4.9 with Example 4.4).

EXAMPLE 4.6 Schumann, *Toccata*, chromatic figures

EXAMPLE 4.7 Czerny, *Systematische Anleitung zum Fantasieren auf dem Pianoforte*, op. 200, ch. 1

EXAMPLE 4.8 Schumann, *Toccata*

Although the *Toccata* has many postclassical traces, Schumann made efforts to distance the work from whatever improvisational history it might have had. The change of title from "etude" to "exercise," and from "exercise" to *Toccata*, supplants its postclassical roots with a more historicist claim. The melodic motive that arrives with the second key area is superimposed upon the *moto perpetuo* figures in a manner that suggests artful "composition" for more than "improvisation." After much experimentation with the work's conclusion, Schumann settled upon a "poetic" slow fade that cancels its association with bravura and renders it more immaterial or fantastical.[28] In all these ways the *Toccata* registers the growing influence of the work-concept in Schumann's thinking. The point of emphasizing the postclassical horizon of the piece is not to reimagine it as a "written out improvisation," which it is not, but to locate its roots in the concrete, material practices specific to the composer-virtuoso tradition, including improvisation. It is not a pure emanation of the composer's imagination, and its fantastical tone is significantly mediated by his engagement with the material, piano-immanent universe of postclassical pianism. Schumann articulated the work's

EXAMPLE 4.9 Fréderic Kalkbrenner, *Traité d'harmonie du pianiste* (1849)

EXAMPLE 4.10 Schumann, *Sonate* [in F♯ minor], op. 11, finale

double horizon in his oxymoronic formulation *exercise fantastique*. With the term
double-sons (double-sounds)—a pun on *double-sens* (double-meaning)—he layers a
second, poetical meaning on top of the prosaic premise of the piano exercise, pressing
material practice into service of compositional fantasy.

In Schumann's early piano output there are only two passages that use explicit improvisational terminology. In the mosaic-like finale to his Sonate in F♯ minor, there is
a short transitional passage linking the first period (*Maestoso*, A major) to a new idea
in the secondary key area of E♭ major (Example 4.10). Not long thereafter, this short

transition returns, in transposition, to pivot back from E♭ to A major, and this time it is marked *quasi improvisato*. The marking offers no easy interpretation as a performance direction since it is also marked *marcato*, leaving little space for rhythmic push and pull. Perhaps it indicates, at the fantastical level, a sudden intrusion of the impetuous improviser Florestan-Paganini, come to ironize or undermine the heroic pretension of the preceding *maestoso* (the sixteenth-note figure strongly resembles a cross-string *spiccato* in the Paganini manner). Yet there are other, more traditional improvisational resonances in this passage. The enharmonic magic that takes the music so quickly from A major to maximally distant E♭ was a specialty of keyboard improvisers. Loose and rapid enharmonic transitions can be found, for example, linking the discrete sections of Kalkbrenner's *Effusio musica*—a piece intended to simulate a free fantasy— as well as the Chopin F-major *Impromptu*, a composition closely related to Chopin's improvising practice.[29] Upon this stunning harmonic shift, Schumann superimposes a comparably radical transformation of the leading sixteenth-note figure. It starts off decisive and martial, but quickly becomes something dreamy and slightly playful. In a sonata obsessed with doubles and polarities, the *quasi improvisato* passage explores a liminal space where various sorts of opposites can be mediated and moved seamlessly through one another.

The second explicit reference to improvisation appears at the opening of the last section of *Variationen über den Namen "Abegg,"* op. 1, which is marked *Finale: alla Fantasia* (Example 4.11). This section contains no traces of free fantasia rhetoric or even paraphrase. It calls for an explanation that leaves Schumann's "romanticism" far

EXAMPLE 4.11 Schumann, *Variationen über den Namen "Abegg,"* finale

Statements 1–3 of chord progression

Statement 4

behind and points more unambiguously toward the practices of postclassical pianism.[30] The finale opens with an arc-shaped phrase lacking all melodic or motivic content. It simply unfolds a four-bar cadential chord progression over a dominant pedal. This progression—the "theme" of the finale—is immediately repeated twice with different *brillante* figurative patterns, until the bass unfreezes and launches an extended progression toward a tonic cadence. The form of the finale is shaped by two reprises of the progression-theme, with intervening free-form digressions, and rounded off with a fade-out *codetta*. Each of the seven iterations of the progression-theme introduces changes of figure, tempo, dynamics, chord voicing. These variations, sometimes minute and subtle, give the impression that Schumann spent considerable time at the piano exploring the variative possibilities of the progression. Returning repeatedly back to the tonic 6/4 sonority, it evokes a circular, quasi-hypnotic sense of time and can be repeated *ad infinitum*.

Such experimental elaboration of simple harmonic progressions was standard practice for the pianist-composers of the 1820s and earlier. Rooted in figured bass practice, but free of numerical figures, such progressions were part of the postclassical pianist's repertoire of tropes and patterns that Jim Samson calls "musical materials."[31] Improvisations by postclassical pianists such as Moscheles and Meyerbeer tended to start from folkish songs and comic opera melodies, usually in some sort of periodic form. But as an exercise for developing extemporaneous skill, the short chord progression served as an ideal vehicle. Kalkbrenner, in his treatise on preluding and improvising, recommended that students begin with simple elaborations of basic, closed harmonic progressions and gradually proceed to greater degrees of elaboration (Example 4.12). The ability to flesh out elementary patterns in variation was particularly valuable for improvising dance music at social salons, as Schubert and Chopin are known to have done. Chopin's *Berceuse*, originally entitled *Variantes*, appears to have been the product of Chopin's improvisational habits, and it represents an extreme case of the short chord progression as the foundation for free elaboration.[32] And as mentioned earlier, Schumann once improvised obsessively on the cyclic bass C-F-G-C.

Schumann was surely aware of the baroque practice of improvising variations on standard progressions, but we cannot assume that he based his keyboard improvisations on such progressions. For all his interest in Bach, he did not obviously think of the baroque master in connection with variations or ground basses.

EXAMPLE 4.12 Kalkbrenner, *Traité d'harmonie du pianiste*

His diaries from 1827 to 1831, when he improvised most, only rarely mention specific tunes he improvised upon, but the few he does mention are typical of the postclassical free fantasy rather than baroque practice. The complete list includes Himmel's "An Alexis send'ich dich," Weber's *Afforderung zum Tanze*, the drinking song "O du lieber Augustin," Schubert's *Sehnsuchtswalzer*, and "the Field concerto" (as he called it in a diary entry). We don't know which motive from the Field concerto Schumann was using, but the other four themes were all familiar, indeed "popular," in the German-speaking world (Example 4.13). Harmonically they are all quite elementary. The first bars of the Schubert waltz, for example, replicate the beginning of Kalkbrenner's model progression. A more striking commonality among these four tunes is that they are all in triple meter, two of them—the Schubert and Weber—being waltzes.

Schumann's strong gravitation toward simple triple meter models favors an interpretation of the conclusion of the "Abegg" variations as some sort of stylization of his improvisational practices ca. 1830. His choice of a waltz theme is unusual for concert variation sets of the time, but it makes sense for a pianist busy in salons rather than public concerts. The "alla Fantasia" finale should clearly be heard as an acceleration of waltz-theme's 3/4 lilt. (Its pace is no faster than Weber's *Aufforderung zum Tanze*.) Other aspects of the finale reminiscent of improvisation are the relatively loose joints between episodes and reprises, the chromatic figures built around the shape of the hand, and the varied repetition of a short cadential formula in the coda. A sense of improvisatory freedom, furthermore, pervades the unmetered music immediately preceding the finale. It opens with a citation of the "Abegg" theme, but instead of launching another variation it becomes an open-ended, improvisatory cantabile that

EXAMPLE 4.13 Himmel, melody of "An Alexis send'ich dich," a common theme taken for improvisations in the 1810s and 1820s; from A. W. Bach, *Variationen für das Piano-Forte über den beliebten Gesang von Himmel "An Alexis send'ich dich"* (Berlin: Lischke, ca. 1818)

dissolves into a cadenza. The potentially improvisatory history of the "Abegg" finale should not, however, lead us to conclude that these variations are somehow less of a "work." For all its debts to the tradition of brilliant virtuosity, the piece in certain ways critiques the conventions of the virtuoso concert work.[33] Its title suggests esoteric or private meanings. The density and detail of the first two variations, the relative compactness of the form, and especially the quiet ending set it distinctly apart from the style of postclassical concert variations. They betray a will to "poeticize" within the variation-set format.

IMPROVISATION, *BILDUNG*, AND ECONOMY

The conflict Schumann felt between the joyful, spontaneous experience of improvisation and the need to rein it in for the sake of compositional productivity points to a larger tension in the *Bildung*-centered model of subjectivity that was consolidating in the German middle classes in the 1830s. Improvisation establishes a situation of open-ended, non-productive play and potentially violates ethical principles of thrift, economy, and efficient productivity that were increasingly enforced as norms of behavior. The moral economy of the German middle classes encouraged freedom and creative play, but simultaneously insisted that such play must be disciplined and channeled toward productive and lasting ends such as scores and compositions or, beyond music, children, respectability, and household income. As moralizing voices sought to control or channel experiences of subjective play and experimentation, they reinforced a conception of improvisation as excessive or transgressive, unwittingly giving it a seductive new aura.

The fascination with improvisation took shape in live performances as well as literary representations. Germans seem to have encountered Italian improvisers mainly on their trips to Italy, but ever since O. L. B. Wolff's breakthrough of the 1820s, German-speaking talents had been appearing to rival the Italians. In Leipzig, Schumann heard a performance by the itinerant improviser Maximilian Langenschwarz and dismissed him as a "charlatan." Schumann undoubtedly knew about the less controversial Wolff, who was now a professor in nearby Jena. And through his friendship with J. P. Lyser he must also have witnessed the poetry improvisations of Karoline Leonhardt-Lyser. As literary historian Angela Esterhammer has shown, the figure of the *improvvisatore* was also appearing in novels and poems. In such works the *improvvisatore* was represented as a poetic genius, but his status as a public performer playing for money made him "an unstable agent potentially disruptive to gender, class, and economic systems," and this disruptive potential was strongest in the German context:

> The representation of the improviser as an inconsistent or unreliable agent, both in literature and in life, takes on its fullest dimensions in nineteenth-century German culture. . . . The young protagonists are exposed in the process of their *Bildung* to a variety of theatrical experiences that include improvisational

performance. But . . . these experiences of improvisation represent the kind of spontaneous, anti-establishment behavior that the young men must learn to sublimate if they are to assume appropriate social roles.[34]

A representative example from Schumann's immediate context is Hans Christian Andersen's breakthrough novel *The Improvisatore*, published in German in 1835. The novel is partly autobiographical: as a teenager Andersen was known to Copenhagen society for his brilliantly acted comic improvisations, earning him commissions to write *Singspiel* librettos.[35] The success of some early books earned him in 1833 a royal stipend to travel through Europe, where he charmed salons with an irresistible manner of reciting his fantastical tales. The trip brought him to Italy, where he continued to visit the salons and began to write his novel. *The Improvisatore* was immediately translated into many languages and propelled Andersen's rise to international fame. Andersen's trajectory bears certain direct parallels with the aspirations of the young Schumann. He was both an author and a performer, but his performer role—his ability to fascinate in the salons with his storytelling—temporarily overshadowed his status as writer. And like many aspiring poets, Andersen was sometimes plagued by the sense that performance and improvisation were achievements of a lesser order. When a Copenhagen colleague criticized his singspiels, Andersen threw up his hands, lamenting, "I am nothing but an improviser!"[36]

These tensions are at the center of Andersen's novel, which is part Italian travelogue, part *Bildungsroman*. The Italian protagonist Antonio, born into poverty and orphaned, is gifted with a natural capacity for extemporaneous poetic invention that gains him entry into the elite salons of Rome. Antonio's problems stem from his incapacity to turn his improvisational genius to socially productive use. His salon connections gain him neither a profession nor an amorous partner. His avoidance of professional and personal commitments makes him stray from the good path, and soon he finds himself running from the law. Antonio's personal growth depends upon channeling his talents to ends that are both productive and public. At a critical point his friend implores him: "You have glorious abilities, which must be developed, but that they must actually be, Antonio! Nothing comes of itself! People must labor! Your talent is a charming society talent; you may delight many of your friends by it, but it is not great enough for the public."[37] The fulfillment of this goal finally arrives when Antonio gives a splendid public improvisation at the San Carlo theater in Naples, in a charity performance for indigent fishermen.

Thomas Mann's debut novel *Buddenbrooks* delineates similar social "problems" with improvisation, but explores the economic relationships more explicitly. Mann's novel first appeared in 1900, and its narrative arc shows a concern with "degeneration" that was under heavy discussion in the previous decade (Max Nordau's *Degeneration* appeared in 1892). Although the novel does not belong to Schumann's time, its meticulous historical realism provides psychological insight into the status of art within bourgeois concepts of economy at mid-century. Taking place in the years 1835 to 1874, it portrays the mores of a merchant-capitalist family from the Protestant north. Life in the Buddenbrook household is characterized by disciplined work, elegant luxury, deep family pride, respect for traditions, religious piety, civic service, and the strategic pursuit of advantageous familial connections. The novel is subtitled "the decline of a family" because the Buddenbrook family's good fortunes are undone by various modern forces: popular revolution, war, unhappy marriage, predatory aristocrats, moral dissipation, and not least, a streak of bad physical health that begins to consume the family members.

Music plays a marginal role in the story until 1861, when the heir to the dwindling family fortune, Hanno, is born. Little Hanno has strong musical inclinations, but his father disapproves of them since they hold no practical value for the family or the business. As Hanno grows into his teens he thinks about his future and muses to a friend: "What should I do with my music, Kai? It does nothing. Should I travel around and play? They [my parents] wouldn't allow it in the first place, and secondly I will never know enough to be able to. I know almost nothing, I can only improvise a little bit when I am alone."[38] Hanno is an instinctive musician, full of fantasy and talent, but he cannot convert his musical inclinations into an economically productive pursuit; he can "only improvise." Taken together with his frail physical constitution, his improvisations emblematize the exhaustion and decay of the economizing discipline that had once brought the family to its prestigious heights. Before he dies, at the tender age of fifteen, Hanno plays one final improvisation, a pianistic *Liebestod* and, simultaneously, a *tour de force* of evocative prose. In the ethos of the Buddenbrook family, improvisation is resolutely anti-economic, and not only because Hanno is drawn to music instead of business. His process of music-making does not even arrive at finished works. As an improviser, he simply channels his energies into improvisations played in solitude, devoid of social impact and leaving no traces.

Hanno's conflict with the Protestant ethos of his family resonates in striking ways with the struggles of Schumann. Over the course of the 1830s Schumann made considerable efforts to streamline his musical labor so that he would improvise less and work his way toward the purely "head"-based manner of 1845. This artistic evolution went hand in hand with changes to his personal and domestic habits for greater efficiency and productivity. Gradually he was adopting economizing habits that infiltrated the lives of the German middle classes in the 1830s and 1840s at various levels, from the personal to the familial and the national. This ethos can be found in the business practices of people such as Friedrich Wieck and August Schumann, in habits of domestic management, in the education of children as "cultivated" subjects, and in principles of the then-modern science of political economy. By showing how Schumann absorbed and adopted practices of economy and self-economization in his life and his music, we will better see the social and ethical factors contributing to the decline of improvisation in European music at mid-century.[39]

Economies of Inventiveness

In common parlance the word "economy" evokes associations with money and with the large-scale management of natural and human resources. Here I want to work with a more multivalent concept of economy that does not presume a primarily monetary or material meaning and does not centralize its capitalist form. Economy is always about a disciplining of productive labor and an organized distribution of products within a discrete network of relations, putatively for the "greater good" (sustenance, perpetuation, stabilization) of the network. But this disciplining and distributing can take place at many levels—cognition, the individual, the family, the profession, the institution, the nation—and the labor thus organized is not always geared toward the provision of material needs. In the Greek city-state, citizens needed to demonstrate effective household management in order to project public virtue and maintain social status. Max Weber was fascinated by the modern western form of capitalism precisely because it seemed to be driven by ethical and religious convictions—the sanctity of work and the responsibility of individuals to make themselves productive—that were relatively independent of, when not in conflict with, monetary or material gain. The concept of economy, in other words, embraces ethical and political factors alongside monetary and material ones.

The ethical aspects of economy come to the fore not only in Max Weber's well-known study of the Protestant ethic, but also in a little-known essay by Vladimir Jankélévitch called "Cognitive Significance of the Principle of Economy" (1928). Jankélévitch rejected a view of cognitive economy that he believed was becoming dominant in empirical philosophy, pragmatic philosophy, and the social sciences. The target of his polemic was the "principle of the least expense of energy"—the idea that the mind, when confronted with the vast array of impressions the world throws at it, selects only a small fraction of them and uses only those needed to solve the immediate task at hand. This interpretation reduced the mind to its passive, reactive, and pragmatic function. It construed the concept of economy only in terms of limitation, reduction, minimization, or conservation. Jankélévitch, committed to a more vitalist philosophy, offered an alternative view of mental economy that stressed the mind's capacity for strenuous, active creation. Borrowing from the conceptual vocabulary of Henri Bergson, he stressed the "intuitional" powers of the mind, which pick up whatever has been brought to immediate consciousness and explore it, probing its essence and developing relationships to other impressions or memories. This is an almost purely mental sort of work, disengaged from pragmatic tasks, but it is creative and productive within that realm.

This cognitive activity can be described as "economic," as opposed to merely "imaginative," for reasons best explained by means of Jankélévitch's example. The economy of Liszt's Sonata in B minor, he argues, lies in "the complex metamorphoses of its four cardinal motives and the unity of their organic growth."[40] In other words, the minimization of motivic material helps concentrate and stimulate the composer's inventive powers, so that through inventive transformations a richly textured musical tapestry emerges. Here Jankélévitch is drawing on a conventional idea of motivic development and extending a line of thought, leading back to E. T. A. Hoffmann, that stresses the beauty of motivic unity. But unlike Hoffmann and his descendants, who emphasized the motive as an agent of identity, Jankélévitch privileges the processes—the "growth" and "metamorphoses"—to which the motive is subjected. While acknowledging the importance of minimized means, he valorizes the diversity and richness of the ends. Moreover, Jankélévitch's conception of the economic "output" is emphatically dynamic and processual in spite of his recourse to a musical work for illustration. He is not particularly interested in Liszt's sonata as a complete musical object, but as a trace of an intellectual procedure, an in-time act of thinking and developing, which he believes to be music's true ontological state. Although Jankélévitch's essay is not primarily about music, its conclusion flows directly from the musical considerations:

> A new application does not bring anything essentially new. . . . But a new application implies a testing, a confrontation of the preexisting formula with certain accidental situations: and the act of integration that results from it lives on only by a mental effort. . . . In the effort of thought to "understand," in penetrating *intellection*, it is the theme itself that has become essentially flexible and dilatable: it has ceased to substantively transcend the stationary discourse of our mind, in order to become immanent to the alleys and pathways of an inventive proceeding.[41]

This account of the economizing intellect also characterizes precisely what happens when an improviser elaborates a given theme. Through strenuous mental exertions and "applications," the theme sheds its static qualities to become a new, "flexible and dilatable" kind of musical object.

Jankélévitch's perspective on cognitive economy, emphasizing expansive and generative process and the laborious work of mental creation, was not only a challenge to his peers in empirical and pragmatic philosophy. It also inverted the concept of economy prevalent in music criticism and aesthetics. Janet Levy has identified "economy" as one of the leading "covert and casual values" in music scholarship and criticism, and correctly identified it as a "legacy of nineteenth-century thought."[42] Economy was perhaps even the master-concept underlying the habitual praise of organic unity, concentration, counterpoint, and thematic work. Promoters of these phenomena stressed the unity and simplicity of motivic material. They located virtue in the minimization or concentration of thematic resources—the economy of means versus the economy of ends. Such values had become completely naturalized in the language of musical criticism: "[economy is] dependent on particular cultural/ideological contexts. But as it tends to be used in writings about music it is an ascription of praise . . . that is seldom made with explicit regard to a particular context."[43] Levy did not try to historicize these cultural/ideological contexts, but she did suggest that the virtue of economy was related to "the Protestant dictate of 'waste not, want not' and the sequel to that, 'a penny saved is a penny earned'."[44] The Protestant vision of economy valorized limitation, subtraction, and minimization at the level of means, and downplayed the inherent value of the products thus generated. Max Weber emphasized this apparent disjunction between the monetary and the ethical aspects of western capitalism. Its goal was the generation of money, but its most successful practitioners, he argued, followed a Protestant ethic of self-abnegation and virtuous conservation.

Concepts of economy, then, are inflected by the ethical systems in which they are embedded. They vary according to the balance they establish between means and ends, and most of them support normative ideas about what constitutes legitimate labor or "good" products. From Jankélévitch's "catholic" perspective, improvisation looks economic in the most positive sense, but from the perspective of Protestant ethics it looks fully anti-economic. Schumann's evolution away from piano improvisation represents a triumph of the latter over the former. If he wavered between different economizations, however, it was not for personal reasons alone. His evolution took place in a historical context where music's cultural status was steeply ascending and, simultaneously, entering a large-scale marketplace organized along capitalist lines. On these shifting sands, conflicts over material and immaterial standards of value, and the proper channeling of musical labor, were bound to arise.

Head vs. Hand

To follow Schumann's gradual absorption of the economizing ethos, which caused him to cease improvising, it will be expedient to start at the endpoint. In 1850 Schumann had accumulated sufficient credibility as a critic and as a composer of larger-scale works that he was appointed to the kapellmeister position in Düsseldorf. Though not very capable as an orchestral or choral conductor, he was happy to wield the baton for symphonic music and leave his identity as improvising pianist-composer far behind. With the recent death of Mendelssohn (1847) he acquired an important symbolic status as a role model for younger generations of musicians and caretaker of Germany's middle-class musical institutions. In this final period Schumann centered his ambitions on large-scale genres for orchestra and choir. He became more concerned with writing in a distinctly national or "folkish" style to reach a larger concert audience, thereby contributing to the development of a musical public sphere. As Reinhard Kapp has argued, his public role and responsibility made him into "Germany's musical preceptor": a teacher issuing advice to young and aspiring musicians from a position of wisdom and experience.[45]

It was in this role that Schumann disseminated his economized model of mental composition. In 1852 he wrote to Carl Debrois, an admiring young composer in Vienna: "Accustom yourself . . . to think of music in the mind itself, without the help of the piano; only this way do the inner sources open themselves up and manifest themselves in ever greater clarity and purity."[46] In the same letter he steered Debrois away from his early piano oeuvre, redirecting him toward the later, public works:

> You praise too highly and do so concerning my earlier works, such as the sonatas, whose occasional weaknesses are only too clear. In my later larger works, such as the symphonies and the choral compositions, such generous recognition might be more justified.[47]

As a matter of pedagogical principle, he wanted younger composers to imitate the composer of the Faust scenes or the "Rhenish" symphony, not the composer of Carnaval.

The mental approach to composition was aligned with a higher, purer, and more objective sort of composition than piano-based composition could ever be. To another composer he wrote: "Free yourself from the subjective piano. Choir and orchestra lift us up above ourselves."[48]

Schumann spread the doctrine of mental composition not only to advanced composers, but also to children. His collection of maxims and aphorisms known as "Musical House and Life Rules" was compiled in 1848–1849 and published as an appendix to the *Album für die Jugend*. They were aimed at establishing "healthy" musical habits early in children's musical development, and they stressed the capacity to imagine or represent musical ideas in the mind prior to their sonic realization:

> If you pick out little melodies on the piano, that is charming; but if they at some point come by themselves, not at the piano, then you enjoy yourself even more, for your inner sense of music is aroused—The fingers must do what the head wants, not the other way around.
>
> What does it mean to be musical? . . . You are musical . . . when you have music not only in the fingers but in the head and the heart.
>
> When you begin to compose, do everything in your head. Only when you have a piece completely finished should you produce it on an instrument. If your music comes to you from inside, if you feel it, it will also affect others.[49]

These pedagogical principles are a direct extension of Schumann's "completely new manner" of 1845. Having learned from his early mistakes, and having arrived at a satisfyingly "objective" method of composition, he now strove to install a particular economy of musical labor in the coming generation of musicians.

A strong ethical current runs through Schumann's musical advice to the young. Indeed the shortest maxim in the "House Rules" asserts: "the laws of morality are also those of art." Developing "inner" musicality thus followed a broader cultural mandate to develop a rich "inner" self. This was not an invitation for students to become introverted. The self Schumann seeks to form is conscious of itself, possessing an objective faculty that allows it to survey its activity and understand its relation to the outside. The ultimate goal of this inwardly conceived self is to "affect others" or "lift it above itself," but the procedure for attaining that goal is a rigorous concentration on inner powers. The ethical dimension of Schumann's rules for the young is perhaps most evident in the exclusive focus on process and procedure. There are no "aesthetic" comments about how good music should sound or what makes it beautiful—only rules for music-making as an activity unto itself, with its own independent principles of right and wrong, and the piano falls on the "wrong" side. Such high regard for the character of labor, and such disregard of concrete outcomes, is reminiscent of the Protestant morality that Max Weber detected in the western world's most successful capitalists. The right thing to do with one's wealth and with one's capacity to work, in this worldview, was simply to produce more wealth through work, and every occasion to profit from this inner potential was to be exploited.[50] Such ethical principles, though originating in religious concepts of the subject's relation to God, also applied to the microspheres of daily life and labor. As Kapp notes, "the very title 'house- and life-rules' is meant to convey that standards of general validity will be conveyed, which will be practiced in the 'house' and in 'life,' the musical as well as the social life."[51]

To witness such conjunctures between practices of economy in personal, household, and musical life, let us return to Schumann's earlier years. Only with great difficulty was Schumann able to discipline his personal and household habits of economy over the course of the 1830s. In letters to his mother written while a student, he often complained that his expenses were spinning out of control and asked her to send more money. As he entered Heidelberg "society," for example, he found himself in need of neo-aristocratic, gentlemanly accoutrements such as carefully tailored clothes, boots, and cigars, and the bills exceeded his means (EL 105). These requests were expressed in the lingo of responsibility to show his mother he aspired to economic control. In the early days of a trip through Switzerland and Italy in 1829, he complained to her that "however economical I am, I spend from three to four thalers a day, and sometimes from five to six. Driving comes horribly expensive. . . . In Italy I hope to manage on two thalers a day" (EL 72). This proved to be hopeful indeed; he was soon penniless and stranded in Milan, saved only by a last-minute loan from a fellow German (EL 73–76).

His personal finances did not improve much after university, when he settled into the Wieck house and committed himself to a professional career in music. Finding himself in insurmountable debt, he wrote his mother in a fit of self-loathing: "This contempt and waste of money is a wretched characteristic of mine. You would not believe how careless I am—I actually throw money away. I am always reproaching my-self, and making good resolutions, but the next minute I have forgotten them, and am tipping somebody with eight groschen. . . . And I fear it will never get any better" (EL 132). But he had a plan: if only his mother would send him 200 thalers to invest, he would have some sort of regular income from interest, and he could supplement it with his occasional musical income: "I have made an exact calculation of my receipts and expenditures up to Michaelmas. But still, I must have the interest of my money. . . . My capital I will never touch. . . . I will manage to earn or otherwise cover the deficit in my expenses. In my next letter I will send you my calculation" (EL 138–39). Apparently his mother believed in the plan, for he soon wrote proudly: "I can assure you that I have never lived so pleasantly, economically, and steadily as during the last three months" (EL 147).

In the aftermath of this breakthrough, Schumann worked resolutely toward house-hold autonomy.[52] He began casting about for work as a music critic and founded his own journal, the *Neue Zeitschrift für Musik*, to feature his distinctive literary voice. Management of the journal seems to have prompted a new commitment to careful accounting at home. But it was his courtship of Clara that gave real urgency to his pur-suit of household and financial management. When Clara informed him that Friedrich Wieck had called him a "spendthrift" he seethed with resentment: "for eight years I have not been out of Saxony, and have been sitting still, saving my money, without a thought of spending it on amusement or horses" (EL 276). In his continuing efforts to justify himself he underlined the meticulousness of his accountability and orderliness with respect to money, communications, and the household:

> The only thing that could possibly make me miserable would be to owe people money that I could not pay. . . . I have proved to you how exact I am in everything for your sake. I am sure you will be pleased with all my domestic arrangements. Would you believe it, the first thing I do every morning is write down all that I have spent the day before, and calculate it to the last penny. Are you aware that since 1835 I have kept a great draft-book in which I give a minute account of every letter written and received?[53]

When Clara and Robert got married, they began keeping a joint household diary in which they wrote to each other, and kept meticulous financial accounts of every transaction in the household.

Schumann's management of his compositional habits over the course of the 1830s followed a parallel trajectory marked by increased discipline and self-monitoring. In 1829 he admitted to Friedrich Wieck, with a blend of pride and embarrassment, that improvisation consumed his productive capacities: "sometimes I am so full of music, and so overflowing with melody, that I find it simply impossible to write down anything" (EL 82). Two years later, when he was twenty-one and aspiring to a professional career, he still did not have a single published opus, prompting one of the Wiecks to urge him: "dear Robert, I beg you—do produce something that's finished."[54] This goading had its intended effect: by the end of the year Schumann had published the "Abegg" variations and *Papillons*. From this point onward he was very conscientious about his work habits, but he continued to struggle. His diary entries often begin with an overview of the previous day's accomplishments: "In general accomplished little. Messy disorderly living. Unbelievably awful weather all the time" (TB 2:32). In October 1837, at the peak of the strife with Clara's father, he was experiencing difficulty concentrating on work. In three consecutive entries he wrote: "Yesterday dreamt away one hour after another. Wake yourself up!"; "What an awful day again yesterday. This cannot go on; get yourself together and get to work with all your powers! It cannot go on like this"; "Overall calmer yesterday. But incapable of work" (TB 2:36–37). This vigilance about time and work eventually paid off. He was particularly pleased at how fluently he was composing in 1838 while writing *Kreisleriana*. Yet there were still phases when he let down his guard. In May 1841, after a slow period, he reflected on his unfinished pieces and the difficulty of continuing them after long interruptions: "But the main thing is just to keep on producing" (TB 2:177). Success in composition depended essentially on steady labor, maintained through rigorous self-monitoring.

These habits of personal and domestic economy, crystallizing in the late 1830s, did not immediately spell the end of Schumann's attachment to the piano. His penchant for improvisation remained strong all through the 1830s, subsiding only later on. The finger injury destroyed his ambition to a pianistic career, but not his will to improvise: "Do not worry yourself about my finger!" he wrote to his mother in 1834, "I can compose without it; and I should hardly be happier as a traveling virtuoso. . . . It does not interfere with my improvising. I have even regained my old nerve in improvising before people" (EL, 222). As late as 1839 his compositional process was still dependent on improvising, even to the point of impeding productivity: "I am quite absorbed in a world of dreams over my piano. . . . If one could only finish everything one begins! But how much time one would need to do that!" (EL 293–94). A year later, while on vacation in Switzerland, he ran across a dilapidated old piano that awakened "the old music-madness that comes upon me when I encounter a piano after a long pause. Thus while in Switzerland I often improvised well into the night."[55]

Schumann, then, was only incompletely "reconstructed" in relation to free playing. The effort to build "objective" control into his creative process met with mighty resistance. Back in 1829 he had frankly celebrated the irrational spontaneity of improvisation and opposed it to didactic theory: "I detest theory pure and simple, as you know, so I have been living very quietly, improvising a good deal, but not playing much from scores" (EL 77). Just three years later, after taking a course in rigorous counterpoint, he changed his mind on the value of theory: "Dorn, my theoretical master, had improved my mind immensely, and, by steady application, I had succeeded in obtaining that beautiful clearness which I used so often to dream of, but never possessed" (EL 167). Thrilled with his rapid progress, he wrote to Friedrich Wieck: "formerly I wrote down everything on the impulse of the moment, but now I follow the course of my ideas more, and sometimes stop short and look round to see where I am" (EL 155). This thought, and its wording, portend his triumphant declarations about "head composition." The benefits of contrapuntal study extended beyond music to include a greater sense of overall personal health. The analysis of Bach's fugues, he wrote, "seems to have a strengthening moral effect upon one's whole system" (EL 179). In 1832, then, "beautiful clearness" entered Schumann's consciousness as an aspiration. At this point he did not yet associate rational control with transcendence of the piano. His orientation to music was still shaped, in the main, by the material and performative ontology of postclassical pianism. He even encouraged a student to keep working diligently on her piano etudes because "without fingers there would be no art, and Raphael and Mozart would never have existed" (EL 243). Instrumental mastery, "handedness," was still conceivable as an integral component of genius.

The next step in Schumann's evolution toward head composition took place in 1838, just as he was gaining confidence in his monetary circumstances and his personal accounting skills. Having recently composed *Davidsbundlertänze, Symphonische Etuden,* and *Kreisleriana,* he told Clara, "I am paying great attention to melody now" (EL 268)— "melody" meaning not lyrical phrases but longer-range planning of phrases and linear trajectories. Statements like this were aimed at pleasing Clara, who had recently urged him to become "clearer" in his compositions and to attempt a string quartet (EL 264). It was thus opportune for him, after announcing his new commitment to "melody," to say that "the piano is getting too limited for me" (EL 268). He warned Clara *not to improvise too much* [emphasis original]; too much gets uselessly lost that way. Make up your mind to get everything down on paper at once."[56] His updated ideal of musical production featured clearness, melody, avoidance of improvisation, and a shift away from the pianistic medium.

In reality Schumann was still far from relinquishing the pleasures and advantages of the piano. Just a few weeks earlier he had expressed pleasure at having attained a certain directness of expression in his compositions and in his performance of them: "my music now seems wonderfully intricate in spite of its simplicity; its eloquence comes straight from the heart, and everyone is affected when I play before people, as I often do now, and like to do" (EL 268). He again praised this economized, improvisation-free mode of production in recounting the composition of *Humoresque*:

> I have been all the week at the piano, composing, writing, laughing and crying, all at once. You will find this state of things nicely described in my op. 20, the "Grosse Humoresque," which is already at the printers. You see how quickly I always work now. I get an idea, write it down, and have it printed; that's how I like it. (EL 288)

There is a touch of overstatement here. Schumann was still capable of indulging in expansive bouts of improvisation, telling Clara that "last night I improvised quite marvelously at the piano" or that "at the piano I am inspiring myself a great deal."[57] The very notion of a musical "humoresque" embraces quirky, irrational psychological turns, and his state of mind—laughing, crying, and composing all at once at the piano—hardly evinces a breakthrough to Apollonian clarity. Only after 1840, the famous "year of song," did Schumann actually begin distancing the piano from his creative process and move in the direction of the "completely new manner" of 1845.[58] In 1841 or 1842, under continuing pressure from Clara, he began turning his attention to chamber works and symphonies. Piano works and songs would always have a limited audience. They were smaller in scale and lacked a significant public dimension. Such genres might be sufficient for the musical economy of the domestic household, but they were not for the macroeconomic musical world—the world of public concerts, oratorios, and operas that Schumann, now acknowledged as a major player, was expected to serve.

Economizing Subjects

Clara was just one influence on Schumann's evolution. His personal transformation was also aligned with economizing ideas and practices that were being advanced in criticism, aesthetics, and pedagogy. The critic and conductor Carl Kossmaly, an associate at the *Neue Zeitschrift für Musik*, published aphorisms and philosophical maxims stressing the need for musicians to manage carefully their creative resources:

> The artist should should seek above all to steadily gather together the powers and energies of his mind, and use them worthily with prudent economy [*mit weiser Oeconomie*]; he should restrain himself from burning away the holy fire of his soul in one permanently fiery, unnecessary, and wasteful [*kostspielige*] fit of enthusiasm.

It is typical of young, gifted, and vigorous musicians everywhere . . . to blow the cannon of their entire knowledge and their acquired studies. . . . It shows poor, foolish housekeeping [*Haushalt*] to give oneself away entirely all at one time.[59]

Kossmaly's ethics of musical labor, like Schumann's "House Rules," was aimed at the education of young musicians and the containment of enthusiastic excess. His perspective is especially relevant here because he, one year after penning these aphorisms, published a long survey of Schumann's piano works that cast aspersions on the early piano works: "the extravagance of which the composer is so particularly fond sometimes degenerates into bombast and complete incomprehensibility, as if the striving for originality occasionally loses its way."[60] These may be surprising words coming from a periodical edited by Schumann, but they matched his own judgment that early works like the Paganini studies, the "Abegg" variations, *Papillons*, and the *Allegro*— were "too small and too rhapsodic to make any great impact."[61] Schumann, Kossmaly, and their associates conceded this in order to strengthen the narrative according to which Schumann had transcended his improvisational past.[62]

An even more explicit voice for musical economization was that of the critic, pedagogue, and composer Adolph Bernhard Marx. The first volume of his most influential treatise *The Study of Musical Composition*, first published in Leipzig in 1837 and updated through the 1840s, merits close attention because it directly links the norms of musical composition with monetary and ethical aspects of economy. Marx's treatise was aimed at young students, not advanced practitioners, and his compositional method stresses untrammeled production. Rejecting the abstract, speculative tone of past composition treatises, he demands concrete activity and tangible productivity: "[the school] is . . . intended not merely to impart knowledge, but action [*That*]. The student, therefore, must by no means be contented with knowing and understanding the different doctrines of the School, but must be able to bring forth works of art, and indeed with ease and certainty."[63] Marx is trying to forge a certain kind of producer: a reliable, steady, and efficient one. To ensure this he is even willing to jettison the principle, repeated in countless treatises of earlier times, that good music begins with an inspired melodic idea or kernel.[64] The needs of musical production cannot wait for some arbitrary epiphany of inspiration that might never arrive: "We may, perhaps, be so fortunate as to possess some good [melodic] ideas. But this alone would be of little use. We must be certain that we shall always be able to produce something new; our productive power must not depend upon the accidental occurrence of a happy idea."[65] Marx does not explain why constant productivity is so important. He lays all value on productive activity itself, not quality of product. His regime is in this way analogous to the moral viewpoint Max Weber associated with capitalism, in which labor is meaningful in itself, and does not necessarily take its justification from the things it yields: "capitalism is identical with the pursuit of profit, and forever *renewed* profit, by means of continuous, rational, capitalistic enterprise."[66] Such a rigorous productive regime naturally entails total dedication to work: "The road toward this goal is unceasing diligence and continual creation." But diligence alone will not suffice. The student also needs to follow a distinct "method of study and practice," one that is rationally regulated, fully conscious of its productive methods, and accountable to its decisions: "We can and must be able to account for every step we take."[67]

Such rigorous standards of production could be met most securely by following Marx's prescribed technique: rational manipulations of a "motivo." Citing the model of Beethoven's Fifth Symphony, he systematically demonstrates how a small motive can be transformed through rhythmic, melodic, and harmonic permutations.[68] The ultimate goal of these generative operations—carried out by what Horkheimer and Adorno called "instrumental reason"—is to extend the motive into a large-scale musical structure, thus germinating a greater yield from the initial cell.[69] In laying out these principles Marx tellingly resorts to the registers of value and money. As if borrowing David Ricardo's labor theory of value and applying it to musical production, he writes: "it is not the motivo for its own sake, but both that *and* the manner in which it is developed, which constitute the value [*Wert*] of any artistic production based upon it."[70] Marx even describes this procedure using the metaphor of the expansion of capital through an investment of a germinal sum:

It is only by thus continually forming, transforming, and developing [the motivo] that the student can acquire the power of producing with facility and certainty; and, without this power, even great fertility of ideas is of little or no value, as every idea will remain fruitless. A piece of gold which I find is worth only as much as its value in money; but a skill which I have acquired, may be a source of constant profit.[71]

A. B. Marx was one of the few theorists in whose work Schumann took active interest. Schumann was reading the *School of Musical Composition* in the early 1840s and met Marx in person in 1842. His encounter with the *School* thus coincides precisely with his turn toward large-scale symphonic works, which called for techniques of motivic development.[72] It is difficult to imagine Schumann embracing Marx's relentlessly rationalistic method without some degree of hesitation. But the favor Schumann gave to "mental" composition could well be borrowed from this emphatic passage in Marx's *School*:

The student should also be able to realize in his mind the effect of any given or required combination of sounds, without the aid of an instrument. . . . To compose without the assistance of an instrument, is also the only way of becoming independent in the development of our ideas, and certain in their artistic representation. . . . Dispense as much as possible with all external assistance, such as the piano, or any other instrument.[73]

As in Schumann's "House Rules," these pronouncements concern not the aesthetic product, but only the process of composing. The goal is to acquire cognitive power in order "to invent and plan with clearness, freedom, and decision," and the means to the end is to concentrate rigorously on a single motive: "Only with limitation does he [the composer] unlock the full power, the entire inner richness of the minimal [*Reichtum des Wenigen*] to which he has confined himself."[74] The principle of adhering to a single motive "must never be abandoned, lest extravagance and confusion should take the place of unity and decision."[75] Passages like these uncannily echo Schumann's and Kossmaly's concerns about proper musical labor, the containment of waste, and the bizarre, irrational qualities of Schumann's early works. Yet Marx did not go quite as far as Schumann in banishing the piano entirely from the creative process. Once the student has developed strong mental powers and has learned to connect motives with phrases, Marx writes, "is it recommended to refresh the mind with improvisations [*Improvisationen*] on the given material, and also to accustom oneself to realizing immediately in tones the ideas unfolding on the inside."[76]

An echo of Marx's head-based principle is found in a didactic article from 1842 entitled "Tips for the Proper Study of Scores." Published in the reform-minded journal *Wiener allgemeine Musik-Zeitung*, the author ("E.") recommends that students strive to unite their reading of scores with concrete sound-impressions or sound-memories. The goal to arrive at a point where "the representations of sight and hearing combine with another in such a way that, when he later sees the same notes he earlier saw written, he believes himself to hear the tones again, and takes them in mentally" (WAMZ 1842, 75). Developing his skills this way, the student will acquire a productive method in which he "does not need the assistance of a pianoforte for the realization and clarification of conflicting ideas, and does not need to interrupt its continuity by hearing part of the piece on the instrument." Toward the article's conclusion, "E." clarifies that the model for such a method is found in Beethoven's creative process. He imagines Beethoven composing not through the medium of the piano, but only with

> a pen that cannot always keep pace with the rapid motions that lift him into the highest spheres. . . . Beethoven sketched his most wonderful tone-paintings in such beautiful blessed moments, and in the hours of cold reflection removed the traces of an overheated, borderline bizarre association of ideas, and only then oversaw the flowing, logical ordering that immortalized them for the public world.[77]

In this author's mind the germinal instant of Beethoven's invention, "the beneficent ecstasy of the moment," is piano-free, and necessarily so. Freedom from the instrument is the source of the vividness of the material and its concentrated unity. If the composer's inventive inspiration has led him to stray, he can later correct it in the working out of the piece, and it can be made legible "for the public world."

A. B. Marx's values for composition and for the education of younger musicians belonged integrally to his larger mission of producing a flourishing musical public sphere. As Celia Applegate has shown, he was a principal architect of Berlin's emerging concert life, exerting himself tirelessly to develop the musical public through criticism and education. He strove to advance music beyond the micro-economies of home, salon, and court, and to establish its "macroeconomic" dimensions with large audience participation in concert halls and theaters.[78] The leading themes of the *School for Musical Composition* are designed to produce the subjects and citizens appropriate to this publicly conceived musical culture. Its subjects will contribute to the musical commonwealth by steering themselves away from the wasted energies of piano-playing and establishing large-scale symphonic or choral canvases whose rational procedures can be followed by a large body of listeners. By coordinating the labor of individual producers with the larger economic needs of artistic life, Marx showed himself to be a political economist in the musical sphere. Schumann, for much of his career, had no such faith in the possibility of a democratic or participatory musical public sphere. But as he evolved into the role of kapellmeister and Germany's musical preceptor around 1850 and became a player in Germany's musical macroeconomy, he became a shining example of Marx's economized musical subject, and helped disseminate it in educational statements about the virtues of mental composition.

Romanticism and the Economy of Generation

To describe Schumann's evolution as one of "economization" risks naturalizing the minimalist, culturally Protestant version of economy, and forgetting that it can bear a less conservationist ethos. Both A. B. Marx and Schumann rhetorically exaggerated the value of "objectivity" in order to correct what they perceived as a dangerous overvaluation of the subjective. They stressed the "objective" virtues of rationality, accountability, and productive steadiness to the point of practically negating the role of subjectivity altogether. Their model of economized music production, in other words, was strongly marked by a *subtraction* of subjectivity. For Schumann, the attainment of objectivity was a way of correcting his earlier overinvestment, induced by romanticism, in the value of subjective inspiration and spontaneity. In his eyes, romantic subjectivity had come to look anti-economic, and improvisation looked anti-economic by association.

There is, however, a way to look at romantic subjectivity as pro-economic, and it is directly relevant to the earlier, improvising Schumann. In his book *The Ego-Effect of Money* Fritz Breithaupt argues that German romantic writers developed a dynamic model of the self that was influenced by recent developments in the science of political economy. After 1800, the discourse of political economy was turning away from Adam Smith's idea of economy as regulated by balance or equilibrium—between supply and demand—and starting to emphasize David Ricardo's notion of surplus—value that can generated and stored in excess of demand. The romantic notion of individuality picked up on this surplus dynamic: "The early Romantics defined individuality as an act of self-extension. . . . Individuality cannot simply be assumed as a given, but as something that has to be brought about. This bringing about takes the form of a reflection of the subject on the subject." The act of reflection, in other words, "generates the reflecting Ich as a surplus to the reflected being."[79] The subject is thus divided into an unreflective being-in-the-world, on the one hand, and a reflective or self-conscious awareness of that being, on the other. Romantic philosophers and poets made a virtue of intensifying the latter, reflective function as a strategy for expanding and enriching the self. They divided the self in order to expand it into something fuller, richer, larger. According to Breithaupt this idea of the self was often metaphorized in images of money and had a strong correlation to the latest theories of capitalism:

> This surplus-individuality is structured like that which Schlegel describes as the dynamics of money and [Karl] Marx later defined as capital: money that reflects on money, thereby growing or "extending itself" (*sich bilden*) by means of interest. . . . It is exactly this "moreness" of capital that connects individuality and money.[80]

Schumann's creative habits demonstrate this *Reflexionsprozess* with rare clarity. By inventing fantasy characters such as Florestan, Eusebius, and Raro, in both his writings and his pieces, he extended his self into a series of reflections—reflections that recursively produced him, Robert, as a deep, complex, multi-faceted individual. A similar dynamic of subjective extension applies to the *Doppelgänger* characters he obsessed over in his letters to Clara, and whose codes he wove into his music. They projected images of a non-self the subject strives to incorporate. Schumann seems to have been quite aware of the centrality of reflective processes. As he gained confidence in his compositions he distinguished himself from other composers in these words: "they deal in musical sentiment of the lowest order, and in commonplace lyrical effusions. . . . Theirs may be a flower, but mine is a poem, and infinitely more spiritual; theirs is a mere natural impulse, mine the result of poetical consciousness" (EL 270–71). What Schumann here calls "poetical consciousness" is in essence romantic reflection, elevating him above the unreflective "natural impulse" of his prosaic peers. Schumann's writings also provide examples of the conventional metaphorization of the self through money. At the height of the conflict with Friedrich Wieck in 1839, Robert urged Clara to remain true with the phrase: "Do not let yourself get sold out." If a person's inner value could be figured as money, the development of that self could be figured as capital accumulation. Thus did the impecunious Schumann beg his mother for more money, assuring her that it would be repaid in inner value: "I have often thought of your charming idea that I should store up a *treasure* in my heart, which will bring me *interest* later on" (EL 103, emphasis added).

Schumann's initiation into romantic reflection undoubtedly came through voracious reading in romantic philosophy and poetry. Yet his ability to convert it into music was crucially nourished by his improvising, for improvisation is in many respects the perfect vehicle of romantic reflection. It joins in a single temporal moment two seemingly contradictory states. On the one hand it channels the direct effusion, the impulse of the moment; on the other hand it engages the "external" faculty that reflects upon the given material. While improvising on a given theme, the pianist both delivers the theme and examines it, assessing its potential for development, generating new and original things from it.

This applies to earlier pianists as well as Schumann, but Schumann alone tied improvisation to the romantic self. Quite unlike previous pianists, he considered the piano a repository of thoughts, ideas, and personages. Such persons and presences seemed to be lodged in the keys or in his fingers—at a site external to the "inward" site of subjectivity. In an early letter to his mother he claimed that his "old grand piano . . . contains the sweetest recollections of my childhood and youth, and has taken part in all that I endured, all my sighs and tears, but all my joys too" (EL 33), and that "my piano tells me all the deep sentiments which I cannot express" (EL 33). In 1834 he told Clara that "when I am thinking of you very intently, I invariably find myself at the piano, and seem to prefer writing to you in chords of the ninth, and especially with the familiar chord of the thirteenth" (EL 233). On other occasions he claimed to "hear" Clara's voice traveling through his instrument from a distance. In these cases the instrument served as a kind of confidante or dialogic partner through which his subjectivity unfolded and extended itself. The piano was both literally and figuratively a sounding board, mirroring back to him images, impulses, and fantasized love objects that fed his fermenting subjective consciousness. In this sense the piano acted as a double of his own self—a surrogate for his many alter-egos and alternate personas. It took on a phantasmic quality of agency and became an essential catalyst of a subject-object feedback process.[81]

Many of Schumann's first published works were the outcome of this improvisation-rich, reflective compositional process. In 1832 he told Friedrich Wieck, "I compose easily and rapidly, but in working it out I am always trying all sorts of experiments, which almost make me despair [of finishing]" (EL 173). Presumably these "experiments" were new combinations and developments of material that he tried out in improvisation. Perhaps he had a hard time fixing them on paper because the various alternatives all seemed good, or because the flow of improvisation suggested a new and better possibility just ahead. There was something indiscriminately productive and expansive about these improvisations. They had no logical end, and there was always more that could be done. Around the same time, as he was working on the *Intermezzi*, op. 4, he wrote in his diary: "How long and how boundlessly I improvised yesterday. The briefest of pauses makes oneself aware of the progressive steps just taken, and one is amazed at the place at which one has arrived" (TB 1:411). Here Schumann marks the strangely unmediated gap between the experience of improvisation, which is completely immersive, and the retroactive faculty of aesthetic judgment. Improvising on the *Intermezzi* materials has taken him to a place that he is unable to recognize while improvising. It has gone its own way. And in this case, importantly, Schumann seems to have been pleased with the outcome. However this faculty of judgment should not be confused with the reflection active *within* improvisational playing, which generates and extends the given materials in time and has only the shortest interval of retrospective distance.

Schumann's improvising practice, then, carried an ethos of unceasing generativity that was economically productive on its own terms. Its logic of abundance was fully reconcilable with a certain dimension of capitalism. His challenge was not finding a way to make improvisation productive, but finding a way to make it *less* productive—in other words, stopping the generative process so that something could take fixed form in a score. Over time, improvisation began to take on an anti-economic appearance because it failed to produce commodities—exchangeable musical objects that could enter the order of monetary circulation. And it was ultimately the notion of the commodity, of concretely stored value, that overtook the understanding of "economy." The theory of mental composition aspires not only to transfer musical conceptions to paper directly, but more radically, to influence the very conceiving of musical ideas with a view to their eventual transfer to paper. The commodity form in this way determines compositional labor from the beginning, not only at its end. It banishes in advance those forms of musical production—improvisation and in-time performance—whose value is temporally and spatially immanent.

The tension between pro- and anti-economic assessments of improvisation is at the heart of little Hanno's fate in *Buddenbrooks*. Hanno's family, symbols of the Protestant-capitalist ethos, can see nothing in his improvisations but counterproductive waste and loss, for such music escapes entirely the circuit of monetary circulation. Mann's narrative of Hanno's final improvisation, however, portrays the performance as richly generative and spiritually redemptive. In several pages of searing prose it evokes the dramatic twists and turns of the frail teenager playing by himself in a curtained drawing room. This is an expansive, epic sound canvas, filled with wild and dangerous adventures, ecstatic triumphs, religious consolations, extreme dynamics, and the full complement of orchestral sonorities. Yet this epic production, for all its maximalism, is generated entirely from the smallest possible source: "It was an utterly simple motive that he presented—a nothing, the fragment of a non-existent melody, a figure of one and a half measures." As he begins to harmonize the motive and develop it through modulations, his performance releases its potency: "[it was] a short-breathed, meager invention, but which was given secretive and significant value [*Wert*] through the precious and solemn decisiveness with which it was presented and brought forth." This motive returns periodically throughout the improvisation as a unifying red thread, returning in an apotheosis at the climax of the entire performance: "it was the motive, the first motive, that sounded! And what presently began was a festival, a triumph, an unrestrained orgy of this very figure, which came forth victorious . . . done up with all the bluster, tinkling chimes, and surging richness of an orchestral setting."[82]

For Hanno, and for Mann's reader, this improvisation leaves nothing to be desired. It is a "perfect" performance insofar as it generates a plenitude of meaning, a completeness of experience not to be found anywhere else in the lives of the Buddenbrooks. It is so fulfilling that it even casts doubt on whether Hanno's imminent death should be considered tragic. His colorful improvisation produces nothing of value to his family or to the world, no commodity that can be exchanged or shared. But it produces everything of value to him—intensity of experience, beauty, sensual pleasure, fullness of purpose—and therefore functions perfectly within his personal and spiritual economy. By narrating the improvisation in a seductive manner, Mann presents Hanno's decadent aestheticism as a legitimate counter-ethic to the prevailing Protestant-capitalist climate of the story. Mann also underlines its internally economic logic. The great expressive and sonorous luxury of the improvisation derives, paradoxically, from an inventive procedure of extreme austerity: "There was something brutal and deafening and at the same time something ascetically religious, something like faith and self-sacrifice in the fanatical cult of this nothing, this piece of melody, this short, childish, harmonic invention of one and half measures."[83] Turning A. B. Marx's goals for motivic economy on their head, Hanno makes the motive a vehicle of radical coloristic and dramatic development, aimed at the provision of purely private aesthetic pleasure. Hanno thus represents, in an exaggerated form, the productive ethics of the younger Schumann—the Schumann who took hedonistic delight in improvising, hour after hour, with motives and fantastical creatures lodged within the instrument.

This chapter has traced a familiar evolution—Schumann's transformation from improvising piano virtuoso to composing kapellmeister—in order to show how personal ethics and the logic of capitalism had an impact on improvisation in the first half of the nineteenth century. The most important factor was a modern notion of what properly constitutes productive labor in music. For the young Schumann, improvisation needed no justification: it gave him experiences of rapture, provided social advantages in society, and linked him with prestigious artists like Hummel, Moscheles, and Beethoven. Over the 1830s, through Herculean efforts, he subordinated this labor to the production of compositions, rethinking piano improvisation as the pre-compositional tool *par excellence*. Having thus conquered the digressive pull of piano-playing, he worked toward an even more streamlined model of productive economy: the pianoless "new manner" of 1845 and beyond. For Schumann, his associates, and his admirers, these stages were signs of a positive "upward" development toward greater maturity and discipline. I have argued that this evolution responded to an ethic of economy shaping the lives of the German middle classes at several levels: in the management of household affairs, in the musical education of children, and in discourses of political economy that advocated the rational apportionment of material and labor for maximal public benefit. Schumann's relentless self-monitoring, the careful way he watched over his personal powers and energies, best exemplifies how this ethos insinuated itself into the life and consciousness of individuals. It induced in him a fear of wasted resources and unproductive musical labor, which he came to associate with his early passions. He eventually viewed piano improvisation, poetic enthusiasm, and romantic reflection as anti-economic, and exchanged them for an economized compositional method free from manual labor, rationally organized, and capable of distributing its fruits into the public space of concert life. Successfully or not, he converted himself into the sort of musical subject appropriate to the new musical economy emerging in the 1840s.

The economizing ethos that militated against improvisation in Schumann's context closely resembles the secular Protestant spirit that Max Weber considered hospitable to western-style capitalism. This does not mean that capitalism is somehow the "ultimate cause" of the decline of improvisation. Indeed Weber opposed the Marxist interpretation of artistic production as a direct outgrowth of society's material base. The first stirrings of modern industrial capitalism were felt in Germany only in the 1850s, and if anything, the economic ethics of the middle classes anticipated *its* development rather than the reverse. Still less can we claim that improvisation in some fundamental way resists or eludes the forces of capitalism. A pianist like Liszt was capable of exchanging his improvisational performances for huge sums of money when he chose to, and such performances could in turn stimulate sheet-music sales that brought in more money still. The case of Schumann does however support the idea that improvisation poses a problem in a culture that defines music chiefly through a particular commodity form—that is, the musical work, the thing that has been *worked on*, thereby storing a quantity of labor value. The antinomy of stored value is transmitted value, as produced and received in time through acts of labor. Such transmitted value is not the unique property of improvisation; it belongs to all performance. It only looks like the special property of improvisation in a context where the work-concept has taken root and reduced the meaning of performance to "interpretation." Thus it is the hegemony of the commodity form, not any inherent quality of improvisation as such, that produces improvisation as antithetical to capitalist logic. The younger Schumann inherited from postclassical pianism a performance-immanent concept of musical meaning largely free of the logic of the commodity, and his blissful improvisations flowed from it. He went beyond his postclassical predecessors, however, in subjecting improvisation to the processes of romantic reflection, whose dynamic of ceaseless self-extension and generativity can align perfectly well, at least at an ethical level, with the dynamic of capitalism.

A familiar vignette of Schumann's later years, told by his friend and biographer Wasielewski, conjures the composer at an asylum in Endenich, improvising at the piano: "it was heartbreaking to have to see the mental and physical power of the noble, great man completely broken. . . . The playing was unpleasant. . . . It seemed as if the force whence it proceeded were injured, like a machine whose springs are broken, but which still tries to work, jerking convulsively."[84] The genius composer, beloved by his public as a kapellmeister, is here reduced to a piano improviser, erratically jabbing at the keyboard in the solitude of his room. Like Hanno Buddenbrook, improvisation is the figural image of his final degeneration. But the image also recalls Schumann's youthful period when he fantasized at the piano for hours on end in a state of blissful solitude. Among his friends and associates those early, improvisation-drenched years were no longer to be idealized, for the mature Schumann had acquired clarity and economy, and redeemed himself from earlier tendencies toward confusion, eccentricity, and waste. Wasielewski's sad portrait is shadowed by an idea of how healthy music-making looks: like a machine, with all the springs working, channeling its force smoothly and steadily. Schumann had once used such a machine, the notorious Chiroplast, to make his hand into a machine of perfect virtuosity and maximally fluent improvisation. But because the Chiroplast ruined his hand, he shifted his labor to the head and left the physical work to the others—the interpreters who did not improvise.

NOTES

1. Ursula Müller-Kerstin. *Stephen Heller: ein Klaviermeister der Romantik* (Frankfurt: Peter Lang, 1986), 15.

2. *Stephen Heller: Lettres d'un musicien romantique à Paris*, ed. Jean-Jacques Eigeldinger (Paris: Flammarion, 1981), 75–76.

3. Ibid., 58–60, 109.

4. Felix Mendelssohn Bartholdy, *Briefe aus den Jahren 1830 bis 1847*, ed. Paul Mendelssohn Bartholdy and Carl Mendelssohn Bartholdy (Leipzig: Hermann Mendelssohn, 1889), 214–15. Letter dated 18 October 1831. This is discussed further in Chapter 2.

5. Robert Wangermée suggests that Liszt wanted to reserve his improvisations for less public circumstances because, as a romantic, he accorded improvisation a "privilege" that might be compromised in the public space. See his "L'improvisation pianistique au début du XIXe siècle," in *Miscellanea musicologica Floris van der Mueren* (Ghent: L. van Melle, 1950), 252–53. This issue is treated in greater depth in Chapter 5.

6. Robert Schumann, *Tagebücher*, ed. G. Eismann and G. Neuhaus, 3 vols. (Leipzig: Deutscher Verlag für Musik, 1971–), 2:402. Hereafter abbreviated as TB.

7. John Worthen, *Robert Schumann: Life and Death of a Musician* (New Haven: Yale University Press, 2007), 37.

8. *Early Letters of Robert Schumann*, trans. May Herbert (London: George Bell, 1888), 168. Hereafter abbreviated as EL.

9. *Robert Schumann: ein Quellenwerk über sein Leben und Schaffen*, ed. Georg Eisman, 2 vols. (Leipzig: Breitkopf und Härtel, 1956), 1:44.

10. *Robert Schumann: ein Quellenwerk*, 1:18. Ellipses original.

11. *Robert Schumann: ein Quellenwork*, 55. Töpken's reminiscence is from 30 September 1856.

12. John Daverio, *Robert Schumann: Herald of a "New Poetic Age"* (New York: Oxford University Press, 1997), 75.

13. Worthen, *Robert Schumann*, 37. For a more detailed chronicle of Schumann's pianistic ambitions see Claudia Macdonald, "Schumann's Piano Practice: Technical Mastery and Artistic Ideal," *Journal of Musicology* 19, no. 4 (2002): 527–63. Macdonald traces Schumann's gradual alienation from the instrument and its social values starting in 1831.

14. Mark Kroll, *Ignaz Moscheles and the Changing World of Musical Europe* (Woodbridge: Boydell Press, 2014), 20.

15. On Hummel's reception see Joel Sachs, *Kapellmeister Hummel in England and France* (Detroit: Information Coordinators, 1977). Moscheles, visiting Carlsbad in 1816, "created quite a furore with his Alexander variations and fantasias." *Recent Music and Musicians: As Described in the Diaries and Correspondence of Ignatz Moscheles*, ed. Charlotte Moscheles (New York: Holt and Co., 1873), 16. We can assume that Schumann heard the same pieces in 1818.

16. [No author], *Carl Wilhelm Taubert. Ferdinand Hiller. Biographen* (Cassel: Ernst Balde, 1857), 57.

17. Quoted in Bodo Bischoff and Gerd Nauhaus, "Robert Schumanns Leipziger Konzertnotizen von 1833: Faksimile, Übertragung, und Kommentar," in *Schumann-Studien 3–4* (Zwickau: Rat der Stadt Zwickau, 1994), 47.

18. In 1831 Schumann wrote to the editor of the AMZ, G. W. Fink, requesting that his review of Chopin's opus 2 variations be published in the journal, and offering his journalistic services (EL 148–49).

19. In an 1834 review of a concert by the young virtuoso Theodor Stein, Schumann dug in his heels on this point, saying that young musicians should not be encouraged to improvise in public, and that they needed to develop their knowledge and skills gradually before being thrust into public concerts (NZM 1834, 14).

20. "Robert Schumanns Leipziger Konzertnotizen," 45. Emphasis added.

21. The changes in nomenclature are discussed in Nicholas Marston, *Schumann, Fantasie, op. 17* (Cambridge: Cambridge University Press, 1992), 17.

22. *Jugendbriefe von Robert Schumann*, ed. Clara Schumann (Leipzig: Breitkopf und Härtel, 1886), 80. Letter dated 6 November 1829.

23. The significant formal difference is that Schumann's introduction is clearly marked as an introduction separate from his exposition in B-minor, whereas Hummel's opening is part of the exposition itself, moving seamlessly toward the second key area. For a full reading of Hummel's formal approach in this movement, see Rohan H. Stewart-MacDonald, "Improvisation into Composition: The First Movement of Johann Nepomuk Hummel's Sonata in F-sharp Minor, Op. 81," in *Beyond Notes: Improvisation in Western Music of the Eighteenth and Nineteenth Centuries*, ed. Rudolph Rasch (Brepols: Turnhout, 2011): 129–52.

24. Jim Samson, *Virtuosity and the Musical Work: the Transcendental Studies of Liszt* (Cambridge: Cambridge University Press, 2003), 46–47.

25. J. Q. Davies, *Romantic Anatomies of Performance* (Berkeley: University of California Press, 2014), 51–55.

26. Claudia Macdonald, "Schumann's Piano Practice," 530, mentions similar exercises that Schumann devised for himself as he tried to master Chopin's variations, op. 2.

27. On the *Toccata*'s origin in improvisation see Worthen, *Robert Schumann*, 415 n.39.

28. For a detailed history of the *Toccata* before its publication, see volume 1 of Wolfgang Boetticher, *Robert Schumann's Klavierwerke: neue biographische und textkritische Untersuchungen*, 3 vols. (Wilhelmshaven: Heinrichshofen, 1976).

29. John Rink makes this case convincingly in "Chopin in Transition," in *La note bleue, Mélanges offerts au Professeur Jean-Jacques Eigeldinger*, ed. Jacqueline Waeber (Bern: Peter Lang, 2006), 52–53.

30. According to Worthen (*Robert Schumann*, 56), Schumann partly improvised the "Abegg" variations at a rehearsal for an 1830 concert, and then repeated the feat in the evening.

31. Samson defines "musical materials" as "a repertory of commonalities . . . everything from formal and generic schemata of various kinds to motivic and harmonic archetypes, and conventional figures, imbued with history" (*Virtuosity and the Musical Work*, 36).

32. Wojciech Nowik, "Fryderyk Chopin's op. 57: From Variantes to Berceuse," in *Chopin Studies*, ed. Jim Samson (Cambridge: Cambridge University Press, 1988), 25–40.

33. Mathias Hansen discusses the work in connection with Schumann's attitudes toward virtuosity in "Robert Schumanns 'Virtuosität': Anmerkungen zu den Abegg-Variationen und ihrem kompositorischen Umfeld," in *Musikalische Virtuosität*, ed. Heinz von Loesch (Mainz: Schott, 2004), 132–41.

34. Angela Esterhammer, "The Cosmopolitan *improvvisatore*: Spontaneity and Performance in Romantic Poetics," *European Romantic Review* 16, no. 2 (2005), 161–63. Esterhammer develops the deviance theme in a follow-up article, "The Improviser's Disorder: Spontaneity, Sickness, and Social Deviance in Late Romanticism," *European Romantic Review* 16, no. 3 (2005): 329–40.

35. Anna Harwell Celenza, *Hans Christian Andersen and Music: The Nightingale Revealed* (Chippenham: Ashgate, 1995), 13–14.

36. Ibid., 25.

37. Hans Christian Andersen, *The Improvisatore*, trans. M. B. Howitt (London: Bonner, 1894), 272.

38. Thomas Mann, *Buddenbrooks: Verfall einer Familie* (Berlin: Fischer, 1908), 515. The conflicts in this passage are glossed in Lothar Pikulik, *Leistungsethik contra Gefühlskult: Über das Verhältnis von Bürgerlichkeit und Empfindsamkeit in Deutschland* (Göttingen: Vandenhoeck & Ruprecht, 1984), 53.

39. The difficulty of squaring musical improvisation with modern economic, legal, and aesthetic regimes of music are addressed broadly in Alan Durant, "Improvisation and the Political Economy of Music," in *Music and the Politics of Culture*, ed. Christopher Norris (New York: St. Martin's Press, 1989), 252-82.

40. Vladimir Jankélévitch, "Signification spirituelle du principe d'économie," in *Premières et dernières pages* (Paris: Éditions du Seuil, 1994), 166. Originally published in *Revue philosophique de la France et de l'Étranger* 105 (1928): 88–126.

41. Ibid., 168.

42. Janet Levy, "Covert and Casual Values in Recent Writings about Music," *Journal of Musicology* 5, no. 1 (1987), 3–4.

43. Ibid., 11.

44. Ibid.

45. Reinhard Kapp describes these aspects of late Schumann, and coins the phrase "musikalische Praeceptor Germanie," in "Schumann nach der Revolution," in *Schumann in Düsseldorf: Werke-Texte-Interpretationen*, ed. Bernhard Appel (Mainz: Schott, 1993), 337 and 343.

46. *Robert Schumanns Briefe. Neue Folge*, ed. F. Gustav Jansen (Leipzig: Breitkopf und Härtel, 1904), 356.

47. Ibid., 355–56.

48. Quoted in Kapp, "Schumann nach der Revolution," 343.

49. Robert Schumann, "Musikalische Haus- und Lebensregeln," *Neue Zeitschrift für Musik*, 3 May 1850, Beilage, 3–4.

50. Max Weber, *The Protestant Ethic and the Spirit of Capitalism*, trans. Talcott Parsons (London and New York: Routledge, 2005 [1930]), 14–18.

51. Kapp, "Schumann nach der Revolution," 337.

52. From early on he had recognized that making a living as a musician would be virtually impossible. He wrote to his mother: *"if ever I could have done any good in this world it would have been in music. . . .* But earning one's bread is another thing!" (EL 90; emphasis original).

53. EL 291. In an 1839 letter to Clara, Schumann explained that Friedrich Wieck was wrong in thinking his "difficult" works wouldn't sell, and gave an exact tabulation of the sales based on the publisher's records (EL 295).

54. There is some unclarity whether this passage should be attributed to Clara or to her father Friedrich. Macdonald favors Friedrich whereas Worthen attributes it to Clara.

55. *Tb* 2:173–74. "So hab'ich in der Schweiz oft bis in die Nacht hinein phantasirt."

56. Robert Schumann and Clara Schumann, *Briefwechsel: kritische Gesamtausgabe*, ed. E. Weissweiler, 3 vols. (Strömfeld: Roter Stern, 1984–2001), 1:307. Although Clara is not generally considered a voluble improviser, she did leave some unpublished preludes that are discussed in Valerie Woodring Goertzen, "Setting the Stage: Clara Schumann's Preludes," in *In the Course of Performance: Studies in the World of Musical Improvisation*, ed. Bruno Nettl (Chicago: University of Chicago Press, 1998), 237–60. The fact that these preludes are written out and in some cases

linked to specific compositions by Robert shows that she too was submitting to the regulation of compositional values and permanence. Eugenie Schumann left an interesting account of Clara's pre-tour practice regime, which is strongly suggestive of improvisation: "Scales rolled and swelled like a tidal sea, legato and staccato; in octaves, thirds, sixths, tenths, and double thirds; sometimes in one hand only, while the other played accompanying chords. Then arpeggios of all kinds, octaves, shakes, everything *prestissimo* and without the slightest break, exquisite modulations leading from key to key. The most wonderful feature of this practicing was that although the principle on which it was based was always the same, it was new every day, and seemed drawn ever fresh from a mysterious wellspring." *Memoirs of Eugenie Schumann*, trans. Marie Busch (London: Eulenberg Books, 1927), 17.

57. Robert Schumann and Clara Schumann, *Briefwechsel: kritische Gesamtausgabe*, 2:704 (28 August 1839) and 3:1091 (21 August 1840).

58. Wolfgang Boetticher, *Robert Schumann: Einführung in Persönlichkeit und Werk* (Berlin: Bernhard Hahnefeld, 1941), 304.

59. Carl Kossmaly, "Musikalische Tageblätter," *Neue Zeitschrift für Musik* 1843, cols. 106 and 113.

60. Carl Kossmaly, "On Robert Schumann's Piano Compositions" [1844], trans. Susan Gillespie, in *Schumann and His World*, ed. R. Larry Todd (Princeton: Princeton University Press, 1994), 310.

61. Quoted from autobiographical sketches in Worthen, *Robert Schumann*, 64.

62. Kossmaly's mapping of Schumann's stages of development had a deep influence on nineteenth-century criticism and twentieth-century scholarship. Hanslick, a strong partisan of Schumann, celebrated his evolution out of the early "Sturm-und-Drang" period: "From this latter work [op. 22] forward one sees a decisive clarification in Schumann's music. The small forms broaden out, the earlier mosaic-like connection of ideas becomes development, poetic willfulness bows to the law of musical beauty. Schumann soon found the transition from genial rhapsode to clear-sighted [*besonnene*] master." Reproduced from *Deutsche Musik-Zeitung*, 14 July 1860, in Eduard Hanslick, *Sämtliche Schriften*, ed. Dietmar Strauß, 6 vols. (Wien, Cologne Weimar: Böhlau Verlag, 2005), I/5:205.

63. Adolph Bernhard Marx, *Die Lehre von der musikalischen Composition*, 2nd ed., 3 vols. (Leipzig: Breitkopf und Härtel, 1941), 1:12.

64. David Trippett comments on Marx's philosophy of motivic germination in *Wagner's Melodies: Aesthetics and Materialism in German Musical Identity* (Cambridge: Cambridge University Press, 2013), 112–15.

65. Adolph Bernhard Marx, *The School of Musical Composition*, trans. Augustus Wehrman (London: Robert Cocks, 1852), vol. 1, 26. Based on Marx's fourth edition. This point was added for extra emphasis after the second edition.

66. Max Weber, *The Protestant Ethic*, xxxi–xxxii. Emphasis original.

67. Marx, *Die Lehre*, 1:12 and 1:26.

68. Trippett gives a useful tabular representation of Marx's system in *Wagner's Melodies*, 115.

69. Marx was clearly aware that his method risked seeming mechanistic. At the opening of the appendices to the second edition he wrote: "The theory of musical composition is thus a fixed system; its methods are in all basic respects established; but . . . it is not a blunt dead mechanism that only produces machines, but a living organism, that gives life and entices lively activity, lively development" (Marx, *Die Lehre*, 1:397).

70. Marx, *School of Musical Composition*, 1:28. In *The Wealth of Nations* Adam Smith famously distinguished between intellectual and manual labor, saying that only manual labor actually yielded products of value, and he subsumed music under the products of intellectual labor. Ricardo's revision of the theory of political economy made the labor invested in a product part of its value, opening the way for intellectual labor to be counted as real value. On Ricardo and the relationship between political economy and subjectivity more broadly, see Sonya Marie Scott, *Architectures of Economic Subjectivity: The Philosophical Foundations of the Subject in the History of Economic Thought* (London: Routledge, 2013), 15–28.

71. Ibid., 34.

72. According to Boetticher (*Robert Schumann: Einführung*, 304), Marx was the theorist Schumann read most closely.

73. Marx, *School of Musical Composition*, 1:13. Less developed iterations of this idea from the second German edition (1841) are found on 16 and 400.

74. Marx, *Die Lehre*, 1:399.

75. Marx, *School of Musical Composition*, 1:33.

76. Marx, *Die Lehre*, 1:17. This point was reiterated in the appendix (404), but tellingly, it was cut during the preparation of the fourth edition.

77. All quotes from E., "Winke zu einem richtigen Studium der Partituren," *Allgemeine Wiener Musik-Zeitung*, 12 February 1842, 75. The first installment of the two-part article is found on page 66.

78. On A. B. Marx's project for public musical culture see Celia Applegate, *Bach in Berlin: Nation and Culture in Mendelssohn's Revival of the St. Matthew Passion* (Ithaca, NY: Cornell University Press, 2005), 104–24.

79. Fritz Breithaupt, "The Ego-Effect of Money," in *Rereading Romanticism*, ed. Martha B. Helfer (Amsterdam/Atlanta: Rodopi, 2000), 229–30. For a more extended treatment of the topic, see by the same author *Der Ich-Effekt des Geldes: zur Geschichte einer Legitimationsfigur* (Frankfurt am Main: Fischer, 2008).

80. Breithaupt, "The Ego-Effect of Money," 230.

81. The subject-position manifested in Schumann's improvisations, then, cannot be reduced to the autonomous liberal subject or monad of consciousness usually summoned as "Robert Schumann." It is rather a porous subject, which has opened itself out toward the "other" of the instrument and the agencies it conveys (or the affordances it offers). The improvising subject surrenders itself to that which lies beyond its immediate grasp, in an aspiration to dynamically expand the self through some sort of reappropriation of its "beyond." This basic tenet of the romantic *Reflexionstheorie* of Schumann's time closely resembles the philosophy of CSI, according to which a person enters into a group improvisation from a bounded subject position, but opens and expands the self through dialogic interaction with others. We will return to this *Reflexionstheorie* when considering its relation to economy later in the chapter.

82. Thomas Mann, *Buddenbrooks*, 523.

83. Ibid., 526.

84. Quoted in Laura Tunbridge, *Schumann's Late Style* (Cambridge: Cambridge University Press, 2007), 151.

5

Liszt and the Romantic Rhetoric of Improvisation

FRANZ LISZT AND Robert Schumann were peers and mutual admirers who recognized in one another common aspirations. The vast temperamental, aesthetic, and ideological differences between them eventually led to a cooling of their friendship, but these differences are sometimes so sharply drawn as to obscure the parallels. Both styled themselves as aesthetic progressives who sought to "poeticize" music. Both were powerfully drawn to the piano and felt a personal, almost physical attachment to it. They built their technical skill on the foundation of postclassical works by Hummel, Czerny, Ries, Moscheles, and others, and they improvised enthusiastically and impressively in their early years. Both traded the piano for the conductor's baton when they accepted kapellmeister appointments—Liszt in Weimar in 1848, Schumann in Düsseldorf in 1850. And as they became kapellmeisters they grew into new roles as institution leaders and administrative directors, sacrificing the fierce independence of their earlier years for the sake of public duty and broader relevance. Each of them downscaled their compositional output for piano and began conceiving large-scale symphonic works and oratorios. And after taking on their new positions, both began curating their earlier works—streamlining them, clarifying their lines, and organizing them into collections.

Two of music's most brazenly forward-looking romantics, then, began as enthusiastic improvisers, submitting only later in their careers to trends in musical life that favored permanence, musical writing, and public relevance. The previous chapter argued that Schumann's evolution into a composer-identity entailed a rejection of improvisation as a legitimate productive resource. Liszt, in contrast, felt no such incommensurability between improvising and composing. To an extent matched perhaps only by

Chopin, his composed oeuvre seems to appropriate, encode, and stylize it. Much of his published music unfolds itself loosely, opens itself to digression and luxurious harmonic turns, and projects a sense of exploratory freedom whose allure sounds deeply indebted to improvisation. Even a piece like the Sonata in B Minor, with its more pronounced aspiration to formal cogency and self-sufficiency, revels in unexpected turns of phrase, abrupt contrasts, and fantastical cadenza-like flights. Liszt in many respects remained an unreconstructed improviser, and although many detractors held this against him, his improvisational "spirit" has been widely celebrated since the late nineteenth century. It is telling, however, that when critics and scholars draw attention to his improvisational orientation, they typically point to examples from his composed and published oeuvre. This habit only confirms that Liszt was, in a deeper sense, already reconstructed—that he successfully channeled his extemporizing impulses into composed pieces that convert improvisation into its aesthetically reflected form.[1] If we try to imagine the improvising Liszt through the lens of his finished compositions, we repress the ontological gap separating performances from works, phenomena from meanings, improvisations from "improvisatoriness."

Even if we cannot always disentangle performed improvisation from aestheticized improvisatoriness, a theoretical distinction between the two is essential to understanding Liszt and the changing fortunes of improvisation in the nineteenth century. During his prodigy years, the 1820s, he improvised free fantasies at nearly all concerts to great acclaim, and did not struggle with the convention. By the end of his virtuoso career in 1847 he was offering free fantasies far less frequently, winning praise instead for playing his own compositions or interpretations of Beethoven and Schubert. At the legendary master classes he gave in Weimar in the 1850s, he promoted "liberty" at various levels of performance but did not actively encourage students to improvise or play free fantasies. Composition had already won the battle for priority, and Liszt had bought into the value system placing composition at a "higher," more prestigious level than improvisation or execution. Indeed his absorption of this value system prompted him to retire from concertizing in 1847 and reinvent himself as a composer. Nonetheless, improvisational swerves and gestures seemed to burst through the surface of his compositions, as if resisting textual inscription. They manifested a wayward romantic force that drew perpetual charges of "formlessness" or harmonic "chaos" from critics and professional peers.

Scholars have recently explored tangents between Liszt's published oeuvre and his improvisational practice, and there is much room for further research along these lines.[2] While some aspects of his published oeuvre will be discussed here, this chapter concentrates on Liszt's path as a performing improviser to document a transition from the practice of the free fantasy—a distinct genre of performance associated with Hummel, Moscheles, and others—toward a more diffuse and generalized concept of "improvisation" as a mode of musical invention implicitly defined against "composition." As a child prodigy Liszt improvised on given themes at nearly every concert, projecting a rare sense of creative liberty and technical control that helped establish his reputation as a natural genius on par with the child Mozart. In the early 1830s he transitioned to adulthood and reinvented his artistic identity in the milieu of French romanticism. In this new context, writers constructed his improvisations as elevated poetic utterances that established a dialectic between the potential and the realized—between the actual and the virtual—and gestured toward a transcendence of the mundane. Whereas musicians in the kapellmeister network had been admired for the learning and authority their fantasies projected, Liszt registered improvisation as a sort of excess—an inexhaustible generative potential or deep reserve of feeling that was released spontaneously in the moment of inspiration. The romantic rhetoric of improvisation also channeled social ideals, crediting extemporaneous performance with a unique capacity to achieve communal intimacy within a closed circle of artists and artistically sympathetic patrons. When Liszt returned to the world of public concerts and undertook his legendary tours (1838–1847), these anti-public values came into conflict with his practice of improvising on audience-given themes, leading him to denigrate it, to do it less often, and to reinvent it in line with ascendant musical values stressing "work"-like craft and integrity. Increasingly, during his virtuoso years, his concert pieces were perceived as "improvisatory" even when written out or fully prepared, and the distinction began losing meaning.

THE PRODIGY (1822–1828)

Like Schumann and Mendelssohn, Liszt emerged in the universe of postclassical pianism populated by heroes like Hummel, Kalkbrenner, and Moscheles. In the early 1820s, when the free fantasy on given themes was at its peak, he was studying in Europe's hotbed of pianism, Vienna, with Carl Czerny. In determining how the young Liszt improvised such pieces, scholars have generally relied on his early published works, but certain aspects of these published pieces fail to match written accounts of his playing.[3] Liszt developed his capacities under the direct tutelage of Czerny, who recalled in his memoirs: "I endeavored to teach him free improvising [Phantasiren] by frequently giving him a theme on which to improvise [improvisieren]."[4] It is significant that Czerny specifies not "several" themes but "a" theme. In his improvisation treatise of 1829, possibly the most valuable single source of its kind, Czerny makes a categorical distinction between "single-themed" and "several-themed" approaches.[5] In his typology there are two types of "fantasy-like" improvisation: improvisation on a single theme, and "freer improvisation on several themes." The methods of elaboration are essentially the same for both types. The main difference is that the multi-theme fantasy provides more opportunities to combine, juxtapose, and recall the various themes.

In working with Liszt on single-theme improvisation, Czerny emphasized the spontaneous transformation of a given motive. The first step in developing this extempore skill, Czerny writes, is to master the art of playing the motive or theme in various different styles: "The performer must devote time and practice to achieve the capability of transforming each motive that comes his way into all these styles with ease and adroitness."[6] Most of these transformations simply preserve the melodic contour of the motive and use it to initiate music in a conventional style or topos—Adagio, Scherzo,

Rondo, Polacca, Waltz, Fugue, etc. Liszt's technique of "thematic transformation," commonly invoked in connection with his symphonic works of the 1850s, clearly owes something to this basic improvisational practice of his childhood.[7] Czerny's examples of "given themes" are always incomplete musical statements, not familiar or complete tunes. The shortest theme contains just three pitches, and the longest is a pair of two-bar phrases in an antecedent-consequent relationship. Contrary to what many scholars have concluded based on printed music, complete melodies, periods, and rounded musical ideas were apparently not the starting points for "fantasy-like improvisation." This would also mean that the classical variation style, where the theme and its underlying chord progression provide the foundation, is not "fantasy-like" improvisation. Indeed, Czerny devotes a separate chapter of his treatise to variations, considering them a separate genre.[8] For the single-themed fantasy, Czerny appears to suggest that pianists start with something akin to a Beethovenian musical motto—a shorter idea that can easily be transposed, sequenced, and taken on modulating journeys.

Although thematic transformation was Czerny's first method in developing fantasy-like improvisation, he ultimately thought the free fantasy should build out to larger forms, and for models he recommended entire movements from symphonies and piano sonatas by Mozart and Beethoven. (He does not mention Schubert's *Wanderer Fantasy*, but his criteria describe the formal model of that piece nearly to perfection.) A main motto—a short and memorable idea stated by the pianist out front—should be used to lead off distinct sections or sub-movements of the extended, unbroken piece, and it can be reprised as a head-motto at formal junctures to provide unity to the entire improvisation. It is highly doubtful that Liszt ever arrived at this advanced, formally conscious stage of fantasy development while under the tutelage of Czerny. There are no traces of such a formal conception in accounts of his early or later performances. All evidence suggests that in these early years his approach was to work up a single motive at length. Nearly all his free fantasies were based on a single theme, featuring simple folkish songs like "Il pleut bergère," "Au clair de la lune," tunes from popular operas by Mozart, Rossini, Boieldieu, and Weber, or when the occasion afforded, a striking theme from another piece just played at a given concert.[9]

The first body of critical response to Liszt's free fantasies comes from 1824, the year of his debut concerts in Paris. Few critics praised them for their roundedness or integral coherence, as they nearly always did with Hummel's fantasies of the same period. Most observers remarked upon the ease and fluency with which he handled harmonic modulation, and the variety of guises in which he made the motive appear: "At first it seemed as though he had chosen as a theme the tune 'Il pleut bergère,' but after a few measures this expectation vanished, and like a new Proteus he took pleasure in adopting all sorts of forms and characters in order to outrun anyone who tried to keep up with him."[10] In an extended review from a few days later we find a more explicit account of the way the fantasy unfolded:

> [Liszt] preluded for a while; then, seizing upon an idea for his opening, which he
> developed and followed artfully, he took as a transition the first measure of the

aria from Mozart's Figaro: Non più andrai. Once seized, this motive was never abandoned by the improviser; it appeared now in the thunder of a fiery bass, then in the exquisite delicacies of the high notes, alternately emerging and disappearing, and constantly supported by rich, varied, and imitative harmony, yet always carrying with it the authentic stamp of improvisation whether through its beauties or its lavishness.[11]

Both descriptions suggest that Liszt reveled in the free development of one short motive, moving it through various harmonic, coloristic, and contrapuntal combinations. Neither suggests that he improvised variations on an entire melody or its chord progression. This differentiates their style from that of his earliest published concert fantasies. In these bravura compositions, the introductory sections and transitions may transmit something close to an extemporaneous style, but the variations themselves do not obviously bear the imprint of improvisation. The variations more likely represent worked out ideas, arrived at through the exploration of texturally and technically complex keyboard resources.

The young Liszt occasionally improvised on multiple themes as well, but it is not clear that these followed a particular formal model. They may well have been potpourris, where one theme at a time is stated and treated, rather than a more integrated model exploring relationships among two or three themes. During a provincial tour of 1825 he was given a theme from Boieldieu's *La dame blanche*, but it veered off into an improvisation on themes by Carl Maria von Weber:

> The artist started off with a motif from *La dame blanche* that was given to him. A sequence of felicitous developments led him to play the hunters' chorus. The motive from Robin [*Der Freischütz*] appeared beneath his fingers. Then all the bluster and verve of Weber's music overcame him. With effects full of energy he led toward the gracious motive of the Waltz [Weber's *Aufforderung zum Tanze*]. He paraphrased it with ever increasing fire and passion until the moment when he completed the subject with a cascade full of grace and a decrescendo.[12]

Liszt finished off this improvisation with a fade-out mimicking the ending of Weber's concert waltz *Aufforderung zum Tanze*. Here again none of the themes was stated *in toto*, and there does not appear to have been a formal plan after the prelude. The chosen motives have common features: the hunter's motive from *Freischütz* is a brief arpeggiation of tonic and dominant chords, and the *Aufforderung zum Tanze* themes are comparably generic melodically and harmonically. (Mozart's "Non più andrai," one of Liszt's favorite motives for improvisation, shares these features as well, with its rhythmically energetic march-rhythm and tonic-dominant chords.)[13] What is interesting about this particular improvisation is that Weber's *Aufforderung*, which contains many themes in series, seems to be treated freely, in the manner of a paraphrase, keeping certain features of the original composition while cutting others and adding new developments. We will see that this free development of

Aufforderung became one of his favorite vehicles of improvisation throughout the 1830s and 1840s.

The stylistic disjunction between Liszt's improvisations and his composed-out concert works suggests that his improvisations resisted the demands of inscription and commodification. They did not deliver complete, familiar tunes with variations, but directed attention toward the pianist's active, transformative act. The popularity of the tunes he chose did not simply convert to an experience of the familiar. On the contrary, the tune's familiarity assisted the listener in following Liszt's process of improvisatory reinvention, development, and de-familiarization. His early improvisations thus demanded a moderately strenuous level of listening engagement. Listeners were not asked to passively take in the familiar melodies and brilliant virtuosity, but were encouraged to "follow along" in his thought process. The improvisations activated a more direct artist-audience bond and suspended the commodity form of music. By evading the logic of the commodity in this manner, Liszt's improvisations aligned themselves with the elite, anti-popular thrust of the free fantasy as practiced by Hummel and his contemporaries. As discussed in Chapter 2, Hummel did sometimes deliver whole melodies and play "straight variations" when improvising, but only when he chose to adapt his style to a less discriminating public. Such improvisations were understood as potpourris or capriccios, which were set apart from what Czerny called "fantasy-like" improvisation. The fantasy style proper, higher in status, entailed the more flexible motivic techniques of "developmental" music and fugal or quasi-fugal combinations. This appears to be the stylistic horizon from which Liszt departed in his single-themed elaborations. He rarely failed to insert a few quasi-fugal passages, however elementary, to claim a link to the free fantasy model of Hummel and Moscheles.

Because Liszt played a total of two or three pieces at his early concerts, the free improvisations had a disproportionate role in audience perceptions. When performing for sovereigns and aristocrats he apparently played improvisations almost exclusively.[14] Concert reviewers typically singled out two pieces for commentary: the concerto (usually by Hummel or Czerny) and the improvisation. In the concerto he displayed his mastery of technically difficult passages and large-scale pieces, while the improvisation showed a quite different side by revealing inventive capacities. As early as 1824 he was being called "the young and famous improviser Litz [*sic*]" (*Corsaire*, 18 February 1824). Improvisation also fed into the dominant trope of his early reception—that he was a reincarnation of Mozart: "he renews among us a musical phenomenon that amazed Paris in 1763. . . . At sixty years' distance the prodigy of Mozart is reproduced in the young Liszt" (*Moniteur universel*, 12 March 1824). Parisian readers were already familiar with anecdotes of Mozart's astonishing improvisations, and Adam Liszt, astutely shaping his son's public image, wanted to cash in on the connection. The predominance of Mozart's "Non più andrai" in his choice of tunes might have underlined the connection still further, since the aria is about a boy who is being asked to behave "like a man." Completing the link between Mozart and Liszt was Johann Nepomuk Hummel, who had studied with Mozart and was still Europe's most admired improviser: "The eleven-year-old Liszt is a *wunderkind* who is arousing endless attention here through his improvisations on the pianoforte. He is truly endowed by nature with the rarest capacities. May he, like Mozart and Hummel, develop from the *wunderkind* into a great artist" (AMZ 1824, 189–90). Liszt's improvisations thus supported a genealogy quite different from the Beethoven-Czerny-Liszt line of transmission that modern scholars have tended to emphasize.[15] It is often forgotten that Czerny had studied with Hummel as well as Beethoven.

The prevailing response to both Liszt and Mozart as improvising prodigies was a feeling of wonder and uncanniness. Their mastery of the piano was extraordinary in itself, but their capacity to generate music off the cuff heightened the sense of awe. Improvisation manifested mental and inventive capacities that were thought to belong to adults alone. In his classic study *Centuries of Childhood*, Philippe Ariès argued that the conception of the child as a different type of being, distinct from adults, became more pronounced over the course of the sixteenth and seventeenth centuries, and took its modern form in the educated middle classes of the eighteenth century. The educational philosophy of Rousseau, in particular, promoted the idea that children lack knowledge and need prolonged tutelage to acquire it. Yet Rousseau's ideas attained general dissemination only in the last quarter of the eighteenth century, after Mozart's prodigy years, and there is a measurable shift of response between Mozart and Liszt.[16] Responses to Mozart were dominated by a discourse of wonder that greeted extraordinary phenomena with assertions of absolute inscrutability. The Englishman Daines Barrington, in his famous 1769 anecdotes of Mozart, did not try to explain *how* the child prodigy did what he did. Bracketing causal explanations, he merely reiterated the "extraordinary facts" and "amazing and incredible" performances he witnessed, in which improvisations figured prominently: "his extemporary compositions also, of which I was a witness, prove his genius and invention to have been most astonishing."[17]

By the time of Liszt, however, the conceptual differentiation of children from adults had become more pronounced, and contemporary observers focused less on the "divine gift" than on the precocious maturity of Liszt's mind. This shift of focus did not entirely kill off the discourse of wonder. A Toulouse paper, for example, reported that "the young virtuoso reawakens the memory of pagan mythology, and it is merely a child that has produced these marvels, this magic, these prodigious feats." This same review, however, invoked more up-to-date psychological ideas, claiming that "this likeable child manifests a superior mental constitution [*organisation*]."[18] The notion that a child might possess a mature, adult musical mind had a latent insurgent potential. It suggested that children were not only behavioral mimics, but might also possess independent cognitive-productive power. This was not only at odds with a general perception of children as "unformed," but also with the way the professional music establishment upheld its authority. As discussed in Chapter 2, improvised free fantasies were often valued for the guild-like learning and professionalism they put on display. Liszt's fantasies threw into doubt the cherished idea that deep study of harmony and counterpoint were really necessary to improvise well. Czerny, recalling Liszt's audition to study with him, was struck by the boy's intuitive grasp of musical rules: "at his father's request I gave him a theme for improvisation. *Without the slightest learned harmonic knowledge* he nevertheless brought a certain intelligent sense [*genialen Sinn*] to his playing."[19] Critics responded similarly, making a categorical separation between the child's technical and mental capacities:

> Performance on the piano is little more than mechanical work. Thinking, so to speak, plays no role in it . . . but the faculty of improvising music, of pursuing a theme long enough to move from one key to another, of vigorously attacking the most difficult modulations without getting lost and without breaching the rule of composition, this talent is truly the effect of a mind quite particular to the young Liszt. (*Pandore*, 14 April 1824)[20]

The baffled responses to Liszt's early improvisations belong to a more general uncertainty surrounding improvisation. The question of its origins, of how it is possible at all, returns perpetually among both insiders and lay spectators. Answers tend to fall into two polarized lines of explanation: a disenchanted one, according to which it is a "mechanical" reshuffling of learned and practiced patterns, and a quasi-theological one, according to which it channels some supernatural agent or spirit beyond human volition (in romantic discourse, "genius"). Even authors who recognize the binary terms of this debate rarely find a way to avoid them. This persistent undecidability about improvisation's originating agency affected the discourse around the young Liszt. Any child who exhibited adult-like behavior seemed to cross a "natural" threshold. Paradoxically, though, "nature" also offered the best account of how a child prodigy could do what he did. Liszt, according to the writer just quoted, was "endowed *by nature* with the rarest capacities." A conceptual conflict arose between the theory that children's minds are shaped by conscientious education and the theory that these minds are formed by natural endowments. Liszt's improvisations pressed this conflict to the fore, and the explanation by "nature" only reaffirmed the mystery of origination.

    With the help of his free fantasies Liszt managed to escape the skepticism and suspicion critics increasingly expressed toward child prodigies. In the fifty or sixty years intervening between Mozart and Liszt there had emerged an entire world of keyboard pedagogy oriented specifically toward children—a world represented well enough by Czerny's incessant stream of private lessons and published exercises. Consequently, musical prodigies and pseudo-prodigies cropped up more often than they had in previous eras. By the 1840s a musical observer could write that "musical child prodigies are shooting up from the ground like mushrooms after a night of warm rain."[21] It was becoming more difficult to resist the impression that an exceptionally talented child was not the product of a punishing educational regime or an overbearing, exploitative parent.

    Most piano prodigies born around the same time as Liszt, such as George Aspull, Anna Caroline de Belleville, and Leopoldine Blahetka, rarely if ever improvised before audiences.[22] In 1834 the Hamburg-born pianist Theodor Stein, fifteen years old, undertook concert tours in which he regularly played free fantasies on given themes, but he failed to make a good impression and his career burned out quickly.[23] In 1838 Friedrich Wieck was asked to take on eight-year-old Charles Filtsch, "who improvises for hours in a state of celestial transfiguration" and who did not restrain himself from embellishing the concertos in his repertoire.[24] Liszt's gift for free improvisation set him apart from these potential rivals and lifted him out of the "child" frame altogether: "Liszt transcends infancy and youth; he is mature with talent, and genius; he not only manages the instrument with precision and speed . . . but he composes, he improvises!"[25] In 1824 King George IV, who had a decent ear for music, gave Liszt the minuet from *Don Giovanni* as a theme for improvisation, and afterward said, "this boy surpasses Moscheles, Cramer, Kalkbrenner, and all the rest of the great piano-players, not only in execution and rendering, but also in the wealth of ideas and the way of carrying them out."[26] It is quite ironic that improvisation broke the childhood frame in this manner, for nineteenth-century biographies of prominent musicians nearly always contained anecdotes in which the child's precocity revealed itself through unsolicited keyboard improvisations.[27] The fact that no contemporaries read Liszt's improvisations as an extension of "childlike" capacities for imagination or creative play, as they might today, shows the extent to which children were viewed as products of education—blank slates who become musical, artistic, or creative through disciplined regimes of training and "cultivation."

When critics faulted Liszt's free fantasies, they usually brought up larger concerns about the decadence of standards and taste in the emergent sphere of public commercial concerts. Liszt had quickly established a reputation based purely on public performances, royal protection, and press recognition, bypassing the professional musicians' establishment represented in Paris by the Conservatoire. And in contrast to other musicians in the city he was not demonstrating "serious" credentials by playing works such as those of Beethoven or other "classic" composers. His improvisations were finding response in the free market of public concerts, where an untutored public could easily submit to the allure of virtuosity and the boy wonder. The music critic for the *Courrier des théâtres* worried that his high-level bravura was potentially trivializing a dignified art:

> His improvisation . . . was much too technical and not musical enough. To constantly shift one's theme into a new key before the previous has been established, to make a storm roar in the bass together with flute-like notes in the upper octaves, to run through chromatic scales with perfect evenness and to connect everything with imperceptible transitions—these are known to be the conditions of all good improvisation, and Liszt did not leave any of them behind; but we advise him again not to forget about charm, which is not to be confused with the tart and trivial melody of vaudeville so loved by some of our peers.[28]

This demand for "charm" and "melody" possibly belongs specifically to French critical discourse, but the invocation of cultural hierarchy does not. The professional music elite in Germany and Austria, clinging to a valuation of free improvisation as a "higher" practice, often lamented the promiscuous spread of the term *Phantasie* or *Fantasie* into the realms of bravura virtuosity and amateurism through the commodification of published works by that name. Echoes of this critique had been heard in the press reception of his Vienna debut, where he also improvised: "We would prefer to call the 'fantasy' a capriccio, for several themes played in sequence and connected by interludes do not yet deserve that honorable title, so often misused in our journal" (AMZ 1823, 53). Liszt's performance belonged to a lesser order of improvisation, and to call it a "fantasy" was to disrespect that genre's high status. Child prodigies were particularly susceptible to such charges because they were so immediately attractive to the general public and were more likely to be understood as entertainers rather than artists. An author observing the glut of musical prodigies asserted that "in our times the artificiality of virtuosity has come to outweigh art, and the taste of the greater public, which leans in the direction of the former, is increasingly preferred to the latter."[29]

In December 1829 the young music critic Edouard Fétis publicly exhorted Liszt to find a new artistic direction: "Ah, Mr. Liszt!, why do you pursue us with your endless improvisations! When one has a talent like yours, is it not vexing to see it wasted on ridiculous things? . . . There are some good ideas in what you played, but they are drowned out in a flood of notes" (*Revue musicale* 1829, 498). These words fell on impressionable ears. Liszt's prodigy years were over, and the recent death of his father, who had presided over his career, awakened a strong desire for personal redefinition. Moreover, Fétis words were printed in the recently founded *Revue musicale*, the first music-specific journal in France. The *Revue* had introduced into the Parisian music world a new kind of authority—that of the professional or semi-professional music critic—and all artists working in the public domain would have to contend with its power. By 1843 the *Revue* was encouraging musical artists to "polish their output by disengaging it from banalities inseparable from improvisation or from too-rapid production" (RGMP 1843, 432). Like Schumann, Liszt started to develop a conscience about improvisation and about the self-sufficiency of piano virtuosity more generally.[30] In the next phase of his career, he would channel improvisation toward different ends.

THE ROMANTIC RHETORIC OF IMPROVISATION (1830–1835)

"Abandon naturel et passion," voilà son devise
CAROLINE BOISSIER[31]

In the early 1830s Liszt and the musical world around him underwent dramatic changes. In the space of just a few years Meyerbeer, Bellini, Paganini, Berlioz, Chopin, Carl Loewe, Schumann, and Liszt had contributed variously to the development of musical romanticism, leaving many aspects of postclassical aesthetics and classicism in the dust. For musicians outside the kapellmeister circuit, the genre of the improvised free fantasy—tied to values of learnedness, communicative clarity, and sociability—lost its appeal. Like Meyerbeer, Loewe, and Schumann, Liszt redirected his improvisational instincts and habits into new creative channels. From about 1830 to 1835 he withdrew almost entirely from public concerts and entered a period of self-absorption. It was a response to disappointed love, existential crisis, and spiritual torment, and at the same time a period of intense musical, spiritual, and intellectual ferment. He was feeding his mind with the poems by Byron and Lamartine, the inspired religious writings of the Abbé Lammenais, and the utopian-socialist philosophical ideas of the Saint-Simonians. Musically, he was keeping close company with fellow romantics such as Berlioz and Chopin and processing his life-altering experience of Paganini in concert, after which he committed himself to raising his technical piano skills to a still higher level. Socially, he was circulating in the top intellectual and artistic salons of the Parisian *beau monde*, where he met the Countess d'Agoult and with whom he initiated a consequential affair.

At the occasional cameo appearances he made at public concerts in this period, Liszt did not play many solos and rarely if ever improvised.[32] He had moved out of the public spotlight into the candlelight of salons, where the press could not track his activities. The best portrait we have of his playing from this period comes from Caroline Boissier, who observed the lessons her daughter Valérie took with Liszt in 1832 and wrote about them in detail.[33] During the lessons Liszt often played and improvised for them, and it is clear that his earlier model—taking a single motive and following it through several combinations and modulations—was no longer his standard method. With his newly developed "transcendental" technique, he had become a habitual embellisher, especially when playing "classic" compositions. In a famous passage from the *Lettres d'un bachelier* he confessed that he had once added "a lot of tricks and organ points" to classical pieces by Beethoven, Weber, and Hummel, and declared, quite implausibly, that he no longer committed such sins.[34] When playing Weber's second piano sonata, Boissier noted, he added thirds, octaves, and sixths at will and with great ease. When not tied down to a specific piece "he improvises like a god using inimitable detours and delicate, sensitive, unexpected notes, embellished with ravishing fiorituras."[35] A London critic judged that "he executed about one-half *more* notes than are to be found in the Concert-Stuck [of Weber]," a level of embellishment substantial enough that it prompted another critic say "his performance had in many respects the vigour and originality of an extemporaneous effect."[36] These techniques of modulating and enriching sound were in line with the postclassical premises of improvisation, though considerably amplified by the resources of the modern instrument. As early as 1827 a critic had noted embellishments applied by Liszt to a Hummel concerto. Another point of continuity between his improvisations of the 1830s and those of his earlier years was a tendency to paraphrase Weber's *Aufforderung zum Tanze*.[37] To judge from Boissier's comments, Liszt profited from Weber's occasional modulations and major-minor turns to intensify and dramatize harmonic contrasts:

> In the passages he improvises there are harmonic detours and modulations into the minor juxtaposed with the melody, with a charming effect. These are like reflections of melancholy thoughts amid happy things, a cloud that passes in

front of the sun and veils its rays momentarily; you can't imagine the effect of these contrasts.[38]

Caroline Boissier was transfixed not only by Liszt's musicianship but also by his personality, behavior, and appearance. Herself from an elite family, she interpreted his intense passion, sensitivity, and moodiness as evidence of an exceptional, "noble" soul (and often told him so, to his grateful recognition). When elaborating on this "performance of nobility" she marked intersections of Liszt's performing persona with other spheres of performance culture. She compared his approach to that of the actor François-Joseph Talma, famous for his lead roles in classical tragedies:

Into the Kessler study he places expressions as detailed, nuanced, motivated and deepened as Talma would in the analysis of a role. He sings, his musical phrases inspire him, and in a state of verve he declaims them like a great actor, searching with his fingers to arrive at the perfect quality of expression.[39]

The reference to Talma is intended to underline the elevated, sublime quality in Liszt's performance, but the image of an inspired man declaiming noble ideas and phrases to a large assembly could also intersect with the image of the orator at the tribune, pulpit, or courtroom. Thus did Boissier once describe Liszt as "a magnificent improviser, an eloquent orator, a vehement, passionate man."[40] The term "improviser" in this context probably refers not to music but specifically to oratory, for in French parlance the verb *improviser* was used mainly to describe political and legal speeches.

Comparisons between rhetoric and musical communication were ubiquitous in eighteenth century aesthetic discourses, and their impact lingered well into the nineteenth.[41] Czerny, however, made a more specific reference to oratory at the opening of the first chapter on the free fantasy: "As soon as the performer sits down before a larger gathering and generally to improvise in front of an audience he can be compared with an orator who strives to develop a subject as clearly and exhaustively as possible on the spur of the moment."[42] Czerny specifies three sorts of skill subtending the arts of both pianist and orator: technical fluency on the "instrument" of communication; a deep reserve of wide-ranging learning; and a fertile, inventive imagination allowing him to create images and embellish phrases to "avoid dullness and boredom"—the latter calibrated to "listeners' powers of comprehension."[43] Unlike eighteenth-century writers, Czerny imagines the free fantasy unfolding before a larger audience—the heterogeneous, boredom-prone audience of the modern or postclassical virtuoso—and it is this situation that brings to his mind the image of the performing orator.

Conspicuously missing from Czerny, however, is any mention of the orator's inspiration—the elevated countenance and the capacity to move the passions of the audience. This is where Liszt's French context differed markedly. Boissier's comparison of Liszt to orators and improvisers was prompted by his inspired and gestural performance manner, which strove "to depict his feelings and to make them join with those of others."[44] Liszt even evoked specific principles of oratory, advising his student that "musical phrases are bound to the same rules as the phrases of a speech; it is forbidden to repeat the same words."[45] These improvisational values were shared by the prominent educator Eugène Paignon. In his extended treatise *Éloquence et improv-isation* (1846) Paignon argued that improvisation was superior to plain speech and worked-out eloquence because it has a greater capacity to charm and affect the soul of listeners: "studied, prepared discourse pales before it." With almost breathless enthu-siasm, Paignon portrayed the relationship of speaker to audience as one of deep social reciprocity and mutual affirmation:

> Improvisation is one of the most beautiful manifestations of intelligence; it is the faculty that understands best how to subjugate the mind. And a society of people gathered to hear an orator, to give themselves to him, stimulating him with their breathing, indeed maintaining by their presence the sacred flame that burns in him and consumes him—is this not the happiest image of social perfection and of civilization?[46]

In 1830s Paris the most famous improviser of this sort was Pierre-Antoine Berryer, who staunchly defended the monarchy in lengthy parliamentary speeches and was admired by liberals for his engagement in favor of freedom of the press. (When Marie d'Agoult was in need of a lawyer in 1839, Liszt insisted she hire Berryer and none other.) Paignon apostrophized him in politically charged words: "Berryer! His talent rises, unfurls; he soars over the assembly, dominates it, forces it to be attentive; but he only has this power when he abandons old ideas that perished with the storm and attaches himself to those same principles that have toppled kings."[47] Improvisation is best, in other words, when inspired by forward-looking, revolutionary ideals—a ro-mantic spin on a traditional discipline.

Paignon pointed out that oral improvisation did not have to take place in the courtroom, parliament, or pulpit alone: "for our pleasure it also makes its way into the salons where elegant conversations shine forth."[48] And the few journals reporting on this smaller-scale, semi-private universe, such as the *Journal des artistes et des amateurs*, did occasionally announce or review oratorical performances. The recep-tivity of the general public to such displays was enhanced by the significant position oratory held in arts academies and educational institutions. In the 1820s and 1830s Eugène de Pradel, stimulated by the revived interest in Italian *improvvisatore*, made himself the first celebrity improviser in the French language. Like Germany's O. L. B. Wolff, he claimed to have validated French as a viable language for poetry improv-isation, and he sought recognition from the learned authorities at the Académie française. In 1836 Pradel challenged the Italian improviser Luigi Cicconi to a contest where each poet improvised a full verse tragedy, speaking all the characters, on a sub-ject solicited from the public. In his letter to the Académie gloating over his success, he defended the unique advantages of improvisation: "You know better than anyone that, in the course of thought, anything unexpected, picturesque in expression, or ca-sual and conventional in style, is enhanced a thousand times by the burning energy of improvisation."[49] He further defended the relative simplicity of the tragedy's plot, which was required because "in a drama created instantaneously . . . the author-actor [*auteur-acteur*], obliged to play all the roles in improvising them, cannot take on all the complications without risk of becoming confusing."[50] This was a performative experiment on par with Liszt—fusing improviser and actor, taking on multiple characters, adopting a tone of sublimity, and projecting them on a large canvas. Pradel and Liszt are not known to have associated, but Pradel often performed alongside musicians and singers at public concerts, taking subjects from the audience and elaborating them in rhymed verses.[51]

The romantic movement, thriving in 1830s Paris, was reclaiming rhetorical aesthetics and giving them a distinctly poetic slant.[52] The popularity of Madame de Staël's novel *Corinne* played a large part in this, as will be discussed later. In Liszt's milieu the most significant performer was possibly the Polish exile and poet Adam Mickiewicz, who arrived in Paris in 1832 with his major literary achievements already behind him. His most famous work, the verse drama *Dziady*, comes to a climax in a long, Byronesque monologue called "The Improvisation." It is a self-portrait of sorts, for Mickiewicz was an extraordinary literary improviser who often displayed his talent in salons and in public situations, usually to the accompaniment of music. When he was invited to lecture about Slavic literature at the Collège de France in the early 1840s, he insisted on improvising the lectures, and by this point he had adopted a mystical philosophy of radical poetic instantaneity according to which the poet channels divine and prophetic power.[53] Reversing the usual pattern, Mickiewicz evolved from a "writing" poet into performing, acting one. George Sand, utterly taken with the Mickiewicz, arrayed him with Goethe and Byron as major exponents of what she called the *drame fantastique*, and excerpted his "incomparable piece 'The Improvisation'" to illustrate the new genre.[54] She was also present at a legendary soirée in 1840 where Mickiewicz traded improvisations with a younger poet and induced a state of quasi-religious ecstasy in the audience.[55]

Liszt's piano performances contributed vitally to these romantic convergences of poetry, oratory, acting, and improvisation. In 1833 the poet Émile Deschamps published a poem in *La France littéraire* called "The Most Beautiful of Concerts!" (*Le plus beau des concerts!*). It is a dreamy, fantastical reminiscence of an elegant musical salon hosted by an aristocratic lady, at the center of which is a performance by Liszt: "Once the marvelous child, now a man,/Seated at the musical tripod, improvising poet,/Liszt, Liszt transforms notes into verses, the piano into a lyre/Without transforming his state of delirium" (*France littéraire* 1833, 206). The poem leaves behind the piano prodigy image of earlier years and constructs Liszt as a poet-musician, inspired and improvising. As an avid propagandist for romanticism, Deschamps had a vested interest in assimilating Liszt's playing to the romantic aesthetics of improvisation.[56] It is entirely possible that Liszt was actually improvising at this soirée, but it is also possible he was playing a movement from a Weber sonata or some other piece in his repertoire. The poem openly transfigures the events it recollects, taking advantage of retrospective distance to represent it as a voyage into the ideal: "As for the *real*, for bitter regions,/I have to bid you adieu." The venue, an aristocrat's hotel, is fantasized as "the palace of the fairies;/It was Rome . . . Bagdad . . . or Califs . . . or César's" (*France littéraire* 1833, 205; ellipses original). Using the poet's fantastical license, Deschamps represents Liszt's performance not necessarily as it was, but as he wishes it to be.

This was the consequential new meaning improvisation acquired in the context of romanticism. It became part of a rhetoric invested with desire—the desire for the perfect performance, the "most beautiful of concerts." The romantic rhetoric of improvisation thrived on a dialectic in which real phenomena oscillate with their idealized representation. An improvisational performance was imagined as less bounded, less finite, less mediated than a performance of a finished piece. It would be infinitely deeper and richer, like poetry glimpsed in the moment of inspiration and invention. Friedrich Schlegel had written: "The romantic form of poetry is still in the process of becoming. Indeed, its true essence lies therein, that it is always in the process of becoming and can never be completed."[57] Improvisation epitomized music in its neverending state of becoming. It was a key romantic emblem of creative genius, rising high above art produced through rules, tradition, and craft. Many writers were responsible for developing these literary and philosophical tropes around Liszt, Chopin, and other pianists in the French milieu. But George Sand was disproportionately influential in establishing and disseminating them. In her 1835 open letter to Liszt (eventually published in *Lettres d'un voyageur*) she recalled the spectacle of a concert she attended with his young protégé Hermann Cohen: "I saw you facing the orchestra of a hundred voices, while everyone kept quiet to hear your improvisation, and the child, standing behind you, pale, moved, immobile as a marble statue, yet trembling like a flower . . . seemed to inhale the harmony through all his pores."[58] In this passage the boy's transfixed attention and ecstatic response is a surrogate for the ideal response of the whole audience; he feels what they would feel if they were still blessed with his innocence and natural receptivity. To support this image of such perfect affective transfer, Sand describes the performance as an "improvisation," conveniently eliminating the object—the composition—that might stand in the way. The real performance she was recollecting, however, was a public concert where Liszt had played Weber's *Konzertstück* with orchestra, and had not improvised.

Sand's portrait, like Deschamps', takes the writer's privilege to evoke an idea of perfect musical performance, and improvisation is a leading figure in this rhetoric. Gone are the values ascribed to improvisation in the kapellmeister network, such as learnedness, mastery, traditional craft, and stylistic diversity. These are displaced by an emphasis on the improviser's free, vivid imagination, and, crucially, on a complete, immediate transmission of divine fire to spectators. It would be difficult to find a construct of the performer more opposed to that of the "interpreter" who dutifully relates himself to the composer or seeks out the mysteries of a work. The interpreter model was unquestionably on the ascendant in this period. It had not yet achieved the hegemony it achieved later in the century, but an avid romantic like Berlioz was actively policing performers who violated the intentions of composers or the texts of great works with alterations, cuts, and embellishments. Liszt himself would soon buy into this composer- and work-centered ideology in public pronouncements, regardless of whether his practice kept pace.[59] The romantic celebration of improvisation did not express what was culturally dominant in the 1830s. It is better understood as a kind of negative critique, expressing a desire for modes of musical experience that were being edged out by the cult of composers, the commodification of music, and the perceived banalization of music in commercial public concerts. It reflected the critical, opposi-tional stance French romantics adopted in relation to the mainstream, which included, in their eyes, the spiritless politics of *juste milieu* and the vapid, commercialized cul-ture of the uncultured "bourgeoisie" whose interests the new regime were supposedly serving.[60]

Other writings by Sand expressed this critique of public convention and commer-cial society by making improvisation the special preserve of artists and intellectuals communing among themselves in the face-to-face situation of salons. Comtesse de Bassanville recalled that Sand, at her country house in Nohant, a "chateau of liberty" where so many artists converged, "almost always opened the concert with some im-provisation in the manner of Liszt, her teacher and friend. While this was happening the guests drew, worked, wrote, or even read, because she did not demand they listen.[61] Sand's notion of improvisation embraced not just music and poetry but the entire spontaneous artistic lifestyle of her bohemian circle. In a semi-fictional account of their life, she wrote:

> In order to inspire himself, doubtless, with the view of the trees and mountains,
> the doctor had a small piano brought in to help him improvise, beneath a very
> cloudy landscape. The hours when the doctor improvises are the most blessed
> of our journey for everyone. Beppa seats herself at the piano and slowly plays
> with one hand a short musical theme which helps the improviser follow his lyric
> rhythm, and thus unfold in one afternoon myriads of strophes, during which
> I doze off profoundly in the hammock.[62]

Here, in the vortex of French romanticism, is a utopian model of community— situated in nature, away from the divisive forces of urban life, and meeting the needs of its members through improvised artistic performance, sympathetic listening, and spontaneous collaboration. Sand's rhetoric of improvisation is fantastical, idealized, and unreal, and self-consciously so. It seduces the reader into a world that has the appearance of reality, but which, as the reader discovers in the aftermath of reading, is too beautiful and frictionless to be *really* real. It is this very unattainability that qualifies it as "romantic." Its critical potential resides in its power to shape conscious-ness about what was perceived to be fatally missing from actual musical performances and from the conditions of exchange and communication in modern life.

The trope of improvisation as the perfect condition toward which performance aspires first crystallized around the playing of Liszt and Chopin, and it became deeply sedimented in critical discourse for the rest of the nineteenth century. The young Charles Hallé recalled his experiences of Chopin in Paris by writing: "you listened, as it were, to the improvisation of a poem and were under the charm as long as it lasted."[63] The influential Berlin critic Ludwig Speidel wrote of Liszt: "nothing is more charming than when he plays Chopin's dance pieces (one wants to say, when he improvises them)."[64] "As it were," "one wants to say"—with such subjunctive locutions these writers signal awareness that the pianist is not really improvising, but giving off a seductive aura of improvisation. They seize the writer's resources to illuminate the aura and channel the desire for improvisation.

Liszt himself was happy to blur the lines in this way. In a letter written from George Sand's retreat in Nohant, a gathering place of numerous artists in the romantic circle, Marie d'Agoult reported: "Liszt was marvelous here the evening before his departure. He played piano—improvised—*as he sometimes says to me*. The fluttering wing of the cherub hovered over him. It was a beautiful and grand soirée."[65] Not only does Liszt spin his playing as improvisation, but the improvisation becomes the central figure of d'Agoult's entire reminiscence of the salon. Other writers did the same. The protagonist of Balzac's 1837 novella *Gambara* is an opera composer who, as he struggles to bring his ideas to fruition, elaborates on his invented themes "in a masterly *fantasia*, a sort of outpouring of the soul after the manner of Liszt."[66] Josef Dannhauser's famous 1840 painting, which circulated in lithographs as "Liszt Improvising [*fantasierend*] at the Piano," performs the same cultural work. It shows Lisztian improvisation in its most natural element: the evening salon, in the company of French romantic writers and leading composers. His improvising resonates fully and completely with the auditors. Conspicuous for their absence are the philistine noblemen, politicians, diplomats, and bankers who often made salons unbearable for artists. This resolutely ahistorical image portrays music not as it was, but as it ought to be.

Because the romantic rhetoric of improvisation thrived on idealization, the historical sources for romantic artists need careful scrutiny. To judge from written sources, Chopin improvised so often in private company that we can consider it his preferred way of performing. But most of the reports we have were written by the hosts and guests at salons, in whose writings, as we have seen, the figure of improvisation could furnish an allure of spontaneity and social exclusivity. There is reason to doubt the literalness of the term "improvise" in a passage such as this one by Heine:

> [Chopin] is not only a virtuoso but also a poet; he can reveal to us the poetry that lives in his soul. . . . Nothing can equal the pleasure he gives us when he sits at the piano and improvises. He is then neither Polish nor French nor German: he betrays a much higher origin . . . his true fatherland is the dream realm of poetry.[67]

Chopin may well have been improvising when Heine heard him; he was unquestionably capable of doing so.[68] But in this passage improvisation also serves a literary purpose, aiding in the construction of an image of the musician-poet whose free-flowing music elevates him above the contingencies of national identity: the pianist is emphatically *not* playing a mazurka or a polonaise. It seems just as likely that Heine was using the term "improvisation" metaphorically when he wrote this well-known passage about Liszt:

> When he sits down at the piano, sweeps his long hair back several times, and starts to improvise, he often hurls himself furiously at the ivory keys, creating a towering wilderness of chaotic thoughts throughout which flowers of the sweetest sentiment disperse their fragrance.[69]

As these various examples show, romantic writers had philosophical incentives for construing any performance as improvisation and for de-emphasizing the fixed, formulaic elements that characterize improvisation in nearly all manifestations. Too often musicologists have been tempted to "go along" with this romantic tendency. Paganini's romantic aura, for example, has often prompted questionable claims about the extent of his improvisations. A recent study argues that "Paganini improvised freely and constantly" and that "his performing style was indeed based on improvisation and poetic license."[70] In fact, most of what we know about Paganini's improvisations comes from his earliest period, when he improvised *cantilena* lines over composed-out basses, invented dialogues between two strings, and played solo capriccios in private company. Improvisation is hardly ever mentioned in the vast body of journalistic coverage of his European concert tours, where he played concertos and variation sets of his own composition, and played them *loco*. It is true that he occasionally improvised a *capriccio* or embellished a *cantilena*, but there is no evidence that in concerts he improvised "freely and constantly." With Paganini, improvisation was more the exception than the rule. His virtuosity and engaging performance manner may well have communicated "improvisatoriness," but this was an aesthetic quality that could emerge from fixed compositions as well as from freely invented pieces.

COMPOSING IMMEDIACY

While the literary construction of improvisation was under way in Parisian salons and in popular literature, Liszt was frantically educating and reinventing himself through extensive reading of the romantic canon. A famous letter from 1832 gives a snapshot of his state of mind:

> For a whole fortnight my mind and my fingers have been working like two lost souls. Homer, the Bible, Plato, Locke, Byron, Mozart, Weber are all around me. I study them, meditate on them, devour them with fury; besides this, I practice four to five hours of exercises. Ah! Provided I don't go mad you will find in me an artist![71]

His musical notebook from this period records this intellectual-spiritual ferment with remarkable clarity. Vague, dissociated musical ideas, some of them lacking metrical indications, sit side by side with quotations from poems and jottings in total disarray. While basking in this stream of consciousness, he was improvising his way toward an original, personal compositional voice. First to appear were a pair of compositions, *Harmonies poétiques et religieuses* (1835) and the set of three *Apparitions* (1834), that are radical by any standard. They are composed in an intense, tempo-less, expressionistic idiom aimed at the evocation of dreaminess, yearning, and ennui. Like the scribblings in the notebook, they are disjointed and fragmented, tracing mercurial, imbalanced shifts of feeling like a stenograph recording the *vague des passions*. In search of a music that follows every nuance of thinking, feeling, and speaking, Liszt overloaded these compositions with detailed performance indications, as though he wanted to transfer to paper a sounding concept he had fully worked out at the keyboard. He was striving for a maximally direct transmission of poetic and musical impulses to paper— capturing inspiration, as it were, at its point of origin. They represent an extreme application of the principle of unrevised spontaneity that made romantic writers celebrate improvisation.

Although these early works have the appearance of written-out improvisations, they simultaneously represent an initial step away from improvisation "itself." In this period of solitude and introversion, Liszt no longer treated improvisation as an event-immanent communication with a public audience, but subordinated it to a precompositional role. Two features of this compositional stylization stand out. First, the sense meter and time is distended beyond recognition. *Apparition* no. 3 is notated with two time signatures, both of which are mere approximations, since Liszt is measuring the music intuitively, according to the rhythm of feeling. It is marked with the extremely rare indication *senza tempo*, and opens *in medias res* as though cutting in on a fit of agitation (Example 5.1). The opening of *Harmonies poétiques et religieuses*, too, is marked *senza tempo*; Liszt doesn't even attempt to indicate a meter, and problems with the alignment between left and right hands have preoccupied editors (Example 5.2). The effect of this atemporal music is to shut down any expectation of linear process or harmonically directed phrase motion. It concentrates the listener's attention on the immediate present, dilating it with a plenitude of atmospheric evocation and expressive intensity. In this way Liszt's experimental compositions stylize the "punctual" focus of improvisational performance.

The second stylistic feature that comes to the fore in these pieces is Italianate *bel canto*, which appears in the form of bare recitative or soaring lyrical phrases. Among the many styles available to Liszt, *bel canto* was the one most associated with expressive immediacy, making it a reliable resource for conjuring the "inspired poet" image. At the opening of *Apparition* no. 3, for example, Italianate melody hosts an affective transition from intense agitation to consolation (see the second and third systems in Example 5.1), and the opening "ennui" phrase of *Harmonies poétiques* is answered by a sudden, unmotivated "cry" in recitative. *Apparition* no. 1 evokes an oneiric world where sensations and images blur into one another indistinctly (Example 5.3). Beginning *in medias res*, the right hand sings *bel canto* melodic phrases while a harmonically vague triplet figure in the left hand suggests ripples in the water—a Venetian gondolier's

EXAMPLE 5.1 Liszt, *Apparitions*, no. 3, from the original German edition
(Leipzig: Hofmeister, 1834)

EXAMPLE 5.2 Liszt, *Harmonies poétiques et religieuses*, opening, from the original German
edition (Leipzig: Hofmeister, 1835)

EXAMPLE 5.3 Liszt, *Apparitions*, no. 1

song transfigured by undulating waves. As the barcarolle fades away, a more full-fledged aria melody, *cantando*, is initiated, but it is broken off after a medial cadence, and a new kind of music takes over. The role of Venetian ambience and *bel canto* style in these works shows that the romantic ideal of expressive immediacy was best mediated through cultural signifiers associated with Italy. As Melina Esse has shown, the 1830s were a moment when the personas of *bel canto* opera singers were converging with literary representations of Italian poetry *improvvisatore*.[72] This nexus of literary, musical, and theatrical relationships subtended Liszt's musical choices as he fashioned himself into a musical poet-orator.

IMPROVISATION AND THE IMAGE OF ITALY (1836–1838)

Apparitions and *Harmonies poétiques* did little to advance Liszt's reputation as a composer. Even his friends suggested to him that such a fragmentary style of music was not sustainable.[73] He was nevertheless determined to invent himself as a composer, and improvisation continued to serve as a critical resource of invention. During his Swiss retreat of 1835–1836, while building up material for the *Album d'un voyageur*, he often improvised "storms." George Sand, writing about his improvisation on the great organ at Freiburg, noted that "the storm appears to be his ideal! Sublime dada, worthy of the brain of Ossian."[74] After a public concert in Geneva, Marie d'Agoult sketched a satirical play that begins: "The artist is at the piano; he has just improvised a storm. Prolonged bravos and applause."[75] Such *Sturm-und-Drang* improvising left an unmistakable imprint on the Swiss compositions *La Chapelle de Guillaume Tell, Orage,* and *Vallée d'Obermann,* not to mention the dramatic storms present in his transcriptions of the *Guillaume Tell* overture and the *Pastoral* symphony. Small wonder he later told Amy Fay that "storms are my forte."[76]

Storm improvisations, an established practice of organists and melodrama accompanists long before Liszt, dispensed with "given themes" in order to evoke colorful canvases with dramatic ups and downs. It is easy to imagine that Liszt raised their pictorial impact with new levels of bravura and chromatic patterns. D'Agoult, indeed, made light of the chromatic richness of his latest pieces and improvisations: "there are never fewer than thirteen flats in the fantasies that you compose, not to mention those you add when performing them."[77] The trope of following the storm with a cheerful shepherd's tune—familiar from Beethoven's *Pastoral* symphony and Rossini's *Tell* overture—was probably deployed by Liszt, and such tunes themselves were understood to be improvisatory. The first piece in his *Trois airs suisses* (1835–1836) is an "Improvisata" on the Swiss herdman's *ranz des vaches,* and it was probably Liszt's working-through of this material that prompted Sand to beg him: "Read poetry to me, go to the piano and improvise those wonderful pastorals that make old Everard and me sob as they remind us of our youth, our hills, and the goats we tended."[78] In Switzerland Liszt also continued to refine a gestural vocabulary that signified "improvisatory" performance. Albertine Rive-Necker, observing him during his Swiss stay, wrote that "his eyes wander upwards. . . . He seems to be reading invisible pages, or rather to be composing and playing according to the inspiration of the moment."[79] While the fascination with improvised storms clearly belonged to the period of his Swiss retreat, it reappeared on his 1840 tour through the British provinces, where he accompanied the declamation *The Inchcape Bell* in melodrama style, including an improvised storm, and in performances of the Beethoven's "Moonlight" sonata, which he embellished with the rumblings of distant thunder.[80]

As Liszt and Marie d'Agoult moved on from Switzerland to Italy, they entered a cultural milieu they perceived to be out of touch with the progressive artistic currents of Germany and France. They also considered Italy a natural home for improvisation, and this stereotypical marking of national differences colored their perceptions throughout. D'Agoult's journals, letters, and memoirs suggest that Liszt's improvisations took on heightened importance while they were present in Italy. In a diary entry summarizing his Milan performances of summer 1838, she contrasted the unanimous success of the improvisations with the relative indifference that greeted his new, original compositions:

> His genius . . . was slow to be understood, and if he had attempted to play serious music . . . he probably would not have succeeded because his fantasies tended too much toward the German genre. He improvised many times, sometimes very well, other times only decently, but always with enormous success.[81]

Shortly thereafter, following a two-month stint in Florence, she again correlated his success with improvisation: "He played in public seven times: twice at the court, twice for the poor and three times for himself. Great success, especially the improvisations."[82] D'Agoult's comments mark a perceived gap between the aesthetic orientation of Italian audiences and the aesthetic of Liszt's bold new compositions. The Italians are especially receptive to the improvisations, but less receptive to the harmonic and developmental intricacies of what she calls the "German genre." Clearly Liszt and d'Agoult were disappointed that, at the very moment Liszt most desired recognition as a composer, he was being "held back" by the Italian preference for free fantasies.

Italian press reports corroborate d'Agoult's perception that the improvisations attracted special attention.[83] For the first time since the 1820s, Liszt was playing free fantasies "on given themes." At his Italian debut concerts of December 1837 he spotlighted his own compositions, but almost immediately afterward he was earning a reputation for free improvisation. A writer at *La Moda* considered him "incomparable as a player as well as improviser and sight-reader, and not superficially versed in literature" (*Moda* 1837, 400).[84] At his concert in Como later the same month (29 December) the printed program announced that he would improvise on themes given by the audience, and the reviewer for *Glissons* singled it out as a concert highlight:

> This was the true triumph of Liszt. . . . The vote fell to a horn chorus from Weber and a motif from *La Sonnambula*, which the performer varied in a thousand ways. The motive from *La Sonnambula* is *grazioso*, and of a German character, with difficult harmonies and chords; but for Liszt nothing is difficult. (*Glissons* 1838, 8)

One wonders whether the "difficult harmonies and chords" really belong to Bellini's source. They more likely belonged to Liszt's improvisational treatment of the motif, as he took the motive through modulations and reharmonizations. Either way, the Italian reviewer heard in Liszt's improvised fantasy something "other"—a harmonic palette unfamiliar to his ears and vaguely associated with "Germany." Crude though this attribution may seem, it points to a real duality in the harmonic atmosphere in Liszt's concert fantasies on Italian operas—that is, between the free chromatic space he opens up in introductions and transitions, and the largely diatonic orbit of the borrowed operatic material.

In the early months of 1838, after the Como concert, Liszt improvised at *every* performance. In a letter to d'Agoult he proudly reported: "Nourrit sang the Duo from *Guillaume Tell* wonderfully. He was applauded enthusiastically. For my part, I improvised on motives from the same opera, with prodigious success."[85] In February, fresh from this triumph, he improvised twice "on given themes" at the prestigious salon of Countess Samoyloff in Milan. At this glorious event paying tribute to the recently retired Giuditta Pasta, he also played the role of master of ceremonies at the piano, accompanying arias from Pacini's *Niobe* and Rossini's *Semiramide*, as well as scenes from Donizetti's *Lucia di Lammermoor* and Mercadante's *Emma d'Antiocha* (*Corriere delle dame* 1838, 82–83.).[86] Just days later *Glissons* announced he would participate in another concert at La Scala "in which he will abandon himself in improvisation to the inspirations of his fantasy, and will play a trio by the other esteemed artist

Pixis" (*Glissons* 1838, 72). The concert at La Scala gave rise to the most explicit words Liszt ever wrote about improvisation, in an open letter on musical conditions in Milan published in the *Revue et gazette musicale*.[87] In the letter Liszt justified his decision to improvise a fantasy on given themes in these words: "As you can see, my friend, I found an excellent way to add some life to a concert—that entertainment so tiresome it can seem like a duty. Besides, in this land of improvisation and improvisers, why shouldn't I say, 'Me too'?"[88]

Two aspects of this passage are very remarkable and call for comment. First, it casts aspersions on public concerts, as though the institution itself was trivial or banal. Second, it implies that Liszt played a free fantasy as a concession to Italian taste, in "the land of improvisation and improvisers." Given Liszt's extensive background in improvisation and public concerts, these were spectacularly disingenuous words. They make more sense when we consider his aspiration to gain acceptance as a composer. For the first time in his career, Liszt was confronting the pejorative associations of improvisation. While its immediacy and spontaneity were widely celebrated, these virtues seemed to come at the cost of permanence and reflection, which composition alone could guarantee. As Esterhammer has shown, this ambivalence had haunted the romantic perspective on improvisation from the very beginning. It was thus expedient for Liszt, striving to define himself as a composer, to "other" improvisation as a cultural possession of Italy. And in this effort, French romantic writers were his best allies.[89] Under the influence of Staël's *Corinne* and German romanticism they had been building up a myth of Italy as a "land of improvisation and improvisers." The myth mixed reality and fantasy. The reality was a culture of actually improvising poets and orators native to Italy, though now spreading to France, Germany, and England. The fantasy was a cluster of ideas, images, and sentiments that romantic authors and European travel writers attached to the signifier "Italy": a land of free and easy poetic invention, full of spontaneous effusions of beauty. Because the idealization of improvisation was so heavily mediated by this construct of Italy, it is worth describing at more length.

The image of Italy that prevailed in Parisian literary circles was overdetermined and can hardly be summarized in all its complexity. A majority of romantic writers— Chateaubriand, Lamartine, Alfred de Vigny, Alfred de Musset, George Sand, and others—made use of Italian ambience. Sand and Musset often set their novels in Italian contexts to give an aura of fantastical remove from the contemporary social situations they mimicked.[90] Liszt's travel essays in *Lettres d'un bachelier ès musique* reproduce all the typical tropes. They fetishize Italy's classical and early Christian past, praise the easygoing naïveté of its people and their closeness with nature, valorize the seemingly unforced beauty of renaissance painters, and express nostalgic longing for Italy's innocence, chivalry, and lack of the neuroses of civilization.

Germaine de Staël's best-selling novel *Corinne: ou l'Italie* was the single most popular and influential disseminator of these ideas. The eponymous heroine is an *improvvisatrice* who, early on, is given a crown of laurels by the Roman public and delivers a lengthy extemporization at the Capitol on the glory of Italy. In the audience is a recently arrived traveler from England, Lord Nelvil, who has been beset with profound melancholy since the death of his father and has come to Italy to help restore his balance. Corinne and Nelvil instantly feel an affinity for one another, but their opposing temperaments and cultural backgrounds block the realization of their love at every path. The novel draws a sharp opposition between them. Lord Nelvil's cold, northern, inward-turned Protestant temperament—brooding and reflective, inured to pleasure and beauty—is contrasted with Corinne's warm, Catholic, Italian temperament, with its love of external beauty, fantasy, and history. Staël complicates the binary somewhat by introducing a Frenchman who represents a third national character (allegorically, "conversation" or "esprit"), but the novel's dramatic tension lies in the prospect that Nelvil's oppressive melancholy will be overcome by Corinne's charm, intelligence, and natural grace. It constructs Italy as an imagined space of improvisation and associates it with feminine charm, intelligence, eloquence, and sympathy.

Liszt's familiarity with *Corinne: ou L'Italie* is beyond doubt. The heroine of Rossini's 1824 opera *Viaggio a Reims*, premiered in Paris just a few months before Liszt's own opera *Don Sanché*, is based on Staël's character, and her "improvisation" is one of its dramatic centerpieces. Saint-Beuve dubbed d'Agoult "The Corinne of the Quai Malaquai," probably in honor of her conversational skill, and Liszt referred to her by this name in a letter of 1833.[91] A comment in d'Agoult's journal during their Italian journey suggests that the couple might have viewed their own relationship in terms of the novel: "As we viewed the beautiful sites and grandiose monuments, [Liszt] told me he needed me so that the beautiful would become manifest to him through me; that I was for him like the speech through which the beauty of things was revealed to him."[92] The relationship described here precisely mirrors the relationship between Corinne and Lord Nelvil: for long stretches of the story, Corinne shows Nelvil the various ancient ruins and museums of Rome, providing expert historical digressions and interpretive commentary on everything.[93] Countless foreign travelers used Staël's novel as a kind of tourist guide, and d'Agoult herself noted in a letter that she was "loving this divine country in the company of Goethe, Byron, Chateaubriand, Corinne."[94]

George Sand based the heroine of her novel *Consuelo* (1842) on Corinne, recasting the poet as an extemporizing Italian opera singer.[95] In Sand's imaginative universe, poetry, improvisation, and florid singing blur into one another and become indistinguishable; they jointly represent the distinctively Italian art of natural, spontaneous expression. In one scene the precocious singer Consuelo annoys her dogmatic teacher (who happens to be named Porpora) by singing the assigned aria with dozens of wild ornaments, all of them in perfectly good taste. Later in life Consuelo gives a prospective student a test:

> Try to improvise something, whether with the violin or the voice. It is thus that the soul manifests itself at the tip of the lips or the fingers. Thus shall I know whether you have, indeed, the divine afflatus, or are only a quick scholar steeped in recollections of the works of others.[96]

The student, whose name happens to be Joseph Haydn, proves that he is indeed gifted with the "divine afflatus." In contrast with Staël, who popularized a fairly rigid southern/northern binary opposition in which improvisation was aligned with the south, Sand lets improvisation belong to "northern" keyboardist Haydn as well.

Berlioz's memoirs of his travels through Italy further exemplify the part-real, part-imaginary connections that French romantics made between Italy, improvisation, and music. Narrating his peregrinations around Rome and Naples, Berlioz describes a song he heard many times in the countryside and the Abruzzi mountains. It was essentially a flexible recitation formula for extemporaneous verses: "[The tune] changes according to the words improvised by the singer, and the accompanists follow along as they can. This improvisation does not demand much poetic skill from this mountain Orpheus; it is simply prose."[97] A month later he unexpectedly encounters this melody again at a country inn:

> In the evening, in Capua, we enjoyed good food, good lodgings, and . . . an im-
> proviser. This good man, after some rapid preludes on his large mandolin, asked
> what nation we were from. . . . Here is the cantata he addressed to us three
> supposed Frenchman, in music likewise improvised, and without the slightest
> pauses. . . . [Berlioz prints the melody and text.][98]

For Berlioz as for other romantics, improvised poetry of this kind embodied various forms of otherness. It was spontaneous, oral poetry joined inextricably with music. It was found beyond the confines of civilization and cities, in rural areas immune to change, close to nature, and populated by simple people. Influenced by the latest literary research, Berlioz further imagined that Italian improvisers represented a modern survival of ancient Homeric recitation.[99] He implied this in his reference to one of the mountain singers as "the Tyrtaean companion"—an allusion to the ancient elegiac poet of Sparta, whose art was often linked with Homeric and epic narrative.

In Italy, of course, such improvisation was not confined to residual "folk" practices. Especially around Rome, one might well have encountered a poetry improviser in a theater, a salon, or a city square. Many acquired their skills through intensive study of Latin philology, law, and rhetoric, and the most brilliant of them could make successful European tours. Although Liszt and d'Agoult did not describe any encounters with improvising poets, such poets were never far away. Two days after Liszt's La Scala concert a lawyer named Antonio Bindocci gave an *Accademia di poesia estemporanea* at the same theater.[100] Bindocci's standard practice was to take six or seven themes from the audience and improvise on them using multiple rhyme schemes and forms.[101] One subject proposed to him was the *duomo decorata*, in honor of the coronation of Ferdinand I which had just taken place at the Milan cathedral.[102] Liszt's ritual of taking themes from the audience for improvisation was similar, and he described it at length in his open letter on Milan. One audience member had even suggested to Liszt the same subject, the *duomo di Milano*, that was given to Bindocci (*Glissons* 1838, 87). Musical and poetic improvisation had separate histories, then, but the transaction with the audience and the heightened sense of occasion made them quite similar as perfor-mance rituals. In addition, extemporaneous poets nearly always performed with onstage musical accompaniment—typically a droning or atmospheric background in-strument such as the harp, guitar, or piano—and the music became gradually more an-imated as the improviser's inspiration swelled. Thus a music-poetic convergence was built into the practice of poetry improvisation—a real-world ground for the images of ancient, Orphic performance that romantic writers liked to summon.

Liszt's visually compelling and theatrical performance manner echoed the de-meanor of the poetry *improvvisatore*. The latter entrained audiences by performing forth their effort and inspiration, dramatizing the labor of invention as they searched out and uttered verses, and employing a conventionalized vocabulary of hand gestures to accent the meanings. It is therefore not surprising that tropes of poetic inspira-tion trickled heavily into Italian journalistic responses to Liszt. A critic at *Il Pirata* claimed "he is at the piano-forte like a poet inspired by his muse" (*Pirata* 1838, 285) and characterized Liszt's playing in terms of vocalization and speech:

> When the harmony then bursts forth like a torrent and speaks the language of all the affections, all the passions, then the eye of Liszt brightens, intensifies, and seems to seize upon some unidentifiable object. He glimpses his own genius, to which he speaks and issues commands, at once gushing out impetuously as though in a transport of disdain, then murmuring softly as if speaking a secret amorous language. (*Pirata* 1837, 197)

This was a one-man drama, comparable to the lengthy verse tragedies improvised by the astonishing Tommaso Sgricci. There is a substantial contrast between these Italian characterizations of the "poetic" musician—which take their cue from the appearance of the performer—and the discourses of "poetic" music in Germany and France, which are more metaphorical. Discourse about the playing of Chopin, Clara Wieck, and Adolphe Henselt uses the word "poetic" to highlight an intensity of lyrical, interiorized, or anti-theatrical concentration—that is, the very opposite of performative poetry. Even as Liszt's performances reminded viewers of improvising poets, the unfamiliar chromaticism of his music redirected the image back to his non-Italian origins. A writer at *Glissons* took note of the "many complicated passages in his compositions, in which the 'enharmonic' genera is frequently used," and concluded that "Liszt is a pianist-poet, whose manner could, in a manner of speaking, be compared with that of Victor Hugo; he is a Titan of audacity and power" (*Glissons* 1838, 58).

Although the French romantic image of Italy was highly idealized, it was counterbalanced by a sharp critique of Italy's political oppression under Austrian rule. Writers imagined Italy as a land filled with unrealized potential, rich in natural endowments, and predisposed to the appreciation of beauty, yet lacking in aspirations to elevation, depth, and reflection. Corinne, the personification of Italy, offers an ex-planation of how political and artistic decadence are intertwined in Italy:

I agree with you that, for the last century or two, unhappy circumstances having deprived Italy of her independence, all zeal for truth has been so lost, that it is often impossible to speak it in any way. . . . The Italians are afraid of new ideas, rather because they are indolent than from literary servility. By nature they have much originality; but they give themselves no time to reflect. Their eloquence, so vivid in conversation, chills as they work.[103]

As a close friend of Italian exiles in Paris, Liszt was highly attuned to Italy's battles against Austrian and papal oppression. In common with other romantics, he admired artists such as Tasso and Dante who had flourished under despotic political conditions.[104] Marie d'Agoult, in letters and diaries from Italy, railed against the decadence of its opera, the climate of political repression, and the lack of vital philosophical culture in Milan.[105] This is the perspective, merging political and artistic critique, that compelled Liszt and d'Agoult in the open letter on Milan to lament the artistic "backwardness" and superficial taste prevalent in Italy:

It was to an audience whose taste had been reduced almost entirely to music derived from opera that I ventured to present two or three fantasies in my own style. . . . They were applauded, thanks . . . to some octave passages played with quite laudable dexterity and to several cadenzas, spun out over the melody, which might have issued from the throat of the most determined nightingale.[106]

The implication here is that Italian audiences, knowing only opera, were incapable of comprehending his "advanced" compositions, and that he improvised bravura cadenzas to compensate for their mediocre level of understanding.[107]

Liszt's decision to improvise a free fantasy in Milan had the same motive: "As my concerts have always been criticized for being too serious, I hit upon the idea of adding a little life to them by improvising on themes proposed by the dilettantes and chosen by acclamation."[108] Here improvisation is a compromise—a capitulation to Italian taste by a composer of elevated artistic orientation. Liszt suggests that the style of his free fantasy was lighter or more accessible than that of his composed-out opera fantasies. Yet at the same time, the humorous tone of the letter permits him to put improvisation in a more positive light. In taking themes from the audience, he writes, "the improvisation becomes a joint effort, a matter of the artist's polishing the jewels that have been given him."[109] Thus improvisation, in contrast to composition, restores a sense of community to the concert event. Liszt had voiced this idea before. In his 1835 essay "De la situation des artistes," written in a far more earnest and utopian spirit, he had asserted that taking themes from the audience was a "way of improvising . . . [that] establishes a more direct rapport between the public and the artist. . . . [The improvisation] becomes a communal work."[110]

In a short space of three years, then, Liszt's attitude toward improvisation had darkened considerably. Though he had previously associated it with a possibility of social regeneration and community through art, he now considered it a symptom of underdeveloped artistic consciousness. If he had formerly treated it as an indispen-sable resource of composition, he increasingly viewed it as pre-compositional or even antithetical to higher composition. Like Italy, improvisation was something not yet realized, lacking elevation, calling out for fuller realization through reflection and development.

REFORMULATING IMPROVISATION

The concerts that Liszt played almost incessantly from 1838 to 1847 demonstrate that for all the distance he wanted to place between himself and improvisation, he could not dispense with it. He continued to play free fantasies on given themes and improvise in other forms, even when most of his rivals were ceasing altogether. Like Chopin, Bocklet, and Moscheles, he kept improvising without inhibition. But it is im-portant not to overstate the case. In many ways his outlook had been deeply reshaped by the emergent order in which improvisational performance occupied a lower status. Consider the 1838 concert series in Vienna—the first outburst of "Lisztomania" and the launching pad of his touring career. The first six concerts of the series were filled with the most diverse possible repertoire, but Liszt improvised at *none* of them. Only at the seventh concert, when he was running out of repertoire and novelties, did he improvise, and on this occasion he did not take themes from the audience, but chose the motive from the piece he had just played: Weber's *Aufforderung zum Tanze*. This, of course, had been his favorite motive for improvisation since his childhood, and it was hardly risky. At the next concert, his farewell, he did not improvise.

The infrequency of Liszt's improvisations did not lessen their impact on listeners and audiences. Heinrich Adami of the *Allgemeine Theaterzeitung* singled out the im-provisation as the highlight of a concert he attended, and formulated a philosophical maxim in response: "The instantaneous moment generates inspiration" (*Allgemeine Theaterzeitung* 1838, 447).[111] That Adami gave special mention to the improvisation is all the more surprising for the fact that, at its thrilling climax, it was interrupted by cries of delight so loud they broke Liszt's concentration. For a moment he left a domi-nant seventh chord lingering in silence, and then abruptly returned to the head motive for a premature close. Critic Carl Tausenau, reflecting on the concert series as a whole, considered it fit to acknowledge "what [Liszt] has achieved in that sphere so distinctive to the piano—the free fantasy" (*Allgemeine Theaterzeitung* 1838, 456). He nostalgically recalled Liszt's debut concerts as a child prodigy in Vienna, when his free fantasies had been admired universally, and expressed regret that during this triumphant return Liszt had only improvised once.

Liszt's itinerant concert tours began properly in late 1839 with more concerts in Vienna. Still seeking to establish himself as a composer, he presented an ambitious new piece entitled "Fragment nach Dante" that eventually became his "Dante" so-nata. Tellingly, at none of the five concerts from October to December of that year did he improvise. Only when he circled back through Vienna two months later

(February 1840) did he improvise publicly. At one concert he again played an extemporaneous encore on Weber's *Aufforderung*. The only other improvisation took place at his "farewell concert," and it was a more traditional free fantasy on given themes. He selected the Austrian national hymn by Haydn, a Thalberg *cantilena*, and a Strauss waltz, and as usual the audience burst out in applause at several climactic moments. Curiously, in the deliberations over themes the audience did not approve his choice of a Strauss waltz, and he ended up more or less imposing it against their will. Evidently he had some special motive for including the waltz. Perhaps his familiarity improvising on Weber's *Aufforderung* made him comfortable with waltz rhythms. Or perhaps he intended the performance as a sort of farewell tribute, delivered in a popular, accessible style, to the city that had helped make his name. The choice of tunes was unusual for the absence of an opera melody and for the heterogeneity of styles represented (something Czerny discouraged in his treatise). All three motives came from beloved Viennese composers, and each emblematized a different facet of the city's cultural-national identity. At the climax of the fantasy Liszt produced a "fusion of such heterogeneous objects into a whole through almost overwhelming bravura" (AMZ 1840, 375)—a phantasmic conflation of the ballroom (Strauss), the concert hall (Thalberg), and the national-imperial ceremony (Haydn).

The patterns established during the Vienna concert series remained standard for Liszt's concert career as a whole. Occasionally, but not very often, he played fantasies on themes solicited from the audience, combining the chosen themes at the end. In Germany he often combined a *bel canto* aria from a current Italian opera with a shorter motive from Weber or Mozart. (For the latter, he often reverted to the "Non più andrai" motive he had favored in his youth.) Normally he introduced a third theme that, *pace* Czerny, could serve as a recurring head-motto binding the parts of the fantasy together.[112] Another common approach was to improvise on a single theme of special relevance to the local audience, thus making improvisation a vehicle of communal pride and sentiment. For audiences in England he improvised on "God Save the King." For the Berlin university students he worked with "Gaudeamus igitur," and for audiences in Spain and Portugal a popular "Jota aragonaise" by the salon composer Nogués.[113] When he passed through Stettin he met the local kapellmeister Carl Loewe, who impressed Liszt by playing his setting of the gothic ballad "Der Mutter Geist." That evening Liszt, stirred by Loewe's performance, opened his own concert with an improvisation on motives from Loewe's composition.[114] When the workers of Toulouse serenaded him with the Provençal song "Campano qué souno," he immediately picked it up and began improvising on its motives, developing it into a fantasy by combining it with a *mélodie hongroise* (*Journal de Toulouse*, 1 September 1844). Nearly all of these improvisations eventually led to published fantasies, doubtless intended as souvenirs for those audiences who had heard them live.

Far more commonly, Liszt improvised on a motive from a piece he had just played, in response to the audience's vociferous demand for an encore. Rather than repeat the same piece, as the convention of encoring dictated, he "reinvented" it with yet more bravura, raising the applause to still higher levels. The most frequent of such "encore-improvisations" was his old standby *Aufforderung zum Tanze*, but he also in this fashion worked up motives from *Erlkönig*, the *Grand galop chromatique*, one of his *Mélodies hongroises*, and other pieces. A representative example comes from a Vienna concert of 1846 whose program closed with his recently composed and published fantasy on Spanish melodies. A young Eduard Hanslick was present and recalled it in his memoirs:

> Stormily called back many times, he once again placed himself at the piano and reworked the same Spanish themes into entirely new, brilliant pictures in completely free improvisation. Liszt was visibly in a good, almost boisterous [*übermutig*] mood, so his improvisation had an incomparably more thrilling effect than the known, printed piece I had before me.[115]

This sort of improvising downplayed the social leveling and democratic exchange implicit in the fantasy "on given themes." Rather than condescend to the mixed audience, meeting it at its level, he built upon the audience's arousal and lifted them to a "higher" level. Such improvisation performed an artist-led idea of community consistent with the vision advanced in "De la situation des artistes." It also evaded the charge of triviality critics had been leveling at the postclassical fantasy on given themes, which had modeled a more heterogeneous and civic idea of community.

The performance aesthetics of the encore-improvisation, too, differed from that of the traditional fantasy on given themes. Liszt was not merely varying or manipulating materials suggested by others, but "recomposing" materials he had chosen for himself. In this way the encore-improvisation blurred the lines between improvising, playing a work, and composing, at a time when the mass dissemination of printed music seemed to be hardening those demarcations. This was consistent with a more general perception, which has never left the discourse around Liszt, that an improvisational sensibility infiltrated his printed fantasies as well as his interpretations of classic works. His intensely poetic style of pianistic delivery, a Königsberg critic wrote, could be detected not only in his original opera fantasies, which bore "the character of a free improvisation," but also in the performances of those works:

> This form [the composed fantasy] and the productions of other composers submit to his individuality; just as Iffland realizes the same character in different ways on two or three evenings, but every time represents the character with such apparent authenticity that one is left in doubt which portrayal is preferable, so does Liszt, when following his immediate impulses, constantly appear in different guises the less limited his field of activity is. (*Königliche Preussische Staats- Kriegs- und Friedenszeitung*, 15 March 1842)

This writer converts improvisation into a rhetorical figure for something more fundamental: the performative moment and the act of musical origination. Improvisation no longer designates a specific type of musical event or situation, but is reinterpreted

as a descriptor for the radically punctual, in-the-moment thrust of Lisztian performance, regardless of whether he is "actually" inventing music or not. Liszt's playing,
to an extent matched only by Chopin's, anchored this amplification of the meaning
of improvisation to embrace not just the inventive act but also the reinventive impression. But this could only have occurred in alliance with romantic writers, whose
rhetorical tropes for improvisation had produced beliefs and expectations about what
keyboardists were doing in performance. Vladimir Jankélévitch was employing a long-
accumulated romantic discourse when he wrote: "Like creation, invention or inspiration, improvisation is a beginning: improvisation is the germinal or initial stage of
song, of music being born."[116]

Critical response to Liszt's improvisations was generally positive, but an intransigent old guard, remembering the days of Hummel, took them to task. Such critics
were not fundamentally against Liszt or against improvisation per se. On the contrary, they highly valued the improvised fantasy genre, but were anxious that the commercialization of musical culture, whose token was the figure of the touring virtuoso,
was leading to decadence. Carl Gollmick, a conservative-leaning critic, compared Liszt
unfavorably to Hummel, who lived in "a worthier time" and whose improvisations
preserved a sense of "order and unity" while embracing the inspiration and freedom
(*Ungebundenheit*) unique to improvisation. Liszt's fantasy, in contrast, "was a casually
thrown-together sequence of criss-crossing flashes of ideas; it was never anything
more than subjective expression of feelings in a thousand fleeting shades of dark
and light" (*Frankfurter Konversationsblatt*, 17 August 1840). Gollmick was bothered,
furthermore, by the entertaining manner in which Liszt negotiated themes with the
audience: "he was playing around with the public, à la Langenschwarz but without the
interest that comes with novelty." As a consequence of the audience ritual, Gollmick
continued, Liszt was left with three tunes—"Non più andrai," Bellini's "Mira, O
Norma," and Mozart's "champagne" aria—that he could only awkwardly attempt to
superimpose at the conclusion. A similar perspective was offered by the Hamburg
critic "Wahrlieb," who reviewed two consecutive concerts at which Liszt improvised.
The first improvisation—on the *Allegretto* from Beethoven's Seventh Symphony, the
drinking song from Donizetti's *Lucrezia Borgia*, and Mozart's "champagne" aria—was
a disappointment, coming out exactly "as such things turn out and will always turn
out in a concert hall, where the freer unfolding of the imagination is blocked and se-
verely limited" (*Freischütz*, 14 November 1840). At the next concert Liszt improvised
on the same Donizetti aria and "Non più andrai," but Wahrlieb became even more
critical:

> As a performing virtuoso Liszt is truly colossal and merits the most unreserved
> praise. But he should not improvise in public. This fantasia showed that the
> one played recently at his third concert was no accidental mishap. . . . On the
> contrary, that previous one was a great success in comparison with today's—for
> Liszt, that is, not for the connoisseurs. To improvise freely one must possess,
> next to all the gifts of genius, a completely thorough, solid foundation of

knowledge, without which one will never arrive at a satisfying result. (*Freischütz*, 21 November 1840)

Wahrlieb was clinging to the elite, professional, and anti-public values that many German authors, Hummel included, had voiced in the 1820s with regard to the free fantasy genre. Liszt, he knew, was not improvising according to the principles and values of the kapellmeister network.

Reverence for Hummel's free improvisations did not necessarily translate into antipathy toward Liszt's modern style. Gustav Schilling, a Stuttgart-based musical writer and committed educator who wrote for a general audience rather than music specialists, voiced a more middle-of-the-road position. Discussing the "Fantasie" genre in his didactic treatise *The Pianist* (1843), Schilling made brief remarks on the improvised fantasy: "This freedom in true musical poetry, this purely improvised musical speech . . . can have an overpowering attraction when the player understands truly how to improvise [*fantasiren*], but this is the case with only very few rare individuals." Schilling considered Liszt one of those rare individuals, but at the same time he felt Liszt exemplified a modern trend in which compositional and improvisational talents had become mutually exclusive. Some pianists were excellent composers but poor improvisers, while others were brilliant improvisers but insignificant composers: "I do not hesitate to name the widely praised Liszt as a perfect example [of the latter]. I have never had occasion to meet a pianist who combined the talent for free improvisation with the calling to true composition with such skill and in such a high degree as Hummel, who died several years ago."[117] Professional specialization, Schilling intuited, was motivating pianists to concentrate their energies on executive skill, or on crafting ambitious compositions, and the capacity to improvise, demanding both kinds of energy without great rewards, was falling between the cracks. In this context Liszt stood out for perpetuating the practice. For every critic who judged Liszt's improvisations trivial or superficial, there were two who praised them. With so few contemporary pianists up for comparison, it mattered less how well he improvised than that he did so at all. Just as he was about to retire from concertizing, a writer at *La France musicale* defended him against his detractors by calling him "a knowledgeable musician, the best sight-reader in the world and a wonderful improviser."[118]

The improvisations Liszt played in Vienna in 1846, toward the end of his performing career, are emblematic of how things had changed since his 1822 debut concerts in that city. Of the ten public concerts he mounted in 1846, only the seventh included a free improvisation on given themes (two of Liszt's favorite motives from Weber, and a comic song known only locally). The relative scarcity of improvisations did not mean he had lost his touch. A week before this seventh concert he made a great impression improvising at a charity concert for the kapellmeister Gyrowetz. After accompanying the popular bass Josef Staudigl in Schubert's *Erlkönig* and Handel's aria "O Ruddier than the Cherry" (both in G-minor), he launched into an improvisation. Using Handel's opening orchestral part as a prelude, he transitioned to the headmotive of *Erlkönig*, and after briefly elaborating upon that, introduced "O Ruddier" in the bass. He freely invented a fantasy that alternated between the motives and eventually interwove them, and according to several sources it was the highlight of the concert. Heinrich Adami emphasized the lack of preparation as a distinct advantage: "Liszt had certainly, definitely not thought about such an improvisation in advance, and it was so successful precisely because it came only from the impulse of the moment and because he surrendered himself completely to the artistic inspiration of the moment and of his genius" (*Allgemeine Theaterzeitung* 1846, 283–84).[119] Adami was far less enthusiastic about the free fantasy at Liszt's seventh concert, which was based on given themes and therefore lacked the spontaneity, as well as the generous social motive, of the earlier charity concert. He claimed that this performance did not come off well and mused that the whole practice of improvising on given themes might be "a misguided thing" (*Allgemeine Theaterzeitung* 1846, 307). The encore-improvisation on Spanish themes that Hanslick so admired took place at the eighth concert, and at the ninth concert, in response to audience demand for an encore, he improvised a mélange of his Hungarian melodies and his recomposed *Aufforderung* (*Wanderer* 1846, 332). But as if listening to Adami's criticism, Liszt did not improvise on given themes at the final three concerts. In contrast to his farewell concert of 1840, where he had taken themes from the audience and improvised, he bade adieu this time with a fantasy on the Austrian national hymn, composed by the person who had instructed him in the art of improvisation, Carl Czerny.

Liszt was still playing improvisations, then, but they were a relatively marginal feature of the 1846 series. He foregrounded instead his "reformed" commitment to works and composers considered "classic." The concert programs stacked up more large-scale pieces by Weber, Hummel, Czerny, Schubert, and Beethoven (late works included) than any of his previous concerts. The implicit message was divined by a journalist in a retrospective essay covering the whole series: "How often classical names appeared in Liszt's concerts! They, and the particular care that he devotes to their performance, clearly betrayed the noble taste Liszt brings to the task" (*Wiener Zeitung* 1846, 822). Liszt was well aware that improvisation could be a liability, and that it was better to develop a reputation for playing classic works. Yet the perceived tension between improvisation and "classic" value was a distinctly recent development. Viennese pianist Carl Maria von Bocklet, discussed in Chapter 2, had a solidly "classic" profile but was widely celebrated for the free fantasies he rarely failed to play at his own benefit concerts. The *Humorist* was expressing common opinion when it said "[Bocklet's] improvisation could hardly find a match among pianists living today" (*Humorist* 1845, 875).

During the 1846 season Bocklet and Liszt collaborated twice under a "classic" banner. At the fourth *concert spirituel* Bocklet played Beethoven's "Emperor" concerto and Liszt conducted Beethoven's Fifth Symphony. And at one of Bocklet's benefits Liszt appeared as distinguished guest artist, joining him for Hummel's Sonata in A♭ for four hands, after which Bocklet played a free fantasy on motives from Schubert's "Der Wanderer" and Weber's *Jubelouverture*. Though only ten years older than Liszt, Bocklet was a completely unreconstructed improviser—a living reminder that improvisation had once been fully compatible with classic aesthetic values and with an attitude of reverence toward works. Yet this compatibility had rested upon Bocklet's small, select audience of admiring connoisseurs in Vienna, and upon his decision *not* to take themes from the audience for improvisation, but to choose his own. No keyboardist, not even Hummel, ever found a full reconciliation between the elite values associated with the free fantasy genre and the communicative requirements of modern public concerts.

THE KAPELLMEISTER

After he retired from the concert stage in 1847, Liszt entered a new phase of his career focused on composition, teaching, conducting, and promoting new music from his kapellmeister post in Weimar. At the court of Grand Duke Carl Alexander he acquired a surprising new stage for his improvisational talent. As Detlef Altenberg has shown, Carl Alexander envisioned Liszt as a key ally in his mission of restoring Weimar to the prominent cultural position it had enjoyed in the era of Goethe and Schiller.[120] Back in 1844, at an intimate literary soirée, he had heard Liszt improvising melodramatic accompaniment to readings from Goethe's *Faust* by the famous poetry improviser O. L. B. Wolff.[121] As soon as Liszt settled into Weimar, Carl Alexander set about reviving this compelling marriage of modern music and classic literature: "I gave a concert where 3 songs by Dante were declaimed to the accompaniment of improvisations by Liszt, whose genius on that evening rendered him truly worthy of the immortal poet whose inspirations he translated."[122] An article of uncertain provenance about this event drew attention to the irreducible power of improvisational delivery:

> There is a form whose transitory and rapid nature, like the imagination from which it takes its life, has an incommunicable brilliance: improvisation! We can't help mention this because Liszt possesses it a degree almost unheard of before. The Grand Hereditary Duke sought to show this by presenting to Liszt 3 different subjects from 3 eras, which would give his intellect as well as his musical genius an opportunity to manifest their brilliance to the fullest extent. And so he accompanied with improvisations the reading of several pieces from *Faust* by Goethe, from *Le Cid* of Herder, and from Dante. Above all else, it is here that one senses the full extent of his capacities both musical and intellectual.[123]

This compliment is double-edged. On the one hand it attributes highest value to improvisation as a manifestation of Liszt's musical inventiveness and broad artistic vision. On the other hand it produces a kind of double subordination: improvisation is put in service of literature as a background or secondary discourse, and the improvising musician acts in service to the hereditary ruler, who commands the concert and dictates the terms of the improvisation. This was not the role Liszt envisioned for himself or for music in Weimar. His reputation for pianism and improvisation needed to be shelved at least temporarily in favor of his compositional projects. Over the next few years he published large-scale compositions on Dante and Faust that represented his goals far better than did any improvisations on those authors. Yet the warm reception of these performances at court underline the point that improvisation thrived in relatively closed, elite circles that deliberately kept distance from the complications of public exchange.

From the Weimar period to the end of his life, as many anecdotes attest, Liszt continued to prelude, embellish, and improvise frequently and brilliantly.[124] The circumstances and the approaches are highly miscellaneous and do not fall into any clear particular patterns or practices. They were received and described in the same reverent tones that greeted Liszt's every activity within his circle of associates. He had preserved his uncanny knack for lending a warm glow to social gatherings and artistic encounters with some unexpected, spontaneous effusion at the piano. Such anecdotes made improvisation an integral motif in the collective memory of Liszt as a person and an artist. It can therefore seem paradoxical that he did not encourage students to improvise, and that very few did so with any seriousness of intent. Adele aus der Ohe was a rare student whose free preludes impressed and pleased him, but instead of encouraging other students to imitate her, he asked her to prepare a volume of preludes and modulations that her classmates could practice to avoid the embarrassment of improvising a bad prelude.[125] Apparently it was preferable to have something prepared that sounded like improvisation than to actually improvise and play something banal. The most prominent of his students probably had the capacity to improvise in varying degrees, but none was inclined to display it or flout their talent for it. In the 1850s and 1860s one was more likely to hear free playing in the company of the aging players—Hiller, Moscheles, or Meyerbeer—than in the presence of any Liszt student.

Liszt, then, might best be described as an incompletely reconstructed improviser. He began his career as a relatively uninhibited and intuitive practitioner, freely developing single themes using the keyboardistic idioms in which Czerny trained him. In the 1830s he began responding to signals, coming from the professional establishment, that questioned the self-sufficiency and aesthetic legitimacy of improvised performance. He first channeled his extemporaneous energies into the production of highly original compositions trying to "capture" improvisation, with limited success. He retreated from the public milieu and reserved improvised performances for the aristocratic and artistic elite of the Parisian salons, a context free from the standards of professional judgment and the communicative demands of the public sphere. While this was happening, the thriving French romantic movement generated an attractive new, anti-establishment defense of improvisation, idealizing it as a practice of transcendent poetic utterance and imaginative freedom. For a while anyway, he could improvise not only with a good conscience, but with a forthright sense of mission. Liszt and his fellow romantics subsumed music into this broader concept, devising a literary and performative rhetoric that valorized improvisation and made it into a signifier of maximally vital, maximally communicative performance.

When he returned to the public concert scene in the later 1830s, though, Liszt found himself caught between the professional-critical censure of improvisation and the progressive-romantic celebration of it. This tension reached its breaking point in the open letter on Milan, where he bizarrely disavowed improvisation and implied it was a trivial "Italian thing." From this point forward, he made his own bravura compositions and classic works the core elements of his concert programs. He significantly tapered down free improvisations on given themes, and devised a new form, the "encore-improvisation," that was more impervious to professional censure.

Liszt thus submitted his improvisational inclinations to two reconstructive trends that were coming from the professional guild: the declining prestige of performance versus composition, and the increasing prestige of the "interpreter" role within the domain of performance. Yet the improviser in Liszt kept bursting out from these ideological restraints, as if unconsciously resisting the ideologies he consciously adopted. And with the exception of the more severe professional critics, responses to them were extraordinarily positive. It is as though his listeners, too, remained unreconstructed, deriving a unique sort of pleasure from his free playing. In this sense he preserved improvisation in an independent zone, beyond the reach of ascendant and eventually dominant musical values. This is not to say that his practice conformed perfectly to the romantic vision of improvisation, which was every bit as much an ideological encroachment. Writings by Heinrich Heine and George Sand reveal less about the actual music-making of Liszt and Chopin than about a longing to construe all good performance, all good music, *as* improvisation. They overtly fantasize into being an idea of perfect music-making where fixed, finished musical phenomena are magically restored to their emergent state.

The romantic rhetoric of improvisation thrived on a repression of its messy realities—its risks, labors, and infelicities—to make it a metaphor for other, more philosophically elevated things. It portrayed the improvising Liszt as an agent of infinite flexibility and radical spontaneity that always succeeds in reaching its target listeners. The rhetoric was out of sync with the realities. As we have seen, Liszt frequently fell back on conventional storm tropes, on certain motives (Weber's *Aufforderung*, Mozart's "Non più andrai," "God Save the King"), and on "encore-improvisations" versus free fantasies on given themes, to ensure that he would get the improvisations across. It was nonetheless the idealizing, romantic rhetoric of improvisation that eventually installed itself into the received image of Liszt. His improvisations never sounded as good as they did in the later nineteenth century, when they were heard least, and talked about most.

NOTES

1. The most celebratory of writers was Vladimir Jankélévitch, whose essays on Liszt are collected in *Liszt: rhapsodie et improvisation* (Paris: Flammarion, 1998). His comments on Lisztian improvisation are scattered throughout the essays, and they always concern the "spirit" of

composed pieces rather than performances per se. He writes, for example: "Whether impromptu or prelude, each work of Liszt is, rather than a masterpiece or piece of jewelry, rhapsody in this sense; indeed the entire output of Liszt, in its totality, unfolds a sort of immense rhapsodic poem jangling with czardas, arpeggios, paintings and sublime exclamations" (162). This is not to claim, however, that Jankélévitch's philosophy is not in other respects exceptionally conducive to performance-centered interpretation.

2. See the chapter "Virtuosity and Interpretation" in Carl Dahlhaus, *Nineteenth-Century Music*, trans. J. Bradford Robinson (Berkeley: University of California Press, 1989), 134–41. On the *Dante Sonata* and improvisation see David Trippett, "Après une lecture de Liszt: Virtuosity and Werktreue in the 'Dante' Sonata," *19th Century Music* 32, no. 1 (2008): 52–93. Kenneth Hamilton discusses Liszt's concert fantasies on "Gaudeamus igitur" (1843 and 1851) and suggests they "tally pretty closely with descriptions of his general approach to concert improvisation, including extensive playing around with fragments of the tune in harmonic sequence, glittering glissandos, and even at one point a loose fugal exposition." See his *After the Golden Age: Romantic Pianism and Modern Performance* (Oxford: Oxford University Press, 2008), 51.

3. Janet Ritterman, in "Piano Music and the Public Concert, 1800-1850," in *The Cambrdige Companion to Chopin*, ed. Jim Samson (Cambridge: Cambridge University Press, 1992), claims: "As reviews indicate, the connection between improvisations and composed fantasies or variations was extremely close" (25). Malou Haine gives a lucid overview of Liszt's childhood early concert improvisations in "Franz Liszt à Paris (1823–1835): de l'enfant prodige à l'artiste compositeur," in *Liszt et la France: musique, culture, et société dans l'Europe du XIXe siècle*, ed. Malou Haine, Nicolas Dufetel, Dana Gooley, and Jonathan Kregor (Paris: Vrin, 2012), 354–56.

4. Carl Czerny, *Erinnerungen aus meinem Leben* (Baden-Baden: Heitz, 1968 [1842]), 27.

5. Carl Czerny, *A Systematic Introduction to Improvisation on the Pianoforte*, trans. and ed. Alice L. Mitchell (New York: Longman, 1983).

6. Ibid., 50.

7. Trippett points this out and gives an example of such transformations from Czerny's treatise, in "Après une lecture de Liszt: Virtuosity and Werktreue in the 'Dante' Sonata," *19th Century Music* 32, no. 1 (2008), 73–74.

8. Zsuzsanna Domokos proposes that the *Impromptu on Spontini and Rossini* is "one of his early works that gives a clear picture of the art of improvisation of the young Liszt," and interprets it according to Czerny's prescriptions for the multi-theme fantasy, in "Carl Czernys Einfluss auf Franz Liszt: Die Kunst des Phantasierens," in *Liszt-Studien 4*, ed. Serge Gut (Munich: E. Katzbichler, 1993), 22. However, the *Impromptu* clearly belongs to the genre of the potpourri, not the fantasy on multiple themes. It introduces four themes, each of which is subjected to a variation, then a short, often quite abrupt transition to the next theme. A couple of ideas are reprised, but the overall formal unfolding is that of the potpourri. In a letter to Czerny dated 17 March 1824, Adam Liszt called this piece "an amusement, or rather, quodlibet, on different themes." See [Dudley Newton,] "Incidents of Franz Liszt's Youth," *Liszt Society Journal* 15 (1990), 3.

9. A thorough index of Liszt's early Paris concerts is found in Geraldine Keeling, "Liszt's Appearances on Parisian Concerts, 1824–1844, I," *Liszt Society Journal* 11 (1986): 22–34. Before 1828, Liszt played mainly on single themes, but that year he improvised a fantasy on three themes including the *Andante* from Beethoven's Seventh Symphony and motives from Auber's *La Muette de Portici* and Rossini's *Siège de Corinthe* (Keeling, 27). The seriousness and grandeur of these pieces, and the choice to improvise on several themes together, announce the onset of a quite different approach to the free fantasy that he would later develop. In an assessment of

improvisational practices in Paris around 1830, Andrea Estero suggests that the more common type was not rooted in the older throughbass practice or in chord progressions, but on a looser sort of thematic elaboration: "pianistic improvisation around 1830 was above all improvisation on a given theme, and not simply harmonic-contrapuntal elaboration" (105). Andrea Estero, "L'improvvisazione pianistica a Parigi intorno al 1830: Permanenze e innovazioni," in *Sull'improvvisazione*, ed. Claudio Toscani (Lucca: LIM Editrice, 1998), 105.

10. AMZ 1824, 113–14 (Paris report).

11. *Moniteur universel* 1824, 286. Liszt again improvised on the Mozart motive in the French provinces in 1825, prompting a similar description of the shape of the improvisation: "The young Liszt, after obligatory preludes and after a certain number of chords, took the motive 'Non più andrai' from the *Marriage of Figaro* and varied it most capably; in guiding it through different keys he even found some very felicitous modulations." Quoted from *Le Diable boiteux*, 15 March 1825, in *Franz Liszt: un Saltimbanque en Provence*, ed. Nicolas Dufetel and Malou Haine (Lyon: Symetrie, 2007), 53.

12. *Journal de Dijon et de la Côte-d'Or*, 20 December 1826, 397–98. Quoted in *Franz Liszt: un saltimbanque en Provence*, 77.

13. That Liszt's improvisations were generated from short and generic motives is suggested by a report on Liszt's 1825 performance before the Royal Society of Musicians in London: "if in any thing we could have discovered the youth of the player . . . it would have been the brevity of the strains of melody, and in the repetitions of favourite passages of execution, which were traits too remarkable to be missed" *QMMR* 1824, 241.

14. In an early letter from Paris, Adam Liszt wrote to Carl Czerny: "Once he played at Madame la Duchesse de Berry's, where the whole royal family was present, and where he had to extemporize four times on given themes—three times at the Duc d'Orléans'." Quoted in Newton, "Incidents of Franz Liszt's Youth."

15. The inclination to trace a genealogy back to Beethoven is especially difficult to resist because Czerny had studied with him and because Czerny revered Beethoven's improvisations. However, it is equally possible that Czerny represented a break in the chain rather than a link. There are no accounts at all of Czerny improvising, which would be a surprising lacuna if he had possessed even a fraction of Beethoven's talent for improvisation.

16. Philippe Ariès, *Centuries of Childhood: A Social History of Family Life*, trans. Robert Baldick (New York: Random House, 1962), 336. On the specificity of the late-eighteenth-century moment, see Hugh Cunningham, *Children and Childhood in Western Society Since 1500*, 2nd ed. (London: Longman, 2005), 4–10.

17. Daines Barrington, "Account of a Very Remarkable Young Musician," in *Philosophical Transactions . . .*, vol. 60 (London: Lockyer Davis, 1771), 64.

18. *Journal politique et littéraire de Toulouse*, 18 February 1826. Quoted in *Franz Liszt: un saltimbanque*, 66.

19. Czerny, *Erinnerungen*, 27; emphasis added.

20. The same journalist had written a few weeks earlier: "This virtuoso is so young, that looking at him you would take him for a child. But hearing him it is another thing: there is not a man who has arrived at a mature age with whom he could not compete, whether with respect to performance or composition" (*Pandore*, 9 March 1824).

21. Quoted from *Der Pilot* (1841, no. 26) in Freia Hoffmann, *Instrument und Körper: die musizierende Frau in der bürgerlichen Kultur* (Frankfurt: Insel Verlag, 1991), 309.

22. In the aftermath of Liszt's first bloom, however, young virtuosos did still play free fantasies. In 1829 the fourteen-year-old Adolphe Henselt played a free fantasy followed by

composed variations on a tune from *Der Freischütz*. This followed a convention—seen in Liszt, Weber. and others—according to which a rondo or variation set could be preceded by a free fantasy, presumably in slow tempo.

23. For brief reports on this tour, see AMZ 1834, 245, 383, 466. Stein more or less completely disappeared from the central European music scene, but he apparently remained active, and even preserved his reputation as an improviser, in the area of Riva and Reval (Tallinn). In the 1870s he taught at the St. Petersburg conservatory. For a rare notice from a central European source (which acknowledges his improvisational talent) see RGMP 1855, 276.

24. *Friedrich Wieck: Briefe aus den Jahren 1830–38*, ed. Käthe Walch-Schumann (Köln: A. Volk, 1968), 81.

25. *Gazette de France*, 9 March 1824; emphasis original. The *Journal des débats* (23 March 1824) chimed in with this line of interpretation: "Liszt must be judged as a man, and has no need for the concessions often made to composers or even pianists of his age."

26. [Dudley Newton,] "Incidents from Franz Liszt's Youth II," *Liszt Society Journal* 16 (1991), 2. From a letter of Adam Liszt to Czerny dated 29 July 1824.

27. Nineteenth-century biographical anecdotes of improvising children usually described simple harmonizations and elaborations of tunes picked up by ear, not free improvisation. The anecdote about Carl Loewe's childhood improvisations, related in Chapter 3, is one example among many.

28. *Courrier des théâtres*, 30 March 1824. Quoted in *Franz Liszt: un Saltimbanque*, 87–88.

29. Quoted from an 1841 source in Hoffmann, *Instrument und Körper*, 310.

30. On Liszt's self-criticism as a virtuoso see Robert Wangermée, "Conscience et inconscience du virtuose romantique: A propos des années parisiennes de Franz Liszt," in *Music in Paris in the 1830s*, ed. Peter Bloom (Stuyvesant, NY: Pendragon Press, 1987), 553–74.

31. Caroline Boissier, *Liszt pédagogue: Leçons de piano données par Liszt à Mademoiselle Valérie Boissier à Paris en 1832* (Paris, 1927), 27.

32. According to Keeling, "Liszt's Appearances on Parisian Concerts, I," he played "improvisations" at an 1833 concert at the Gymnase musicale, apparently at the intermission of a drama. This is mentioned only in one source and we know nothing else about it.

33. On the Liszt-Boissier relationship see John Rink, "Liszt and the Boissiers: Notes on a Musical Education," *The Liszt Society Journal* (2006): 5–36.

34. *An Artist's Journey, lettres d'un bachelier ès musique*, ed. and trans. Charles Suttoni (Chicago: University of Chicago Press, 1989), 17–18.

35. Boissier, *Liszt pédagogue*, 38.

36. Quotes respectively from *Musical World*, 14 May 1840, and *Spectator*, 16 May 1840. Quoted in Dudley Newton, "Liszt and His Glass," *Liszt Society Journal* 13 (1988), 53–54.

37. On the embellishing of Hummel and on his *Aufforderung* improvisation, see William Wright, "Liszt's London Appearances in 1827," *Liszt Society Journal* 16 (1991), 9–12.

38. Boissier, *Liszt pédagogue*, 73.

39. Ibid., 61. The impulse for this musician/actor comparison may have been Liszt himself, who at the time intended to produce a treatise, a "course in musical declamation," and was teaching Valérie Boissier according to its principles (85).

40. Ibid., 84.

41. See for example George Barth, *The Pianist as Orator: Beethoven and the Transformation of Keyboard Style* (Ithaca, NY: Cornell University Press, 1992); Mark Evan Bonds, *Wordless Rhetoric, Musical Form and the Metaphor of the Oration* (Cambridge, MA: Harvard University Press, 1991); and Martin Kaltenecker, "The 'Fantasy-Principle': Improvisation between

Imagination and Oration in the Eighteenth Century," in *Beyond Notes: Improvisation in Western Music of the Eighteenth and Nineteenth Centuries*, ed. Rudolph Rasch (Brepols: Turnhout, 2011), especially 31–34.

42. Czerny, *A Systematic Introduction to Improvising*, 42.

43. Ibid., 42–43.

44. Boissier, *Liszt pédagogue*, 84.

45. Ibid., 87.

46. Gorgias [Eugène Paignon], *Éloquence et improvisation: l'art de la parole oratoire au barreau, à la tribune, à la chaire* (Paris: Cotillon, 1846), 24. A German translation of this treatise was published in Weimar in 1848.

47. Ibid., 62–63. Comtesse de Bassanville's memoir of a Paris salon underscored the political dimension (in this case conservative) of salon improvisations: "The salon of [Marquise] Osmond received at that time a large number of renegades; however, because the marquise did not have to make concessions to attract her guests, it was kept intensely and frankly royalist, before, during, and after; nuance did not make a difference. And so every newcomer was held to improvising a couplet against the republic; the tune and the theme being given in advance, the poet of the occasion had to perform without stumbling. It is true that because this test, to which every newcomer was submitted, was widely known in society, he was free to prepare his improvisation in advance, all the more so as the tune was quite old and the poetry sometimes quite mediocre." Bassanville, *Les salons d'autrefois. Souvenirs intimes*, 3rd series (Paris: P. Brunet, 1862), 212–13.

48. Gorgias, *Éloquence et improvisation*, 24.

49. Eugène de Pradel, *Lettre à l'Académie Française, à l'occasion de la lutte littéraire* (Paris: Vinchon, 1836), 13. An account of this improvisation duel is found in "Lutte d'improvisation," *Ménestrel*, 15 May 1836, n.p.

50. Ibid., 11.

51. Bruno Moysan makes insightful remarks on Liszt's relationship to the public culture of oratory in *Liszt: virtuose subversif* (Lyon: Symétrie, 2009), 253–54.

52. See the chapter "Romantisme, littérature, rhétorique," in *Histoire de la rhétorique dans l'Europe moderne 1450–1950*, ed. Marc Fumaroli (Paris: Presses universitaires de France, 1999), 1044ff. and 1156ff.

53. Angela Esterhammer, *Romanticism and Improvisation, 1750–1850* (Cambridge: Cambridge University Press, 2008), 210.

54. *George Sand Critique, 1833-1876*, ed. Christine Planté (Tuson, Charente: De l'Erot, 2006), 101.

55. Esterhammer, *Romanticism and Improvisation*, 155. For a comparison of Liszt's performance to that of Mieczkewicz based on the "language of sentiments," see the review cited in Jean-Jacques Eigeldinger, *L'univers musical de Chopin* (Paris: Fayard, 2000), 257.

56. On Deschamps' advocacy for romanticism against French classicism, see the manifesto at the beginning of his collection *Etudes françaises et étrangères*, 2nd ed. (Paris: Urbain Canel, 1828).

57. Friedrich Schlegel, *Kritische Schriften*, ed. Wolfdietrich Rasch (Munich: Carl Hanser, 1958), 38.

58. George Sand, *Lettres d'un voyageur* (Paris: Michel Lévy Frères, 1869), 228–29. An English translation of this entire letter is found in Suttoni, *An Artist's Journey*, 206–217. Curiously, Suttoni mistranslates the French phrase "écouter votre improvisation" as "to hear you perform" (214).

59. In his January 1837 open letter to George Sand he wrote: "I no longer divorce a composition from the era in which it was written, and any claim to embellish or modernize the works of earlier periods seems just as absurd for a musician to make as it would be for an architect, for example, to place a Corinthian capital on the columns of an Egyptian temple" (Franz Liszt, *An Artist's Journey*, 18).

60. On the fictive nature of the category "bourgeoisie" under the July Monarchy, see chapter 6 in Sarah Maza, *The Myth of the French Bourgeoisie: An Essay on the Social Imaginary 1750–1850* (Cambridge, MA: Harvard University Press, 2003).

61. Bassanville, *Les salons d'autrefois*, 209.

62. Sand, *Lettres d'un voyageur*, 48.

63. Jean-Jacques Eigeldinger, *Chopin: Pianist and Teacher, as Seen by His Pupils* (Cambridge: Cambridge University Press, 1986), 271.

64. Cited from *Fremden-Blatt*, 11 April 1884, in Edward Blickstein and Gregor Benko, *Chopin's Prophet: The Life of Pianist Vladimir de Pachmann* (Plymouth: Scarecrow Press, 2013), 68.

65. Daniel Stern, *Correspondance générale*, ed. Charles F. Dupêchez, 4 vols. (Paris: Honoré Champion, 2003–), 2:39. Emphasis added.

66. H. de Balzac, *A Father's Curse and Other Stories*, trans. James Waring (London: Dent and Co., 1898), 234.

67. Quoted from Heine's collection *Über die französische Bühne* (1837) in *Chopin: Pianist and Teacher*, 284.

68. The sixty-seven documented instances of Chopin improvising are gathered together in Krystyna Kobylanska, "Les improvisations de Frédéric Chopin," in *Chopin Studies 3* (Warsaw: Frederick Chopin Society, 1990), 77–104.

69. Quoted from *Über die französische Buhne* (1837) in Franz Liszt, *An Artist's Journey*, 221.

70. Philippe Borer, "Paganini's Virtuosity and Improvisatory Style," in *Beyond Notes: Improvisation in Western Music of the Eighteenth and Nineteenth Centuries*, ed. Rudolph Rasch (Brepols: Turnhout, 2011), 191.

71. Letter to Pierre Wolff dated 2 May 1832, in *Letters of Franz Liszt*, ed. La Mara, trans. Constance Bache (New York: Charles Scribner's Sons, 1894), vol. 1, 8.

72. Melina Esse, "Encountering the *improvvisatrice* in Italian Opera," *Journal of the American Musicological Society* 66, no. 3 (2013): 709–70.

73. In his open letter to George Sand of 1837, he looked back at these pieces with a somewhat critical eye: "About that time I wrote a number of pieces that inevitably reflected the kind of fever that was consuming me. The public found them strange and incomprehensible, and even you, my dear friend, criticized me at times for being vague and diffuse." *An Artist's Journey*, 18.

74. George Sand, *Oeuvres autobiographiques* (Paris: Gallimard, 1970), vol. 1, 912.

75. "Un concert à Genève, Trilogie et proverbe (historiques et philosophiques)," in Franz Liszt, *Sämtliche Schriften* (Wiesbaden: Breitkopf & Härtel, 1989), 1:403.

76. Amy Fay, *Music Study in Germany* (London: Macmillan, 1893), 221. I thank Kenneth Hamilton for this reference.

77. Franz Liszt, *Sämtliche Schriften*, 1:403.

78. Quoted from Sand's *Lettres d'un voyageur* in Suttoni, *An Artist's Journey*, 215.

79. Quoted from an August 1836 diary entry in Robert Bory, *Une Retraite romantique en Suisse: Liszt et la comtesse d'Agoult* (Geneva: Editions Sonor, 1923), 36. James Davies gives historical context for this performance habit in *Romantic Anatomies of Performance* (Berkeley: University of California Press, 2014), 167.

80. Ludwig Rellstab, *Franz Liszt: Beurtheilungen-Berichte-Lebensskizze* (Berlin: Trautwein, 1842), 7.

81. Daniel Stern, *Mémoires, souvenirs, et journaux de la Comtesse d'Agoult*, ed. Charles F. Dupêchez (Paris: Mercure de France, 1990), vol. 2, 161.

82. Ibid., 192.

83. The best gathering of Italian sources for Liszt's concerts is the appendix in Luciano Chiappari, *Liszt a Como e Milano* (Pisa: Pacini, 1997). Several of my citations are borrowed from this source. Most of the journals were founded just two or three years before Liszt arrived in Italy, constituting the first flush of a critical arts press in Italy, making it difficult to document the presence of improvisation in Italian concert life before Liszt. See Marcello Conatti, "I periodici teatrali e musicali meta Ottocento," *Periodica musica* (1989): 13–18.

84. This writer might have heard about the improvisation Liszt sprang upon Ricordi when he first arrived in Milan in September 1837. In one of the *Lettres d'un bachelier* Liszt describes himself stumbling upon the Ricordi store: "a publisher is the musical republic's Resident Minister . . . the Providence of a wandering musician. So, I enter and promptly sit myself down at an open piano. I begin to improvise, which is my way of presenting my credentials." Franz Liszt, *An Artist's Journey*, 62.

85. Franz Liszt, *Correspondance Franz Liszt Mme. D'Agoult*, ed. Serge Gut and Jacqueline Bellas (Paris: Fayard, 2001), 305.

86. See also Chiappari, *Liszt a Como e Milano*, 70. The concert took place 21 February 1838.

87. Franz Liszt, *An Artist's Journey*, 72–99.

88. Ibid., 91.

89. Liszt's Milan article was written at least in part by Marie d'Agoult. See Daniel Stern, *Correspondance générale*, 2:180, and Suttoni's comments in *An Artist's Journey*, x and 84 n.27. For a more exhaustive treatment of the question of the authorship of these writings see the editorial commentary by Rainer Kleinertz in Franz Liszt, *Sämtliche Schriften*, vol. 1.

90. See Annarose Poli, *L'Italie dans la vie et dans l'œuvre de George Sand* (Paris: Collin, 1960), and Urbain Mengin, *L'Italie des romantiques* (Paris: Plon, 1902).

91. *Correspondance Franz Liszt Mme. D'Agoult*, 69. Marie d'Agoult reminisced about being called "la Corinne du quai Malaquais" in her *Mémoirs, souvenirs, et journaux de la comtesse d'Agoult*, vol. 1, 262. Nicolas Dufetel describes two quotes from *Corinne* in Liszt's sketchbooks of the early 1830s, in "'Une grande idée: celle du renouvellement de la Musique par son alliance plus intime avec la Poésie'. Les citations littéraires dans les esquisses et l'œuvre imprimée de Liszt: le laboratoire d'une modernité?", http://www.bruzanemediabase.com/Parutions-scientifiques-en-ligne/Articles/Dufetel-Nicolas-Images-et-citations-litteraires-dans-la-musique-a-programme-de-Liszt-pour-un-renouvellement-de-la-Musique-par-son-alliance-plus-intime-avec-la-Poesie.

92. Journal entry dated 24 July 1837, quoted in *Mémoirs, souvenirs, et journaux de la comtesse d'Agoult*, 133.

93. D'Agoult clearly resembled Corinne far more than Liszt resembled Nelvil, but the Liszt-d'Agoult relationship, in which the woman's knowledge and verbal skill reflect the beauty of Italy's visual splendors to the inexperienced male character, in a manner simultaneously educational and personally bonding, is unmistakable. It is as easily as relevant as the Dante-Beatrice parallel discussed by Sharon Winklhofer in "Liszt, Marie d'Agoult, and the 'Dante' Sonata," *19th Century Music* 1, no. 1 (1977): 15–32.

94. Daniel Stern, *Correspondance générale*, 2:157.

95. Angela Esterhammer, *Romanticism and Improvisation 1750–1850* (Cambridge: Cambridge University Press, 2008), 187.

96. George Sand, *Consuelo*, trans. Fayette Robinson (Philadelphia: T. B. Peterson, 1870), 331.

97. Hector Berlioz, *Mémoires de Hector Berlioz, comprenant ses voyages en Italie, en Allemagne, en Russie, et en Angleterre, 1803–1865* (Paris: Calmann-Lévy, 1878), vol. 1, 225.

98. Ibid., 257–58.

99. See Esterhammer, *Romanticism and Improvisation*, 59–77.

100. Chiappari, *Liszt a Como e Milano*, 168.

101. See, for example, the review of an *accademia* he gave in July 1838 in Milan, in *Glissons 1838*, 234.

102. Raffaello Barbiera, *Il salotto della contessa Maffei*, 7th ed. (Milan: Baldini, 1903), 89.

103. Madame de Staël, *Corinne, or Italy* (New York: Mason, Baker & Pratt, 1873), 112.

104. Anna Harwell Celenza draws attention to the themes of exile and political repression in "Liszt, Italy, and the Republic of the Imagination," in *Franz Liszt and His World*, ed. Christopher Gibbs and Dana Gooley (Princeton: Princeton University Press, 2006), 3–38.

105. D'Agoult's private writings from this period are strewn with comments such as "the decadence of music in Italy is complete" (*Mémoirs, souvenirs, et journaux de la comtesse d'Agoult*, 144), and "to judge from La Scala music is in complete decadence in Italy; composers and singers are beneath contempt" (Daniel Stern, *Correspondance générale*, 2:101).

106. Franz Liszt, *An Artist's Journey*, 89.

107. Liszt's condescending view of Italian musical taste provoked scandal and inspired rebuttals from Italian journalists. When he returned to Milan the following fall he tried to appease the public by promising a free fantasy that he announced as "Réminiscences de La Scala"—a gesture of respect to the house he had insulted. On this improvisation and its probable connection to Liszt's *Guiramento* fantasy, see Hamilton, "Reminiscences of a Scandal— Reminiscences of La Scala: Liszt's Fantasy on Mercadante's *Il guiramento*," *Cambridge Opera Journal* 5, no. 3 (1993): 187–98.

108. Franz Liszt, *An Artist's Journey*, 90.

109. Ibid. When Liszt says his concerts had been criticized as too serious, he was probably alluding to a series of concerts he gave in Paris in 1837 featuring little-known chamber works by Beethoven. Critical responses to these concerts made much of the difficulty and seriousness of Beethoven's works for the general public, and he was not trying to play Beethoven to Italian audiences. See Dana Gooley, "Franz Liszt: The Virtuoso as Strategist," in *The Musician as Entrepreneur, 1700–1914: Managers, Charlatans, and Idealists*, ed. William Weber (Bloomington: Indiana University Press, 2004), 145–61.

110. *Franz Liszt, Artiste et société*, ed. Remy Stricker (Paris: Flammarion, 1995), 125–26. The essay is an 1838 installment of his series *Lettres d'un bachelier ès musique*. For the English language version see Liszt, *An Artist's Journey*, 90. The social values Liszt invokes here are closely related to communitarian and socialist philosophies that he strongly advocated in the 1830s. His association with Saint-Simonism and the ideas of Ballanche led him to see art as a vehicle of social regeneration and a significant antidote to the divisive forces of modern industrial society, and the modern virtuoso as a figure that could contribute to these ends through his priest-like role.

111. Although a variety of reception sources for Liszt's Vienna concerts are now easily accessible and searchable using Austrian National Newspapers Online (ANNO), a useful collection of them is found in *Franz Liszt: unbekannte Presse und Briefe aus Wien, 1822–1886*, ed. Dezsö Legány (Wien-Köln-Graz: Böhlau-Verlag, 1984).

112. Czerny, *A Systematic Introduction to Improvisation*, 73.

113. Montserrat Bergadà, "Franz Liszt et les pianistes espagnols," *Quaderni dell'Istituto Liszt* 10 (2011), 230.

114. Albert B. Bach, *The Art Ballad: Loewe and Schubert* (Edinburgh and London: William Blackwood, 1890), 79–80.

115. Eduard Hanslick, *Aus meinem Leben* (Berlin: Allgemeiner Verein für deutsche Literatur, 1894), vol. 1, 82–83.

116. Vladimir Jankélévitch, *Liszt: Rhapsodie et improvisation*, 121. Gary Peters has written compellingly about how Kant's philosophy of genius relates to improvisation and artistic origination in *The Philosophy of Improvisation* (Chicago: Chicago University Press, 2009), 36–39 and 118–22.

117. Gustav Schilling, *Der Pianist; oder, Die Kunst des Clavierspiels in ihrem Gesammtumfange theoretisch-praktisch dargestellt* (Osterode: A. Sorge, 1843), 302. Surprisingly, Schilling's pioneering biography *Franz Liszt: sein Leben und Wirken* (Stuttgart: Stoppani, 1844), gives very little attention to improvisation. It notes that the boy's concert debut in Ödenburg included an astonishing free fantasy (32), and reproduces in an appendix (245–48) a translation of George Sand's narrative of Liszt's organ improvisation in Freiburg, but otherwise improvisation is barely mentioned.

118. *La France musicale* 1847, 366–67.

119. This performance was also recalled by Wilhelm Kuhe, *My Musical Recollections* (London: Richard Bentley and Son, 1896), 140–41. A few days later, Liszt performed a similar sequence: after accompanying a singer in Schubert's "Der Schiffer" he took its main motive and combined it with Schubert's "Ständchen" in free improvisation (*Wanderer* 1846, 298).

120. Detlef Altenburg, "Franz Liszt and the Legacy of the Classical Era," *19th Century Music* 18, no. 1 (1994): 46–63. See also *Liszt und die Weimarer Klassik*, ed. Detlef Altenburg (Laaber: Laaber-Verlag, 1997).

121. Letter from Carl Alexander to Soret, 25 February 1844, cited in Dufetel, 82. This event was also briefly reported in the *Neue Zeitschrift für Musik*, 4 March 1844, col. 76.

122. Letter of Carl Alexander to Soret of 3 February 1850, cited in Dufetel, 6.

123. This passage was copied down by Carl Alexander from an unidentified source, and is found in D-WRgs 59/27, 12 A, dossier 1 (E 31–32). I thank Nicolas Dufetel for sharing this with me.

124. See, for example, Goby Eberhardt, *Erinnerungen an bedeutende Männer unserer Epoche* (Lübeck: Otto Quitzow-Verlag, 1926), 104–106; Kuhe, *My Musical Recollections*, 141–42, recalls an improvisation from Liszt's 1886 visit to London; and Wendelin Weissheimer, *Erlebnisse mit Richard Wagner, Franz Liszt, und vielen anderen Zeitgenossen* (Stuttgart: Deutsche Verlags-Anstalt, 1898), 16–17. In an unpublished journal entry from 1869, kindly shared with me by Nicolas Dufetel, Liszt's Weimar patron Carl Alexander wrote: "He improvised again—I don't remember ever having heard him play better. You could say his fingers are but accessories—you forget technique and believe that a magnetic fluid emanating from his person is engendering these wondrous sounds. . . . We were in ecstasy!"

125. David Cannata, "Adele aus der Ohe (Tchaïkovksy & Rachmaninoff)," *Quaderni del Istituto Liszt* 10 (2011), 93. Ohe promptly created the volume and dedicated it to Liszt, though it remained unpublished.

6

Improvisatoriness

THE REGIME OF THE IMPROVISATION IMAGINARY

IN 1847 TWO events dealt a considerable blow to the future of concert improvisation at the keyboard: the death of Felix Mendelssohn and the retirement of Franz Liszt from the concert stage. These two brilliant players, starkly opposed in their aesthetic orientations, were the last pianists whose free fantasies achieved widespread celebrity and acclaim. The future of advanced piano virtuosity lay in ever more difficult technical feats of speed and sound, in the subtle mysteries of "interpretation," and in the art of shaping the piano recital as a self-sufficient theatrical event. As Kenneth Hamilton has shown, many concert pianists continued to improvise preludes and transitional links between movements or pieces. These practices perpetuated values of inventive liberty and interpretative liberty that lay at the heart of the concert virtuoso tradition and resisted the regulative force of "interpretation."[1] But free fantasies, improvised cadenzas, and other sorts of extended free playing largely vanished from the universe of advanced pianism. Even Liszt's students, who had occasional opportunities to hear their master extemporize, hesitated to venture into the same territory. The memoirs of pianist Wilhelm Kuhe, published in 1896 after fifty years of steady concertizing, give a hint about what remained of public improvisation in the second half of the century. After describing "Liszt's phenomenal powers of improvisation," which he had witnessed at a Vienna soirée in 1846, Kuhe wrote:

I may mention here that in after-years I heard three great masters improvise on the piano. At a Philharmonic concert at the Hanover Square Rooms, in 1847—the year of his death—it was my privilege to hear Mendelssohn improvise cadenzas to Beethoven's Concerto in G—a wonderful performance. The improvising of

Stephen Heller was highly original, and that of Ferdinand Hiller quite masterly. I think I am correct in saying that Moscheles was one of the last pianists who excelled in that now almost forgotten art.[2]

The disappearance of free improvisation from public concerts, however, did not spell its "death" everywhere, and one task of this chapter is to identify those pockets where it survived or resisted reconstruction. In the organ world, improvisation not only persisted but enjoyed a sort of renaissance in 1870s when, for the first time since Vogler, a career as "concert organist" seemed to be viable. At conservatories, students were required to improvise as an integral part of their training in theory, score-reading, and musicianship. This occurred less in the advanced, specialized piano classes where students worked on building technique, sound, and interpretation, than in the classes in *accompagnement*, which perpetuated the older thoroughbass practices and were geared toward a more general sort of musicianship. Pianists both professional and amateur continued extemporizing in private and in the company of peers and friends, though the private and amateur spheres are unusually difficult to document.[3] Aging musicians trained in the kapellmeister circuit, such as Hiller, Moscheles, and Meyerbeer, were found improvising here and there, and occasionally an ambitious young pianist would venture a free fantasy in public. There was even some life remaining in poetry improvisation, as exemplified by Emmanuel Geibel in Germany and Giannina Milli In Italy.[4] But the near-extinction of improvising heroes from public life did leave an experiential and social vacuum. Where could the public—increasingly a "mass" public in the modern sense—now find the virtue-in-spontaneity, the natural inventive power, and the communal bonding they had once enjoyed and celebrated in the presence of top improvisers? The charismatic orchestral conductors who emerged in the second half of the century may have filled the void to an extent, but greater compensation was found in the consolidating improvisation imaginary—the representations and fantasies that gave improvisation an aura of perfection, naturalness, and desirability.

Literary representations were at the core of the improvisation imaginary. At mid-century, poets, fiction writers, playwrights, critics, and musicians enriched the field of representations with gypsies, shepherds, troubadours, snake-charmers, and other character-types who delivered "perfect" performances of an improvisatory character. In such representations the music-making is packed with liveliness, charm, and expressiveness. It is never labored or forced. The improvising musicians derive complete pleasure, fulfillment, or catharsis from it. They play for listeners and audiences who are fully attentive, naturally sympathetic, and eager to show gratitude through applause. There is no break in the circuit of communication, and the solo performance always succeeds at producing communal bonds. Many of the stock figures of the improvisation imaginary are exotic Others—belonging, like improvisation itself, to distant places, distant times, or distant social classes. They look nothing like the kapellmeisters, organists, piano virtuosos, conductors, or opera divas of the post-1850 public world. And the wholesomeness of their music-making appears as a desirable alternative to modern musical conditions marked by splintering commodity markets and a firm division of labor between composers and performers. In previous chapters we have encountered ancestors to these figures—the epic bard, the political orator, the Italian *improvvisatore*, and the Venetian gondolier. What is different about the later-nineteenth-century context is that the field of representations circulates in a near vacuum of actual improvised performances. Representations now have the potential to normalize a simulacrum of improvisation as the essence of improvisation. In the absence of actual improvisation, they offer an *ersatz* form: improvisatoriness.

Improvisation thus persisted in the later nineteenth century in two different forms: in certain lines of musical practice, and in a fantasy realm sustained by visual and literary representational media. The practitioners perpetuated values traditionally associated with improvisation: the ideal of a well-rounded musician, the authority of contrapuntal learning, the professional pride of musicians bonding among themselves, the pleasurable communion of artist with public audience, and the hedonistic pleasure of the amateur. The improvisation imaginary, in contrast, channeled utopian longings. It generated idealized, nostalgic, otherworldly images of music-making that critiqued what seemed to be missing from, or unattainable in, modern musical experience: freedom, naturalness of production and reception, and the achievement of harmonious community. This chapter surveys various ways improvisation was performed, imagined, represented, and discussed after Mendelssohn and Liszt in order to show how the imaginary, while detaching itself from practice and experience, preserved the aesthetic and social values that had been associated with improvisation since the early nineteenth century. To this end, a heuristic distinction between free playing and imaginary-receptive dispositions is indispensable, but as we will see, the two levels often intersected and had been co-constituting the meaning of "improvisation" for some time already. The improvisation imaginary triumphed not simply by imposing a fictive vision of improvisation on a naïve, uncritical public, but more deeply, by infiltrating the attitudes and beliefs of composers and performers themselves. Increasingly, virtuosos and composers convinced themselves that what they were doing when they interpreted a masterpiece, or when they composed one, was a kind of improvisation.

PRACTICES
The Cavallo-Blanchard Alliance

As seen in earlier chapters, professional musicians and high-toned critics had been campaigning against improvisation since the early nineteenth century. Critics initially accused "charlatans" such as Vogler and violinist Franz Clement of turning improvisation into an entertaining cheap trick that thrilled the public while violating the dignity of "higher" improvisation, but in the era of Hummel and Moscheles this accusation faded. Critics now aimed their fire at dilettantism—the "fashion" for free fantasies imitated by aspiring artists incapable of improvising well, as well as indulgent amateurs who emulated the "inspired" creation of the best players. They treated improvisation as a symptom of musical decadence as pianos became ubiquitous and *soi-disant* virtuosos started appearing everywhere. There was still some critical steam remaining in 1847, when critic Ludwig Granzin published a philosophical dialogue entitled "Today's Virtuosity and its Effect on Dilettantism." Granzin's essay marks a new turn in critical opinion by taking a strong stance against the free fantasies of Hummel and Mozart, previously treated as exceptions to the problem: "That Mozart, in his improvised fantasies before a larger concert public, played nothing other than trivialities on request, is certain." Granzin had only slightly less negative things to say about Hummel's free fantasies, an example of which he had heard in person twenty-six years earlier: "I do not want to denigrate what Hummel improvised on that evening. I am only saying that a musical improviser before a concert public can hardly give his best. Even if I could improvise better than Hummel did at that time, I would hardly want to do it at a public event." Asked by his interlocutor whether younger artists should aspire play free fantasies, he responds "decidedly not," since improvisation can only "manifest divination" and cannot "produce artistic education."[5] Free improvisation might be legitimate on its own terms, but it does not belong in concert life because, as a manifestation of pure mystery, it has no power to educate or develop the public.

Granzin probably had little to worry about, since very few pianists seemed to be offering free fantasies in the later 1840s. Yet around this time a young keyboardist out of Munich named Peter (born Pietro) Cavallo began attracting international attention for his virtuosity and his exceptional talent for improvisation. Cavallo made concert debuts in German cities but had his greatest impact in Paris and remained there the rest of his life. He was equally comfortable on piano and organ and remained active on both instruments. Never a touring virtuoso or a major public figure, Cavallo held organ chairs at a handful of smaller parishes in Paris, played at the Salons Pape as a sort of "house pianist," published salon pieces, and co-directed an amateur choral society. He was a local, second-tier virtuoso who bridged professional and dilettante spheres. Some of the interest he aroused in Paris when he arrived in 1843 came from liturgical music reformers, who were looking to elevate French organ music with an infusion of German severity and depth.[6] Cavallo's advocate, the critic Henri Blanchard, immediately identified him as a product of the German network: "formed by the German school, he is distinguished by the deep learning he deploys in his improvisations" (RGMP 1843, 252). At the concert in question Cavallo, playing piano, first improvised on the "prayer" from Rossini's *Mosé* in the presence of its venerable composer. To prove he had really just improvised, he asked Rossini to write down a fugue theme "which he immediately treated as a consummate contrapuntist" (RGMP 1843, 252). Blanchard also emphasized what he perceived to be a rare spontaneity of invention: "[Cavallo is] an artist cut from the same cloth as Hummel for improvisation, though he has more fire. . . . With him, caprice is not mediated; it emerges instantaneously from his imagination" (RGMP 1844, 104).

If Cavallo's early performances put contrapuntal learning on display, he soon adjusted his style to render it more popular and ingratiating. In performances at the semi-public Salons Pape, partnering with singers and instrumentalists, he most often improvised first on a single theme, then again on two themes given by the audience. His choice of tunes was fairly standard ("La cì darem la mano," the *Mosé* prayer) but he also sometimes drew from popular, ephemeral romances, comic songs, and dances, especially if they had just been sung at the same concert.[7] At a later performance he improvised a "storm" after a maritime romance had just been sung (RGMP 1847, 43). A German journalist visiting Paris became irritated at Cavallo's penchant for popular material and provocatively requested he improvise on "a fugue by Bach," but this suggestion was silently passed over (AMZ 1846, 45). The manner in which Cavallo elaborated on the given themes must have been somewhat different for organ and piano, but in both cases he reined in learned divagations and kept the style accessible. After taking a pair of themes from the audience, Blanchard wrote, the pianist

> treated them separately, reprised them, combined them, mixed them with different rhythms, but in the midst of it he never lost the view, or rather the ear. M. Cavallo created these *tours de force*, by which many of our great masters have distinguished themselves, more as a harmonist than as a contrapuntist or fuguist, which is not the same thing. (RGMP 1845, 84)

Most descriptions, however imprecise, suggest that he kept the melodic motives in the listener's ear throughout, rather than outfitting the thematic work with digressions, introductions, and cadenzas—an approach consistent with that of the young Liszt and Rudolf Willmers. Even when fleshing out a relatively "serious" subject on the organ, such as a choral motive from Handel's *Samson*, he approached the task in a spirit of variegation: "he walked it around and reproduced the phrases in different keys while surrounding it with extremely varied harmonies and effects which gave them a new charm each time they reappeared" (RGMP 1847, 307).

Cavallo astutely adapted his improvisational style to the intimate, salon-like atmosphere of the Pape showrooms and the other semi-public spaces in which he played. On the occasion when Rossini was present, for example, he improvised both times on themes by the celebrated guest. When he rebuffed the German journalist's suggestion of a Bach fugue, he did so in favor of an opera melody by Halévy, who was in the house that day. When he chose the *Samson* chorus motive, according to Blanchard, it was "doubtless to favor someone in the audience." Cavallo often improvised in tribute to the song just performed, its performer, or a special guest in the room. On one special occasion the *aides-de-camp* of Emperor Maximilian of Bavaria visited the Salons to support their compatriot's concert, and Cavallo immediately changed the course of his improvisation: "[he] intercalated into his fantasy a Polka composed by the prince of Bavaria himself, while enriching it with a flood of accessory ideas and brilliant effects. Though this seems a bit courtier-like, it undeniably had the merit of being smartly suited to the occasion" (RGMP 1844, 133). In all of these ways Cavallo showed a flair for making the best of the immediate circumstances and using improvisation to support the interpersonal cohesion of the salon.

Cavallo's performance venues differed in one important sense from both the older aristocratic salons and the romantic salons that had emerged around 1830. The salons of Pape and of Cavaillé-Coll were instrumental showrooms for pianos and organs, respectively, bringing artistic and commercial motives into full alignment. As Paris hosted more and more commercially minded keyboard "expositions," improvisations made the perfect vehicle of demonstration, since there was no musical work to distract attention from the instrument and its player.[8] This was especially important to Cavaillé-Coll, who wanted to ensure that players were free to show off the novel sounds and combinations of his instruments. For the rest of the century, newly installed Cavaillé-Coll organs were consistently inaugurated with concerts featuring star improvisers, nearly always culminating in a simulated "storm."[9] Pape, for his part, specialized in the creation of keyboard instruments designed to resemble elegant salon furniture, and might have welcomed the light style and relaxed sociability of Cavallo's improvisations as a suitable ambience for their display.[10] The ephemeral popular songs heard before and between Cavallo's performances, too, belonged to the domestic salon market toward which Pape and Cavaillé-Coll directed many of their products. In this way the growth of musical industries and commerce in France provided a new and surprising outlet for improvisation.

Cavallo was one of the very few keyboardists whose reputation rested primarily on improvisation. After only a couple of years in Paris, journals noted that he "stands apart among pianists by a quite rare specialty, that of *improvisation* [emphasis original]" and that "he makes a specialty of the vast field of instantaneous inspiration."[11] Leipzig's correspondent reported that "Cavallo is here known especially as an improviser on the organ" (AMZ 1846, 45), and the Vienna correspondent considered him "without a doubt the leading musical improviser in Paris" (*Wiener Zeitschrift* 1848, 159). Such "branding" of improvisation, as a mark of a performer's distinction, betrays a small but distinct shift of perception that occurred in the mid-1840s. Audiences were no longer hearing free piano improvisation with any regularity and were losing a sense of how to judge it. It was no longer understood as a natural, familiar extension of the professional pianist's range of skills, but as a rare and specialized skill that, when done well, could set someone apart in a dense field of competing musicians. One popular journal referred tellingly to "the brilliant improvisation of Cavallo, *pianist of a particular genre*" (*La Sylphide* 1847, 61; emphasis added). The aura of authority and tradition that had hovered around Hummel was completely absent in Cavallo. Improvisation made him interesting and different, but not a representative of learning or tradition. The commercial network in which he was imbricated valued novelty and pleasure, and had no need for an aura of authority.

Henri Blanchard, the critic who wrote most often and most enthusiastically about Cavallo, merits independent attention for his views on improvisation. Born in 1787, he was a critic of an older generation and of somewhat dated persuasions. He was modern enough to uphold Beethoven as the supreme ideal of instrumental music, but old-fashioned enough to find romanticism—especially Berlioz's fantastical variety—quite intolerable.[12] Though well informed, he did not style himself as a "serious" critic. He sometimes ironically signed articles as "The Rover of Concerts" and wrote them in a light, witty vein. His warm embrace of Cavallo was rooted in nostalgia for an art he had experienced in its blooming years. "The faculty of improvising," he wrote in 1848, "too neglected by pianists of our time, is cultivated successfully by M. Cavallo. . . . Amidst a counterpoint that is not too rigorous, he knows how to unite two given subjects with contrasting melodic, rhythmic, and characteristic forms, and how to draw from them new, piquant effects" (RGMP 1848, 140). Blanchard's affirmation of variety and "effects" sets him apart from the severe critics who saw the decline of free improvisation as a symptom of musical decadence. Cavallo's "not-too-rigorous" counterpoint was not only acceptable, but a palpable gain for listeners. Blanchard was one of the last critics to affirm the hedonistic strain of improvisational aesthetics, which had benefited both Hummel and Moscheles in the 1820s.

In the middle of the Exposition Universelle of 1855, which brought many keyboardists to the French capital and put hundreds of instruments on display, Blanchard published an article entitled "On Musical Improvisation." It reflected upon concerts he had recently heard by Peter Cavallo, pianist Theodor Stein (whose free fantasies, as seen in Chapter 4, had been widely criticized two decades earlier), and Hamburg-based organist Carl Schwencke. In response to these concerts he nostalgically recalled what improvisation had once been:

> The improvising musician—he is like an orator at the national tribune or sacred pulpit; this is speech, sound, full of life, colorful, passionate; it is also, we should say, the most rare faculty among our present-day pianists, even the best ones. In earlier times people knew how to draw out a thought by means of a fugue; there was logic, progression, and variety in the constant or discretionary breaking of monotony and of the plain perfect cadence. Since the revolution . . . of romanticism [ellipses original], all of that has changed; we have set the heart aside. . . . Melodic and especially harmonic ideas, so easy to discover on the keyboard, simply succeed one another, and thus the *lieu commun* [in rhetorical theory, a trope or figure] becomes linked to the musical common-place. (RGMP 1855, 276)

Blanchard's emphasis on improvisation as a form of vivid musical eloquence, combining sentiment and logic in equal measure, sounds almost like something out of the eighteenth century. His pathos is born of frustration with present-day improvisation, which he blames on romanticism and its formless enchainment of disconnected phrases. He summons the fugue genre not for its learnedness but for its discursive economy—the thematic and developmental focus that provides a sense of unity not found in newer music. The excellent improvisations of Cavallo and Stein did not inspire in Blanchard hope that history could be reversed and improvisation could be recovered. They inspired only the memory of a better, more artful, and articulate musical past.

Accompagnement, Harmony, and Modulation

Had Blanchard looked beyond the concert life in which his journalistic career was enveloped, he might have viewed things otherwise. The teaching of chordal harmony at conservatories and schools rested on more traditional foundations and kept certain practices of improvisation alive well beyond 1847. The classes in *accompagnement* at the Conservatoire in particular placed a prime on the practical application of harmonic theory through improvisation. The harmony treatise officially adopted for the Conservatoire in 1854 carried the title "Treatise on Practical Harmony and Modulations, for the Use of Pianists."[13] These "pianists" were not the advanced students concentrating on solo performance. The treatise's author, M. A. Panseron, was a voice teacher, and the committee evaluating it for potential adoption included only professors of opera composition, oboe, violin, and *solfège*—no professors of piano. It was intended primarily for use in vocal classes and other sorts of accompanying, which included the transduction of orchestral and choral scores to the piano for rehearsal purposes. In short, it was for the enrichment of musicians who needed piano as a secondary instrument.

This secondary status did not make it any less valuable. Halévy, the director of the Conservatoire, argued for adopting Panseron's treatise because "the piano has been taken up by more or less all musicians today."[14] The piano was now considered an essential resource for any complete musician's education. The majority of students were probably expected to work through Part I, on basic harmony. Part II, devoted exclusively to modulation, was in Halévy's words "a matter mainly for pianists" and thus broaches questions of improvisation more directly. In the preface to Part II, Panseron very briefly touches on pragmatic applications of modulation, explaining that it can be useful "whether giving oneself over to improvisation, or following the directive of someone else, always keeping *the time* in such a way that you seem to modulate without reflection."[15] It is not entirely clear what situation he has in mind here. It seems to indicate that the keyboardist is improvising a transition between two separate pieces, or possibly accompanying a vocal lesson where a singer is being led through modulating exercises. Whatever the intention, he does specify that the modulating chord sequence should be realized "by means of arpeggios."

Panseron's teaching of modulation is generally conservative in spirit. He proudly advances his treatise as an update of Catel's original harmony book for the Conservatoire (1802), in which all possible modulations are demonstrated in a sequence of four chords with neighbor-note motions, à la Vogler. Panseron's own table demonstrates all possible modulations from a major key to another key, using a route consisting of three, four, or five mediating chords. In such rapid modulations the soprano line should be "as melodic as possible" in order to give the harmony "elegance and great sweetness."[16] The governing logic is one of smooth melodic connection, and the style of improvisation seems to be directed at pianists who are accompanying soloists in chords or, in the case of church organists, accompanying liturgical hymns. The same foundation could nevertheless serve as basis for free improvisation if the player was so inclined. Panseron thus approves of Kalkbrenner's treatise on preluding, in which the music "proceeds from the imagination of the improviser," while also qualifying it as a book for advanced pianists and "in no way theoretical." Panseron further recommends the prelude collections and improvisation treatise of Czerny as concrete, non-theoretical guides to free improvisation: "It is with the erudition of all these preludes and all these works that you equip your head and make yourself able to improvise with facility." In his final recommendation Panseron entices readers with the thought that, if they internalize the preludes and fugues of Bach and Handel, they might be able to rise to the level of "great improvisers such as Hummel, Moscheles, Liszt etc."[17]

The study of modulation, in sum, had a wide range of benefits and applications, from the performance of elementary linking transitions to the most advanced brilliant improvisation. There is little evidence, however, that students took advantage of the latter path. Pianists training for high-level solo performance may have dropped in on the *accompagnement* classes, but it was not central to their training. It appears that neither Marmontel, who took over the piano department in 1848, nor his predecessor Zimmerman taught improvisation at all. It is true that Kalkbrenner's treatise was published in 1849, but this may not have been in response to a need or demand. It was the year of his death, and it was more likely a tribute.[18] The top French pianist of the 1840s and 1850s, Émile Prudent, seems not to have improvised, at least not in public. In this same period the precocious Camille Saint-Saëns was studying with Kalkbrenner's disciple Camille Stamaty, but again there is no evidence that piano improvisation was part of the program. Saint-Saëns' conservatory training in harmony and fugue bore fruit in his extraordinary organ improvisations of the 1850s and 1860s, but there are precious few examples of him extemporizing at the piano.

The Conservatoire also trained instrumentalists, especially violinists, in harmony and *accompagnement*, with the intention of making them at least capable of improvising a prelude. Pierre Baillot's violin treatise, adopted in 1834 by the Conservatoire, gave examples of both "harmonic" and "melodic" preludes, the former based on arpeggiation and the latter somewhat more free in style, but still based on elementary chord progressions. It is difficult to determine whether violinists practiced these exercises or used them to support actual improvisation.[19] But there are signs that the practice was still alive, if rare, later in the century. Panseron indicated that the principles of keyboard modulation were "equally applicable to all instruments; to the violin, among others, they give results as fine as the piano."[20] Charles de Bériot's treatise *l'Art du prélude*, billed as the "second annex to the *Méthode de violon*" and published in 1875, five years after his death, also suggests that the practice may have been ongoing. De Bériot had been educated in the French school and probably used his preluding manual with students after becoming the chief violin instructor of the Brussels conservatory in 1843. His exercises, like Baillot's, consist of little more than chord progressions for arpeggiation, starting with simple formulas and progressing through inversions and modulation.

Unlike Baillot's examples, however, De Bériot's are written out with piano accompaniment, linking them decisively to the Conservatoire's *accompagnement* pedagogy and ensemble playing. Émile Sauret, a student of De Bériot, is one of the few concert violinists we know to have improvised in the post-1850 context. Violinist Goby Eberhardt recalled that they "played duets as well as concertos in unison, where he [Sauret] then suddenly overtook the accompaniment on the violin and improvised things on it"—an indication of his training in *accompagnement*. Eberhardt further mentioned that Sauret played "preludes and improvisations" that gave forth "a pleasure of a completely special kind."[21] In addition to becoming one of the top violinists of his time, Sauret was also a reasonably prolific composer. He embodied the conservatory's ideal of the complete musician in whom theory, performance, and composition are united and mutually informing. De Bériot expressed this holistic philosophy with a memorable phrase: "To improvise is to compose rapidly, to compose is to improvise slowly."[22]

It is not clear that Sauret's facility in improvisation was a product specifically of his Franco-Belgian training, for he also studied composition in Leipzig at a relatively young age. The basic principles of thoroughbass, harmony, and modulation found in Panseron's treatise were international and are also found in the conservatory pedagogy in Vienna and Leipzig. In Leipzig there was a close parallel to the Conservatoire's *accompagnement* classes in the teaching of Ernst Friedrich Richter, whose *Lehrbuch der Harmonie* was first published in 1853 and became the foundational text in harmony for quite some time. It is rooted in eighteenth-century thoroughbass practice, and as Leonard Phillips has noted, Richter "attempted to make the object of his studies the production of actual music through a study of melody and types of accompaniment."[23] Eberhardt, trained in Germany, was capable of playing two-violin improvisations like Sauret: "It made my uncle especially happy when I freely improvised with [pianist Fritz] Steinbach; he would play, for example, an accompaniment, to which I improvised all manner of themes."[24] In Leipzig as in Paris, advanced piano classes seem to have been largely improvisation-free. The main piano professors at the Leipzig conservatory from its founding year 1843 through the 1860s—Louis Plaidy and Ferdinand Wenzel—focused exclusively on technique, touch, and interpretation. Mendelssohn was the great exception. He led his own classes with the advanced pianists, in which technical questions were set aside to concentrate on "higher" concerns such as counterpoint, composition, and improvisation:

More than once, the lesson was devoted to extemporisation upon given subjects; during the course of them Mendelssohn would sit beside the *improvisatore* and, without interrupting the performance, suggest, from time to time, certain modes of treatment which would take two well-defined motives, and work them up into a model of sonata-form, in order to show how much might be accomplished by very simple means. He insisted strongly upon the importance of a natural and carefully arranged system of modulation; and would frequently call upon one pupil after another to pass from a given key to some exceedingly remote one, with the least possible amount of effort.[25]

Had Mendelssohn lived beyond 1847, one of the students in this class might well have carried the free fantasy tradition forward. But when he passed away, no one remained to model free playing, and what was left of improvisation in the curriculum was found in the *accompagnement* classes where piano was treated as a secondary instrument.

The revival of baroque music, a movement that gained steam after 1850, brought a new level of historical consciousness concerning harmony and keyboard improvisation. Musicians and publishers faced a dilemma concerning the figured bass parts in old scores by Handel and Bach. If they published the barren figured basses, much of the public would be unable to play them. If they offered full keyboard realizations, they would partially misrepresent the composer's intention and thought process. Moreover, a realization designed for piano might sound poor on an organ, and vice versa. The question of what constituted a good piano transcription of orchestral parts added yet another level of complexity. In the 1860s composer Robert Franz prepared editions of baroque works with thoughtful, historically informed keyboard arrangements, and the anonymous review of one such publication made revealing comments about the position of *accompagnement* and improvisation in contemporary musical life:

> The old art of accompanying [*accompagnements*] is lost. It will never come back to life, and if it did it would be nothing but a living contradiction to all of modern art education, which now raises higher, more serious expectations, and at heart cannot content itself with what arrives at the fingers of a talented artist in fortunate moments, but only values that inspiration which the artist himself preserves beyond the moment and converts into fixed artistic form. Our score-readers [i.e., people trained in score transduction and *accompagnement*] practice their art for their own use and pleasure in times of solitude, or before narrower, more intimate circles—the public however makes no demand to hear it because it no longer believes in these arts, valuing them at most as a special talent. It is the same transformation that has pushed free fantasies and even improvised cadenzas out of the public sphere. (AMZ 1865, 453)[26]

With such discouraging voices coming from the establishment, it is little surprise that few students in the harmony and modulation classes sought to develop their improvisation skills at an advanced level. Even the open spaces that baroque music had opened up to performerly initiative were now being reserved for serious composers like Robert Franz. At this point in history, mere knowledge of the requisite harmonic theory was not enough to motivate students to improvise and keep it vital. Nor was the invitation to explore modulation improvisationally, issued to the more advanced instrumentalists by authors like Panseron and De Bériot, sufficient to sustain it in practice. The prestige accorded to "public" music and to composers had consigned private music-making—the locus of conviviality, pleasure, and intra-artist exchange—to a lower position on the scale of values, and improvisation was dragged down with it.

Aspects of free improvisation remained in the living practice of concert virtuosos, particularly in introductory preludes, in transitions between pieces (a specialty of Hans von Bülow), and in the faking of one's way through memory slips (a specialty of Anton Rubinstein). There are indications that such forms of improvisation were perceived as a trademark of the modern, post-Liszt virtuosity, rather than a contin-uation of older practices. In 1865 a young virtuoso from Meiningen named Theodor Scharffenberg was identified as "a specialist virtuoso of the modern school who, con-trary to all concert practice, does not refrain from beginning his work with an *ad libitum* prelude" (AMZ 1865, 445). The vogue for such elaborations, utterly out of sync with the ideology of *Werktreue*, helps explain some of the peculiarities of Felix Draeseke's *Anweisung zum kunstgerechten Modulieren*. This is a fairly traditional harmony-and-modulation treatise, listing in tabular form the strategies and routes of modulation through short chord progressions. Its publication at the relatively late date of 1876 is best explained by Draeseke's appointment to the faculty of the Dresden conservatory that year. Perhaps because of its late date, and because Draeseke was not a theorist, it has a refreshingly up-to-date perspective on modulation practice. Draeseke explains that his treatise is not for "creative artists"—that is, composers of serious music like himself—but for informed amateurs and higher-level piano teachers, people who al-ready know basic harmony and voice-leading: "Most amateurs are pianists, and anyone among them who seeks theoretical knowledge will also make sure they can use it prac-tically. Its most natural application is found in preludes and in transitions from one piece to another."[27]

Also modern is Draeseke's dismissal of counterpoint instruction, which he considers an outdated expense of labor and a hindrance to the student's acquisition of the most relevant theoretical knowledge. (In this he differs from his predecessors Czerny and Kalkbrenner, who paid lip service to the importance of fugal improvisation even while their treatises gave it only marginal attention.) The appendix "Recommendations for Performers" departs from all previous modulation treatises in demonstrating how the relevant chord progressions can be fleshed out with arpeggio figures extending well beyond two octaves—that is, in the manner of modern, romantic bravura. As the realizations become increasingly elaborate, Draeseke advises the player to devise arpeggio figures without doubling the bass note, following the more modern chord spacings and sonorities of Chopin.[28] Whether pianists actually used this treatise for performance purposes is difficult to say. Liszt might have found it helpful, since he was not pleased with the improvised preludes and modulatory interludes he was hearing in his master classes, and even asked one student to prepare a volume of examples for memorization.[29]

Remainders

In the 1860s and 1870s, free fantasies on the piano were usually heard, when heard at all, from the hands of older masters. When in 1864 Moscheles was given an honorary banquet in Vienna to celebrate the fiftieth jubilee of his concert debut in that city, he reciprocated by playing the pieces that had launched his fame: the Alexander Variations and "free fantasies."[30] In 1871 Hiller travelled to London to mount a series of solo recitals and a grand concert at the Crystal Palace and played free fantasies on given themes, including one on Schubert's "Wanderer" and "Steam and Mill" which, in the traditional manner, treated the motives independently and later combined them contrapuntally.[31] The Crystal Palace concert included a performance of Mozart's "Coronation" concerto, in which "the cadenzas introduced in the first and last movements . . . were improvised by Dr. Hiller, according to the true intention of the blanks formerly left by the composer of a concerto, in order to exhibit the skill and ready invention of the player" (*London Daily News*, 21 March 1871). Evidently cadenza improvisation had become rare. The last time London audiences had heard improvised cadenzas was probably 1847, when Mendelssohn had improvised cadenzas in Beethoven's Fourth Piano Concerto.

Composer and pianist Stephen Heller, who barely ever performed in public, came out of the woodwork in 1862 at Charles Hallé's instigation. Hallé, the hero of public musical life in Manchester, had heard that his friend was in need of money, and he had never forgotten the improvisations Heller had played when they were together in Paris in the 1830s:

> [Heller's] shyness . . . left him entirely when he was improvising, a gift in which he excelled all great musicians that I have known. The change that came over him and his execution in such moments, or hours, was marvelous. . . . When improvising all difficulties seemed to vanish. . . . Whether he improvised quite freely, or on subjects self-chosen or given to him, he was equally fascinating, dominating his listeners and pouring out a wealth of ideas of which his published compositions give no idea.[32]

Hallé was determined to make a big impression on Manchester's public by showing off Heller's remarkable improvisational talent: "I insisted on his including in the programme an 'Improvisation on subjects given by the audience.' After a hard fight he submitted, and my expectations of a crowded house were fully realized." Heller finally came around and played a fairly traditional free fantasy, but Hallé, a classically oriented pianist who did not improvise, was in awe:

> He had an extraordinary faculty of combining the most dissimilar themes, and proved it once—the only time, I believe, he ever improvised in public [i.e., 1862]— where the opening of "Don Giovanni," "Notte e giorno faticar," Pedrillo's "Viva Bacco, Bacco viva," from "Il Seraglio," and his own "Wanderstunden," were given to him, and after the one and the other had been treated most ingeniously for

some time, they were all three, or the semblance of them, heard at the same time, a feat so difficult of execution that it would have required long practice . . . and here it was accomplished spontaneously.[33]

The idea that improvisation might be a special, exotic attraction for provincial audiences had occurred to the impresario Bernard Ullman several years earlier, when he brought piano virtuoso Henri Herz to the United States (1846–1847). Herz published a memoir of the tour in 1866 and took an ironic view of his improvisations. Early in the tour, when asked by Ullman whether he could improvise, Herz replied: "I have never made a special study of improvisation, nevertheless I can pull it off like any other when needed."[34] When Ullman suggested he actually do it, though, Herz protested: "Improvise in public, how awful! One might not be in the mood, and it is cruel to deliver such pretentious impotence to a large audience." Herz had in fact discouraged his own students from improvising in his *Méthode complète de piano*, saying that even Hummel had his bad days.[35] Ullman nonetheless insisted that American audiences required improvisations on given themes and that Herz had no choice. Herz would need only to accompany the melody with arpeggios and chromatic scales in the left hand, "dispensing with all harmonic combinations."[36] At the debut improvisation in Baltimore, Herz collected the scores submitted by the audience and there ensued a lively exchange in which the themes were applauded or rejected, often with "great tumult." One musically illiterate audience member over-participated, singing a melody to Herz several times in a terrible voice until Herz was able to decipher it correctly. Ultimately he chose five or six themes and worked them up as a potpourri, played in a light style "full of feats and attractions for the American public of that epoch." Although Herz took a condescending view of this undereducated audience, his up-close encounter with the irreverent ethos of participatory democracy did have a slightly transformative effect upon him: "that which I liked very little at first ended up entertaining me enormously."[37]

Two younger pianists emerged in the 1870s with strong reputations as free improvisers, and each submitted in some measure to reconstructive pressures. Alfred Grünfeld was the first great player to come out of Berlin's Neue Akademie der Tonkunst, the conservatory founded in 1855 with an emphasis on piano training. His teacher Theodor Kullak was the conservatory's director. He had studied with Czerny, and it is likely the conservatory placed some value on improvisation within a pianist's complete education. Kullak's brother Adolph, also on the faculty, published a treatise called *The Aesthetics of Pianism* that devoted a few pages to improvisation as a "completely special and specific" component of the instrument's expressive universe.[38] Grünfeld, at his 1871 debut in his hometown of Prague, played an "Improvisation" on themes given by the esteemed critic and music historian A. W. Ambros, and continued to play fantasies of this kind on his international tours (AMZ 1871, 526). Shortly before the 1876 premiere of Wagner's complete *Ring*, however, he offered in London an improvisation of a different sort:

The "sensation" of the evening was Herr Albert Grünfeld. . . . His "improvisation" consisted of going from one of Wagner's operas to another, joining all the themes with consummate art. After immense applause, Herr Grünfeld selected for his next "Improvisation" Mozart's operas, and concluded with several of Strauss's most popular waltz themes, embellishing them in an extraordinarily clever manner. (*Musical World* 1876, 488)

Notably, these were not fantasies on given themes, but fantasies honoring a single composer, and more specifically still, a single genre within the composer's output. Here, for the first time, the free fantasy genre was showing the influence of canonic and repertorial values by pulling away from shared popular tunes characteristic of the older free fantasy tradition. The press reception of Grünfeld further reveals that these "improvisations" were more like concert transcriptions and paraphrases rather than freely developed fantasies. His Wagner "fantasies" kept using the same material from *Lohengrin* and *Tannhäuser*, and when he returned to London after a pause of three years the Wagner "improvisations" had not changed much, prompting an irritated critic to remark: "we care not greatly for improvisations that be not improvised" (*Musical World* 1879, 400). In the 1880s and 1890s, Grünfeld improvised less and less in public. At his 1886 Vienna recital, a grand event reviewed by Eduard Hanslick, he adopted a conspicuously serious physical demeanor and chose conspicuously serious repertoire. Though known as a brilliant technician, he was trying to shed his reputation as a popular, charming, somewhat superficial virtuoso, and tellingly, he did not improvise (*Die Presse*, 25 February 1886). Around this time he also began publishing pieces under titles like *Fantasie* and *Paraphrase* on the music he had been "improvising" upon. Critics started losing track of the difference, crediting him for improvising when he played a published *Fantasie*, and vice versa.

While Grünfeld was making his name in the late 1870s, the child prodigy Ferrucio Busoni (b. 1866) was being trotted around various northern Italian and Austrian towns by his father, who showed off his son's precocious talents in composition, performances of classic works, and free improvisations on given themes.[39] Busoni's skills, honed under the tutelage his father rather than in a conservatory, were at this point almost completely intuitive and void of theoretical training, as if the many classical works he was learning were simply lodging their patterns in his fingers. At concerts he played everything from memory, even the piano part in a Haydn trio. Reports of the boy's improvisations tell us little other than that he tended to elaborate on a single, short theme. At the earliest Vienna concert of the nine-year-old, Hanslick "gave the boy several motives at the piano, which he immediately developed in the same serious style, mostly imitative and contrapuntal" (*Neue freie Presse*, 12 February 1876). In these improvisations, then, there was no trace of the free fantasy genre. What A. W. Ambros wrote about Busoni's six short, published piano pieces probably applied to the improvisations as well: "With these ideas he plays like another child plays with his toy: he amuses himself with it until he is tired of it, then throws the toy into the corner quickly and for good" (*Wiener Abendpost* [Beilage], 12 February 1876). To judge from one such piece, the "Studio contrappunto," the counterpoint was none too learned or severe, elaborating the material in a manner that emphasized the separation of the hands. Busoni's precocious improvisations were mobilized to convey his surfeit of musical inventiveness, and this phase inevitably passed. When he returned to Vienna in 1883 for a serious debut as a composer-performer he did not improvise, and his concert programs thereafter show no signs of improvisation.

Although improvisation did not stay in Busoni's concert practice, his childhood experience, in which composition, interpretation, and improvisation were indissolubly united, left a lasting imprint on his aesthetic vision. In his aesthetic writings he privileged living, emerging music over reflection and composition: "Notation is to improvisation as the portrait is to the living model. It is for the interpreter to resolve the rigidity of the signs into the primitive emotion."[40] As late as the 1920s he proselytized in favor of improving cadenzas to classic concertos, and when his student Gottfried Galston suggested publishing his concerto cadenzas he rejected the idea: "In the 8th Mozart concerto cadenzas I invent something. The idleness of virtuosos is lamentable. My Beethoven Violin Concerto is completely improvised [in the cadenzas]. Why always this Joachim cadenza, which doesn't even sound good?"[41] These comments can be confusing because Busoni had in fact fixed his own cadenzas in notation: otherwise Galston would not have suggested publishing them. Moreover, Busoni would not literally have improvised the cadenzas on the violin. Yet despite of these two levels of mediation Busoni considers them "completely improvised." The difference between actual improvisation and its aesthetically reflected form is completely lost.

In the decades after 1850 organ improvisers began acquiring more public attention. In France, as seen earlier, the drive for technological and commercial eminence at the international expositions created new alliances between artists and instrument-making firms. The blue-chip organ-building firm Cavaillé-Coll found its artistic partner in L. J. A. Lefébure-Wély, organist at the church of the Madeleine from 1847 to 1858. In an echo of the "branding" discourse surrounding Cavallo, his early biographer wrote: "M. Lefébure is before all else an improviser. That is the distinctive feature of his talent. Whatever the merit of his written compositions, one does not find in them that verve, power, majesty, and elevation so admired in his improvisations on the organ."[42]

Lefébure acquired an extraordinary reputation because the Madeleine was not only a sacred space but also a political symbol—a neoclassical structure associated with Napoleon's victories—as well as a showroom for the grand Cavaillé-Coll instrument Lefébure had inaugurated in 1847. During the Second Empire visitors were encouraged to visit for both musical edification and a wondrous encounter with French technological splendor: "For eleven years, there were few music-lovers, tourists, or distinguished foreigners, whether in the spheres of politics, science, or diplomacy, who did not hasten to go to the Madeleine to hear M. Lefébure."[43] What they heard, without exception, were improvisations elaborated at strategic points in the liturgical service. At one service he elaborated "at some length" on the three versets of the Magnificat with "three musical ideas on the viola da gamba, the celestial voices, and the human voice."[44] In the freedom offered by improvisation, Lefébure could show off the colorful variety of the instrument, changing stops at will, and combine musical pleasure with technological display.

As a genuinely popular musician, Lefébure did much more propaganda work for Cavaillé-Coll in their Paris showrooms and in churches beyond France. He improvised at nearly every organ inauguration of the 1850s, becoming one of the key celebrities of these grand civic ceremonies. When he was summoned to Belgium to inaugurate a new Cavaillé-Coll, his improvisations were applauded "by the congregation and even the Archbishop" (RGMP 1856, 90). The manner in which the organ broke through to secular relevance is reminiscent of J. G. Vogler, who in the late eighteenth century had paraded his technologically innovative, colorful orchestrion with the intention of giving organs a more public and more universal identity, and had done so by playing flashy, accessible improvisations. The main difference was that Vogler had worked in a largely pre-capitalist milieu, and his motivations for improvising were guided by enlightened ideals of progress. In Second Empire France, it was international commerce and industry that was issuing a new call to improvisation.[45]

French industry also propagated organ improvisation at the Exposition Universelle of 1878 when a massive Cavaillé-Coll was built at the Trocadéro, a space that accommodated two thousand people. The concerts played there by Alexandre Guilmant were so popular that the Trocadéro became a permanent site for organ concerts for over a decade, Guilmant sharing the glory with Eugène Gigout. The programs of Guilmant and Gigout were celebrated for giving the public little-known repertoire by Bach and Handel, but they also regularly included free fantasies on given themes, usually as the penultimate number. One of Guilmant's fantasies from the 1878 series went as long as fifteen minutes.[46] At a later concert he forgot one of his scores and substituted a long programmatic improvisation that featured a dramatic storm. A receptive critic took this as an occasion to reflect on the value of improvisation:

> He left his music at home: all the better: isn't improvisation the triumph of the organist? . . . In such moments the organist is the equal of the orator and the poet; he commands his public and transports it with him into the ether. Neither the painter nor the sculptor exercises such an empire over the crowd. I have occasionally expressed surprise that M. Guilmant does not give more space to improvisation at his organ concerts.[47]

Gigout's reputation as an improviser was even stronger. César Franck, the revered teacher of organ improvisation at the Conservatoire, declared that "Gigout is a great one, a very great organist and the most astonishing improviser."[48] Another witness claimed that Gigout "always improvised; I never saw him with music in eyesight."[49]

Both Guilmant and Gigout toured internationally and played free fantasies on given themes to large, unfamiliar audiences. Their superior talents as improvisers, which made even Lefébure-Wély look dated, can be attributed to the success of church music reforms that took off in France after 1850. Reform leaders such as François-Joseph

Fétis and Louis Niedermeyer encouraged organists to study older medieval and baroque styles in order to reinvest liturgical music with a sense of solemnity and make it
sound less similar to secular music. The key organist involved in these reforms was the
Belgian Jacques-Nicolas Lemmens, who was deeply versed in German contrapuntal
idioms. Guilmant studied under him directly, and Gigout published an edition of his
École d'orgue. Lemmens's original 1862 edition of the *École* emphasizes the importance
of improvisational facility and seems to attack Lefébure's more attractive, colorful
approach:

> [The organist] must be well trained in harmony, counterpoint and fugue, other-
> wise his improvisations will be of no value and full of mistakes. . . . [Avoid] that
> continual changing of stops which is such an abuse nowadays. . . . Many organists,
> in a vain attempt to conceal the poverty of their improvisations, sacrifice style
> and true sentiment to material effects which may please certain hearers, but will
> always be disapproved by connoisseurs.[50]

When Gigout republished the treatise in 1920 he drew special attention to Lemmens's
section on modulation and exhorted readers: "it is indispensable that the organist—
indeed the musician—know how to improvise."[51]

French interest in German organ traditions played a role in converting Anton
Bruckner into a concert organist, thus bringing improvisation still further out into
the open. Bruckner was an irrepressible improviser, famous for losing control of
his choir and congregation at St. Florian, but his reputation as a wide-ranging and
learned contrapuntist was unsurpassed.[52] In 1869 he was invited to play at an organ
festival in Nancy and improvised at both of his concerts. At the first performance
he became uncommonly enthusiastic in the culminating pedal-point and botched
the conclusion, but the audience responded with wild enthusiasm.[53] On the strength
of these appearances Bruckner was invited to Paris where he improvised at two
concerts. The first was a more private event for musicians and connoisseurs where he
elaborated on themes from his first symphony. At a second and more public concert
at Notre Dame he was given a theme by organist Alexis Chauvet, "whose three parts
I reworked first into a prelude, then into a fugue, and finally symphonically. . . . At
the conclusion I played an interrupted organ-point, which was in Paris completely
new and stopped them in astonishment."[54] Saint-Saëns, Franck, and the entire press
singled out the improvisations as the concert's highlights. Predictably, Bruckner was
next invited to London, where he played concerts in the grand, non-liturgical spaces
of Royal Albert Hall and the Crystal Palace in 1871. At the Royal Albert Hall concert he improvised on classical pieces by Bach, Handel, and Mendelssohn, which not
all critics were happy to hear "reworked." At the Crystal Palace concerts, however,
he improvised on audience requests, faring particularly well with a German patri-
otic song at the first concert, an event billed as a "Great National German Festival,"
and at the second, arousing British patriotism with the unavoidable "God Save the
Queen."[55]

The values that critics and observers associated with free piano improvisations in this period do not seem to perpetuate the celebration of communicative potency and social idealism that had grounded the reception of Hummel and Liszt. The improvisations of Moscheles, Herz, Heller, Busoni, and Grünfeld discussed here were all presented and received as somewhat exotic curiosities, fascinating in their effect but not part of a living tradition. Yet there was enough momentum left in improvisation to pick up newer historical trends and tendencies. The free fantasies of Grünfeld and Bruckner accommodated themselves to the growth of the canon and to the prestige of modern symphonic music. Herz flexibly adapted his old training to the popular and participatory ethos of concerts in the New World. And most conspicuously, the free fantasy tradition gained new life as the organ acquired a modern, quasi-secular identity networked with the interests of industry, technological development, public concerts, and national or civic festivals.

REPRESENTATIONS

In improvisational performance there is often uncertainty on the part of the listener about what the performer is doing or intends to do. This uncertainty is responsible for both what is pleasurable and what is unpleasurable in the experience. Historically, the gap between what the player knows and what the listener knows has generated extensive, sometimes anxious discourse. Is the performer "really" improvising or is she "faking" it? Is improvisation the unthinking action of mechanical, well-trained hands, or is it the product of a thinking, sovereign mind? Such questions, and suspicions of fraudulence, seem to return perpetually.[56] In previous chapters we have seen several examples: Liszt and other child prodigies were suspected of being mechanical automatons. Kalkbrenner's supposed improvisations were revealed to be a fixed composition. Schumann carefully tuned into Wilhelm Taubert's improvisations for signs of iterative formulas. Opponents of the free fantasy genre lambasted mediocre musicians who passed themselves off as "inspired" artists, and Hiller defended Hummel against skeptics who criticized his reuse of the same motives. The uncertainty endemic to improvisation is mitigated mainly by experience and familiarity. Listeners can understand better what a player intends by hearing many performances of a single artist, by hearing other players who improvise in a similar vein, or simply by improvising themselves, developing an intimate, insider's knowledge of exactly what problems and choices the improviser faces. This is the main reason top improvisers have derived the most enjoyment from playing for and listening to each other. With peers they are fairly certain they will be understood.

For nonprofessional listeners, the uncertainty hovering around improvisation can be made pleasurable through the activation of beliefs and assumptions about what is occurring. The belief, for example, that an improviser is channeling deep feelings, or catching a ray of divine inspiration, or mobilizing deep reserves of contrapuntal knowledge, can enter the listener's mind as an explanatory account that displaces the uncertainty and converts it into an occasion for amazement, delight, or appreciation. In the post-1847 period, as the rarity of improvisations exacerbated listener uncertainty, the work of these beliefs—the improvisation imaginary—was increasingly called into play. The idea of musical improvisation ceased to be constituted by performed phenomena and reconstituted itself more fully in the realm of representations and discourses defining how it originated and what it represented. In the era of Staël's *Corinne* the improvisation imaginary had thrived on exchanges between literary representations and the living tradition of poetry performance found in Italy and on international stages. And as seen in the cases of Moscheles, Loewe, Schumann, and Liszt, such intersections of literary culture and performance culture were also present in the musical world. New to the post-1847 period was the circulation of these representations in the relative absence of actual experiences of improvisation. Now the representations took on a free-floating life of their own, and improvisatoriness—a reflected or constructed image of improvisation—became a surrogate for improvisational events.

The improvisation imaginary of the latter half of the nineteenth century included many of the same figures we have encountered in previous chapters: Italian *improvvisatori*, epic bards, folk balladeers, street entertainers, young soldiers, Venetian gondoliers, and historic keyboard giants such as Mozart and Beethoven. The imaginary also included discursive tropes and patterns—appearing in music criticism, journalism, and pamphlets—that contoured the perception of what was happening in improvisation and what it meant. Compositions, too, enriched the realm of representations with notated simulations of improvisation in pieces with titles such as *Rhapsody, Impromptu*, and *Improvisation*. Certain threads within the improvisation imaginary, such as the image of the political or religious orator, or of Mozart extemporizing, lost much of their force, while other threads, such as ethnically exotic entertainers or folk pipers, became denser. These discourses and representations sustained a positive, desirable image of spontaneous musical or poetic invention through an era that was in other respects unreceptive to it. We cannot hope to track all the representations and discourses here. The examples discussed below are only a selection from well-known authors and musicians who attributed special aesthetic, social, or political value to improvisation. Collectively they built up a strong, dense network of ideas and associations around improvisation that endured well beyond the nineteenth century.

Wagner's Troubadour

It can seem paradoxical that Richard Wagner, famously opposed to performers' liberties, would publish an essay including a paean to the power of improvisation. But that is exactly what he did in "On the Destiny of Opera" (1871), which originated in a public lecture summarizing his dramatic philosophy. Wagner's reflections on improvisation begin with spoken theater. The astonishing magic of Shakespeare's dramas, he argues, lies in their rare coordination of overall plan and local accident: "Though the main plan of a play was easy to perceive . . . the marvelous 'accidentiae' in its working out . . . were inexplicable on any hypothesis of deliberate artistic planning. Here we found such drastic individuality, that it often seemed like unaccountable caprice."[57] Wagner concludes that this rare balance was a consequence of Shakespeare's close relationship with his improvising actors. The playwright was in constant contact with them, allowing the actors to assimilate his creative vision without textual mediation. The actors, with their strong mimetic skills and improvised variants, kept the drama lifelike, while the poet defined the drama's main ideas and gave them formal shape. Wagner thus describes the Shakespearean drama as "a fixed mimetic improvisation of the very highest poetic value." But he does not consider this drama perfect, for it is still missing one thing: music. Without music, dramatic words fail to attain full ideality, and the drama can only fulfill its destiny completely with the infusion of music.

From these theatrical considerations Wagner moves directly to instrumental music: "We have statements from trustworthy sources that Beethoven made an incomparable impression upon his friends through extended improvising at the piano. We can consider unexaggerated the laments that these same creations were not committed to paper."[58] Beethoven's improvisations, in other words, were at least as good as, if not better than, his written works. This idea had been floating around the Beethoven lore for some time. Beethoven's most "trustworthy" source was probably Carl Czerny's memoir, first published in 1842, which recalled weekly concerts where Beethoven played "with a richness of ideas that distinguished his improvisations as much as, indeed often even more than, his written works."[59] More unusual is Wagner's follow-up point: "far inferior musicians, whose penwork was always stiff and stilted, have quite amazed us in their 'free fantasias' by a wholly unsuspected and often very fertile talent for invention."[60] Here Wagner must have had in mind Hummel and Moscheles, pianists he would have been able to hear in his early years. Another possible source was the English critic Henry Chorley, who had once heard Hummel improvise for "an hour and a half" on four themes from Auber's *Masaniello,* and marveled at the control and inventiveness sustained through the entire performance. In Chorley's opinion Hummel's improvisations were superior to his written compositions: "he commanded the individual force, fire—most of all, fancy—of a poet capable of extempore utterance. . . . It is hard to conceive, that he who was the most various and the most masterly of modern *improvisatori,* should have been a mere machine into which so much learning had been crammed; and thus it is with regret that I have always fancied him undervalued and disparaged."[61] With the examples of Beethoven, Hummel, and Moscheles in mind, it was possible to imagine improvisations more completely satisfying than the best finished works.

For Wagner, the stories of Beethoven's lost improvisations gave forth the idea of a surplus or excess—a freer, more flexible music that only existed in improvisation and did not, perhaps *could* not, find translation into the conventions of written music. They suggested a sort of music the composer might have written but did not yet know how to write, since the rules of composition did not allow such "freedom" to appear on paper. In this way Wagner justified himself as the inheritor of Beethoven's

Fantasies of Improvisation

legacy: he would perpetuate it by composing out the freer, more flexibly unfolding music of Beethoven's improvisations. And by composing out such irregularities he could free Beethovenian music from the strictures of classical periods and architectonic forms. The music would finally achieve "its final liberation from each remaining fetter" and would possess an "untold newness."[62] Wagner valued not only the radical novelty of Beethoven's improvised music, but also its communicability to listeners. In apprehending the artwork of the future, he claimed, "the new and fitting standard might aptly be sought in the impression received by those fortunate hearers at one of those unwritten impromptus by the most peerless of musicians."[63]

Wagner's entire conception of improvisation was of course metaphorical. It took for granted the priority of the composer's or poet's creative resources. The reason he could attribute philosophical meaning to it, making it sound perfect and transcendent, is that there was no real improvisation in his environment to test or verify such attribution—certainly not the enthusiastic improvisations of Nietzsche, which he mercilessly ridiculed, nor a recording of Beethoven's actual improvisations. From his standpoint improvisation was not primarily performance, but one facet of the composer's interior dialectic. Wagner thus had the opportunity to load it with ethical and philosophical content, and took advantage by constructing two heros, Tannhäuser and Walther von Stolzing (from *Die Meistersinger von Nürnberg*), who demonstrate virtue and genius in spontaneous, unpremeditated singing. Wagner's heroes belong to an imaginary, preindustrial past in which composition and performance are united—a place where there are no publishers and scores, and all noble song is "improvisation." They embody a critique of the industrial division of labor and of the forces of alienation in the modern musical world. Though rooted in medieval sources, the troubadours are also descended, in literary terms, from Staël's Corinne insofar as their performances mark dramatic climaxes and carry an intensified charge as "in-the-moment" invention. The French poetry improviser Eugène Pradel had in fact made the troubadour a predecessor of the modern improviser, asking, "What were the rhapsodes, the bards, the troubadours, if not improvisers?"[64]

In the song-contest in Act II of *Tannhäuser*, the hero faces off with another singer, Wolfram von Eschenbach, to determine which of the courtly singers is more worthy of the love of Elizabeth. All the contestants are understood to be improvising, but Wolfram's poem-song demonstrates only his command of the rules and conventions of the courtly love tradition—a mastery of technique and of received vocabularies. Tannhäuser's song, by contrast, releases the kernel of freedom—the potential for error, the possibility of unplanned digression—that always lurks as a potential in improvisational events. He begins his song in an apparently courtly fashion, but suddenly veers off into a fervent song in praise of sensual, pagan love. It is an irruption of his "real" self, his authentic feelings and impulses. It is ostensibly also a revelation of a scandalous "truth" about the nature of love, which the courtly conventions hold in denial. Improvisation here is the medium of a moral transgression. It exposes a higher or deeper truth that conventional Christian morality cannot accept or even acknowledge, and in consequence Tannhäuser is cast out almost irredeemably. By improvising "freely" rather than conventionally, he makes himself a social outcast, and the authenticity of his improvisation fails to achieve any social or ethical transformation. Tannhäuser's improvisation, or more precisely, his unleashing of the radical potential of improvisation, is revolutionary in character. His song is a type of music neither heard in nor reconcilable with the existing Christian world, yet it suggests another possible world.

In *Die Meistersinger*, the context for music-making is the musician's guild rather than a grand medieval hall. Here what is prized is not moral chastity but respect for the rules and traditional principles of composition. When the outsider Walther von Stolzing arrives in Nürnberg and seeks entry into the guild, he auditions with a song that breaks many of the rules, since he has not been properly tutored. He has learned to sing only through intuition and through lively contact with nature. He is merely a performer and improviser—not yet a composer. He embodies Wagner's understanding of improvisation as "the natural process at the beginnings of all art."[65] His poem-song, too, is constructed to sound improvisatory: it digresses, takes unexpected turns, and does not flow in symmetrical phrases (although it does betray an instinctive, unrefined understanding of the rules). For these reasons his song, though promising, is still deficient and in need of a composer's reflective capacities. Over the course of the opera Walther's improvisatory waywardness is subject to correction and instruction by the master-singer Hans Sachs. Sachs's gentle, antididactic pedagogy ensures that the hero's innate gifts—his sensitivity to all the marvelous *accidentiae* that his apprenticeship in nature his given him—come to their full realization and can be reconciled with the guild's compositional values. Walther's improvised song, thus corrected and channeled, becomes a medium of integration into the Nürnberg community, and he ends the opera as an emblem of the city's artistic regeneration.

The ethical and political differences between Tannhäuser's and Walther's improvisations are a measure of how ideas of improvisation had evolved between 1845 (*Tannhäuser*) and 1865 (*Die Meistersinger*). In the pre-1848 period, a period when Liszt was thrilling audiences with unregulated improvisation and wild virtuosity, it was possible for a romantic revolutionary like Wagner to imagine improvisation as an agent of excess and insurgent liberation. The chastened, post-revolutionary Wagner, however, was more inclined to view improvisation as insufficiently elevated or insufficiently complete—as something fresh and spontaneous but in need of redemption through the artist's "higher" shaping powers. Whether it is Wagner fulfilling the destiny of Beethoven's unwritten improvisations, or Hans Sachs bringing Walther's improvisation into socially acceptable form, improvisation needs to submit to the supremacy of the compositional principle.

Liszt's Gypsies

European writers, musicians, and listeners had been engaging with Roma music and fictional "gypsy" characters long before the 1850s. In the most influential writings that preceded Liszt's, music received plenty of emphasis, but improvisation was mentioned only rarely. Grellmann's pioneering *Versuch über die Zigeuner*, for example, from which many nineteenth-century writers borrowed, described music is the one "fine art" the Roma people cultivated, but said nothing about improvisation in connection with music.[66] Nor was improvisation a dominant marker of gypsy character in the novels of Walter Scott, which played a disproportionate role in disseminating ideas and images throughout Europe. Liszt's *Des Bohémiens et de leur musique en Hongrie* (1859), a book probably ghost-written to a considerable extent, was thus a pioneer in giving great emphasis to the *improvised* character of the music.[67] It set out to challenge prevailing comical and fantastical stereotypes and celebrate the musical gypsy as a kind of unsullied, primitive artistic genius, and to this end it used improvisation is a key literary motif: "Gypsy art [*l'art bohémien*], more than any other, belongs to the domain of improvisation, and cannot subsist without it."[68]

Improvisation here is not only a metaphor for the wandering, day-to-day existence of the gypsies, but also for an intensity of expression and direct transmission of feeling absent from music produced through mediation and reflection. The music is strong and vital because it is "so eminently inspired, so little dominated by the laws of reflection or constraint, so spontaneous, and until recently so inseparable from improvisation."[69] In gypsy performances there is furthermore no conflict between the player's authenticity of expression and the formation of communal bonds. It is true that the lead instrumentalist "becomes indifferent to everything that in the moment could contradict or block his full absorption in the art that he creates for himself . . . [and] ends up forgetting that he has an audience."[70] But this solitary absorption, rather than hindering communication, concentrates the music's expressive force and draws in the audience irresistibly:

> He who is called to transmit his feeling to his public and his listeners, without preparation and without any meditation, in its initial flight and in the first form that comes upon him, must be inspired by the most spontaneous and most personal impulses, so that this feeling will attract sympathy and gather around him a naively attentive crowd.[71]

The gypsy's improvisation is thus an ideal, perfectly communicative performance in which there are no unmet needs and no gaps of understanding. As an exotic, "other" mode of music-making, it overcomes the various forms of alienation endemic to Europe's modern concert culture.

However, gypsy music was only semi-exotic. It was heard all over Europe in cafes and public squares, existing on the margins of mainstream culture rather than in a purely alternative fantasy-land.[72] Indeed the fiddle and the cymbalom, its two most representative instruments, were a kind of mirror image of the most prestigious instruments of concert virtuosity, the violin and piano. The cultural proximity and exchange between Europeans and gypsies is an important element of Liszt's polemic. In recent times, he argues, contact between gypsy musicians and European publishers and arrangers has led to the notation of their music, and consequently, to a misrepresentation of the beauty of their orally transmitted tradition:

They even try to compose, which is to say notate their improvisations, hardly knowing how to treat their musical materials otherwise. . . . The infidelities of the publications made by this procedure have of necessity been excessively numerous. . . . It demonstrates a good intention, if you will, but evinces an ignorance of the secret of *gypsy art* since it deprives them of their wildest inspirations. Examining the *dead letter* of these improvisations, which you find everywhere you go in our country . . . one can hardly find an idea of the *brio* of the performance of gypsy virtuosos, of the incessant mutations of rhythm, of the burning eloquence of their musical phrasing and the expressive accent of their declamation.[73]

Liszt implies that in gypsy music the performance, because improvised, always exceeds what can be transcribed and notated. A true understanding of the people and of their music must acknowledge, and celebrate, the improvised character of their music.

Liszt's book was a philosophical companion to, and defense of, his *Hungarian Rhapsodies*, a collection of pieces intended to recover qualities of improvisatory vitality that had been fatally lost to notated music. These compositions are unquestionably closer in style and flow to actual Roma music than the music of previous composers. In other respects they are firmly ensconced in the literate concert music tradition. The motives are taken from printed sources, and their rhetorical language borrows much from Liszt's opera fantasies, though condensed to a smaller, miniaturized scale. Liszt seems to avow the connection to his own concert fantasies when he writes:

The true gypsy artist is he who takes a song or dance motive, like a text for commentary, like an epigraph of a poem, and who wanders around with and divagates upon this idea, which he never lets fall from view through an eternal improvisation. . . . [He] enriches his subject with a profusion of figures, appoggiaturas, tremolos, scales, arpeggios, diatonic and chromatic passages, and groups and *grupetti* of sound. . . . Nearly always these inventions of the moment have something surprising. They proceed in the most unexpected cadenzas, unanticipated fermatas, which upend the habits of our ears, but having no less powerful an effect for it.[74]

This reclamation of improvisation is nonetheless meant to explicate and defend Liszt's *compositions* and the right of the *composer* to break laws of composition in the name of folk authenticity. Its intent is to establish a climate of reception for the *Hungarian Rhapsodies* where the difference between improvisation and the compositional inscription thereof—improvisatoriness—will be forgotten, repressed, or fantasized away. If listeners, having read Liszt's book, could imagine a performing gypsy band when listening to a *Hungarian Rhapsody*, the improvisation imaginary would be doing its good work.

Liszt's book further tapped into the improvisation imaginary when arguing that the repertoire of Roma music constituted "the national epic of the bohemians."[75] Lacking a literary tradition that told the people of their history and of their national destiny, the gypsies allowed their musicians serve as a surrogate. The lead improviser reflected completely and transparently the soul of the people and his nation, channeling its deep sorrows and ecstatic joys in the characteristic alternation between *Lassan* and *Friska*. Gypsy musicians were thus assimilated to the figure of the epic bard or epic poet, a figure widely imagined as an improviser as he told traditional stories in a lively manner to attentive audiences in a ritual of intensive community. As seen in Chapter 3, this romantic ideal had informed Carl Loewe's project of reviving ballads and song improvisations. In the case of gypsies, the social collective did not need to be figured only as a listening or spectating body, for there was also a distribution of agency within the ensemble that made it a participatory form of collective improvisation:

> The cymbalom player shares with the first violin the right to develop certain passages, to prolong indefinitely certain variations at his momentary whim. He is a necessary partner in directing the musical poem, having created it at leisure or improvised it instantaneously; he imposes on the others the duty to surround him, to sustain him, even to divine his intention, in order to sing the same funereal hymn or give itself over to the same mad joy. One even sees from time to time a distinguished cello or a clarinet challenge him and claim for himself the prerogatives of unlimited improvisation.[76]

It is conspicuous that Liszt's celebration of gypsy improvisation was written after he had ceased playing piano recitals, after he had acquired a decent reputation as a symphonic composer, and at a historical moment when pianists had ceased to improvise almost entirely. The book portrays improvisation as a marvelous agent of artistic beauty and social cohesion, but does not convert this into a call for reviving the practice in "European" music. It strives rather to ensure that the music of the gypsies, the "other" music, is fully recognized in its improvisational richness. Rhetorically the book elevates improvisation to a very high level of aesthetic value, but the higher aesthetic value of composition seems to be taken for granted, and is never directly challenged. A similar ambivalence applies to the book's attitude toward the gypsies as a nation. It asks readers to recognize the much-maligned people as a noble, artistically rich nation, while denying them the reflective consciousness that would enable them to organize themselves and enter European society as social equals. Both musical improvisation and the gypsy people who embody its principle most authentically are stuck in a sort of pre-reflective state, full of potential but in need of redemption through a reflective agent that can only come from outside, and above.

The Improvising Interpreter

The post-1847 improvisation imaginary was increasingly populated by characters who were historical, social, and ethnic Others—troubadours, street entertainers, gypsies, shepherds, and the like. By virtue of this otherness, it seemed to define a fantasy space completely disjoined from the world of mainstream concert artists and their audiences. The fantasy of improvisation as a free-flowing, natural, unalienated mode of musical production, however, may have worked its deepest effect on perceptions of mainstream performers, for although such performers hardly ever improvised in public, writers started praising them for giving an *impression* they were improvising. As seen in the previous chapter, this aspect of the improvisation imaginary was well under way in the 1830s and 1840s, becoming particularly pronounced in the discourse around Chopin and Liszt. Liszt overtly sought to give an impression of improvisation even when he wasn't really doing it. It enabled him to claim a kind of artistic superiority to the banality of the "mechanical" virtuosos in the musical mainstream.

The virtuoso who carried the impression of improvisatoriness most powerfully in the second half of the century was violinist Joseph Joachim. As Karen Leistra-Jones has noted, "Joachim's relationship to his late-nineteenth century audiences and the fantasies and desires surrounding live performance that his performances activated in his listeners were . . . important in constructing an illusion of improvisation."[77] Leistra-Jones identifies a sort of unwritten contract between listeners and performers: everyone agreed to forget that the violinist was not literally improvising so that they could collectively reap the pleasures gained from imagining he *was* improvising. To call this an illusion is not to deny its efficacy, for it was unquestionably a productive illusion, intensifying listener response through a repression of what was actually happening. The illusion found effective expression in the finale of Joachim's "Hungarian" concerto, where he borrowed from the gypsy style. But it was arguably most potent in performances of his signature piece, Beethoven's Violin Concerto, where he played the role of master interpreter. The improvisation imaginary, then, allowed Joachim to be both "interpreter" and "improviser" at once, without any sense of contradiction. This had not been an option for the romantics of the previous generation. With discourses and practices of improvisation Liszt had marked himself as romantic outsider, retreating from convention and preserving poetry in the private social margin. For Joachim, however, the acquisition of improvisatoriness only cemented his position at the center of the culture of classical instrumental music, as the strongest exponent of "interpretation," masterpieces, and public concerts. This was only possible because improvisatoriness, as an aesthetic effect, was taking over the meaning of "improvisation." The illusion became so entrenched that it could even be summoned to characterize the orchestral conducting of Hans von Bülow in his painstaking dedication to the classics:

> We seem to have the score laid out before us; we see the compositional process at work, built up motive by motive before our very eyes—but the music does not disintegrate in Bülow's hands, no—and this is the remarkable thing—he fuses the whole thing together in a veritable act of genius. Each element succeeds the other with such inevitability that it leaves the impression of a spontaneous improvisation.[78]

As improvisation faded from practice, musicians and writers showed themselves increasingly willing to submit to the improvisation illusion. The memoirs of Goby

Eberhardt serve as an illustrative case, since in them the fantasy and reality of improvisation often comingle. Recalling the once well-known organist and pianist Theodor Kirchner, Eberhardt wrote: "everything he played appeared to be improvisations, as if they surfaced from his soul."[79] The phrase sounds romantic and hackneyed, but the impression was grounded in reality, since Kirchner was one of the few musicians who improvised publicly in the 1860s. It was a talent Kirchner had already shown at a young age. When he arrived in Leipzig in 1838 at age fifteen to study at the conservatory, Mendelssohn gave him a theme for improvisation and was impressed by "the abandon and the extraordinary skill with which the boy fulfilled his task."[80] As organist in Winterthur and Zürich, Kirchner played free fantasies that struck many observers as dilettantish or eccentric: "A quite insignificant improvisation transitioned into the A-minor prelude of Bach, which then dissolved back into improvising, into which the A-major *Song without Words* of Mendelssohn dripped like morning dew. That's what we call flirting with the classics!"[81] The AMZ reviewed an organ concert in Winterthur where Kirchner "improvised on themes from Schumann's *Faust* and Beethoven's Ninth Symphony. What is there to say when artists of such talent and knowledge as Kirchner lead themselves astray like this?" (AMZ 1863, 554) And in a reminiscence from the later 1860s, Eberhardt evoked Kirchner's long blond hair and blue eyes as he preluded before Schumann's piano quintet:

> Finally Kirchner appeared on the podium, gently bowed down from above to the assembled Frankfurt audience and placed himself in a relaxed position at the piano. Impatiently he took off his gloves and began to prelude. Sweet, perfumed chords, interlaced with motives from the quintet of Schumann, were heard as if from far beyond the hall. All of a sudden he closed with a short, questioning motive, turned his head toward his companions and gave the signal to begin. Now he was sitting transfigured at the piano, as though sunk in dreams, and played the quintet without a score as only he could play it.[82]

It is difficult to sort through what is real and what is fantasized in this description. Eberhardt is evidently describing an actual improvised prelude, but his description conspires to assimilate the entire performance to improvisation, as though Schumann's quintet itself "surfaced from his soul."

Eberhardt knew the difference between improvising and seeming to improvise. As noted earlier, he was capable of playing extemporaneously himself and held the improvising of Émile Sauret in especially high regard. These concrete experiences, however, did not keep him from forgetting the difference when he praised his teacher August Wilhelmi: "His playing was grand, noble, passionate, full of fantasy and life. 'He did not play pieces, he improvised them.'"[83] Improvisation is summoned here metaphorically to describe the ideal performance of a work, in which the performer is so fully absorbed that the work appears to be originating all over again. Eberhardt's conflation of improvisation and improvisatoriness further influenced his perspective on the popular Viennese pianist Alfred Grünfeld. In a general attack on the persistence of superficial virtuosity, he pointed to Grünfeld as a pianist from whom "he still heard fantasies on given themes, mainly from Wagner and Strauss."[84] This attack is confused, since Grünfeld's supposedly improvised fantasies on Wagner and Strauss were not based on "given themes." Eberhardt probably heard the later, pseudo-improvising Grünfeld, who played concert fantasies imitating the style of improvisations. Eberhardt's confusion evinces not a weak mind but the deep influence of the improvisation imaginary, where improvisatoriness, as an aesthetic effect, is mistaken for the real thing.

Organ Fantasies

Literary works about improvising organists enriched the field of representations with fantasies of grandeur and power whose tone is quite different from the discourses surrounding violinists, singers, and pianists. In these stories improvisation has nothing to do with a "public" scene including performer and audience, but with the lone organist's sense of exaltation and transcendence when playing the otherworldly instrument. The indefatigable George Sand published in 1873 a *conte fantastique*, "The Organ of the Titan," that opens with an improvisation at the piano by Master Angelin. As soon as he begins to improvise he shudders with anxiety and shouts out "go away, Titan!" to the bafflement of his pupil. Master Angelin's fear is rooted in a traumatic and transfiguring experience from his childhood, taking place "at the beginning of the century," when he was studying music under the eccentric organist and teacher Jean. On a long walk Jean has led Angelin to a wild, rocky landscape. Upon discovering a natural formation resembling an organ, he asks Angelin to play a composition, an Introit, on the "instrument." At first Angelin is totally baffled by the request, but soon he is infected by his teacher's fantasy and begins to hallucinate: "In proportion as my hands became those of a Titan, the organ melody that I thought I heard acquired a frightful power."[85] Jean reprimands him for not playing the requested Introit, but Angelin continues to improvise on the "strange, sublime or stupid motive that raged through my brain."[86] The fantasy comes to an end when the rock formation, pushed to the limits of vibration, collapses and leaves both teacher and student with bloody wounds. At the end of this fantastical experience instigated by his mentor, Angelin has come into his own as an artist. He has channeled the creative potency of nature and improvised into existence a brand-new kind of music, quite unlike the traditional sacred music of his teacher. Sand's allegory is strongly reminiscent of the story Léon Kreutzer told in 1853 about the organ classes of J. G. Vogler discussed at the opening of this book. In Kreutzer's romantically tinged narrative, the dual improvisations of Vogler and his students Weber and Meyerbeer had mediated a productive exchange between the older kapellmeister dispensation ca. 1800 and the more adventurous musical orientation of his students.

Vogler himself entered into the improvisation imaginary in 1864 when Robert Browning, a connoisseur of music history, wrote his poem "Abt Vogler (After He Has Been Extemporizing Upon the Musical Instrument of His Invention)." The poem is cast as a dramatic monologue, a vast and obscure metaphysical mediation on the

polarities of heaven and earth, life and death. It is at the same time an attempt to imagine Vogler's experience improvising on the organ. As in Sand's story, improvisation
is a vehicle of drastic self-expansion and transcendent elation, even as it originates in
immanent physical contact between player and instrument:

> All through my keys that gave their sounds to a wish of my soul,
> All through my soul that praised as its wish flowed visibly forth,
> All through Music and me!

The sensation of elemental power that Vogler sustains throughout, like Angelin's exaltation while "playing" the stone organ, cannot last forever. It must eventually return
to sober, mundane reality. Improvisation offers him a fulfillment so complete and intense that he can only return to everyday reality with a sense of loss. Nevertheless,
after descending from his fantastical flight Vogler is able to find a sort of reconciliation by putting his hands on the keys one last time. He moves his fingers around to
neighbor-notes, discovers an expressive phrase in a digression through the minor, and
finally expires in a satisfying, perfect resolution:

> Well, it is earth with me; silence resumes her reign:
> I will be patient and proud, and soberly acquiesce.
> Give me the keys. I feel for the common chord again,
> Sliding my semitones till I sink to the minor, yes,
> And I blunt it into a ninth, and I stand on alien ground,
> Surveying awhile the heights I rolled from into the deep;
> Which, hark, I have dared and done, for my resting place is found,
> The C Major of this life; so, now I will try to sleep.

At the beginning of this book we saw Vogler improvising at the organ and piano for
his admiring students Weber, Meyerbeer, and Gänsbacher, and instructing them in the
rules of musical creation through improvisational exercises. In those lessons Vogler
was transmitting a living tradition of free playing that followed the imperatives of the
eighteenth century's kapellmeister regime, which called for a combination of compositional, instrumental, and theoretical skills, and did not strongly mark "improvisation"
as a separate, special form of music-making. Half a century later, Browning's poem
converted Vogler into a cultural memory—the memory of a bygone era when an organist, alone at his instrument, could lose himself in deep improvisational reverie,
dissolving all ties to the mundane world and arriving on a plane of philosophical elevation. This "memory" was heavily inflected with romantic notions of aesthetic disjunction and subjective self-expansion, while also conserving traces of the historical Vogler
such his predilection for elevated style, his "handed" approach to modulation, and his
reputation as a superior improviser.

In the regime of the improvisation imaginary, improvisation was nearly always figured this way. It was a thing of the past, something lost, distant, or unattainable. It

belonged to an earlier, pre-capitalist era when musical communication was uncluttered by the commerce of sheet music, competing virtuosos, and mass urban audiences, or it belonged to "organic" folk cultures that were similarly unencumbered. It was somehow more whole, complete, or perfect than other kinds of music-making. In the later nineteenth century, an era we often view as content if not smug with its museum of musical "works," people kept remembering the improvisations of Mozart, Beethoven, Vogler, Hummel, Mendelssohn, and Liszt, as if the act of remembering could compensate for some irretrievable loss. Although concrete experiences of free playing had become rare, the representation of improvisation as a wholesome, desirable mode of music-making was never so strong.

NOTES

1. Kenneth Hamilton, *After the Golden Age: Romantic Pianism and Modern Performance* (Oxford: Oxford University Press, 2008), 101–38.

2. Wilhelm Kuhe, *My Musical Recollections* (London: Richard Bentley and Son, 1896), 140–41.

3. An unsigned article from *The Musical World* (31 December 1864, 836) entitled "Improvising" suggests that elementary improvisation was not rare among young amateurs, even without the encouragement of their teachers. "Many a young pianist, or would-be pianist without labor and without price, has a certain trick of 'improvising,' which he mistakes for talent. . . . We know the astonishing effects which these so-called improvisers obtain, and which mostly consists in giving the melody to the left hand, and letting the right hand rattle over the keys in Arpeggio Passages or Chromatic Runs." As the mocking tone suggests, this author was against improvisation: "Five finger Exercises will make you a better performer than all your improvisations." Philosopher Adolphe Kullak, in his book about the aesthetics of piano playing, argued that piano improvisation engaged the "physical-anatomical" aspect of artistic production in disproportional relation to the mental aspect. In this respect, he continued, improvisation opened itself to the realm of amateurism or "dilettantism" more readily than the interpretation of works. Instead of dismissing amateur improvisation, though, Kullak argued that this less strenuous kind of playing "has its own justification," as it offers an "intimation of the beautiful." Adolph Kullak, *Die Aesthetik des Klavierspiels* (Berlin: Guttentag, 1861), 22.

4. Michael Caesar, "Poetic Improvisation in the Nineteenth Century: Giuseppe Regaldi and Giannina Milli," *Modern Language Review* 101 (2006): 701–14.

5. L. Granzin, "Das heutige Virtuosenthum in seiner Wirkung auf den Dilettantismus," *Neue Berliner musikalische Zeitung* 1/21 and 1/22 (1847), 177–80 and 185–88.

6. This initiative peaked in 1844 when the German organ virtuoso Adolphe Hesse played a series of highly acclaimed concerts in the French capital. See Hans-Jürgen Seyfried, *Adolph Friedrich Hesse als Orgelvirtuose und Orgelcomponist* (Regensburg: Gustav Bosse Verlag, 1965). Although Hesse was an accomplished improviser, his Paris concerts of 1844 were focused exclusively on German repertoire.

7. *La France théâtrale*, for example, reported that he improvised on "La Feuille et le serment," a *romance* that had just been sung by its composer Léopold Amat (27 April 1845, 3). A few weeks earlier the same journal reported that he improvised on a motive from the vaudeville tune "Il est un petit homme" (16 March 1845, 4).

8. Malou Haine, "La Participation des facteurs d'instruments de musique aux expositions nationales de 1834 et 1839," in *Music in Paris in the 1830s*, ed. Peter Blume (Stuyvesant, NY: Pendragon Press, 1987), 365–86.

9. Fanny Gribenski, "L'Église comme lieu de concert: pratiques musicales et usages de l'espace ecclésial dans les paroisses parisiennes (1830–1905)," PhD diss., École des hautes études en sciences sociales, Paris, 2015.

10. See the images at the end of H. Pape, *Notice sur les inventions et les perfectionnements de H. Pape* (Paris: Maulde et Renou, 1845, n.p. [55–58]).

11. *Ménestrel*, 16 March 1845, emphasis original; RGMP 1847, 43.

12. On Blanchard's aesthetic orientation see Katharine Ellis, *Music Criticism in Nineteenth-Century France: La Revue et gazette musicale de Paris, 1834–80* (Cambridge: Cambridge University Press, 1995), 161–63.

13. M. A. Panseron, *Traité de l'harmonie pratique et des modulations, à l'usage des pianistes* (Paris: Brandus, 1855).

14. Ibid., preface (n.p.).

15. Ibid., 130, emphasis original.

16. Ibid., 144.

17. Ibid., 197.

18. Had there been a demand for such a work by Kalkbrenner, it would probably have been printed earlier. In the preface listing the illustrious line of theorists from whom the treatise is descended, the most recent work is Fétis' *La Musique mise au portée du monde*, first published in 1830; and Kalkbrenner's only other pedagogical work was published in 1831. Conceptually his recommendations fall completely in line with older harmony treatises, the principal difference being that the examples are fleshed out in the *stile brillante* and are clearly intended for advanced pianists.

19. See Dana Gooley, "Violin Improvisation in the Early Nineteenth Century: Between Practice and Illusion," in *Exploring Virtuosities: Heinrich Wilhelm Ernst, Nineteenth-Century Musical Practices and Beyond*, ed. Christine Hoppe, Mai Kawabata, and Melanie von Goldbeck (Hildesheim: Olms, 2018), 109–21.

20. Panseron, *Traité de l'harmonie pratique*, 130.

21. Goby Eberhardt, *Erinnerungen an bedeutende Männer unserer Epoche* (Lübeck: Otto Quitzow-Verlag, 1926), 67.

22. Quoted from De Bériot's treatise in Renato Ricci, "Charles-Auguste de Bériot e l'improvvisazione virtuosistica per violino," in *Beyond Notes: Improvisation in Western Music of the Eighteenth and Nineteenth Centuries*, ed. Rudolf Rasch (Lucca: Brepols, 2011), 220.

23. Leonard Phillips, "The Leipzig Conservatory: 1843–1881," PhD diss., Indiana University, 1979, 134–40.

24. Eberhardt, *Erinnerungen*, 35.

25. W. S. Rockstro, *Mendelssohn* (London: Sampson, Low, Marston & Co., n.d.), 111–12.

26. On Robert Franz's goals for editing baroque compositions see his *Offener Brief an Eduard Hanslick über Bearbeitungen älterer Tonwerke* (Leipzig: Leuckart, 1871).

27. Felix Draeseke, *Anweisung zum kunstgerechten Modulieren* (Freienwalde: Verlag Ferd. Draeseke, 1876), 4–5.

28. Ibid., 105–15.

29. David Cannata, "Adele aus der Ohe (Tchaïkovksy & Rachmaninoff)," *Quaderni del Istituto Liszt* 10 (2011), 93.

30. Johann Nepomuk Dunkl, *Aus den Erinnerungen eines Musikers* (Vienna: Rosner, 1876), 55.

31. *Morning Post*, 20 March 1871; see also *The Standard* [London], 27 March, 1871.

32. *Life and Letters of Sir Charles Hallé*, ed. C. E. Hallé and Marie Hallé (London: Smith, Elder & Co., 1896), 54–55.

33. Ibid., 55.

34. Henri Herz, *Mes voyages en Amérique* (Paris: Achille Faure, 1866), 170.

35. Laure Schnapper, *Henri Herz: Magnat du piano* (Paris: Editions HESS, 2011), 146.

36. Herz, *Mes voyages en Amérique*, 170–72.

37. Ibid., 181–82.

38. Adolph Kullak, *Die Aesthetik des Klavierspiels*, 20–22.

39. Edward Dent: *Ferruccio Busoni: A Biography* (Oxford: Clarendon, 1933), 20–41.

40. Ferruccio Busoni, *Three Classics in the Aesthetics of Music* (New York: Dover, 1962), 84.

41. Gottfried Galston, *Kalendernotizen über Ferruccio Busoni* (Wilhelmshaven: Noetzel, 2000), 117. These notes are all from Busoni's classes of the period 1921–1925.

42. Abbé Lamazou, *Biographie de Lefébure-Wély* (Paris: E. Repos, 1863), 22.

43. Ibid., 16.

44. Ibid.

45. The organ historian Kurt Lueders writes that "under the second empire improvisation at the organ is led by Lefébure-Wely, Cavallo and Batiste and Vilbac" and calls them "interprètes-improvisateurs." See Lueders, "Alexandre Guilmant (1837–1911): Organiste et compositeur" (PhD diss., University of Paris [Sorbonne], 2002), 367–76.

46. Archives Nationales, F12 3487, dossier 8. Timings of the 7 August 1878 concert.

47. Jacques Trézel, "Les concerts d'orgue de M. Guilmant," *Moniteur universel*, 23–24 May 1884, 567. This is a review of the Trocadéro concert of 22 May 1884.

48. Quoted in G. Fauré, *Homage à Eugène Gigout* (Paris: H. Floury, 1923), 25n.

49. Charles-Augustin Collin, "Eugène Gigout, sa carrière, son oeuvre," *La Musique sacrée* 25, no. 5–6 (1926), 18–19.

50. J. Lemmens, *Ecole d'orgue*, ed. Eugène Gigout (Paris: Durand, 1920), ii.

51. Ibid., n.p. (introduction).

52. Erwin Horn, "Zwischen Interpretation und Improvisation: Anton Bruckner als Organist," in *Bruckner-Symposion: Zum Schaffensprozess in den Kunsten* (Linz: Musikwissenschaftlicher Verlag, 1997), 121.

53. Erwin Horn, "Anton Bruckner—Genie an der Orgel," in *Bruckner-Jahrbuch 1994/95/96* (Linz: Musikwissenschaftlicher Verlag, 1997), 217.

54. Quoted in Horn, "Zwischen Interpretation und Improvisation," 127.

55. Erwin Horn, "Anton Bruckner—Genie an der Orgel," 218–19.

56. Edgar Landgraf points out that "it is not only the layperson that may have difficulties clearly delineating improvised from non-improvised doings; experts and even performers themselves often note how they cannot determine with certainty how much of an improvisation was indeed improvised and how much was planned and repeated." Edgar Landgraf, *Improvisation as Art: Conceptual Challenges, Historical Perspectives* (New York: Bloomsbury, 2011), 24.

57. Richard Wagner, "Über die Bestimmung der Oper," in *Richard Wagners gesammelte Schriften*, ed. Julius Kapp, 14 vols. (Leipzig: Hesse & Becker [1914]), 9:142.

58. Ibid., 142.

59. Carl Czerny, *Erinnerungen aus meinem Leben* (Baden-Baden: Heitz, 1968 [1842]), 37.

60. Wagner, "Über die Bestimmung der Oper," 143.

61. Henry Chorley, *Modern German Music*, 3 vols. (London: Smith, Elder & Co., 1854), 2:8–9.

62. Wagner, "Über die Bestimmung der Oper," 149.

63. Ibid., 150. This was another point he is likely to have taken from Czerny, who had written: "no matter what company he found himself in, he understood how to make an effect on every listener" (Czerny, *Erinnerungen*, 45.)

64. Eugène de Pradel, *Lettre à l'Académie Française, à l'occasion de la lutte littéraire* (Paris: Vinchon, 1836), 7–8. As mentioned in Chapter 2, a writer for the *Musical World* claimed: "the improvisator, like his predecessors the Troubadours, is accustomed to deliver his thoughts to an instrumental accompaniment" (*Musical World* 1837, 154).

65. Wagner, "Über die Bestimmung der Oper," 143.

66. H. M. G. Grellmann, *Historischer Versuch über die Zigeuner* (Göttingen: J. C. Dieterich, 1787), 153.

67. For literary context on this book see Jonathan Bellman, *The* style hongroise *in the Music of Western Europe* (Boston: Northeastern University Press, 1993), 69–92.

68. Franz Liszt, *Des Bohémiens et de leur musique en Hongrie*, 2nd ed. (Leipzig: Breitkopf und Härtel, 1881), 379. Italics original.

69. Ibid., 403.

70. Ibid., 380.

71. Ibid., 379.

72. On this point see Shay Loya, *Liszt's Transcultural Modernism and the Hungarian-Gypsy Tradition* (Rochester, NY: University of Rochester Press, 2011), 66–85.

73. Liszt, *Des Bohémiens*, 386. Italics original.

74. Ibid., 404–5.

75. Ibid., 12.

76. Ibid., 370.

77. Karen Leistra-Jones, "Improvisational Idyll: Joachim's 'Presence' in Brahms's Violin Concerto, Op. 77," *19th Century Music* 38, no. 3 (2015), 250.

78. Quoted from *Musikalisches Wochenblatt*, 21 February 1884, in Kenneth Birkin, *Hans von Bülow: A Life for Music* (Cambridge: Cambridge University Press, 2011), 308.

79. Quoted in Reinhold Sietz, *Theodor Kirchner: Ein Klaviermeister der deutschen Romantik* (Regensburg: Gustav Bosse, 1971), 72.

80. Ibid., 18.

81. Ibid., 72.

82. Eberhardt, *Erinnerungen*, 217.

83. Ibid., 14. The intention of the quotation marks is not clear.

84. Ibid., 237.

85. *Oeuvres complètes de George Sand: Contes d'une grand-mère* (Paris: Calmann Lévy, 1896), 171.

86. Ibid., 172. On the organ in romantic literature see Jean-Michel Bailbé, "l'Orgue dans l'imaginaire romantique," *Etudes Normandes* no. 2 (1983): 65–73.

Postlude

IMPROVISATION AND UTOPIA

THE FOREGOING CHAPTERS about free playing and discourses of improvisation could leave the impression that improvisation was "everywhere," or at least common and familiar, in European music of the nineteenth century. It was not. One can read through hundreds of pages of musical periodicals reporting on symphonic music, amateur choirs, domestic parlor music, concert virtuosos, opera, and oratorios without discovering a single mention of an improvisation. In the one sphere where free playing was actually standard—the world of liturgical organists—it was barely recognized as improvisation and was described simply as "organ-playing" or "accompaniment."[1] Elsewhere, in the worlds of pianism, singing, and violin playing, it was probably encountered from time to time, but not especially often. As stated in the introduction, improvisation was distributed through the various subspheres of music unevenly, in a patchy way, rather than in continuous fields. It was called into being more by individual inclination and initiative than by convention or demand. Even within the kapellmeister network it was not obligatory or universal.

My main argument has not been that improvisation was more common than previously realized—though I hope some readers have discovered this as well—but that in those places and circumstances where it survived it was intensely valued by producers, critics, and listeners. The fact that improvisational practices met with strong, vehement criticism only proves that it was recognized as a significant phenomenon carrying a certain prestige or value. This conclusion runs contrary to a widespread view that

European music of the nineteenth century organized itself around a hegemonic system of values—epitomized by the normative concept of the musical "work"—that was fundamentally inimical to improvisation. As Wagner's 1871 essay on music drama shows most explicitly, the philosophy of the work could positively embrace improvisation as an essential, indispensable component of what made art-works vital and powerful. The most celebrated performances of Beethoven's Violin Concerto were those of Joseph Joachim, and they were admired *because* he seemed to be improvising it. In the philosophy of the work improvisation was subordinated—conceptually and aesthetically—to a "higher" principle, but it was not denigrated or devalued as something completely contrary to its essence.

The decline of improvisation as a living practice in European concert music was not the result of a deep philosophical incompatibility between the work idea and the idea of improvisation. The deep incompatibility lay, rather, between the communicative logic of improvisational performance and the demands of communication in the public sphere—the latter acquiring unprecedented regulative power in the nineteenth century. Serious critical opposition to musical improvisation first emerged in tandem with the emergence of a musical public sphere of commercially organized concerts in the decade after the Congress of Vienna. These larger, socially heterogeneous events were regulated by a demand for efficacious, "successful" communication that improvisations were less likely to fulfill than performances of pieces. They also constituted the audience as a body in critical judgment, capable of deciding whether a performance was "good" or "bad"—a situation that called for common, shared norms that improvisation could not reliably provide.

It is easier to see the negative, juridical side of these two regulative ideas—efficacious communication and shared standards of evaluation—than it is to recognize their positive, productive motivations. The demands of public-sphere communication were intended to suspend the operation of class differences and educational differences in a socially heterogeneous concert context, and to intensify genuine participation by making every person an independent, capable "judge." Their impetus was in this sense entirely democratic if not emancipatory. When an improviser like Hummel succeeded in meeting the demand, it was celebrated as the highest possible musical and social achievement. An event in which popular melodies, loved and appreciated by everyone as a sort of common property, are given to an artist by an audience and turned by the artist into new music—where melodies are recognized but imaginatively transformed in an unfamiliar, "fantasy" space, a space inhabited by both the artist and the listeners—is an event full of emancipatory meaning. For as Jacques Rancière has written, emancipation "is not the transmission of the artist's knowledge or inspiration to the spectator. It is the 'third thing' that is owned by no one, whose meaning is owned by no one, but which subsists between them, excluding any uniform transmission, any identity of cause and effect."[2]

But Hummel, everyone knew, was an exception. At public concerts an average free fantasy was more likely to fall flat than a performance of a set of brilliant variations. Making free improvisation thrive in the public sphere would remain an uphill battle. It persisted and thrived in areas of musical culture most insulated from the public sphere and its communicative demands: mainly the sphere of church organ playing, but also in the spheres of amateur and private music-making. The discourse of critical improvisation studies (CSI) has given relatively little attention to questions of public communication, aesthetic judgment, and the division between professional improvisers and lay audiences implicit in any concert scenario.[3] It tends to valorize the professional formation of the self-sustaining, self-sufficient artist's collective, a formation that consciously breaks away from the public sphere and derives political strength and solidarity from that gesture. In artist collectives the audience are the players and the players are the audience—or are at least imagined that way—and there is no need whatsoever to communicate beyond the circle. This spirited strength-in-narrowness, and the associated indifference to public communication, has always been good for the health of improvisation. It was present in the school of Vogler, in the circles of French romanticism where Liszt and Chopin thrived, and in the organ guild where players impressed one another with complex improvised fugues (and still do).

CSI's commitment to the power and dignity of elite, closed musical formations, however, sits uneasily with its most emphatic claim: that improvisational practices naturally—by sheer virtue of being improvisational—invite democratic participation and model more desirable social arrangements. The kinds of collective engagement and participation that give strength to artist collectives, CSI argues, could be socially transformative if they were made the model for social and political action in the world at large—indeed the public world. The drive to make improvisation relevant on a "public" scale does not seem sufficiently attentive to the potential of improvisation to fail to communicate, especially to highly heterogeneous audiences. The consequences of a freely improvised performance that does not "succeed" may not seem significant to performers—who are aware of, and accept, the risk—but they can be significant for a public audience that has invested in them affectively. In nineteenth-century Europe, the solution was to keep the idea of improvisatoriness alive while playing written pieces whose prospects for successful communication were more secure.

I have argued here that the values surrounding improvisation in the nineteenth century harbored positive visions of society and community, even though free playing normally took a soloistic form. Improvisation powerfully bonded musicians of the professional class to each other in the manner of a club or a guild, since its complexities were best appreciated by highly informed listeners. The school of Vogler is an early example, and the duo improvisations of violinists Émile Sauret and Goby Eberhardt a later example. The improvised duos that Moscheles, Hiller, and Mendelssohn played together, trading phrases and picking up where the other left off, were pleasurable and playful exercises held together in a unified "language" while allowing for quite divergent and digressive articulations from the individuals. This intra-artistic bonding was blended with sentiments of friendship and intimacy that all three musicians cultivated among themselves beyond their professional musical activities. The free fantasies of Hummel and Moscheles were socially invested insofar as they seemed to bridge the greatest axis of social difference in musical life of the time the gap between connoisseurs and amateurs. And the romantic circle—Liszt, Chopin, de Musset, Sand, and Delacroix—leaned on the analogy between improvised sociality, as manifested in their free bohemian lifestyle, and artistic improvisation, as manifest in the performances of the musicians, poets, and painters in the circle. Among them this enchanted, improvisatory aura was politically invested—a living critique of the banality of bourgeois society and the spiritless materialism of the post-1830 *juste milieu*.

The strongest investment, perhaps, that nineteenth-century musicians and listeners made in improvisation was more ethical than it was social and political. Starting with Germaine de Staël and the romantic cult of Corinne, improvisation was viewed as an emblem of an elevated or "higher" freedom. It became the object of intense fantasies, desires, and longings, as if it could somehow lead to a better world free of alienation and conflict. Under the influence of these ideas, musical improvisation was imagined as a perfect performance, or perfect music *tout court*. Characteristic of the romantic perspective is the idea that improvisational spontaneity and novelty originate in a mysterious, external agent that visits or inhabits the artist's fantasy. As Edgar Landgraf has put it: "German Romantic theory no longer anchors artistic creativity in the special abilities of the artist, but rather attempts to understand the fashioning of art as autopoietic."[4] We have encountered many examples of this autopoietic myth: the story of how Carl Loewe improvised "Wallhaide" in the forest, the image of Liszt overtaken by demonic forces while improvisation, and George Sand's narrative about Master Angelin, who invents new music by "playing" the massive rocks of a sublime landscape as though they were an organ. Romantic autopoiesis asserted that there was a source of generation and creation "outside" or "beyond" the human, so that we might not be trapped in the finite limits of our material and cognitive worlds. This was the utopian promise of improvisation. As the improvisation imaginary accrued more and more characters and figurations in the nineteenth century—troubadours, gypsies, shepherds, saltimbanques, etc.—most of them took on the appearance of unalienated, effortless producers, integrated with nature and with their communities.

In its utopian element—which is at once optimistic and socially critical—the discourse of CSI works in the tracks of this nineteenth-century concept of improvisation. Many of its concerns emerge from the specific history and experience of African-American artists, and its arguments are keyed to a contemporary climate characterized by ethnic pluralism and neoliberal regimes that little resemble the nineteenth century. But the idea that improvisation harbors a potential to bring something novel and something better into the world—that it can model reform or revolution in ethics, politics, and society—has been around a long time. A utopian vision of this kind lurked in the background of Ernst Ferand's *Die Improvisation in der Musik*, a monumental work and one of the only full-length historical studies of improvisation. A closer look at Ferand's perspective, which assessed improvisation in "nine centuries" of western music, will help put the nineteenth-century situation in broader perspective. The 1938 date of Ferand's book—lying roughly between the nineteenth century and the era of modern jazz—makes it a suitable vehicle for understanding the long-term continuity of utopian longings articulated around improvised music.

The specifically historical aspects of Ferand's book have little bearing on the nineteenth century. Drawing on a "developmental" model of history and covering fully nine centuries of music, he suggested that European improvisational practices peaked in the vocal and instrumental polyphony of the fifteenth and sixteenth centuries. Ferand proposed that the moment pedagogues printed exemplary models of extemporaneous elaboration in significant numbers—namely, in the early seventeenth century— musicians no longer relied on attentive listening and memory to guide their music-making, and the impulse to improvise began to abate. The rise of monophony and of figured bass further constrained improvised elaboration, delegating extemporaneous invention to the soprano voice (whether instrumental or vocal) or to the smaller sphere of the continuo group. The practice of improvisation, in Ferand's narrative, narrowed still further in the eighteenth century with the rise of *galant* texture, slowly confining improvisation to the limited sphere of the keyboardist playing preludes and free fantasias. In the nineteenth century nothing was left but the dying embers of a once-thriving tradition.

It is easy to detect in Ferand's narrative the influence of early German-language musicology, which accorded a certain special honor to the Renaissance and to those aspects of baroque music most clearly descended from polyphonic traditions. He located the "drive to improvise" (*Improvisationstrieb*) in devotional singing practices of the early middle ages, where florid singing expresses the pleasurable *gaudeam* of religious ecstasy. Polyphony of the high middle ages and the Renaissance, from this perspective, represented a communal, multi-voiced expansion of this religious inspiration. Such freely expressed joy, in Ferand's narrative, went into decline with the emancipation of instrumental and vocal music from the regulation of church institutions—an emancipation that cut improvisation off from its religious motivation and resituated it in the domain of human artifice, individual agency, and instrumental mechanism. As music expanded its secular presence, a certain natural dignity of improvisation was lost: "This spontaneous musical manner of expression was observable at its purest at the beginning of its development."[5] Here Ferand reiterates a valorization of Renaissance polyphony that, as James Garratt has shown, extended back to romantic authors of the early nineteenth century.[6]

But unlike those romantic authors, who celebrated Renaissance polyphony for its ethereal, disembodied aura, Ferand imagined the music in terms of performing bodies and voices, and this seems to be more forward-looking. He did not think of vocal polyphony in the *res facta* of the written score, but in the performing ensemble's freewheeling embellishment of those notes. By focusing on improvisation he wanted to restore our understanding of music to its living practice and to social, communal action. His historical perspective was thus shaped by an idealized vision of improvisation as the uninhibited, "natural" expression of individuals engaged in coordinated social practice, geared toward the establishment of harmonious community. This vision is not as different from that of CSI as it might initially appear. Although CSI often promotes what it calls "dissonant" or "discrepant" engagement, and interprets improvisation in pluralistic social contexts where sharp differences of social position must be mediated, it unequivocally overrides these tensions and conflicts with a rhetoric of mutual understanding, sensitive listening, and social harmony achieved by the accommodation and reconciliation of social differences.[7] Both Ferand and authors in CSI idealize improvisation, presenting it as the embodiment of some unsullied ethical virtue—in Ferand's case, humanistically informed notion of the "good" as human fulfillment; in the case of CSI, a politically utopian construction of the "good" as the active, participatory making of one's world.

Although Ferand's positive view of improvisation had its roots in academic humanism, his passion for it was not purely contemplative. In the two decades before he published his *summa* he was teaching at the Hellerau-Laxenburg School near Vienna, attempting to put the ideas of Jacques-Dalcroze into action. Early in the century Dalcroze, who had taught harmony and ear-training in the 1890s in Geneva, developed a method of unifying music and movement by having students practice semi-automatic physical responses to improvised music. One goal was to develop a more wholesome, organic musicianship that united bodily movement and gesture with musical sound by tapping into their common underlying foundation in rhythm. Dalcroze was summoned to create his school by idealistic reformers of the Deutsche Werkbund who, anticipating the Bauhaus, sought to combat the alienation and anomie that had entered the life of laborers under industrialization. The commune in Hellerau was intended to "produce a synthesis of work, life in nature, and art, and lead to a renovation of social life."[8] Dalcroze's curriculum stressed the ability of students not only to recognize or reproduce musical patterns but also to produce their own. In a 1914 prospectus he listed "Improvisation (development of imagination)" as one of the many tasks, and the school offered regular classes for keyboard improvisation as well as group exercises.[9]

In 1914 Ferand became the main person in charge of the music curriculum. During the 1920s he drew on the latest innovations in psychological research, including Gestalt Theory and the intuitionist musical theories of Ernst Kurth, and advocated for the irreducible pedagogical benefits of extemporaneous music-making. Improvisation could reconnect performers, especially those who normally considered themselves "reproducers," to the primal source of musical creativity and invention. It stimulated a rare psychological feedback loop between player and musical discourse: "It is one of the most appealing characteristics of improvisation that apparently unforeseen accidents or lapses influence the development of the ideas and give fresh impetus to the imagination of the player"; in this way it became "an indispensable chain-link between productive and reproductive music-making."[10] Ferand was also attentive to the juncture between physical reflex—developed by instrumental habits—and inventive impulse in the heat of improvisational music-making:

On the path of artistic inspiration (ultimately not analyzable because rooted in the deepest depths of the unconscious)—through its shaping and forming of musical thoughts that are still completing themselves in the mind, through its linear and vertical organization and its temporally controlled transmission on an instrument, achieved through steady contact with the instrument—on this tangled path there is a vast field of possibilities for all manner of obstacles of a purely physical or psychological or even psycho-physical nature, which can place themselves in the way of an unimpeded flow. But it is precisely the overcoming of such limitations and obstacles that constitutes the value—we might call it "ethical," or as one wishes, educational—of the improvisational achievement.[11]

In these framing ideas of Ferand's study and in the idealistic intentions of Dalcroze, we find clear adumbrations of themes that have guided the recent revival of improvisation in pedagogy and scholarship. The notion that improvisation represents a kind of embodied cognition or "corporeal thinking"—thereby bypassing a mind-body dualism that is as artistically unproductive as it is philosophically suspect—has proven most appealing. Whether argued from the perspective of western philosophy or from that of cognitive science, these studies tend to invest improvisation with a special, exceptional virtue. They understand it as a musical practice more aligned with the "natural" embeddedness of the mind in the body—a practice more organic or more whole because it does not start from the false Cartesian duality of mind and body.[12] Ferand's pedagogical mission, for its part, is being perpetuated by some of the programs of CSI, which bring children and laypersons together with professional musicians to carry out exercises in free group improvisation. A combination of educational and social benefits is also attributed to improvisation in the collection *Musical Improvisation: Art, Education, and Society*, whose major areas include not only "improvisation and the creative process" and "improvisation in social and political processes," but also "improvisation in the educational process," with seven essays devoted to the latter area.[13]

   The idea that improvisation can reform music education by restoring active engagement goes back further than Ferand. In the early nineteenth century, the rise of educational philosophies stressing the gradual development of a well-rounded, generally cultivated person (*gebildeter Mensch*) kept this ideal alive under a different regime of value. In 1802 A. E. M. Grétry published a treatise on keyboard improvisation in which he regretted the recent disappearance of improvisation from music pedagogy: "Why is it not taught! Why are so many people strong in the execution of sonatas while knowing so little about how to improvise [*préluder*] with knowledge of the [harmonic] rules!"[14] In a short space Grétry takes the student progressively from very basic triadic harmony all the way through to advanced fugal and enharmonic improvisations. He explicitly intends the treatise to simplify and democratize a practice that, through its association with *maîtres de chapelle*, had acquired the appearance of something esoteric, specialized, or inaccessible. Any fifteen-year-old girl, he claims, can get through his method in a mere three months of steady application. Grétry was not, however, so democratic as to permit a completely intuitive approach to improvisation. He was wedded enough to eighteenth-century ideals of theoretically grounded practice as to demand that the student improvise with knowledge of the harmonic rules. An echo of Grétry's pedagogical concerns is found in Kalkbrenner's treatise on harmony and improvisation, published at some point in the 1840s but possibly written earlier:

> There is a vice in the manner of teaching composition that makes the student learn all the chords and their inversions without knowing how to employ them. . . . How many of our best pianists can produce even a minimally satisfying prelude? And among our students there is not one in a thousand who, in his improvisations, tries to go beyond the perfect cadence. We thus thought that this volume, offered here to conscientious amateurs, would serve art by lifting a corner of the veil that conceals the technical aspect of music and makes it almost incomprehensible to those who are not deeply initiated into it.[15]

For Kalkbrenner, as for Grétry and others, the teaching of improvisation would have a meliorative effect on composition and performance, and on the teaching of those subjects, by resisting overspecialization and shaping a more complete musician. Improvisation had a new role to play as an antithetical critique of what modern musical culture had become.

With the exception of Bruno Nettl's pioneering "Thoughts on Improvisation," which took a resolutely neutral tone, most authors supporting the teaching and practice of improvisation have shared an ethically affirmative vision of it. In various ways and with different degrees of explicitness, they suggest that improvisation is good for music, good for people, and good for the world. More often than not, its virtuousness resides in its marginal status—its antithetical relation to what is aesthetically, culturally, or politically dominant. As a strategy for educational reform, improvisation promises to give classical musicians some of the play, creative engagement, and inventive freedom they have lost due to a traditional overemphasis on instrumental technique, discipline, and fidelity to the score. In its strongest and most idealistic form, represented by CSI, it is nothing less than a refuge for many types of positive and aspirational behavior—democratic participation, intersubjective understanding, community building, recognition of others and cultural differences—that are under threat by dominant political and economic regimes. It is in the nineteenth century that improvisation began acquiring such meanings. Amid the growing authority of "works" and composers, of orchestral and choral institutions, of scores and other musical commodities, improvisation acquired the potential to signify a freedom that was difficult to find elsewhere. This utopian vision of improvisation emerged in the wake of, and in response to, a declining practice. Indeed Ferand, though heavily influenced by contemporary thinkers, carried forward this earlier utopian vision in his writing on the subject. As he put it toward the end of his magnum opus, "the satisfaction a person finds in the simultaneity of idea and realization is at the same time a piece of a lost art-paradise."[16]

NOTES

1. The question whether improvisation needs to be recognized as improvisation in order to count as improvisation has been taken up by Edgar Landgraf. His general argument opposes the romantic account of improvisation as a resource of radical spontaneity or raw inventiveness, since improvisation is always mediated by a discursively iterative system (language, acting, musical codes): "Especially with regard to art, it should be apparent that is not inventiveness itself, but rather its staging that is central to improvisation. For the distinction between improvised and un-improvised creative acts cannot be based on categories surrounding the idea of inventiveness alone." Edgar Landgraf, *Improvisation as Art: Conceptual Challenges, Historical Perspectives* (New York: Bloomsbury, 2011), 38. The recognition of improvisation, in other words, is constitutive of it, and we cannot access it in some purely phenomenal form.

2. Jacques Rancière, *The Emancipated Spectator*, trans. Gregory Elliott (London: Verso, 2009), 15.

3. A recent challenge that accounts for the professional/lay distinction has been offered by Scott Currie, "The Other Side of Here and Now: Cross-Cultural Reflections on the Politics of Improvisation Studies," *Critical Studies in Improvisation* 11, nos. 1–2 (2016). Access at www.criticalimprov.com. DOI: http://dx.doi.org/10.21083/csieci.v11i1–2.3750

4. Landgraf, *Improvisation as Art*, 9.

5. Ernest Ferand, *Die Improvisation in der Musik: eine entwicklungsgeschichtliche und psychologische Untersuchung* (Zürich: Rhein-Verlag, 1938), 414.

6. James Garratt, *Palestrina and the German Romantic Imagination: Interpreting Historicism in Nineteenth-Century Music* (Cambridge: Cambridge University Press, 2002), especially chapter 2.

7. For an insightful critique of this tendency see Gary Peters, *The Philosophy of Improvisation* (Chicago: Chicago University Press, 2009), 21–25.

8. Herta Hirmke-Toth, *Rhythmik in Hellerau-Laxenburg: Die pädagogische Arbeit der Schule Hellerau-Laxenburg 1925–1938* (Saarbrücken: Südewester Verlag für Hochschulschriften, 2009), 9.

9. Ibid., 43–44, 52–53.

10. Ferand, *Die Improvisation in der Musik*, 424, 425.

11. Ibid., 425–26.

12. Vijay Iyer, "Exploding the Narrative in Jazz Improvisation," in *Uptown Conversation: The New Jazz Studies*, ed. Robert G. O'Meally, Brent Hayes Edwards, and Farah Jasmine Griffin (New York: Columbia University Press, 2004), 393–403. Jairo Moreno, "'Body 'n' Soul?': Voice and Movement in Keith Jarrett's Pianism," *Musical Quarterly* 83 (1999): 75–92. An older and more idiosyncratic but widely read argument about the links between improvisation and corporeal practice was made by David Sudnow in *Ways of the Hand: the Organization of Improvised Conduct* (Cambridge, MA: Harvard University Press, 1978). The tendency of these studies to advance a physiology-centered viewpoint on improvisation, against the errors of Cartesianism or romantic idealism, finds a striking anticipation in a treatise on the aesthetics of piano playing by Adolph Kullak, brother of the eminent piano teacher Theodor Kullak. In the pages devoted to improvisation, Kullak challenged Hegel's definition of art as the "sensual appearance of the idea," countering it with the claim that it is "a phenomenon of human agility, and a handling of sensory material. . . . The pleasure of improvisation is actually a physical-anatomical one, a glimpse into the amazing mechanism that brings the creation forth, transmitted through the form of the optimal material." Adolph Kullak, *Die Aesthetik des Klavierspiels* (Berlin: J. Guttentag, 1961), 20–22.

13. *Musical Improvisation: Art, Education and Society*, ed. Gabriel Solis and Bruno Nettl (Urbana: University of Illinois Press, 2009). The most recent addition to this literature is *Improvisation and Music Education: Beyond the Classroom*, ed. Ajay Heble and Mark Laver (New York: Routledge, 2016).

14. A. E. M. Grétry. *Méthode simple pour apprendre à préluder en peu temps avec toutes les ressources de l'harmonie* (Paris: Imprimerie de la République, 1802), 2–3.

15. Fréd. Kalkbrenner, *Traité d'harmonie du pianiste, principes rationnels de la modulation pour apprendre à préluder et à improviser, op. 185* (Amsterdam: Heuwekemeyer, [1849?, repr. 1970]), 1.

16. Ferand, *Die Improvisation*, 426.

INDEX

Abbate, Carolyn, 152

accompagnement (free harmonization), 27, 250–54

Adami, Heinrich, 99–100, 226, 231

Adorno, Theodor, 185

Agoult, Marie d', 135, 208, 210, 214, 218, 219, 220, 222, 223, 225, 240

Allgemeine musikalische Zeitung (Leipzig), 65, 67

Altenburg, Detlef, 232

Ambros, August Wilhelm, 256, 257

Andersen, Hans Christian, *The Improvisatore*, 134, 174

Anton, Karl, 139–40

Applegate, Celia, 186

Ariès, Philippe, 204

Arnold, Charles, 67

Aspull, George, 205

Auber, Daniel, 81, 235, 263

Bach, August Wilhelm, 102

Bach, Carl Philipp Emanuel, 9, 10, 18, 27, 34, 43, 162

Bach, Johann Sebastian, 29, 46–47, 101, 182, 247, 251, 253, 259, 260, 270

Bailey, Derek, 20, 115

Baillot, Pierre, 2, 251

ballad (Ger. *Ballade*), 116, 120, 137–41, 152

Balzac, Honoré de, *Gambara*, 214

Bärmann, Heinrich, 40

Barrington, Daines, 204

Bassanville, Comtesse de, 213, 238

Batka, Richard, 148

Beethoven, Ludwig van, 2, 6, 7, 9, 10, 11, 18, 22, 23, 25, 27, 31, 39, 42, 62, 64, 65, 66, 76, 85, 90, 95, 96, 97, 98, 99, 101, 104, 105, 106, 159, 160, 185, 186, 191, 199, 201, 204, 206, 208, 219, 231, 236, 241, 243, 248, 255, 258, 262, 269, 270, 273, 278; *Fantasia* op. 77, 9, 34, 45; *Allegretto* from Seventh Symphony, 82–83, 94, 99–101, 229, 235

Belleville, Anna Caroline de, 205

Bellini, Vincenzo, 229

Bemetzrieder, Anton, 38

Benjamin, Walter, 148–49

Bennink, Han, 107

Berger, Ludwig, 102, 160

Bergson, Henri, 176

Bériot, Charles de, 251–52, 254

Berlioz, Hector, 12, 122, 207, 208, 212, 223, 248

Berner, Friedrich Wilhelm, 39, 40, 59, 67, 92

Bernstein, Susan, 20

Berryer, Pierre-Antoine, 210

Bindocci, Antonio, 223

Blahetka, Leopoldine, 205

Blanchard, Henri, 94, 96, 246, 248–49

Bocklet, Carl Maria von, 12, 15, 63, 97–101, 154, 226, 231–32

Böhner, Johann Ludwig, 67, 68, 109

Boieldieu, François-Adrien, 201, 202

Boissier, Caroline, 207, 208–209

Bothwell, Julie (Loewe), 117, 118, 121, 139, 150

Brandt, Caroline, 40

Breithaupt, Fritz, 187–88

Browning, Robert, "Abt Vogler," 271–72

Bruckner, Anton, 14, 56, 260–61

Bülow, Hans von, 254, 269

Bürger, Gottfried August, 119

Busoni, Ferruccio, 11, 257–58, 261

Byron, 87, 208, 211, 215, 222

cadenza, 22, 114, 258

capriccio, 27, 65, 76, 203, 207, 215

Carl Alexander, Grand Duke, 232

Carl von Mecklenburg, Prince, 123

Carus, Agnes, 157

Catel, Charles-Simon, 250

Cavaillé-Coll (organ firm), 248, 258

Cavallo, Peter, 246–49

Chateaubriand, François-René de, 221

Cherubini, Luigi, 65

Chopin, Frédéric, 2, 6, 7, 11, 16, 53, 64, 82, 154, 159, 169, 171, 199, 207, 208, 212–14, 224, 226, 229, 234, 235, 269, 279, 280

chorale, 12, 34, 46–47, 85, 101, 121

Chorley, Henry, 88, 263

Cicconi, Luici, 210

Clement, Franz, 71, 245

Clementi, Muzio, 10, 27, 64, 88, 102, 166

Cohen, Hermann, 212

community; of artist and audience, 147–49, 225, 227–28, 241, 244, 256; civic, 104–106; of connoisseurs and amateurs, 41, 63, 69, 76–79, 84, 98–99, 106–107; of musicians and artists, 39, 53, 92, 213, 245, 279

Congress of Vienna, 65, 67, 70, 80, 92, 108, 278

Corelli, Arcangelo, 1

Corinne, ou l'Italie (novel), 5, 6, 14, 18, 87, 134–35, 142, 143, 145, 211, 221–22, 224, 262, 264, 280

Cramer, Johann Baptist, 10, 48, 49, 64, 65, 66, 88, 159, 206

CSI (Critical Improvisation Studies), 3–4, 14, 77, 89, 107, 197, 279, 280, 281–84

Czerny, Carl, 8, 72, 154, 159, 198, 204, 205, 227, 231, 233, 235, 236, 251, 256; single-theme fantasy, 50, 73, 74, 76, 200–201; several-theme fantasy, 200–201; oratory, 209–10;

head-motto, 74, 227; fugue, 254; as Liszt's teacher, 200–201, 204–205; on Beethoven's improvisations, 9, 263; embellishment, 22; free fantasia, 23; prelude, 55, 166–67; capriccio, 76, 203; potpourri, 76, 203; variations, 201

Dalayrac, Nicolas, 82–83

Dannhauser, Josef, 214

Dante, 225, 232–33

Davies, James, 165

Debrois, Carl, 178

Delacroix, Eugène, 280

Deschamps, Émile, 211–12

Devrient, Eduard, 123, 137

Dolphy, Eric, 107

Donizetti, Gaetano, 220, 229

Dorn, Heinrich, 182

Draeseke, Bernhard, 146

Draeseke, Felix, 55, 146; modulation treatise, 254

Dusch, Alexander von, 39

Dussek, Jan Ladislav, 10, 34, 64, 92

Eberhardt, Goby, 252, 269–70, 279

economy/economization, 16, 155, 173–78, 180–81, 183–92

Egarr, Richard, 1

embellishment, 22, 121–22, 208, 239

epic, 117, 138–40, 147–49, 223, 245, 267–68

Escaich, Thierry, 1

Esse, Melina, 218

Esterhammer, Angela, 5, 6, 118, 134, 138, 147, 173, 221

Esterházy, Prince Nikolaus, 64

Ferand, Ernst, 280–83

Fétis, Edouard, 207

Fétis, François-Joseph, 85, 103, 260

Field, John, 159, 172

Filtsch, Charles, 206

Firmian, Count, 38–39

Forkel, Johann Nikolaus, 25

Fouqué, Friedrich de la Motte, 41, 147

Franck, César, 14, 56, 259, 260

Franz, Robert, 253

free fantasia (style/genre), 9, 18, 27, 34, 41–42, 53, 162–64 free fantasy (genre), 10, 12, 13, 28, 65–67, 200–201

free playing, 7–8, 10, 27–28, 53

fugal style, 34, 37, 43, 52, 59, 81, 100, 254, 283
see also learned style

galant style, 10, 17, 27, 32, 34, 50, 70, 93, 281

Galston, Gottfried, 258

Gänsbacher, Johann, 25, 28, 37, 38–39, 48, 50, 272

Garratt, James, 281

Geibel, Emanuel, 130, 136, 244

George IV (king of England), 206

Gessheim, Professor, 130

Giesebrecht, Ludwig, 130, 136

Gigout, Eugène, 259–60

Gjerdingen, Robert, 17–18, 50

Gluck, Christoph Willibald, 85

Goertzen, Valerie, 7

Goethe, Johann Wolfgang von, 93, 94, 101, 103, 117, 118, 124–26, 129, 130, 136, 137, 146, 147, 211, 222, 232; on the ballad genre, 137–38, 140

Gollmick, Carl, 229

Gottschalk, Louis Moreau, 74, 75

Graham, William A., 148

Granzin, Ludwig, 246

Grave, Floyd, 28, 29

Grétry, André Ernest Modeste, 8, 283–84

Grillparzer, Franz, 2, 11

Grünfeld, Alfred, 256–57, 261, 270, 271

Guilmant, Alexandre, 14, 259–60

Gyrowetz, Adalbert, 48, 230

Halévy, Fromental, 250

Hallé, Charles, 213, 255

Hamilton, Kenneth, 7, 235, 243

handedness, 128, 165, 189

Handel, Georg Friedrich, 81, 85, 101, 102, 104, 230, 247, 251, 253, 259, 260

Hanslick, Eduard, 31, 89, 228, 231, 257

Haydn, Franz Joseph, 27, 41, 227

head-motto, 74, 81, 84, 227

Heine, Heinrich, 16, 214–15, 234

Heller, Stephen, 154, 244, 255, 261

Henselt, Adolf [Adolphe] von, 95, 224, 236–37

Henze-Döhring, Sabine, 52

Herder, Johann Gottfried, 118, 138, 139, 147, 232

Hérold, Ferdinand, 74

Herz, Henri, 70, 78, 113, 256, 261

Hiller, Ferdinand, 11, 13, 15, 51, 63, 76, 79, 90–91, 92–95, 102, 105, 108, 135, 137, 154, 233, 244, 255, 261, 279

Himmel, Friedrich Heinrich, 172

Hoffmann, E. T. A., 68, 176

Hohenzollern, Marie von, 130–31

Horkheimer, Max, 185

Horn, David, 107

Hummel, Johann Nepomuk, 2, 7, 11, 13, 15, 39, 42, 43, 62–65, 70–79, 81, 84, 130, 135, 155, 156, 157, 160, 161, 165, 191, 198, 199, 200, 201, 203, 204, 208, 229, 230, 231, 232, 245, 246, 248, 249, 251, 256, 261, 263, 273, 278, 279; students of, 92–97, 113–14; *Fantasie*, op. 18, 72, 73, 76; Sonata in F-sharp Minor, 162–64

improvisation imaginary, 2, 11, 13, 16, 26–27, 41–42, 86–87, 96, 106–7, 122, 199, 212–13, 234; gypsy, 265–68; improvising interpreter, 269–70; troubador, 264–65; shepherd, 219, 244, 268

Jacques-Dalcroze, Émile, 282, 283

Jankélévitch, Vladimir, 176–78, 229, 234–35

jazz, 1, 3–4, 24, 89, 107, 281

Joachim, Joseph, 22–23, 269, 278

Junker, Carl, 34

Kahlert, August, 130

Kalkbrenner, Friedrich, 8, 10, 12, 23–24, 42, 49, 64, 70, 78, 84, 88–89, 102, 113, 159, 162, 166, 168, 169, 171–72, 200, 206, 251, 254, 261, 284

Kanne, Friedrich August, 43, 93, 103

kapellmeister (profession), 13, 24, 63–70, 109–10, 120–22, 178, 198

kapellmeister network, 13, 63, 79

Kapp, Reinhard, 178, 180

Kent, Duchess of, 85

Kirchner, Theodor, 270

Knecht, Justin Heinrich, 55

Körner, Theodor, 117, 118, 119, 120, 147

Kossmaly, Carl, 183–84, 186, 196

Kreutzer, Conradin, 67

Kreutzer, Léon, 26, 27, 28, 271
Kuhe, Wilhelm, 243–44
Kuhlau, Friedrich, 65, 66, 84
Kullak, Theodor, 256
Kurth, Ernst, 282

Lamartine, Alphonse de, 221
Lamennais, Félicité de, 208
Landgraf, Edgar, 56, 280, 285
Langenschwarz, Maximilian, 136, 141, 142, 173, 229
Lauska, Franz, 49
learned style, 66, 71, 75
Lefébure-Wély, Louis James Alfred, 258–59, 260
Leistra-Jones, Karen, 269
Lemmens, Jacques-Nicolas, 260
Leonhardt-Lyser, Karoline, 141–47, 173
Levin, Robert, 1
Levy, Janet, 177
Lewis, George, 4
Lichtenstein, Hinrich, 41–42, 49
Liszt, Franz, 2, 6, 7, 8, 11, 13, 16, 64, 70, 84, 95, 102, 137, 155, 156, 160, 176, 177, 192, 243, 245, 247, 251, 254, 261–262, 265, 269, 273, 279, 280; compared to Mozart, 201–205; on gypsies, 265–68; as child prodigy, 200–207; *Harmonies poétiques et religieuses,* 216; *Apparitions,* 216–18; storms, 218–19; encore-improvisation, 227–28, 234; *Aufforderung zum Tanze* (Weber), 202–3, 208, 226, 227, 228, 231, 234
Loewe, Carl, 2, 6, 11, 13, 15, 207, 227, 262, 268; "Wallhaide" 117–19, 120, 124, 127, 140, 149, 280; "Die Zauberlehrling" 124–29
Louis Ferdinand, Prince of Prussia, 92
Lyser, Johann Peter, 141, 173

Mann, Thomas, *Buddenbrooks,* 174–75, 190–91, 192
Marmontel, Antoine François, 251
Marschner, Heinrich, 81
Marx, Adolph Bernhard, 184–87, 191, 196, 197
Marx, Karl, 188
Matthison, 130
Mehrdeutigkeit (polysemy), 36–37, 44, 55
Méhul, Étienne, 40, 48, 96
melodrama, 119–20, 123, 136–37, 219, 232

Mendelssohn, Felix, 2, 6, 11, 14, 63, 70, 89–92, 101–106, 107, 154, 156, 160, 178, 200, 243, 245, 252–53, 255, 260, 270, 273, 279
Mercadante, Saverio, 220
Meyerbeer, Giacomo, 11, 13, 14, 15, 25, 26, 27, 28, 38, 48–53, 54, 56, 66, 67, 92, 94, 103, 104, 119, 171, 207, 233, 244, 271, 272
Mickiewicz, Adam, 211
Mill, John Stuart, 2, 11
Miller, Julius, 39
Milli, Giannina, 244
Monteiro, Gabriela, 1
Moore, Thomas, 86
Moscheles, Charlotte, 79, 82, 87, 90, 91
Moscheles, Ignaz, 8, 11, 15, 34, 39, 43, 49, 63, 65, 70, 78, 79–92, 99–100, 101, 154, 155, 156, 157, 159, 160, 164, 171, 191, 198, 199, 200, 203, 206, 226, 233, 244, 245, 249, 251, 255, 261, 262, 263, 279
Möser, Carl, 124, 160
Mozart, Franz Xaver, 66–67
Mozart, Wolfgang Amadeus, 1, 7, 25, 27, 31, 34, 45, 64, 69, 74, 75, 77, 85, 87, 90, 91, 93, 95, 96, 97, 99, 100, 101, 182, 199, 215, 227, 229, 234, 246, 255, 257, 258, 262, 273
Müller, Adolf Sr., 142–44
musicians' guild, 39, 53, 80, 90, 92
Musset, Alfred de, 221, 280

Nettl, Bruno, 3, 284
Neukomm, Sigismund, 67
Niedermeyer, Louis, 260
Nietzsche, Friedrich, 12, 264
Nordau, Max, 174
Nourrit, Adolphe, 220

Ohe, Adele aus der, 233
oratory, 97, 146, 209–11, 245, 249; *see also* Czerny, Carl
organ and organists, 13, 25–26, 29–30, 54–56, 121, 218, 246, 258–60, 271–73
Ossian, 86

Pacini, Giovanni, 134, 220
Paganini, Nicolò, 2, 16, 158, 160, 169, 207, 208, 215
Paignon, Eugène, 210
Panseron, Auguste-Mathieu, 250–52, 254
Parker, Evan, 107

Pasta, Giud... 67
Payer, Hie...
Phillips, ...
Pierson, ...88
Pistrucc...
Pixis, Jo..., 60, 70, 221
Plaidy, ...
...play, 34... -90, 173
...artin, 148
poetry... sation, 5-6, 87-8, 141... 174, ... 221, 223-24, 24... see a... Corin...nel)
popular... 70, 71, 74, 79-8, 203... -47; see also c...ccio; see also potpo...
postclassica...anism, 7, 10, 15, 98... 15..., 19...60, ...04-73, 18..., 192, 198, 2...-08, 209, 22... see also *stile brillante*
potpourri, 44, 65, 66, 71, 74, 75, 89, 93, 99, 100, ...202, 203, 235, 256; see ...rny, potpourri
Pradel, Eugène de, 210-11
preluding (and preludes), 7, 8, ...
Prudent, Émile, 251
public sphere, 13, 30, 63, 67, 76... 122, 178, 186, 187, 233, 253, 2... communication in, 10, 16, 9..., 106, 213; anti-public values, 66-... 206, 213, 225, 230, 278

Queen [Therese] of Bavaria, 4...

Radziwill, Anton, 50, 124, 130
Reissiger, Carl Gottlieb, 95
Rellstab, Ludwig, 103
Revue musicale, 83-84, 207
Ricardo, David, 185, 187, 197
Richards, Annette, 9, 18
Ries, Ferdinand, 23, 67, 159, 1...
Ritter, Ernst Friedrich, 252
Rive-Necker, Albertine, 219
Rochlitz, Friedrich, 49
romanticism, 5-6, 16, 86-88, ..., 134-35, 147, 155; French, 200, 207-..., 212, 233; instantaneity, 211, 215-18; ...flection, 187-89; and Italianness, 21-25; see also Scott, Walter; see also *Corinne* (novel)
Rossini, Gioachino, 66, 85, 87, 99, 134, 201, 219, 220, 222, 235, 246, 247
Rousseau, Jean-Jacques, 204

...les Augustin, 134, 222
Sa...mille, 14, 251, 260
S...o, 79, 82
...38-39, 48, 134, 147, 157, 208, 213,
...e, 246, 247, 248
...ff, Countess, 220
...n, Jim, 7, 164, 171
...George, 6, 8, 16, 52, 53, 211, 212-13, ...4, 218, 219, 221, 234, 271, 280; *Consuelo*, ...222-23; "The Organ of Titan," 271
...auret, Émile, 252, 270, 279
Scharffenberg, Theodor, 254
Schiller, Friedrich, 117, 120, 123, 130, 137, 142, 212
Schilling, Gustav, 230
Schlegel, Friedrich, 188, 212
Schmitt, Aloys, 67, 92-93
Schneider, Friedrich, 67, 69, 95, 96, 109, 150
Schoberlechner, Franz, 113-14
Schönfelder, Ludwig, 55
Schubert, Franz, 6, 11, 55, 97, 99, 122, 160, 171, 172, 199, 201, 230, 231, 255
Schumann, August, 175
Schumann, Clara (Wieck), 7, 12, 157, 180, 181, 182, 183, 188, 189, 195-96, 224
Schumann, Robert, 6, 11, 12, 13, 15, 38, 64, 95, 138, 198, 200, 207, 261, 262, 270; and Beethoven, 161-63; *Toccata*, 166-68; *Variationen über den Namen "Abegg,"* 169-73
Schuncke, Carl, 70
Schuppanzigh, Ignaz, 97
Schwencke, Carl, 249
Scott, Walter, 86-87
Seibert, Peter, 147
Sgricci, Tommaso, 87, 224
Shakespeare, William, 262-63
Small, Christopher, 17
Solis, Gabriel, 3
Speidel, Ludwig, 214
Spitta, Philipp, 140, 147
Spohr, Louis, 68-69, 70, 74
Spontini, Gaspare, 81, 123
Staël, Germaine de, see *Corinne* (novel)
Stamaty, Camille, 251
Staudigl, Joseph, 230
Steibelt, Daniel, 27, 48
Stein, Theodor, 205-206, 249

Steinbach, Fritz, 252
Stendhal (Marie-Henri
stile brillante, 10, 23, 63, 6
   see also postclassical piar   4;
Stoepel, François, 72
Strauss, Johann Jr., 257, 271
Strauss, Johann Sr., 227
Sudnow, David, 44
Szalay, Joseph von, 67

Talma, François-Joseph, 209
Tasso, Torquato, 225
Tatum, Art, 107
Taubert, Wilhelm, 123, 160–61, 261
Tausenau, Carl, 226
Taylor, Cecil, 107
Thalberg, Sigismond, 12, 95, 96, 98, 135,
   160, 227
thematic combination, 82, 84, 1
thoroughbass/figured bass, 4, 10, 18, 82,
   98, 121, 171, 244, 252, 253, 281; *see also*
   accompagnement
Tieck, Ludwig, 120, 130, 146
Todd, R. Larry, 102
Töpken, Anton, 157–58
Treitler, Leo, 17, 18
Türk, Daniel Gottlob, 120–22
Tyrtaeus, 86, 122, 223

Uhland, Ludwig, 130, 137, 147
Ullman, Bernard, 256

Veit, Joachim, 44
Vigny, Alfred de, 221
Vogler, Georg Joseph, 8, 11, 13, 14, 15, 63,
   75, 119, 120, 244, 245, 250, 259, 271, 272,
   273, 279; as teacher, 25–27, 37–38, 46–47;

progressivi
30, 259; as pe   4; orchestrion, 25,
25, 34–37, 55   34; as theorist,

Wagner, Richard, 3,
   on Beethoven's im 257, 278;
   troubadors, 264–65   ns, 263–64;
Waselewsk Wilhelm Jo
Web   Bernd Anselm, 1, 192
Weber Carl Maria von, 13,   27, 28,
   37–4 9, 54, 66, 67, 75   99, 119,
   159,   20 208, 211, 212, 2   227,
   230, 2 71 72
Weber   fried 25, 28, 37, 38   56
W belax, 176, 177, 179, 184,
W Grand Duchess of, 92
W hn, Carl Friedrich, 55
W rdinand, 252
W muel, 88, 112
W ristoph Ernst Friedrich, 34, 67, 84
Wi drich, 156, 157, 159, 160, 161, 175,
   1 182, 188, 189, 206
Will ugust, 270
Will aymond, 55–56
Will udolf, 63, 95–97, 247
Wint r, 48
Wolff Ludwig Bernhard, 135–37, 141,
   151 73, 210, 232
Wölfl, h, 27
work-c t, 2, 62, 165, 212–13, 278
Worthe n, 159

Zelter, riedrich, 102, 103, 120, 123, 124,
   126; "Zauberlehrling" 128, 129, 130
Zimmerm Pierre-Joseph-Guillaume, 251
Zumstee nann Rudolf, 119–20